GOING TO THE PALAIS

Going to the Palais

A Social and Cultural History of Dancing and Dance Halls in Britain, 1918–1960

JAMES NOTT

OXFORD
UNIVERSITY PRESS

OXFORD
UNIVERSITY PRESS

Great Clarendon Street, Oxford, OX2 6DP,
United Kingdom

Oxford University Press is a department of the University of Oxford. It furthers the University's objective of excellence in research, scholarship, and education by publishing worldwide. Oxford is a registered trade mark of Oxford University Press in the UK and in certain other countries

First Edition published in 2015

Impression: 1

Published in the United States of America by Oxford University Press
198 Madison Avenue, New York, NY 10016, United States of America

British Library Cataloguing in Publication Data
Data available

Library of Congress Control Number: 2015933890

ISBN 978–0–19–960519–4

Printed and bound by
CPI Group (UK) Ltd, Croydon, CR0 4YY

Acknowledgements

I am indebted to many friends and colleagues for supplying information, advice, and assistance of various kinds and owe particular thanks to John Hudson at St Andrews and Ross McKibbin at Oxford for their sustained guidance. Thanks also to David Salter and Jeremy Crang at Edinburgh, who offered invaluable feedback on earlier drafts of the manuscript. To the various libraries and archives that I have used I also owe considerable debt, not only for the right to use material but also for the friendly and supportive atmosphere in which to work. The staff at the National Library of Scotland were always most helpful as were those in the British Library. I must also give particular thanks to the archivists at the Liverpool Record Office; Manchester City Archives; City of Birmingham Archives; Glasgow City Archives; and Tyne and Wear Archives, not to mention the café staff at those various institutions who sustained me during my various visits. I am particularly indebted to those throughout the country who helped me to organize and conduct the various oral history interviews. From Liverpool, I must give especial mention to Jackie Ross, formerly of the National Maritime Museum and a huge inspiration, together with all the staff at the Liverpool League of Welldoers. From Dundee, I must thank Amina Shah of the Dundee Central Library. All were extremely forthcoming with their help and made available facilities without which I could not have carried out my interviews. I am also indebted to Alison Turnbull, Fiona Kingston, and Eleanor Marshall who worked as research assistants on my oral history project, generously funded by the School of History at St Andrews. In addition George West was extremely forthcoming with information and oral history interviews undertaken in Rochdale in the 1980s. Similarly Andrew Schofield of the North West Sound Archive was also very helpful indeed. Of course, I also offer my heartfelt thanks to all of those volunteers who allowed themselves to be interviewed—not only have their recollections proved invaluable in the writing of this book, but they willingly let me into their private worlds without a second thought.

I would like to thank the following for permission to reproduce material: Extracts from Mass Observation reproduced with permission of Curtis Brown Group Ltd, London, on behalf of The Trustees of the Mass Observation Archive. Extracts from BBC WW2 People's War Archive reproduced by permission of the BBC. WW2 People's War is an online archive of wartime memories contributed by members of the public and gathered by the BBC. The archive can be found at http://bbc.co.uk/ww2peopleswar. Extracts from recordings from the NWSA, permission granted by North West Sound Archive. Extracts from Manchester City Records reproduced courtesy of Manchester Libraries, Information and Archives, Manchester City Council. Extracts from Liverpool Record Office reproduced with permission from Liverpool Record Office, Liverpool Libraries.

I would like to thank the following for permission to use photographs and other illustrative material: Herald and Times Group for Figures 1.1, 3.2, and 3.3;

Figure 1.2—Courtesy of Glasgow City Council Archives; Figure 1.3—Image courtesy of A P Knighton and www.picturethepast.org.uk; Figure 1.4—Image courtesy of Nottingham City Council and www.picturethepast.org.uk; Figure 1.5—Image courtesy of Nottingham City Council and www.picturethepast.org.uk; Figure 1.6—Image courtesy of Nottingham City Council and www.picturethepast.org.uk; Figure 1.7—Image courtesy of www.picturethepast.org.uk; Getty Images for Figures 2.1, 3.1, 5.1, 7.2, and 9.3; Scotsman Publications Ltd for Figures 3.4, 4.2, and 7.1; © Mirrorpix for Figures 4.1, 5.2, 8.1, 8.2, and 9.1; and the Imperial War Museum for Figure 9.2.

Lastly, and by no means least, I must give my heartfelt love and thanks to my family, especially my parents, Barbara and Terence, who not only helped out with the transcribing of interviews and collating of material, but, even more significantly, provided the inspiration for this book. Like millions of people in Britain at this time, they met at the palais. This book is therefore dedicated to them.

Contents

PART II. DANCING AND BRITISH SOCIETY, 1918–60

PART III. CONFLICTS AND CONTROL: MORAL PANIC AND THE DANCE HALL, 1918–60

List of Figures

Abbreviations

CBA	City of Birmingham Archives
DDHI	Dundee Dance Hall Interviews Oral History
DET	*Dundee Evening Telegraph*
DM	*Daily Mirror*
DN	*Dance News*
DT	*Dancing Times*
EEN	*Edinburgh Evening News*
GCA	Glasgow City Archives
GDHI	Glasgow Dance Hall Interviews Oral History
LDHI	Liverpool Dance Hall Interviews Oral History
LDN	*Lancashire Dance News*
LRO	Liverpool Record Office
MCA	Manchester City Archives
MDD	*Modern Dance and Dancer*
M-O A	Mass Observation Archive (TC= Topic Collection; FR = File Report; DR = Directive Reply; MDJ = Music, Dancing, and Jazz)
NA	National Archives, Kew
NAS	National Archives of Scotland, Edinburgh
NWSA	North West Sound Archive
PMDW	*Popular Music and Dancing Weekly*
PP	*Picture Post*
PWA	BBC WW2 People's Archive
TWA	Tyne and Wear Archives
WL	Women's Library

Introduction

From the mid-1920s, the dance hall occupied a pivotal place in the culture of working- and lower-middle-class communities in Britain—a place rivalled only by the cinema. Whilst the enjoyment of dancing had been taking place long before the twentieth century, the period after the First World War saw Britain develop a love affair with social dancing that was unprecedented. At no time before had so many people danced, so regularly and with so much contemporary interest and debate. Britain was dance mad. As early as October 1919 the *Sunday Sun* explained:

> There is a big boom in dancing. Ever since the silencing of the guns last November it has loomed large in the social life of the individual. Where it was once an art it has now become a craze . . . if things go on as they are at present, it is safe to assume that dancing will shortly become an obsession with the majority of our younger citizens.[1]

Yet dancing was to become more than just a craze, and it was not merely a fad for young people. As the *Aberdeen Press and Journal* put it in 1926: 'today there is probably the greatest dancing wave that this country has ever seen. Not only do young people—almost without exception—dance, but their parents dance, too.'[2] Moreover, such popularity was not only maintained but extended as the decades progressed, by which time dancing had become big business. In February 1953, for example, the *Economist* named the dance hall industry 'the second biggest entertainment industry' after cinema. It estimated that weekly audiences in Britain's dance halls were around four million, and annual audiences were around 200 million, compared with only eighty to ninety million for football, and that these generated revenue of £25 million (a 'conservative estimate') compared with only about £15 million from broadcasting.[3] Furthermore, the dance hall that had sprung up to cater for this unprecedented demand for dancing was a unique social space, with its own set of conventions and characteristics. This impression was recorded by a London 'Mass Observer' visiting a dance hall in Bolton in 1938:

> Made my way up to the second floor of building. Met man at head of stair. He came forward, looked at me. Near him were roll of tickets labelled 9d. I said 'how much?' He said 'Sixpunce'. Paid. Walked into darkened dance room. Turned left to deposit coat in cloakroom, where attendant was sitting in wicker chair, both feet on counter, reading American magazine. He got up, gave me ticket number 56. Pegs nearly full, coats, hats, waistcoats. On floor brown parcels of outdoor shoes. Went on to dancefloor . . .

[1] *Sunday Sun*, 26 October 1919, 5.
[2] *Aberdeen Press and Journal*, 22 November 1926, 3.
[3] *Economist*, 14 February 1953, 401.

> Orchestra, nine men in dinner jackets (no one else wore these), on raised dais in one corner, start a tune. Large groups of each sex, segregated and concentrated round door, break up and mingle into couples. Common mode of approach is simply to touch girl on elbow; she moves out, dance. Within a minute only dozen of the hundred or so in the room . . . are not dancing. A girl has just come up to me. SHE wants me to dance with her. I say this is a new one on me, 'Doesn't the man generally ask the girl for a dance?' She says she is on the staff, one of eight, job is to dance with anyone. Paid by owner of the hall. Three minutes, dance stops. All couples stay on floor, slight applause. Band do encore. Three minutes, same again; encore. It's hard work steering on small floor among crowd; couples constantly bump; no apologies, just grins. At end of second encore (there are three automatically all evening) men walk straight away from their partners, not escorting them off the floor. Sexes accumulate into their original separate groups around door.[4]

The voluntary segregation of the dance hall into single sex groups coming together almost magically when the band began to play and then returning to their separate spheres, was not, however, exclusive to Bolton. Neither were the crowded dance floors, stage managed encores, the professional dancing partners, or smartly dressed band. Many of the public dance halls in Britain shared these characteristics and they provided a ritualized leisure pursuit of great social importance. We can gain some sense of this importance through an examination of why so many people chose to go to dance halls. A precursory glance at comments from a 1939 Mass Observation survey on the topic reveals a range of reasons and social functions for dancing: 'I enjoy the Rhythm-impelling bands, the cabarets, the catering and the zest creating programmes', 'Excellent to get to know people', 'Ideal exercise for fitness', 'Makes one light-hearted', 'an excellent medium for the opposite sex to make friends without obviously "picking up"', 'they are very valuable for developing the social nature of the community'.[5] Not everyone saw them so positively, however. As early as May 1919 the *Derby Daily Telegraph* noted: 'The recent extraordinary increase in the popularity of dancing amongst all sections of the community is compelling the attention of social workers to the dance problem . . .'[6] This was one of countless warnings against the 'problem' of dancing that were to be sustained throughout the next forty years. Considered immoral and indecent by some, the Church and political authorities launched a series of attacks on the dance hall industry. Thus, examining why this huge expansion in the popularity of dancing occurred how and when it did, and the responses to it, can tell us a great deal about British society and culture at this time.

A social and cultural history of dancing and dance halls in Britain, *c.*1918–60, *Going to the Palais* has four main objectives. First, to examine the expansion of the dance hall industry and the development of a 'mass audience' for dancing between *c.*1918 and 1960. Second, the impact of these changes on individuals and communities will be examined, with a particular concentration on working- and

[4] T. Harrisson, 'Whistle While You Work' (1938) (Winter) *New Writing* 47.
[5] Quotations from M-O A: MJD, 6/F and M-O A: Directive Reply: 'Jazz 2, July 1939'.
[6] *Derby Daily Telegraph*, 5 May 1919, 4.

lower-middle-class communities and on young men and women. Third, the cultural impact of dancing and dance halls will be explored. A key aspect of this debate is to examine how Britain's dance culture held up against various standardizing processes (commercialization, Americanization, etc.) over the period, and whether we can see the emergence of a 'national' dance culture. Finally, an assessment of wider reactions to dance halls and dancing in the period will be examined. There is more, however. This book is concerned with the complex relationship between discourses of class, culture, gender, and national identity and how they overlap—how cultural change, itself a response to broader political, social, and economic developments, was helping to change notions of class, gender, and national identity.

It is important to note that this book will not be a history of 'ballroom dancing'. Ballroom dancing developed into a quite distinctive activity as early as the 1920s and 1930s, taken over by professional and semi-professional dancers. Although I will mention this development, I am predominantly concerned with social dancing and social dancers. This also explains why I wish to confine this study to the period up to the mid- to late 1960s. Although ballroom dancing survives up unto this day, the dance hall was a specific social and cultural phenomenon belonging to a specific historic moment. By the mid- to late 1960s, it had transformed into something quite different. It deserves a study of its own, rather than being part of a 'general history' of dancing in this country. I should also clarify what is meant by the term 'dance hall'. Although it appears self-explanatory, throughout this book I will use 'dance hall' to describe all of the major venues where dancing took place, whether this was a permanent commercially run venue or a temporary public venue utilized regularly for dancing. The 'palais' in the book's title refers more specifically to the palais de danse, purpose-built commercial dance halls which appeared on Britain's high streets from the 1920s onwards. When necessary a distinction will be used to distinguish the two, and where I am talking about a specific venue that also will be made clear.

Despite its importance, the dance hall has attracted little academic attention. This book aims to reverse the dearth of historical scholarship on this subject. It is true that the study of popular culture in late nineteenth- and twentieth-century Britain has proliferated in recent years. There are now numerous and excellent studies of subjects as diverse as cinema, darts, smoking, and the juke box, all part of a sustained and extensive study of Britain's leisure and recreation culture during this period.[7] The work on dance halls and social dancing in Britain is much more limited, however, and most of it focused on the earlier period or on specific aspects of dance culture. Of that literature which does exist, most studies brush over the topic whilst exploring other subjects in more depth, particularly leisure and music. Clare Langhammer, for instance, looks at dancing as part of her study of women's

[7] See for example P. Chaplin, *Darts in England 1900–39: A Social History* (Manchester: Manchester University Press, 2012); J. Richards, *The Age of the Dream Palace: Cinema and Society in 1930s Britain* (London: I.B.Tauris, 2009); A. Horn, *Juke Box Britain* (Manchester: Manchester University Press, 2010); M. Hilton, *Smoking in British Popular Culture 1800–2000* (Manchester: A & C Black, 2000).

leisure in England in the period 1920–60.[8] Michael Brocken also examines some aspects of Liverpool's dance halls in his excellent study of the city's music scene from the 1930s to the 1970s.[9]

Histories of gender also contain acknowledgement of the importance of dancing to women. For example, Leanne McCormick's study of interactions between American troops and Northern Irish Women during the Second World War, notably titled 'One Yank and They're off', contains some details of dance hall liasons between the two groups.[10] Similarly, Sonya O'Rose in her examinations of wartime 'Good Time Girls' also highlights the role of dancing in creating negative stereotypes of women.[11] Such studies, however, inevitably contain little sustained examination of the topic. Turning now to studies solely focusing on dancing in Britain, Liz Oliver made an early foray into the topic with her article on public dancing in Bolton from 1840–1911, where she makes important observations concerning the role of dancing amongst women and the moral reactions against it.[12] A much more complete study of social dancing in Britain is provided by Theresa Buckland, whose monograph examines the period 1870 to 1920. This is the fullest work on the topic to date. The focus of this groundbreaking work is the world of upper-class dancers and society, however, and although there is a foray into twentieth-century popular dancing, this comes at the end of the study, which is from the discipline of Dance Studies rather than that of History.[13] Coming to the later period, there have also been some useful examinations of dancing in particular locations. Tricia Jenkins' study of dancing in Liverpool, carried out in conjunction with the University of Liverpool's Institute of Popular Music, is particularly insightful as it utilizes oral history to gather the views and opinions of Liverpudlian dancers of the 1920s and 1930s. Their testimony is then collated and contextualized, though the audience for this popular history work limits the extent to which that analysis is sustained.[14] Raymond Thomson also produced a case study of dance halls and dance bands in Greenock, Scotland in the later period, 1945–55.[15] A cultural historical approach to the shaping of British dance culture has also been adopted by other scholars. Pioneering in this field was cultural geographer Timothy Cresswell, who explored the construction of the so-called English style of

[8] C. Langhamer, *Women's Leisure in England, 1920–60* (Manchester: Manchester University Press, 2000).

[9] M. Brocken, *Other Voices: Hidden Histories of Liverpool's Popular Music Scenes, 1930s–1970s* (Farnham: Ashgate, 2010).

[10] L. McCormick, '"One Yank and They're off": Interaction between US Troops and Northern Irish Women, 1942–45' (May 2006) *Journal of the History of Sexuality* 228–57.

[11] S. O. Rose, *Which People's War? National identity and citizenship in Britain 1939–1945* (Oxford: Oxford University Press, 2003).

[12] L. Oliver, 'From the Ballroom to Hell: a Social History of Public Dancing in Bolton from *c.*1840–1911' (1995) 2(2) *Women's History Notebooks* 15–23.

[13] T. J. Buckland, *Society Dancing: Fashionable bodies in England 1870–1920* (Basingstoke, Hampshire: Palgrave Macmillan, 2011).

[14] T. Jenkins, *'Let's Go Dancing': Dance band memories of 1930s Liverpool* (Liverpool: Liverpool Sound Series, 1994).

[15] R. A. Thomson, 'Dance Bands and Dance Halls in Greenock, 1945–55' (1989) 8(2) *Popular Music* (May) 143–55.

dancing in the 1920s.[16] Similarly, Allison Abra has examined the role of the dance hall group Mecca in shaping dance trends in the 1930s and 1940s.[17] Both have, to some extent, built on my own work touching on these topics. I pioneered examination of dance halls in my earlier monograph *Music for the People*, which contained two exploratory chapters on the topic, as part of a wider survey of the popular music industry (live and mechanized) in interwar Britain.[18] More recently I have explored the shaping of dance culture and dance music in the 1920s in a study examining the contestation of popular culture at this time. I have also explored the campaign by the Conservative Home Secretary William Joynson Hicks to close down interwar nightclubs, wherein dancing formed an important part of the study.[19] Even here though, the focus of investigation has not been full-square on the palais. The dance hall and popular dancing have remained major missing links in our history of popular culture in twentieth-century Britain.

However, although scholarly literature on the dance hall as a whole is scarce, there have been numerous antiquarian works on various aspects of the history of the dance hall. Despite their obvious limitations such works provide a valuable introduction to the subject, but even their coverage is narrow. Of huge help to the historian is P. J. S. Richardson's early work from 1947, a history of English ballroom dancing that provides a pioneering account of the development of dancing styles and dancers.[20] More recently, one of the best works is Elizabeth Casciani's history of ballroom dancing in Scotland.[21] There are other local studies too, with the important dancing centre of Glasgow covered by Jimmy Brown and Manchester's later dance scene explored by Alan Lawson.[22] Together such works provide useful and tantalizing glimpses of the larger picture.

The obvious corollary to these scattered and fragmentary approaches, however, is to attempt a more complete study of the dance hall in Britain. The fact that their history remains unwritten is a staggering omission. One reason why it has been unwritten, I believe, is that the sources lie far and wide and are usually unconventional—the scale of scholarship involved in producing this book has

[16] T. Cresswell, '"You cannot shake that shimmie here": producing mobility on the dance floor' (2006) 13 *Cultural Geographies* 55–77.

[17] A. Abra, 'Doing the Lambeth Walk: Novelty dances and the British nation' (2009) 20 *Twentieth Century British History* 346–69.

[18] J. J. Nott, *Music for the People: Popular Music and Dance in Interwar Britain* (Oxford: Oxford University Press, 2002).

[19] J. J. Nott, '"The Plague Spots of London": William Joynson Hicks, the Conservative Party and the Campaign Against London's Nightclubs, 1924–29' in C. Griffiths, J. J. Nott, and W. Whyte (eds), *Classes, Cultures and Politics: Essays in Modern British History for Ross McKibbin* (Oxford: Oxford University Press, 2011) and 'Contesting Popular Dancing and Dance Music During the 1920s' (2013) 10(3) *Cultural and Social History* (September) 439–56.

[20] P. J. S. Richardson, *A History of English Ballroom Dancing (1910–45): The story of the development of the modern English style* (London: Herbert Jenkins, 1947).

[21] E. Casciani, *Oh, How we Danced! The History of ballroom dancing in Scotland* (Edinburgh: Mercat Press, 1994).

[22] J. Brown, *Glasgow's Dancing Daft!* (Ochiltree, TX: Stenlake Publishing, 1994) and A. Lawson, *It Happened in Manchester: The True Story of Manchester's Music 1958–65* (Multimedia, 1998).

been quite simply enormous and has necessitated a number of different methodological approaches.

The book is based on archival reconstruction and analysis, together with extensive use of oral history. The economic history of the industry is dealt with first and this, broadly, can be divided into two. The first, and most important, concerns the commercial dance halls. Archives remain which detail the history of individual companies and the historian is also well served by a large trade press. Journals such as *Dancing Times*, *Modern Dance and Dancer*, *Popular Music and Dancing Weekly*, and *Danceland* are used to establish the salient themes in the economic development of different sectors of the industry. The national press also contains some useful data on the dance hall industry's economic fortunes, and the regional press is also used to get a sense of provision in different areas of Britain. Secondly, numerous non-commercial venues, such as church and assembly halls, are also examined. All dance venues were the subject of official regulation and local government authorities issued licences for dancing which had to be renewed annually. Surviving records from local authorities in several towns and cities have been used to give an estimation of the size of the industry over time.

The question of audiences also required several approaches. Establishing the age, class, gender, and regional distribution of the various audiences for dance halls and dancing is complicated. Mass Observation carried out detailed surveys of the audiences for dancing and dance music from the late 1930s to the 1950s and material from these investigations is extremely valuable. The large number of contemporary social surveys is another rich source, together with a wide range of contemporary literature on leisure and recreation. The impact of these developments on individuals and society is perhaps the most important aspect of this study. In addition to social survey material, one of the most significant sources for this book is personal testimony. Following a radio appeal on BBC Radio 4 and engagement with local history societies and other groups throughout Britain, oral history interviews, together with an inter-linking questionnaire, were gathered for this study. As well as a nationwide survey, there were several more in-depth regional studies, in Glasgow, Dundee, and Liverpool, where over thirty oral history interviews were conducted. This provides the most extensive nationwide oral history of dancing and dance hall culture in Britain conducted to date. This oral history has been used to discover the impact of dancing and dance halls on individuals and communities, chiefly in the wartime and post-Second World War period. This is not all, however. A large body of personal testimonies already exists in various oral history archives that touch on this subject. Amongst the most important utilized here was the North West Sound Archive based in Clitheroe. Furthermore, a huge number of written personal testimonies were gathered by the BBC as part of its WW2 'People's War Archive', now deposited at the British Library. These have proved to be an invaluable source.

Finally, cultural, moral, and political reactions are examined using numerous sources too. The national and trade press provides a ready source with readers' letters, articles on dancing, and debates concerning the dance halls themselves. Regional newspapers also echoed this national debate with concerns about particular local dance halls. In addition contemporary 'moral' surveys commissioned by various quasi-religious groups (the National Vigilance Society, The Public Morality Council, etc.) and the Home Office (including the Metropolitan Police) provide illuminating evidence of the debate aroused by dancing and dance halls. Minutes from various regional licensing committees and watch committees are also utilized. There is extensive use therefore of material from the City of Birmingham Archives; the City of Glasgow Archives; the City of Manchester Archives; Liverpool Record Office; and the Tyne and Wear Archives, Newcastle-upon-Tyne.

Turning now to the book's organization, the volume is divided into three main sections: Part I: Dancing, the Dance Hall Industry, and its Audience; Part II: Dancing and British Society, 1918–60; and Part III: Conflicts and Control: Moral Panic and the Dance Hall, 1918–60. Broadly speaking each of these sections takes a particular approach to the subject, though there are multiple approaches within each. Part I is largely an economic history; Part II largely a social history; and Part III is predominantly a cultural history.

Taking each section and the chapters within them, we start with Part I: Dancing, the Dance Hall Industry, and its Audience. This first section examines the expansion of the dance hall industry and the development of a 'mass audience' for dancing between 1918 and 1960. There is an examination of the economics of dancing, looking at the main businesses involved, how the industry organized itself, and who controlled it. It asks: how great was the variety of venues available for dancing? Also, the size and structure of the audience for dancing is assessed, detailing how many danced, who exactly went dancing, and how often. It charts the changes to audiences over time. There is also an examination of the emerging dance culture: what people danced and how they danced. Each of the first three chapters deals with a specific time period within this longer history. Chapter 1 looks at the birth of the palais in the period 1918–39. It asks: why was there a 'dance craze' following the First World War? This period is particularly notable because of the emergence of the purpose-built dance hall, or 'palais de danse' and its development is examined in detail. The scale of the dance hall industry nationwide is also detailed, together with regional case studies. Chapter 2 then moves on to examine the wartime boom in dancing, looking at the dance hall industry at war from 1939–45. This chapter examines the challenges to dancing that the war provided, asking how the industry responded to government restrictions, loss of personnel, wartime shortages, and the dangers of the conflict. The causes of the wartime boom in dancing are also explained and the changing experience of the dance hall, and the changing nature of the audience, examined. Chapter 3 ends this survey of the dance hall and its audiences, focusing on the period 1945–60. The post-war period saw dancing achieve the height of its popularity, and the late 1940s and 1950s in particular were a 'Golden Age'—this chapter charts the rising fortunes of the dance hall industry, examining the burgeoning provision of dance facilities and the increase in the size of the audience. It will also examine why this boom occurred, and, ultimately, why the dance hall fell into decline by the end of the period. Finally, Part I concludes with an examination of dancing in Britain at this time, in

Chapter 4, exploring the popularity of particular dances and examining how people learned to dance, or indeed whether they bothered to learn at all. In doing so, Chapter 4 will explode many of the popular myths about particular dances to take a more nuanced approach to Britain's dancing culture.

Turning now to Part II: Dancing and British Society 1918–60, this second section looks at the impact of these changes on individuals and communities. It considers the behaviour of patrons and the conventions they observed. There is a particular concentration on working- and lower-middle-class communities and on young men and women. Thus, this section assesses the importance of dance halls in the fabric of working- and lower-middle-class communities and explores the extent to which they increased the social and expressive possibilities of such communities. The section starts, in Chapter 5, by looking at the importance of dancing and dance halls to youth in the period 1918–60. The development of a separate 'youth culture' in the post-Second World War period is of particular significance, and this chapter discusses the important role of the dance hall in this youth culture. However, it also examines the links between youth and dance in the period before 1945 thus adding to the growing body of scholarship that sees the emergence of youth culture before the end of the Second World War. The chapter examines how youth was deliberately targeted by the dance hall industry, and the ways in which young people made dancing their own. In addition, the important social functions that dancing and dance halls performed for young people, particularly in their transition to adulthood, are a key focus of this chapter. Next, Chapter 6 looks at the impact of dancing and dance halls on women. As we will see, the most frequent dancers were women and dancing's importance to them was perhaps one of the most significant impacts of all the groups examined here. This chapter examines the extent to which dancing offered an important form of independence and physical expression for women. It explores how women behaved at the dance hall, the preparations they made for dancing (dressing up and notions of 'glamour' are significant), and their reasons for dancing. The chapter also discusses the advice that women were given on how to behave, from various dancing manuals, magazines, parents, etc. It shows the extremely important functions dancing performed for women and elaborates its importance in their growing emancipation across the century. Finally in this section, Chapter 7 examines the dance halls' social function as a venue for romance and intimacy. This chapter will investigate the role that the dance hall played in the interaction between the sexes and explores the extent to which the dance hall was an arena for sexual activity. It asks: how much sexual activity was there in dance halls? How did people 'pick up' in dance halls? Who took the initiative? What advantages did the dance hall have over other venues? It shows that the dance hall became central to courtship in twentieth-century Britain.

Having examined the development of a mass audience for dancing, and the important social functions that it performed, the final section the book, Part III: Conflicts and Control: Moral Panic and the Dance Hall, 1918–60, makes an assessment of wider reactions to dance halls and dancing in the period and relates them to the political, economic, and social contexts of the time. Chapter 8 deals with the issues of morality and gender. A great deal of concern was created by the coming together of men and women in a supposedly intimate manner on the dance floor. This chapter identifies the moral panic created by the new music and new dances. It examines how the behaviour of men and women in the dance hall was seen to reflect changing notions of femininity and masculinity and new attitudes towards sex. Race was also an issue intimately related to dancing and it too caused considerable debate, which is considered in Chapter 9. Although the bulk of 'non-white' migration to Britain came in the period after 1960, race was an 'issue' in the history of dance halls before that date. Much of the music danced to was black in origin, and this created both positive and negative responses. This chapter also offers an interesting insight into developing race relations in the period before mass immigration. The associations of dancing with jazz music in the 1920s, and the racist reaction to that music will be examined. Wartime tensions between white and black GIs present in Britain and the British public's reaction to this conflict are also discussed. In the post-war period, West Indian immigration in the 1950s and colour bars in dance halls are explored; anti-Semitism and anti-Americanism also feature in this chapter. Next, in Chapter 10, we consider the reaction to dancing based on its associations with youth and youth culture. The dance hall became associated with criminal behaviour amongst youths from as early as the 1920s and this chapter explores the reaction against dance halls based on an assumed link with gangs, fighting, and juvenile delinquency more generally.

Within each of these final three chapters there is an additional focus on the shaping of Britain's dance culture, examining how the anxieties detailed caused conflict over the direction of Britain's dance culture. The fight to control the physical space of the dance hall, and the battle to control dancing and dance forms, are outlined. These chapters examine how the churches, certain politicians, and the dance halls and dance teachers themselves sought to 'clean up' dancing and the dance hall, for a variety of reasons and how dances, dance music, and dance halls were changed a result.

As is evident, therefore, the analysis that follows is thematic and often circular rather than strictly chronological, and certain key events and issues recur throughout. This is an intentional effort to explore dance halls and dancing from more than one perspective, and to stress the links between the various themes covered. That being said, attempts have been made to avoid unnecessary repetition. It is hoped that such an approach provides a more nuanced assessment of the experience and impact of dancing in British society.

PART I

DANCING, THE DANCE HALL INDUSTRY, AND ITS AUDIENCE

Chapter 1

The Birth of the Palais

Dancing and Dance Halls, 1918–39

INTRODUCTION

Social dancing in Britain started well before 1918. Prior to the emergence of the palais de danse there were public ballrooms, dancing salons, and all manner of public venues where dancing took place, often on an impromptu or ad hoc basis. What is significant about the period after the First World War, however, is the enormous growth in the audience for social dancing and the development of a sophisticated business both catering for, and to some extent, creating this huge demand. Moreover, this period saw the working and lower-middle classes dancing more regularly and in greater numbers than in any previous period. In short, there was a revolution in popular dancing.

THE GROWTH OF A MASS MARKET FOR DANCING, 1918–39

The dance hall had various roots in the emerging leisure industry of late nineteenth-century Britain. At one end of the social scale, the dance hall emerged from the ballrooms of large hotels, restaurants, and private clubs frequented by the upper-middle and upper classes. Its working-class origins were more diverse. As with music halls, dance halls often started as impromptu 'get togethers' in public houses, and other public places, where singing, pianos, and other simple instruments would provide the music for working-class people to dance to. Like the music hall alongside which it grew up, we can see a similar process of formalization, commercialization, and cartelization in its emergence as a distinctive cultural form. Enterprising publicans saw the possibilities of providing more professional musical accompaniment, sectioning off parts of the pub for dancing and charging a small fee. Later, entrepreneurs from the wider leisure industry saw the potential for profit and opened up separate dancing rooms and dancing halls in urban areas. More frequent public dancing was also a product of the proliferation of municipal halls, assembly rooms, and church halls in the Victorian era; symbols of the spirit of philanthropy and the emergence of a new civic pride given legislative power by the Local Government Act of 1888. This coincided with an unprecedented degree of live music as cafés, restaurants, and hotels employed bands, orchestras, and quartets to accompany their clientele. Bandstands in public parks added to this growing musical culture. In addition, the development of seaside holiday resorts in the nineteenth century, with their numerous facilities for amusement, also provided the physical spaces and business experience necessary for the emergence of the dance hall.

That being said, before the First World War, the public dancing facilities available to the working class were restricted. Those that did exist were either poorly managed or expensive. Moreover, dancing lessons were required to learn the complicated steps and this was not only expensive but often socially unacceptable for working-class males. Holding dances also involved the hiring of musicians and a public hall and the provision of refreshments—all of which served to confine it, for the most part, to special occasions organized by large groups of people. As Llewellyn Smith noted in 1935, not only was dancing not popular among the working class, when it did occur it was fairly disorganized:

> Dancing was not a very popular amusement forty years ago. There were no 'palais-de-danse'... and the dance club was unknown. Privately organised dances, or the occasional public dances at places like the Albert Hall, the Crystal Palace or Covent Garden, did not of course touch the lives of the working class. Dances in which workers took part were run by the various settlements and clubs at Christmas time and on special occasions, but the dancing was often very rough. The men had little idea of steps, the girls were not much better, and the dance sometimes turned into a 'rough house.'[1]

The majority of public dances open to the working class between 1900 and 1919 were held in assembly halls, which could be found in most towns or cities.[2] There were very few purpose-built public dance halls run exclusively for dancing, though some did exist. Dancing schools also provided dancing facilities, holding cheap weekly dances in addition to their normal lessons and larger monthly dances in town halls. The best opportunities for dancing were found outside London and other major towns and cities, in seaside resorts such as Blackpool, Morecombe, New Brighton, Great Yarmouth, Margate, and Douglas. Here dances were held more frequently than elsewhere in the country, often every night of the week in the holiday season, and there were large public dance halls. However, before the widespread adoption of 'holidays with pay' opportunities to visit such resorts were limited for the working class. By 1914, therefore, what little organized dancing there was in working-class communities was centred around dance schools and dancing instructors.

In the period before the First World War, the most enthusiastic dancers in Britain were the upper and middle classes. Styles in dancing, music, and dress were focused on this group and the facilities that were available to them far outnumbered

[1] H. Llewellyn Smith, *The New Survey of London Life and Labour* (London: P. S. King & Son, Ltd, 1930–6), ix, 42.

[2] For a history of dancing before 1919 see P. J. S. Richardson, *A History of English Ballroom Dancing (1910–45): The story of the development of the modern English style* (London: Herbert Jenkins, 1947), 1–35, from which information in this section is taken.

those for the working class.[3] At the higher levels of society private dances were regularly held by the nobility, together with County Balls held by property-owning families in the shires. In London, the Grafton Galleries, the Wharncliffe Rooms, the Portman Rooms, the Savoy Hotel, and the Princess Galleries were popular locations for society dances. London was the centre for the balls of the 'Season' and its large hotels, particularly the Ritz, greatly influenced the nature and popularity of dancing in Britain at this time. There were also innumerable 'subscription dances' organized for charity or by a tennis, football, cricket, or rowing club, which were held in the ballrooms of big hotels in London and throughout the country. Their tickets, usually from 6s 6d to 10s 6d, including supper, and even more for charity events, indicate that the clientele were of above average income.[4]

The provision of 'public' facilities catering for the middle and upper classes was particularly good and the Edwardian period saw a marked shift away from private to public dances. Between 1900 and 1914 numerous 'dance clubs' were formed in the West End of London but they were not fixed features, owned no permanent premises, and hired hotels and other ballrooms for their meetings. These clubs held a series of dances, up to twice a week, for which payment was made in advance. One of the more important of these clubs, the Boston Club, had evolved from the famous KDS or Keen Dancers' Society established in 1903. The Boston Club was one of the first to organize 'dinner dances'. With the development of dinner dances, London's top restaurants also began to run dances. The dance clubs also catered predominantly for the upper and upper-middle classes. Two of the most important were the Royalist Club founded in 1910, which held dances in the Connaught Rooms, and the Public Schools' and Universities' Dance Club established at the Savoy Hotel in 1911.

The increasing popularity of dancing among the upper and upper-middle classes by 1913 resulted in the appearance of the first permanent dance clubs that owned their own premises and provided regular dancing. Again they were exclusively for the rich. The most popular were located at prestigious addresses: The Lotus Club, Garrick Street; Murray's Club, Beak Street; the 400 Club in Old Bond Street; and Ciro's Club in Orange Street all established themselves as fashionable spots. At about the same time, tea dances began to be held at the Princes, Carlton, and Waldorf Hotels.

Several factors allowed dancing to break away from its exclusively upper-class following. Of these developments, the most important was a rise in real wages and increased leisure time for the working population. Between 1914 and 1938 the average working week fell from 54 to 48 hours. Average weekly money wages rose from £1 12s in 1913 to £3 10s in 1938, by which time nearly 42 per cent of workers received paid holidays. This gave rise to annual spending on leisure estimated at between £200 to £250 million during the 1920s and 1930s.[5] More specifically and of direct consequence to the popularity of dancing were the changes

[3] See Richardson, *A History*, 10–21. [4] *DT*, October 1935, 49.

[5] R. Stone and D. A. Rowe, *The Measurement of Consumers' Expenditure and Behaviour in the United Kingdom, 1920–1938*, vol. ii (Cambridge: Cambridge University Press, 1966).

in musical and dancing styles imported from the United States just prior to, and during, the First World War, the development of purpose-built dance halls, and the subsequent creation of large chains of dance halls by big business concerns. Each of these developments will be considered. As a result, the immediate post-war period saw a massive growth in the popularity of dancing. It is estimated that nearly 11,000 dance halls and nightclubs opened up between 1919 and 1926 and contemporaries spoke of a 'dance craze'.[6] Whilst such figures undoubtedly overestimate the extent to which dancing provision grew, there was a huge boom in demand for dancing immediately following the end of the war. Certainly, the press was fascinated by the enormous popularity of dancing at this time. Speaking of the 'Craze for Dancing in London' in January 1919, for example, the *Dundee Evening Telegraph* noted: 'London has gone dancing mad . . . dancing establishments in London are crowded morning, noon, and night with eager pupils studying all the curiosities of the fox-trot, the one-step, the Jazz roll . . . whilst dancing halls are booked up for months ahead.'[7] That year *The Times* also commented on the dance craze in the capital, though it was inclined to withhold approval:

> To one freshly returned from the devastated areas of France and the gutted workshops of Belgium, London presents a wild atmosphere of amusement, recalling some of the worst of the bad old days . . . the present Jazz-madness makes us inclined to sympathize with the rather snobbish Plutarch, who held that dancing . . . held sway in senseless, uncritical theatres, spurned by the intellectual and lofty-minded . . . As for the Jazz, judging from the seriousness of the faces of some of its celebrants it may be religious.[8]

Outside London, regional newspapers noted the enormous popularity of dancing. In 1919 *The Derby Telegraph* reflecting on the 'recent extraordinary increase in the popularity of dancing amongst all sections of the community'[9] reported: 'The craze has not nearly exhausted itself. Syndicates continue to be formed to buy up big places for dancing halls and floors to cost a small fortune . . . and in the meantime the newspapers are full of the latest creations . . .'[10] Talking of the popularity of dancing in northern English towns in 1920, the *Cheltenham Chronicle* noted: 'Dancing, with "the pictures" and football, fill in all the non-working hours in our great manufacturing towns, and, as a consequence, dancing masters not only teach the young how to step, but provide handsome dancing halls for them.'[11] In Edinburgh too in 1920 it was recorded:

> Last year's boom in dancing was attributed to a craze which would soon pass. Such is not the case, however. A visit to any of the numerous halls in the city will convince the most sceptical. Particularly on a Saturday night large numbers can be seen at any dance hall. Indeed, there is every indication that the present dancing season is going to be a

[6] J. McMillan, *The Way it Was, 1914–34* (London: Kimber, 1979), 76.
[7] *DET*, 7 January 1919, 7. [8] *The Times*, 29 April 1919, 15.
[9] *Derby Daily Telegraph*, 5 May 1919, 7. [10] *Derby Daily Telegraph*, 1 September 1919, 3.
[11] *Cheltenham Chronicle*, 18 December 1920, 8.

> record one in Edinburgh. Halls of every size and description that can be adapted for dancing purposes are in great demand.[12]

Firms soon rushed to cater for the demand. In Burnley there were already four permanently licensed places for public dancing in operation by 1919.[13] In Scotland too it was noted: 'There is no lack of enterprise being shown in Edinburgh to meet the demand for dancing halls' highlighting a £40,000 venture in the city.[14] The adaptation of buildings to accommodate the new dancing crowds became commonplace, as new dance halls sprung up all over the country. In Arbroath in 1919, for example, permission was granted to convert St George Hall into a new dance hall by the local magistrates.[15] In Edinburgh the former Player's Riding Academy, Tollcross, was also converted into dance rooms in 1920.[16] Where there was no provision for the new dancing craze, locals complained. In Dundee in 1919, for example, the press noted local demands for dancing in parks and other public places, highlighting the concerns of those 'who proclaim that dancing has become *the* popular recreation, and that ample facilities should be provided'.[17]

Such was its success that alternative leisure forms seemed to suffer as a result of dancing's new-found popularity. The annual report of the Cinematograph Exhibitors' Association for 1922 voiced its concern at the rise of the dance hall:

> The public with depleted pockets after a mad orgy of spending, have largely deserted their annual forms of entertainment and have been to a considerable extent devoting such spare cash as they possess to dancing. The head has given way to the feet. Drama (legitimate and otherwise), the music-hall, and the concert room are all suffering from an unprecedented slump. The cinema is sharing the same fate.[18]

Such was the popularity of informal dancing that members of the British Association of Teachers of Dancing, meeting at their annual conference in Aberdeen in 1922, had complained of 'the evil effects arising from the unrestricted granting of dancing licences to hotels, clubs, dancing palaces, and adventurous persons'.[19] Certainly the number of venues where dancing was taking place seemed to mushroom. In Liverpool, for example, whilst only 79 places were permanently licensed for dancing in 1919, this had risen to 130 by 1922, and 152 by 1925.[20] Similarly, in Newcastle-upon-Tyne, seventy places were licensed for dancing in 1920, rising to eighty-two by 1923 and ninety-nine by 1926.[21] The city's largest dance hall, The Oxford Galleries, opened in 1925 with capacity for 2,500 dancers.

Whilst entrepreneurs rushed to convert existing premises to dancing, levels of business were given an enormous fillip by the arrival of 'palais de danse' in Britain.

12 *EEN*, 17 November 1920, 3.
13 *Burnley News*, 15 February 1919, 7.
14 *EEN*, 23 September 1920, 2.
15 *DET*, 13 August 1919, 7.
16 *EEN*, 8 December 1920, 7.
17 *DET*, 17 April 1919, 2.
18 *The Times*, 15 March 1922, 9.
19 *The Times*, 29 June 1922, 10.
20 LRO: 347/JUS/1/5, 'Register of Licenses for Music, Singing and Dancing 1919–26'.
21 TWA: Newcastle Magistrates Court Collection, MG.Nc.7/4, 'Licensing Minutes 1917–35'.

Adopting a French name to add a note of 'glamour', palais de danse had been first established in North America. They were permanent, purpose-built public dance halls that evolved specifically to cater for a large working- and lower-middle-class audience. Being purpose-built they were able to offer first-class dance floors, orchestras of musicians and other facilities, such as cafés or restaurants, which no Assembly Hall or dancing school could provide. Furthermore, whereas the dancing schools had clung steadfastly to the older dance steps and dance music, as P. J. S. Richardson observed: 'These Palais . . . differed from the previous "Assemblies" not only in their design and their equipment but also in their programme. The modern palais offered an up-to-date programme with an up-to-date orchestra instead of the old programme largely made up of sequence dances and play by a "Quadrille Band".'[22] This modernity was vital to their success.

The first palais de danse to be built in Britain was the Hammersmith Palais, opened on 28 October 1919. It was the brainchild of North American entrepreneurs, Howard Booker and Frank Mitchell.[23] Booker was a British-Canadian but also a citizen of the United States, and Mitchell was American. Both were serial entrepreneurs and had attempted to introduce other American leisure pursuits to England, including baseball. Together they were directors of twelve companies, including the London Baseball Association Ltd, The International Institute of Beauty Culture Ltd, and the Universal Mail Order Company. Booker and Mitchell had witnessed the enormous explosion in interest in dancing in the United States where purpose-built dance halls had opened to cater for a new mass market. Seeing similar growth potential in Britain they set out to emulate the American dance palaces by creating the most adventurous dancing facility in Britain to date. The venue in Hammersmith was chosen because of its proximity to the underground and railway station, which was located immediately behind. Trams and buses also stopped near the entrance. Centrally located and well connected to the transport system, it was believed that it would allow people from all over London to dance there. Size was also important. The large hall needed to cater for a mass dancing audience had previously been a tram depot and then a skating rink. It could accommodate about 2,000. The amount invested in the Hammersmith venture was impressive. The share capital was worth £30,000 and the original shareholders included the margarine manufacturer Sidney Van de Burgh. It was luxurious, with an expensive 'sprung' floor, brilliant decorations, a café, restaurant, and, of course, the most modern style in music playing every night. The contemporary fashion for Chinese-style decoration was picked up; with two pagodas in the dance floor and in the centre was a model mountain with a replica Chinese village and a fountain. Silk Chinese lanterns adorned the ceiling. At either end of the dance floor was a bandstand, to allow multiple bands to play for the dancers. People thought the partners were mad to contemplate so large and magnificent a hall for public dancing, and assumed that it would be a failure.

[22] *DT*, October 1935, 49.

[23] Information in this section from National Archives: BT 31/24605/155007 'Hammersmith Palais de Danse' (1919–32).

Booker and Mitchell were vindicated, however. It made over three times its original capital in the first twelve months and on opening night, a crowd of 7,000 dancers queued to enter, eager to listen to its music, provided for the first nine months by the Original Dixieland Jazz Band on tour from America. Even when the Original Dixieland Jazz Band left, the Hammersmith Palais was able to attract many of the best dance bands in Britain and was often the venue for visiting American bands, notably Sidney Bechet soon after the ODJB. It was a huge hit. The Hammersmith Palais attracted actors, sportsmen, film stars, and even royalty, with a list of patrons that included the Prince of Wales (a keen dancer), the Duke of York, Mary Pickford, Douglas Fairbanks, Lady Diana Duff Cooper, and George Carpentier. It was estimated that three million dancers had danced there by 1928 and it became a national attraction, known throughout Britain. Its manager, M. E. Dowdall, estimated that less than 5 per cent of its patrons were drawn locally, the rest coming from all over London and farther afield.[24]

The success of the Hammersmith venture was so great that its owners opened a second 'palais de danse' in Birmingham shortly afterwards. It provided inspiration for hundreds of others too, as businesses rushed to imitate Booker and Mitchell's success. The spread of palais throughout Britain was rapid. In Edinburgh the Palais de Danse, Fountainbridge opened in 1920—though the Wemyss Ballroom also advertised itself as 'Edinburgh's Palais de Danse', a sign of the fashionability of both the word and the concept.[25] In the space of a few years, Britain's dancing facilities were transformed as large, luxurious ballrooms emerged (see Figs. 1.1–1.3). In Glasgow the Dennistoun Palais and Plaza opened in 1922,[26] the F&F Palais de Danse opened in Partick in 1925,[27] The Locarno on Sauchiehall Street opened in 1926[28] together with The Imperial Palais,[29] and Green's Playhouse opened in 1927 with a huge dance floor with capacity for 6,000 dancers.[30] In Manchester there was similar growth. The Arcadian dance hall opened up in 1921, followed by the Casino Ballroom in 1922, the Rivoli Palais de Danse and the Dance de Luxe in 1923, the Savoy Ballroom in 1925, the Majestic in 1926, and the Plaza, the Blackeley Palais de Danse, Levenshulme Dance de Luxe, and Embassy in 1927. The Ritz Palais de Danse followed in 1928.[31] In Liverpool the Grafton Rooms opened in 1924 and in Birmingham, in addition to Booker and Mitchell's second palais opened in Sparkbrook in 1920, Tony's Ballroom opened in 1926 as did The West End Ballroom which had accommodation for 900 dancers.[32]

[24] *DT*, March 1928, 843–5.

[25] E. Casciani, *Oh, How We Danced! The history of ballroom dancing in Scotland* (Edinburgh: Mercat Press, 1994), 46–7.

[26] GCA: City Assessor's Department: D-CA 8/2636, 'Dennistoun Palais'/'Plaza'.

[27] GCA: City Assessor's Department: D-CA 8/988, 'F&F Palais de Danse'.

[28] GCA: City Assessor's Department, D-CA 8/2930, 'Locarno Ballroom'.

[29] GCA: City Assessor's Department D-CA 8/2753, 'Imperial Palais' and Green's Playhouse'.

[30] GCA: Mitchell Library, Gf 381 GLA, 'Ritz Palais de Danse'.

[31] MCA, M117/4/4/2, Register of Music and Dancing Rooms, 1902–27.

[32] *Birmingham Dispatch*, 17 August 1926, 4.

Fig. 1.1. Dance hall architecture: exterior of Glasgow Locarno, 1938
Source: Herald and Times Group.

It was not just in the larger cities of Britain that palais appeared either. Almost immediately, palais sprang up in smaller towns throughout the country. In Nelson, Lancashire the 'New Palais de Danse' was opened in 1920, as was the Palais de Danse in Miller Arcade, Preston.[33] Dover too had a palais de danse operating by 1920[34] and in 1922 the 'Palais De Danse Rosyth Company' started work on a palais for the shipbuilding town.[35] In 1923 Exmouth, Devon got the Arcadian Hall.[36] In 1924 Perth got the go-ahead for a new dance hall in York Place.[37] In Penzance the Marina Ballroom opened in 1926,[38] whilst in Grantham that year the

[33] *Burnley News*, 11 December 1920, 4. [34] *Dover Express*, 10 September 1920, 5.
[35] *DET*, 24 November 1922, 8. [36] *Exeter and Plymouth Gazette*, 27 November 1923, 7.
[37] *DET*, 17 April 1924, 3.
[38] *The Cornishman and Cornish Evening Telegraph*, 3 November 1926, 4.

Fig. 1.2. Dance hall architecture: exterior of Dennistoun Palais, 1936
Source: Courtesy of Glasgow City Council Archives.

Fig. 1.3. Dance hall architecture: exterior of Nottingham Palais de Danse, 1925
Source: Image courtesy of A P Knighton and www.picturethepast.org.uk.

building of a new dance hall was also approved.[39] In 1927, Loughborough got a new luxury dance hall, with accommodation for 800 dancers, with cloakrooms and a ballroom whose ceiling was adorned with hand-painted lanterns and painted butterflies, balloons, dragonflies, and birds.[40]

The growth of purpose-built dance halls providing first-rate facilities at affordable prices, with proper organization and orderly conduct, shifted the focus of dancing by the mid-1920s away from its former upper-class strongholds in the West End of London towards an urban lower-middle- and working-class patronage. The palais de danse were providing the facilities that would, by the mid-1930s, make dancing a truly mass leisure pursuit. Regular, cheap, and modern, dances at a palais de danse were ideal for those with lower incomes who were interested in the new dance steps and the new dance music. However, despite the eventual triumph of the palais, the development of popular dancing in Britain at this time was not without its problems. The reality of dancing's popularity in Britain during the 1920s was more complex than the notion of a 'dance craze' and the appearance of the palais suggest.

The growth in the popularity of dancing during the 1920s was impressive but it was not continuous. Dancing had become a 'craze' in the immediate post-war boom but it was hit by the economic cycles of the interwar period as much as any other business. It was not until the mid-1930s that it could claim to be a mass leisure pursuit and the development of the Mecca circuit of dance halls and the resolve of other dance hall businessmen played a leading part in this revival. Before coming to that development, let us examine some of the factors which affected dancing's popularity and highlight the fluctuating fortunes of business in the 1920s. For a variety of reasons, the immediate post-war boom in dancing was not sustained and the numbers of people dancing began to stabilize after about 1922–3, despite the peak of excitement created by the Charleston craze. Firstly, during this period the cinema was not dislodged from its dominant position in entertainment. The acceleration in the rate of construction of cinemas was testimony to the growing popularity of the film as entertainment. By 1926 there were 3,000 cinemas in operation, a rate of growth given a further boost with the advent of sound films in 1925, rising continually to 5,000 by 1939,[41] Secondly, the dancing profession attempted to raise the status of dancing by incorporating complicated dance steps, difficult to execute and requiring expensive lessons—factors which combined to deter some from entering dance halls. Thirdly, radio was emerging and although not yet the mass medium it was later to become, it already had a large following, with over half a million licensed listeners by 1923, rising rapidly to five million by 1932. Radio began to consume money and occupy leisure time. Fourthly, the appearance on the market of increasingly cheap portable gramophones was moving the focus of some leisure activities back into the home. More importantly,

[39] *Grantham Journal*, 27 November 1926, 12.
[40] *Nottingham Evening Post*, 12 September 1927, 6.
[41] J. Richards, *The Age of the Dream Palace: Cinema and Society in 1930s Britain* (London: I. B. Tauris, 2009), 11–12.

all of these developments were taking place in the context of regionally based economic decline after the post-war boom, especially in those areas affected by high unemployment. Thus, whilst the media saw dancing as a 'guilt-edged' business, the reality was more nuanced. As a 1927 editorial in the *Dancing Times* discussed, the validity of claims concerning the popularity of dancing was suspect:

> We refer glibly to the present 'dancing craze' and a year or two ago wrote about the 'boom' in dancing. There is no such thing to-day as a dancing craze, neither has there been a boom in dancing during the present generation. Listen to this. A director of a company which owns more important Dance Halls than any other in the country estimates that on a Saturday night in London not more than twenty thousand people are at dances whereas on the same day of the week upwards of half a million people visit the cinema in the Metropolitan area. The dancing craze has not yet come . . . we have scarcely reached the fringe of it.[42]

It is also important to remember that for much of the 1920s, the popularity of dancing was subject to seasonal fluctuations. Winter was the most popular season for dancing, and this was when dance halls recorded their best business. In the summer months, business in town and city ballrooms could drop off considerably and some had to close altogether. This was due to a variety of factors—the lure of seaside holidays, the desire to be outside during better weather, but also the stuffiness of many overcrowded dance halls. Some businesses tried to overcome this lull by employing top London dance bands over the summer season, or adopting stunts or themed dance programmes. Yet it was not until the widespread adoption of more effective air-cooling systems in dance halls that seasonality began to decline.

Of greater importance to the popularity of dancing was the economic downturn caused by the worldwide depression of 1929. At first this hit the popularity of dancing hard. In July 1929 the *Daily Mail*, for example, gloomily stated that '[d]ancing in Manchester is declining in popularity'. It pointed to the closure of the Rivoli ballroom in Oxford Road and the Blackley Palais de Danse and their conversion to cinemas. It went on: 'The slump in dancing began about eighteen months ago. Five ballrooms closed permanently at the beginning of last summer, and not have re-opened for dancing.' The downturn created considerable introspection from those involved in the dance business, which resolved to try and find out why business was declining. In Manchester, for example, local opinion blamed draconian restrictions on licensing of late hours by magistrates, but also the economic climate. The *Daily Mail* opined: 'The slump is caused by a shortage of money amongst the younger people, who, because of the slump in Manchester's cotton industry, cannot afford to dance every night in the week, as many of them used to.'[43] As the downturn got worse, disquiet in the dance business grew and a number of scapegoats were sought. 'Sitter Out', regular columnist in the *Dancing Times*, in June 1929 speculated that it was 'poor management' and heavy overheads (especially paying bands too much) that led to the failure of some dance halls.

[42] *DT*, October 1927, 2. [43] *Daily Mail*, 27 July 1929, 20.

He also claimed that the boards of directors of such companies had insufficient knowledge of how to run a palais de danse.[44] Later that summer, dance teachers blamed the 'immense variety of arduous and complicated new steps which all self-respecting dancers have to learn' for damaging business.[45] Competition from other leisure forms also affected business in this harsher economic climate. Skating became a popular alternative to dancing around the end of 1929 and beginning of 1930 and its impact on Britain's dance halls was even picked up by the *New York Times*, which stated that 'the dance craze has been hard hit by the vogue of skating'.[46] It reported that the Hammersmith Palais had been converted into an ice rink, together with the Locarno, Glasgow (only opened the year before as a dance hall) and dance halls in Edinburgh and Birmingham, which had four skating rinks. Yet this skating craze proved short-lived, as did the slump in dancing.

Despite the fears that the dance craze was over, and even with the initial slump it caused, in fact the depression of 1929 reinforced the centrality of dancing, and in particular the palais, to British leisure habits. As early as the middle of 1930, there was evidence that attendance levels at dance halls were picking up again and business was strong enough to encourage new enterprises to open. In Edinburgh, for example, a new ballroom opened at the Grosvenor Hotel in November 1930, followed by the Lido Dance Club, Cockburn Street in March 1931, and the Havanna Dance Club, Princess Street in July.[47] But it was not just the higher end of the dance business that saw a revival. Edinburgh's Palais de Danse was booming and it was observed: 'never has the Palais been so successful than it is at present'.[48] Even in some of the worst affected parts of the country the depression was not deterring dancers. From Belfast, where unemployment was amongst the highest in the country, in August 1931 ballrooms reported their 'best season for some years' and the 'record crowds' prompted some to comment that there was 'an opening for some ambitious individual to provide another suitable dance hall'.[49] The following month, the new Celtic Ballroom was duly opened in Portrush together with the Regent Palais in Bangor, followed a few months later by 'one of the largest halls in Ireland', a new ballroom on the top floor of the Co-op Building.[50] In Glasgow too there was confidence despite the economic troubles. Alex Warren of the Albert Palais described October 1930 as the 'best start' to the autumn season for over two years.[51] That month a new hall, the Norwood Ballroom, was opened and it was reported that 'notwithstanding the fact that there is still considerable trade depression in Clydeside, the numerous dance halls in the City report fairly good business' with the Plaza and Dennistoun Palais both doing 'exceptionally well'. It went on that at 'that popularly priced hall, Dennistoun Palais, the business is really wonderful, nightly attendances of 800 to 1000 dancers are quite regular'.[52] It would seem that the mainstream palais with

[44] *DT*, June 1929, 220.
[45] *DT*, August 1929, 414.
[46] *New York Times*, 23 February 1930, 53 (New York City, New York).
[47] *DT*, December 1930, 409; April 1931, 89; and July 1931, 397.
[48] *DT*, January 1932, 509.
[49] *DT*, August 1931, 495.
[50] *DT*, August 1932, 503.
[51] *DT*, October 1930, 101.
[52] *DT*, December 1931, 389.

their excellent value for money entertainment were doing particularly well as times became harder. In Liverpool, also badly hit by economic woes, Alderman John Clancy described his home as 'the dancing city,' so numerous were the licences being issued for dances.[53] The *Dancing Times* was able to report that Liverpool 'ballrooms have all re-opened and the floors of most of them are crowded . . . Both around the districts and across the river, the halls are being well patronised and the main dance centres in the city have provided novelties and good bands.'[54] In Manchester too business seemed buoyant by the end of 1931. The Ritz was 'attracting capacity audiences' and the Plaza Ballroom underwent an expensive refurbishment,[55] both indications of a return to confidence in the industry. At the Nottingham Palais de Danse, profits were high. In the 1930–1 season it was possible to declare a dividend of 7 ½ per cent and carry forward a balance of over £3,000. As one of its shareholders commented: 'In view of the fact that Nottingham has been hit as hard, if not harder, than a great number of industrial towns, this is an extraordinarily gratifying financial report.'[56] By the next year, attendance figures for the 1931–2 winter season were 50,000 higher than for the previous year. Profits were also up, at £4,683 9s 6d compared with £3,207 the year before. The shareholders dividend also rose to 12 ½ per cent.[57] It was also reported that the popularity of dancing had saved the Mecca group in 1931. Business in the restaurants was the worst for many years but the development of the dance halls was strong enough to ensure increased profits in all branches.[58] Seasonality also seemed to be disappearing. By 1931–2, many dance halls were remaining open during the summer months too. At the Locarno Streatham, attendances in July 1931 sometimes exceeded 2,000 per night, and averaged 1,500 daily for the whole month.[59]

Dancing, it would appear, was depression proof. Far from damaging dancing, the economic downturn actually seemed to encourage its popularity. In particular, the slump secured and extended the success and dominance of the palais de danse. Why was this? The economic downturn forced the general public to prioritize, jettisoning those leisure activities considered less essential to enjoyment. The palais thrived in hard economic times because they offered excellent dancing facilities at very reasonable prices. As Russell Pickering, general manager of the dances at the Royal Opera House Covent Garden noted:

> [T]he public today are very discriminating and very critical of the music provided and the accommodation available. The effect is today one has to be a specialist to give the public good dancing; the days of an indifferent floor with mediocre music and poor amenities are over—hence the popularity of the well-organised dance hall.[60]

Palais de danse also offered a range of other amenities and entertainments for a single admission price and in hard times the audience wanted more for their

[53] *DT*, December 1931, 377.
[54] *DT*, November 1931, 201.
[55] *DT*, October 1931, 87.
[56] *DT*, August 1931, 446.
[57] *DT*, July 1932, 330.
[58] *DT*, December 1932, 460.
[59] *DT*, August 1931, 499.
[60] *DT*, October 1934, 42.

money. As we shall see later, the businessmen behind the palais de danse worked hard to capture and extend the market for dancing. The depression saw them triumphing over other competition for the depleted pockets of pleasure seekers.

As significant as the resilience of dancing to the economic downturn was, by the end of 1931 not only had dancing regained its previous levels of popularity, it had now passed beyond the status of a 'fad' and had established itself as a key feature of Britain's social and cultural life. Indeed, its survival during a time of unprecedented economic turmoil was testament to its popularity. As the proprietors of the Masque Ballroom, Birmingham, were able to state that year: 'Ballroom dancing is no longer a craze—it has now become a habit, a well established and exceedingly healthful form of amusement.'[61] Nottingham's S. J. Fallon concurred: 'dancing is neither a "craze" nor is it by any means "over." It is a habit'.[62]

MECCA AND THE DEVELOPMENT OF THE DANCE HALL INDUSTRY

To satisfy this habit new dance businesses began to spring up in cities throughout Britain as the revival in the industry was sustained, and business extended. 1932 saw new dance halls opened in Leeds (the New Gallery Palais de Danse); Bristol (the Astoria Dance Salon); Edinburgh (the Eldorado Ballroom); Glasgow (Cadova Restaurant); Croydon (Mecca Lido).[63] By 1933, business was so good in Glasgow that several dance halls in the city had to turn dancers away and the Dennistoun Palais announced alterations to accommodate more dancers in January of that year.[64] It was not just the depression and subsequent revival that entrenched the dancing habit and allowed palais to triumph, however. Dance hall owners and the emerging chains of dance halls did this too. The rapid commercialization of the dance business is nowhere more typified than in the development of the largest of these dance hall chains, the Mecca chain.

The Mecca chain was co-founded by Cyril L. Heimann and Byron Davies.[65] Heimann, a Dane who moved to England in 1913, started his career in the catering business, working for a firm called 'Mecca Cafes'. After providing catering facilities for the dances that started to be held at the Royal Opera House Covent Garden in 1925, Heimann was quick to recognize the potential mass market open to dance halls if they were properly organized and targeted the mass market decisively enough. He persuaded 'Mecca Cafes' to purchase Sherry's dance hall in Brighton, and in 1927 Heimann entered the dance business by taking over Sherry's as general manager. Heimann worked hard building up the business for several years and was able to persuade financial backers to support him as he expanded his business.

[61] *DT*, October 1931, 79. [62] *DT*, October 1929, 24.

[63] *DT*, March 1932, 723; August 1932, 491; January 1932, 509.

[64] *DT*, January 1933, 511.

[65] Much of the following information is taken from interviews of C. L. Heimann and B. Davies carried out by Tom Harrisson and Alec Hurley. M-O A: MJD 3/A: 'C L Heimann' (1938) and MJD 3/E: 'Facts about C L Heimann' (1938) and 'Byron Davies' (1939).

Sherry's was followed by the Ritz Manchester, in 1930, The Locarno Streatham Hill, southwest London, in 1931 and the Lido Croydon in 1932. In 1933 Heimann and Byron Davies founded the Mecca Agency Limited. Davies had previously been involved in numerous forms of business and commerce and had a keen sense of what was needed to succeed in the increasingly sophisticated consumer and service industry of the interwar period. Davies started in the dance business after visiting the Hammersmith Palais in 1919. Starting without prior knowledge of the industry he built up his own dance halls, which provided greater facilities, high quality floors, and good quality dance bands and musicians. Such direct experience was to prove vital to the success of Mecca.

Mecca was an enterprising concern and its method of business was to acquire cheaply existing dance halls that were faltering or just surviving and then turn them around. In 1935, Heimann started a joint venture in Scotland with Alan B. Fairley, an important operator in the amusement and leisure industry in Scotland. In 1936, Heimann and Fairley became joint Managing Directors in the Locarno, Glasgow, a city that some experts believed had the best dancers in Britain. The Mecca circuit of dance halls then accelerated rapidly and by 1938 Heimann and Fairley had become Associate Directors of dance halls throughout the country; the Palais de Danse Edinburgh; Mecca-Locarno Leeds; Grand Casino Birmingham; and The Royal Tottenham. They were also joint general managers of the Paramount dance hall Tottenham Court Road. By 1940, they even controlled the Royal Opera House Covent Garden from where Heimann had derived his first inspiration. In addition to the halls, by 1938 the Mecca Agency also controlled 300 dance bands playing in some 2,000 establishments throughout the country, more than any other organization in Britain. This agency dealt with virtually all aspects of the dance hall business from management to laying dance floors, building bandstands, supplying bands, cabarets, professional dancers, accounting services, publicity, and so on. There was also a subsidiary, 'Dance Hall Equipment Ltd', that specialized in supplying everything needed for the running of dance halls along the Mecca line 'from carpets to cups, from tea urns to tea spoons; from bandstands to balloons; from shades to streamers. We're decorators, electricians, constructors . . .'[66] The original catering firm, 'Mecca Cafes' was still trading but business grew so that the Mecca Head Offices, located in Dean Street, Soho, expanded from a single floor in 1930 to the occupation of the whole building—six floors—and a staff of nearly 1,000 by 1939. A fine example of both vertical and horizontal expansion in action, Mecca, together with its co-directors Byron Davies and Cyril Heimann, was the most influential dance hall and dance music concern in the country.

Yet Mecca was not alone. In May 1928 one of the largest dance hall and theatre chains was formed when General Theatres Ltd took over the interests of the Szarvasy-Gibbons Syndicate which controlled one hundred dance halls, including the New Casino Palais and Rialto dance hall in Liverpool and The Astoria, Charing Cross Road, London.[67] In addition to these dance halls, General Theatres Ltd also

66 Anon., *Stepping Out* (Danceland Publications, 1940), backpiece.
67 *Melody Maker*, May 1928, 519.

took over the old LTV variety halls and leading dance bandleader Billy Cotton was given the post of Musical Director to the company. As Musical Director, Billy Cotton directed the dance band arrangements at the group's dance halls as well as the newly acquired variety theatres. Management of the chain's ballrooms was left to E. W. Bourne who had opened Southport Palais and managed the Regent Brighton. They were, therefore, a major factor in dance hall provision. Many other theatres and cinema groups, such as Gaumont British and Odeon, also diversified into dance hall ownership. For example, by 1929 The Gaumont British Picture Corporation and Provincial Cinematograph Theatres Ltd owned the Astoria; Dalston Dance Salon; the Palais de Danse Tottenham, Wimbledon, Ilford, and New Cross; the West End dance hall, Birmingham; and the Regents at Brighton and Weymouth.[68]

The businessmen involved in these chains and other dance hall owners were vitally important in extending the market for dancing. Even though dancing had a natural popularity, dance hall owners worked hard to increase the size of the audience for dancing, recognizing the limits which dancing alone had in attracting customers. One of their most important strategies was the investment of huge amounts of money into infrastructure. In order to take its place in the newly emerging commercial leisure industry, and in particular in order to compete with cinema, businesses invested heavily in dance hall buildings. Dance halls took their place alongside cinemas as the new 'people's palaces' of the high street, offering a degree of comfort and value for money typical of the new leisure industry. Thus, a spate of 'luxury' dance halls opened up in major towns and cities throughout Britain in the 1920s and 1930s. Some examples illustrate the extent to which businessmen up and down the country invested time, energy, and capital into the new dance hall industry. The Ritz dance hall in Manchester opened on 11 December 1928. Claiming to be 'the most up to date ballroom in the north of England', it had a sprung parquet floor, a restaurant open from noon 'til midnight, a ladies' hairdressers, and a staff of eighteen headed by two championship dancers, and was managed by Parisian dance teacher Henri Jacques. The excitement that such new leisure facilities created locally is illustrated by the fact that although it had capacity for 1,300, on the opening night 600 dancers were turned away as there was insufficient space to accommodate them.[69] In September 1929, the Locarno Streatham was opened, advertising itself as 'England's Super Dance Hall' it cost £60,000, with £10,000 spent on the ventilation system alone. It had sprung floors in Austrian Oak, and employed Billy Mayerl's Orchestra—a leading London dance band.[70]

Businessmen went to great lengths in order to ensure that they were providing the latest styles and facilities in their dance halls. A sense of the impetus for opening dance halls can be gained from the study of a Lancashire dance hall, the Carlton, Rochdale, that opened in September 1934. The dance hall was the original ideal of two local entrepreneurs, Messrs Blincoe and Travis, who, inspired by the success of

[68] *DT*, October 1929, 26. [69] *DT*, January 1929, 613.
[70] *DT*, September 1929, 551.

dance halls in nearby Bury, saw an opening for a large dance hall in Rochdale. Travis had run this hall, which was always overcrowded, and convinced Blincoe, who had no knowledge of the industry, that money could be made. They found a large disused mill in the centre of Rochdale and persuaded several others to buy it, forming the company Embassy Entertainments. All the investors were local people with no knowledge of the industry but who considered the proposition a relatively safe one. Considerable effort was put into making sure that the newly opened dance hall was up to date and in keeping with the best in the industry. Tours were made to dance halls in Manchester, London, and Scotland and the best features of these halls were communicated to their architects. Once the designs had been decided on, no expense was spared to make the dance hall as comfortable and stylish as possible, and considerable effort was taken with the furnishings:

> It was a lovely place, although I say it myself. And well furnished. And then we got all the settees and tables. And I know we were very, very keen that tables should be the right size. Size enough to . . . comfortably sit four, not sort of just big enough to put your plate on, and your cup and saucer somewhere else. But there was all the crockery to be bought. And we had good service in the restaurant, the café was well equipped and, well, there was nothing skimped about it at all. The tables, the linen and everything in the café. And then the ballroom—of course, the floor was the thing of the ballroom. That was a maple floor. It had to be maple. And there was a great, great lot of discussion and talk about that. It was set on rubber to make it more resilient. And it was beautiful when it was finished, the floor. It was really inviting. You know, a long stretch of this maple flooring. It looked really good altogether . . . It was very nicely done. It was tastefully done. Because . . . we were doing it because it was something we wanted to make it into the best possible.[71]

Big spending was not just a feature of newly opened dance halls either. Rolling programmes of investment were maintained in the better halls and efforts were made to constantly update and extend the facilities and attractions, often at considerable cost. This indicates the continuing profitability of dancing and the determination of those in the dance industry to keep abreast of changing tastes. As the proprietors of the Masque Ballroom Birmingham commented after a renovation in 1931, they hoped 'to provide the acme of comfort for dancers'.[72] The beginning of a new dance season in the autumn was often the occasion for a new face-lift. In October 1930, for example, the Palais de Danse Birmingham was redecorated in Japanese style and a new electric cooling and heating system was installed.[73] Edinburgh's Maxime's Dance Club had also been 'entirely re-decorated' in October 1931 'use having been made of herbaceous landscape scenes, Riviera painting and flood lighting principles'.[74] That same month, the Plaza Ballroom in Manchester was also refurbished and 'an elaborate system of multi-coloured and diffused lighting' was installed, and the West End cast of 'It's a Boy' led by Leslie Henson attended the re-opening, together with the British 'film

[71] The Carlton Rochdale: Oral History, Mrs Rose Blincoe, nd (1990s), Rochdale, Lancashire.
[72] *DT*, October 1931, 79. [73] *DT*, October 1930, 85. [74] *DT*, October 1931, 99.

star' Miss Dodo Watts.[75] Dance floors were one of the biggest areas of expenditure. In September 1931 the Nottingham Palais de Danse spent over £1,000 laying a new dance floor and the hall was 'further enhanced by the addition of new carpets, new lighting and a new decorative scheme'[76] (see Figs. 1.4 and 1.5). In October 1933 the Hammersmith Palais spent £5,000 on a new maple dance floor. Such changes were not one-offs either. In Nottingham, just one year after installing a new dance floor, in July 1932 the Palais de Danse installed a new bandstand, described as an 'entirely new departure in design, with a unique scheme of decoration, and possessing extraordinary acoustic properties'.[77] The following month it employed Louis Armstrong as a guest performer, and later that year Jack Hylton.[78]

Fig. 1.4. Dance hall architecture: exterior of Nottingham Palais de Danse, 1920s
Source: Image courtesy of Nottingham City Council and www.picturethepast.org.uk.

[75] *DT*, October 1931, 87. [76] *DT*, September 1931, 595. [77] *DT*, July 1932, 403.
[78] *DT*, September 1932, 599.

Fig. 1.5. Dance hall decor: ballroom and fountain, Nottingham Palais de Danse, 1925
Source: Image courtesy of Nottingham City Council and www.picturethepast.org.uk.

In addition to investing heavily in dance halls and their facilities, businessmen also sought to increase the size of the dancing audience by utilizing the latest marketing and publicity strategies. The most successful dance halls spent considerable energy trying to keep abreast of changing tastes and anticipating the needs of their customers. As M. E. Dowdall, manager of the Hammersmith Palais de Danse, stated, the 'golden rule' for managing a dance hall was 'never to stand still'. He went on: 'One must always be "polishing up" as it were, embellishing here, redecorating there, eliminating things which have had their day, anticipating and installing the things of tomorrow.'[79] Nottingham Palais de Danse manager Mr Fallon also believed in the importance of keeping up with changes. 'One cannot relax efforts to draw the public into the ballroom. A constant succession of stunts, competitions and divers attractions, must be arranged to hold your patrons.'[80]

Competition to attract dancers was fierce. Special events and party nights were used to woo dancers away from other halls, or alternative leisure forms, and indicate that the dance hall industry was particularly 'go ahead', with a keen appreciation of the demands of its target audiences. A pioneer in this respect was Byron Davies, who came to work for the Mecca Group. Davies was one of the first to make sustained use of press agencies to promote dancing and he advised others in the dance business to adopt the mentality of 'showmanship', highlighting that

[79] *DT*, March 1928, 845. [80] *DT*, December 1930, 331.

businesses needed 'an angle', something to mark them out from the crowd. He was also aware of the power of fashion and changing tastes. Writing in 1928 he claimed: 'In dancing, as in every other walk of life, it is the originator who scores. The craving is ever for "something new", and change is the spice of "variety."'[81] He advocated the use of a number of 'stunts' to liven up the dance hall. Getting dancers to change dance partners more readily was one focus of these stunts. Davies advocated the introduction of dances such as the Paul Jones and the Excuse Me and the idea of 'hidden partners' where a black curtain or screen would be operated by an MC and behind it lady partners would be paired up with male partners one by one. Making dancers feel special by providing small 'gifts' for everyone was another idea. Tombolas, a 'Surprise Night' whereby every tenth or twentieth visitor was awarded a prize, ranging in size and cost, with the prizes progressing in value according to the size of the audience, were also used. There was also the 'Bargain Basement' night whereby the management purchased cheaply a 'job lot' of articles—scissors, key rings, ink bottles, etc.—cheaply and then each visitor, having been charged 6d more than usual, was allowed to rummage in a 'bargain basement' table in the hall.[82] Entertainment variety was also provided by encouraging 'talent nights' whereby the cabaret would be provided by the visitors themselves, with prizes for the best, and offers of a week's engagement for the winner. Band Stunts were also suggested whereby individual band members would be asked to do something special—such as donning special outfits for particular songs, getting one member to dance or sing a chorus in a juvenile voice, or even having a 'massed band parade' when two bands merged and paraded the dance floor.[83]

VENUES FOR DANCING IN INTERWAR BRITAIN

Having outlined the development of the palais and a mass market for dancing, it would be useful to explore in more detail where people danced. During the 1920s and 1930s, dancing was everywhere in Britain. There were an unprecedented number of public and private dance facilities, permanent and temporary, available throughout the country. From Aberdeen to Torquay, not only urban but also rural areas could offer a wide range of options for dancers. We have already seen how the permanent public dance hall helped revolutionize dancing in Britain. Yet, to focus purely on the development of palais de danse and circuits of dance halls would be to ignore the numerous other locations for dancing which existed in even the smallest of communities.

That permanent dance halls were not the only places to dance can be seen from the *New Survey of London*. In 1933 H. Llewellyn Smith counted twenty-three palais de danse in the County of London.[84] However, he reckoned that this was only about one tenth of the total number of locations for dancing, as there were

[81] *DT*, November 1928, 187. [82] *DT*, December 1928, 361.
[83] Ibid. [84] Llewellyn Smith, *New Survey*, ix, 64.

numerous halls and rooms where dancing regularly took place and to which the public were admitted. Local and county councils would grant licences for dancing and music in locations as diverse as church and mission halls, club rooms, municipal halls, assembly halls, swimming baths, hotels, and restaurants. Typical of the variety of locations that each town or city would offer is the description of a 'seaport' town (probably Portsmouth or Southampton) given by Renee Radford in 1927:

> In this particular seaport there are estimated to be some four hundred works, big and small. Few are without their annual whist drive and dance, many have Welfare Institutions that hold weekly 'hops' in the works hall . . . Church social clubs, private dancing clubs, professional dancing halls, the bakers, confectioners, grocers, drapers, dairymen, butchers, police—almost every occupation runs its dances. The Territorials' Drill hall is pressed in to service on an average once a week. Each detachment of territorials gives its dance, with officers and non coms' dances thrown in besides. About sixty to seventy times a year one local cafe alone holds dances, at which from a hundred and fifty to two hundred people attend each time. At another restaurant there would be about fifty a year and at many more anything from four to forty functions during the 'busy' season. At the larger halls the attendances may run up to a thousand, and four or five hundred at a time are commonplace. At one of these such halls over two hundred functions, most of them dances or whist drives and dances, take place—one every night of the week.[85]

An examination of the licensing statistics of several key cities in Britain at this time indicates how varied and numerous opportunities for dancing were. The rise in the number of venues can be seen clearly in Newcastle-upon-Tyne, for example. In 1918, seventy-two locations were licensed for dancing in the city, rising to ninety-five by 1925, 144 by 1930, 245 by 1935, and 251 by 1939.[86] In Birmingham too there was a similarly large increase. In 1919 there were eighty-two locations licensed for dancing, rising to 143 in 1925, 173 by 1930, 176 by 1935, and 179 by 1939.[87] A closer look at the composition of these aggregate figures reveals that the variety of venues for dancing was great. In Liverpool in 1926, for example, there were some 199 different venues licensed for dancing. This included forty-nine public halls, twenty-four church halls, fifteen political clubs, eleven cafés and hotels, four dance halls, and three dance schools, amongst other venues, including Co-op halls, swimming baths, schools, and parks.[88] In Manchester between 1918 and 1932

[85] *DT*, April 1927, 84–5.

[86] TWA: Newcastle Magistrates Court Collection, MG.Nc. 7/4 Licensing Minutes 1917–35 and MG. Nc. 7/5 Licensing Minutes 1936–60.

[87] CBA: PS/B 4/1/1/4 and PS/B 4/1/1/5, *Third Annual Report of the Public Entertainments Committee of Justices* (1920); *Ninth Annual Report of the Public Entertainments Committee of Justices* (1926); *Fourteenth Annual Report of the Public Entertainments Committee of Justices* (1931); *Nineteenth Annual Report of the Public Entertainments Committee of Justices* (1936); *Twenty-Third Annual Report of the Public Entertainments Committee of Justices* (1940). NB up to 1930 these figures also include licences for 'music' and 'music and singing' as well as 'dancing' so will exaggerate the dancing opportunities slightly. After that they only include dancing licences.

[88] LRO: 347/JUS/1/5 'Register of Licenses for Music Singing and Dancing 1919–26'.

there were 245 venues licensed for dancing. Of these, nineteen were permanent dance halls and sixteen were dance schools. Dances were also held in seventeen Co-op halls; eight town halls; thirty-one other public halls; eight assembly rooms; nineteen church halls; twenty-five hotels and restaurants; twenty-five political clubs; thirty-two cinemas and theatres; thirteen works clubs; twelve social clubs as well as five swimming baths, amongst others.[89] In Glasgow in 1937, 256 were venues licensed for dancing, with a capacity of over 32,000. There were twenty-two corporation-owned halls; sixteen public dance halls; eleven social clubs; eleven masonic halls; ten sports clubs; nine works clubs; eight public halls; eight trade halls; eight political clubs; seven Orange Halls; six church halls; five dance schools; five Co-op halls; five institutes; four hotels/cafés; two cinemas; and two private clubs.[90]

Yet it was not just in large cities that such variety could be found. In 1938 the National Institute of Industrial Psychology conducted a survey into 'Leisure Pursuits outside of the Family Circle' in several places in England, including a 'county town' (Ipswich) and a 'satellite town' (Slough). It found widespread evidence of the popularity of dancing, and outlined the provision for it, in both places. In Ipswich (with an estimated population of 92,500) it found that there were twenty-eight venues where dancing regularly took place. They included nine works' clubs which arranged five monthly, two fortnightly, and two weekly dances; five political clubs which arranged two monthly, one fortnightly, and two weekly dances; five church halls which arranged five monthly dances; seven social clubs which arranged three monthly, one fortnightly, and three weekly dances, and two Territorials units which arranged alternately a monthly dance. Put another way, there were an average of sixty-seven dances per month in the town, and the survey estimated a regular dancing audience of about 4,000.[91] In Slough (population 55,000) it found that there were seven halls where dancing took place regularly, including two in hotels, one in a cinema, and two in halls belonging to the YMCA and the Leopold Institute. There were also dances held in five works' canteens and two church halls, though less regularly. The total number of dances organized were forty-five per month—with eight weekly, seven monthly, and eight fortnightly.[92] Rural districts were not immune from the popularity of dancing either. The same 1938 study found that in a 'rural district' (the West Kesteven District of Lincolnshire, 1931 population 16,106) dances were held 'fairly regularly in most of the villages that have halls'. Indeed about one third—seventeen—of the forty-seven villages in the district held dances, including three of the twenty-nine 'small villages'; six of the nine 'middle-sized' villages, and eight out of nine of the 'large' villages. The smallest populations had the most difficulty running dances due to the numbers needed to make them viable. In the largest villages sampled dances were

[89] MCA, M117/4/4/2 'Registers of Music, Dancing and Rooms 1902–37'.

[90] GCA, E7/4/1 'Register of Music Halls etc, 1934–52'.

[91] S. M. Bevington, *Leisure Pursuits outside the Family Circle* (National Institute of Industrial Psychology, 1939), 20.

[92] Bevington, *Leisure*, 72–3.

held fortnightly or weekly; in the middle-sized villages, half held them monthly and half fortnightly; in the smallest villages dances were no more than occasional with two or three per season.[93] Circumstances were certainly aiding dancing in the countryside, however. The number of village halls grew substantially between the wars. The National Council on Social Services, for example, built over 400 village halls and a further boost was given in 1937 by the Physical Training and Recreation Act that allowed for grants for the construction and improvement of village halls.

That village halls, town halls, assembly rooms, and church halls provided opportunities for dancing is perhaps unsurprising. It would be useful to examine the provision of dancing in some of the more unusual venues, however, in order to give an impression of the range of dancing experiences, and dancing audiences, that existed in interwar Britain.

Perhaps one of the most ingenious dance venues was public swimming baths. In the interwar period, many baths experienced a lull in popularity during the winter season as cold weather put off potential bathers. However, enterprising individuals recognized that the buildings could be put to good use as dance halls. Wooden boards were used to cover the swimming pool and became dance floors. Decorations and lighting were installed to create a suitable atmosphere, and the results could be impressive.[94] The facilities provided at the municipal baths at Glossop, for example, reveal how sophisticated swimming bath dance halls were. The decoration of silk Chinese lanterns, dimmed to create atmosphere, the use of plants and the distinctive dancing, seating, and balcony areas were a direct copy of those found in permanent dance halls (see Fig. 1.6). Thus, for several months a year, baths became dance halls, extending the provision of dancing facilities in numerous towns and cities throughout Britain.

Department stores in some provincial towns and cities also provided facilities for dancing on a more permanent basis. In the Lewis's department store in Manchester, for example, a new extension on the fifth floor built in 1927 included a large dance and concert hall where shoppers could dance during the day.[95] One of the biggest providers of dance facilities in this respect was the Co-op. The Co-op had a large number of department stores and other public buildings throughout the country, particularly in the north of England and in Scotland. By 1914 there were 1,371 retail Co-operatives in Britain, with a membership of over three million[96] and by 1937 the Co-operative movement employed over 57,000 people.[97] The Co-op was particularly keen on establishing close links with the communities in which it operated and to this end it engaged in a considerable amount of social and cultural activity, organizing outings, competitions, classes, and dances. Dances were run for members and more significantly, many Co-operative properties had halls at

93 Bevington, *Leisure*, 112.

94 As the 'Charleston/dance derby' scene from the 1946 American film, 'It's A Wonderful Life' reconstructed.

95 *DT*, May 1927, 153.

96 J. F. Wilson, *Building Co-operation: A business history of the Co-operative Group, 1863–2013* (Oxford: Oxford University Press, 2013), 100, 139.

97 P. Redfern, *The New History of the C.W.S.* (London: J. M. Dent & Sons, 1938), 469.

Fig. 1.6. Dancing in the baths: Noel Street Baths, Nottingham, 1929
Source: Image courtesy of Nottingham City Council and www.picturethepast.org.uk.

which public dancing was organized on a regular basis (see Fig. 1.7). In Glasgow in 1937 there were five Co-op halls licensed for dancing with a capacity of 928.[98] In Manchester, capital of the Co-operative movement, there were considerable numbers of Co-op halls used for public dancing. Between 1918 and 1932, there were seventeen that ran regular weekly dances.[99] These dances were well run, with good local bands, refreshments and food for sale, and usually cheap entrance prices. Dancing was a good way of making connections with local communities, as well as making money.

Political groups and organizations also saw the benefits of operating dances on a regular basis, both private and public. Most large towns had buildings occupied by each of the major political parties, with Liberal Clubs, Conservative Clubs, and Labour Clubs being fixed features of a town's social life. As well as providing a focus for political activities, these political clubs also opened themselves up to the general public, for the same reasons that the Co-op did—to reach out, and to make money. In Glasgow in 1937 for example there were eight political clubs licensed for dancing—seven Labour, one Unionist—with a capacity of 860.[100] Manchester had a particularly large number of political clubs where one could dance on a regular

[98] GCA: E7/4/1, 'Register of Music Halls etc, 1934–52'.
[99] MCA: M117/4/4/2, 'Registers of Music, Dancing and Rooms 1902–37'.
[100] GCA: E7/4/1 'Register of Music Halls etc, 1934–52'.

Fig. 1.7. Dancing in the Co-op: New Co-op Hall, Co-operative Society, Ilkeston, Derbyshire, 1939
Source: Image courtesy of www.picturethepast.org.uk.

basis—twenty-five in the period between 1918 and 1932.[101] Enlightened employers also saw the benefits of providing dances for their employees. This could be done in a number of ways. Many large firms had their own premises for social activities—particularly large industrial concerns. At these, social and sporting facilities were provided, and even when dedicated dance floors were not available, gymnasia could easily be converted for the purpose. As early as 1919 Keiller's, the marmalade manufacturers who employed 1,000 in Dundee, began the construction of a dance hall for their employees to go alongside the canteen, library, and sports pitches.[102] They were not alone. In Manchester between 1918 and 1932, there were thirteen works clubs that had full time licences for dancing, including those at Crossley Motors; the LNWR Club; Metro-Ashbury works club; Manchester Tramways Employees Club; Armstrong Whitworth; and the Victoria Mills.[103] In Glasgow too, in 1937, nine large employers provided dancing facilities on their premises, with a total capacity of 2,759 dancers.[104] Alternatively, as we shall see later, many companies hired out public dancing facilities to provide regular dances for their employees. This gave rise to a large number of so-called 'private bookings' in public dance halls, town halls, and other large dance venues. The 1930s also saw the development of 'roadhouses', institutions that took advantage of the growing

[101] MCA: M117/4/4/2 Registers of Music, Dancing and Rooms 1902–37.
[102] *Dundee Courier*, 10 December 1919, 6.
[103] MCA: M117/4/4/2 'Registers of Music, Dancing and Rooms 1902–37'.
[104] GCA: E7/4/1 'Register of Music Halls etc, 1934–52'.

ownership of cars and also provided nightlife in suburbia and the countryside. These were more exclusive than the venues discussed so far, however. Imported from America, roadhouses were entertainment complexes situated outside major towns and cities, usually involving dance bands, entertainers, restaurants, and cocktail bars. Swimming pools were also available in the summer and some even provided landing grounds for private aircraft. Purpose-built, often from concrete and some with modernist exteriors, they nevertheless joined the growing trend of mock tudorism found in suburbia, with panelling and oak beamed interiors. They offered a bizarre contrast between nightlife and countryside. As James Burke observed, they were:

> . . . a way of having a night in town in the country; because, however Arcadian the situation of the place might be, once you entered the doors you were back in Shaftesbury Avenue or Coventry Street. It gave you the feeling of one of those dreams in which you are in two places at once. You could sit in a Jermyn Street snack-bar, and through the window, fifty yards away, you saw the moonlit countryside.[105]

Such roadhouses were very popular and it was only the outbreak of the war in 1939 that prevented their further development. Keen not to miss out on the dance craze, some of the new cinemas that opened in the 1920s and 1930s also provided dancing facilities. The largest of these 'super cinemas' had their own dance floors, and offered dancing on a permanent basis, thus hoping to capture the dancing audience, many of whom were dancing at the expense of cinema-going. Manchester was particularly well served by large cinemas with facilities for dancing in the interwar period. Between 1918 and 1932 there were nearly thirty cinemas with dancing licences including the Carlton Super Cinema, the West End cinema, and the Lido Super Cinema.[106]

AUDIENCES FOR DANCING IN INTERWAR BRITAIN

The presence of Mecca and other chains, together with the business strategies outlined earlier, catalysed the development of a mass market and raised the profile of public dance halls among the working and middle classes. By 1938 it was estimated that two million people went dancing throughout Britain each week, of which about three-quarters of a million patronized public dance halls whilst the remainder went to private dances, restaurants, and clubs.[107] There were, of course, seasonal fluctuations but these figures suggest that annual admissions to dances were near to one hundred million in 1938. Although most people in Britain during the interwar period could claim to have attended a dance at least once, there was a large section of society that went dancing on a regular basis. Representing its transition

[105] T. Burke, *English Night-Life: From Norman Curfew to present black-out* (London: B. T. Batsford, 1941), 141.

[106] MCA: M117/4/4/2, 'Registers of Music, Dancing and Rooms 1902–37'.

[107] P. Holt, *Daily Express*, 16 November 1938, 16.

from an upper-middle-class pastime to one with a mass market, this regular dancing public was found to be young, predominantly female, and largely working class.

Dancing had cross-class appeal and yet by the mid-1920s it was predominantly a working- and lower-middle-class activity. This verdict is supported by virtually all surveys of the period. *The New Survey of London Life and Labour*, conducted in 1928, illustrates that point:

> To-day dancing as an active recreation appeals to many people of all classes . . . The dance-halls are within the range of nearly everybody's purse, and typists, shop assistants and factory girls rub shoulders in them . . . People drop into a palais after the day's work or on Saturday evenings as casually as they go to a cinema.[108]

A national survey conducted in 1939 by Mass Observation among its panel of volunteers of all classes and all ages suggests that this continued to be the case into the 1930s.[109] Although the Mass Observation sample may not be wholly reliable, it is one of the best available on the subject. That survey showed that 69 per cent of people went to dances, with 22 per cent claiming to go 'regularly'. When looked at from a class perspective, 76 per cent of working-class respondents said that they had been dancing, 21 per cent regularly, and 67 per cent of middle-class respondents said they had been dancing, 24 per cent regularly. From this it can be seen that a large proportion of the population went dancing at least occasionally, with a hard core being regular attenders.

What makes the post-First World War period unique is the engagement of so many working-class people in regular public dancing. The low cost of dancing, from 6d up to 2s 6d, also indicates that dance organizers and commercial dance halls were aiming at a predominantly working-class audience. The manager of a dance hall in Bolton suggests that this was the case:

> We get steel workers, lots of mill girls and men, textile workers, machinists, cloths, rayon people, plumbers, joiners, de Havilland workers . . . , building traders, office workers.[110]

Robert Roberts, writing about dance halls in Salford in the 1920s, confirms that a largely working-class audience frequented them:

> The great 'barn' we patronised as apprentices held at least a thousand . . . at 6d per head (1s on Saturdays) youth at every level of the manual working-class, from the bound apprentice to the 'scum of the slum', fox-trotted through the new bliss in each other's arms.[111]

[108] Llewellyn Smith, *New Survey*, ix, 64–5.

[109] Calculated from a sample of 100 respondents (50 male, 50 female) in M-O A: DR: 'Jazz (Jan 1939)', (1939).

[110] M-O A: Worktown Collection: 48/D: A. H, 'Manager. Aspin Hall. Bolton', 8 January 1940, 11.

[111] R. Roberts, *The Classic Slum* (Harmondsworth: Penguin, 1983), 188.

Patterns of attendance for the 1930s also emerge from the detailed studies made by Mass Observation of dance halls in London and Bolton. Attendance for some of the working class was habitual, as one Bolton dance hall manager pointed out:

> We rely on a class here that comes 4 or 5 nights a week. They have about 5/- spending money a week and they don't want to spend it all on one night. So for their 3–4/- they can get 3 or 4 nights dancing out of it.[112]

Tom Harrison of Mass Observation confirmed this:

> People arrive before 8.30, and as with pubs so with dance-halls, people become regulars, visit the same one once or twice or up to four times a week, especially Saturday and paynight (Friday).[113]

It should be noted, however, that dancing had appeal to the middle class too. In particular, the private function became an established part of the social calendar of middle-class professionals up and down the country. A keen dancer writing in the *Dancing Times* in 1932 explained:

> In the large provincial town where we dance, our three or four dance halls are booked up night after night from October to March with what are called 'party nights,' when sports clubs and many other associations hold their dances. These nights mean crowded floors . . . the usual midnight closing hour extended to one or two in the morning, novelty competitions, cabarets, a drink licence, and the hall often closed to the public.[114]

Further evidence of the popularity of dancing amongst the middle class can be found from a July 1939, Mass Observation survey of the dancing habits of 370 people in the London district of Wandsworth.[115] Twenty-six per cent of the families of those questioned said that they danced. When broken down on a class basis, 76 per cent of those who said that they danced were working class. However, this is less significant than it first appears, because the sample was taken in a predominantly working-class district and so is heavily skewed. When we look at the proportion of working- and middle-class people in the sample who said that they danced, the results are 23 per cent and 41 per cent respectively. The latter figure is, perhaps, untypically high but it does indicate a growing trend towards middle-class patronage of dance halls. We can see further evidence of the split between middle-class- and working-class dancers in a 1938 survey of Ipswich. Using the rather complex notion of 'person-evenings' it was found that an average of about 7,900 person-evenings a month were spent dancing, with *c*.3,000 (38 per cent) of these taking place in places catering chiefly for professional people and office workers, and about 4,900 (62 per cent) in places favoured by factory workers.[116] As we have

[112] M-O A: Worktown Collection: 48/D, A. H, 'Manager. Aspin Hall. Bolton', 8 January 1940, 14.

[113] T. Harrisson, 'Whistle While You Work' (1938) (Winter) *New Writing* 50.

[114] *DT*, July 1932, 364.

[115] M-O A: MJD: 8/B 'Wandsworth Jazz Survey, July 1939' (1939).

[116] Bevington, *Leisure*, 20.

seen, the economic downturn may have forced more middle-class people to patronize the palais de danse on public nights too. A correspondent for the *Dancing Times* wrote in 1931 that the palais was 'becoming more and more patronised by the type of person one usually sees at the more expensive hotels, who in these days of increased taxation cannot afford the hotel prices'. Of the Ritz Manchester he declared 'one is treated exactly as though it cost half a guinea to come in instead of eighteen-pence.'[117]

In particular, however, dancing found a large audience among the new lower-middle class, typified by the spread of suburban housing estates and the growth of the service sector in interwar Britain. The palais de danse became part of the fabric of the new estates, along with cinemas, public houses, modern churches, and terraces of shops. In Ipswich, for example, it was noted in 1938 that three of the town's halls where dancing took place were situated in the 'new estates'.[118] Despite the predominance of the working class in the majority of halls therefore, this new audience favoured some of the 'better' palais de danse. Speaking of the clientele of his dance hall, the manager of The Grafton Rooms in Liverpool stated:

> It is hard to say what class people are in today. The girls work in Littlewoods, Vernons, and Ogdens Pools. The boys are mainly in shops. They are not labouring workers. They are what you may call the sedentary occupations—clerks, shop boys etc. There are not many labourers. They are too tired after a hard day's work.[119]

A dance hall manager in suburban Wimbledon confirmed this trend: 'I should call them lower middle class. There is a large residential area here and the place is a hot-bed of dancing.'[120] Some in the industry tried to promote the idea that the palais was 'democratic' and particularly tried to appeal to the aspiring middle classes. In the eyes of Carl Heimann, co-director of the Mecca chain, dance halls were a place where class distinctions disappeared:

> In the dance hall there is no differentiation between the patrons—they are all on the same 'floor level', all pay the same price of admission; there is no class distinction whatsoever; complete freedom of speech for all and sundry.[121]

In reality, in the normal course of business there was not a great deal of social mixing within the halls and each catered for its own section of society. Of the four main dance halls in Edinburgh at this time, for example, the Edinburgh Palais de Danse was the dancing centre for Scottish 'society', with royal patronage and a number of 'high-class private functions' held every week. The Havanna Dance Club also provided for a varied but predominantly upper-middle-class clientele. The remaining dance halls provided for the group who were most keen on dancing, the working and lower-middle class. However, there were exceptions to this rule. Private functions, especially those organized by employers, could be an occasion for

117 *DT*, November 1931, 151. 118 Bevington, *Leisure*, 20.

119 M-O A: MJD: 5/F, A. H., 'Manager Grafton Rooms Liverpool', 18 May 1939, 2.

120 M-O A: MJD: 5/F, A. H., 'Manager Wimbledon Glider Rink', 13 February 1939, 1.

121 C. L. Heimann, 'Dancing after the War' in Anon., *Stepping Out* (Danceland Publications, 1940), 54.

cross-class mixing. Indeed, the works dance and the dance halls where they took place were a key part of the 'democratization' of public life in interwar Britain. Managements were often very generous with funds for such events, and this went down well with employees.

Within these social groups, dancing was an activity that was more popular among women than men, as the 1934 *Social Survey of Merseyside* pointed out:

> Dancing is one of the very few activities in which women engage more frequently than men. Of the women 20 per cent, but of the men only 7 per cent, made entries under this head. The predominance of women in most dance halls is, indeed, well known. Among men, only Classes A and B seem to dance, while among women the largest—and very similar—proportions are found in B and C. Several of the Reports commented on the regularity with which working-class girls dance; dances are particularly popular in the slums.[122]

A 1938 survey of Ipswich found that dancing was 'more popular with girls than with young men' and went on to note that one works' club ran highly successful weekly dances for girls only, with an average attendance of 200.[123]

Evidence from Mass Observation supports this view that more women danced than men too. In one national survey, it was found that 29 per cent of women danced regularly compared with a mixed total of 26 per cent. When examining which social class of women were the most regular dancers, however, there is some conflicting evidence. All the surveys suggest that high numbers of both working-class- and middle-class women danced, but Mass Observation's Wandsworth Survey disagrees with the *Social Survey of Merseyside* and argues that more lower-middle-class women danced than working-class women. It found that 26 per cent of working-class women danced compared with 41 per cent of middle-class women. Even in rural areas, girls were keener on dancing than men. In a 1938 study of rural Lincolnshire, for example, it was noted 'there can be no doubt that the chief supporters of all dances are the girls, and this is particularly the case with the young domestic servants in the neighbourhood.'[124]

Significantly, opportunities for women to dance varied according to age, and more importantly, marital status. Dancing was predominantly the pastime of the young single woman. Indeed, once they were married and had children, it was often difficult for women to find the time for any leisure pursuits. Claire Langhamer has drawn attention to the concept of the 'life cycle' when considering women's leisure. She highlights how for most of the twentieth century 'leisure' was a much more abstract concept for women than men, as there was often no clear demarcation between periods of 'work' and 'time off'. Langhamer notes how youth and old age were the only significant times of their lives when working-class women could expect to enjoy any significant opportunities for clearly designated leisure time and

[122] D. Caradog Jones (ed), *The Social Survey of Merseyside* (Liverpool: Liverpool University Press, 1934), 3, 277–8. Class A = Professional, administerial, technical, and managerial positions. Class B = Ordinary clerks, shopkeepers, and shop assistants. Class C = All manual workers, domestic, hotel, and café workers.

[123] Bevington, *Leisure*, 20.

[124] Bevington, *Leisure*, 112.

leisure activities. When young, most working-class women went out to work and got paid for it. When old, age and retirement left time, if not energy, to partake in pastimes.[125] As well as age, marital status could be key to determining whether women danced. In the interwar period, dancing when married was not very common for women. Margery Spring Rice's 1939 study of *Working Class Wives*, for example, found that many women had little more than a life of work and sleep.[126] Such circumstances prevented married working-class women from dancing in large numbers, for even when leisure time was available it was difficult to find or afford suitable child-minders. In addition, many working-class women came under pressure from their husbands to stop dancing once married, as men tended to regard the dance hall as an arena chiefly for forming sexual relations. One married woman dancer told Mass Observation in 1939: 'The woman is fond of dancing and not the man and when they get married the man stays at home and the woman goes out. That starts jealousy when she meets another man.'[127] However, whilst not common, there is evidence to suggest that some working-class women continued to dance when they were married. In 1939, for example, Mass Observation carried out a survey of dancers at the Peckham Pavilion in London that specialized in 'Old Time' dancing. There it found numerous married women dancing on a regular basis. Moreover, it would appear that dancing performed a number of important social functions for married women, allowing them sociability and escape from the monotony of housework. A few comments from those interviewed reveals how important dancing could be for them. A 36-year-old housewife from Hammersmith explained: 'In such a happy atmosphere one can forget that Monday is washday.'[128] Another married 36-year-old from Upper Norwood claimed: 'You are sure of a good time, which greatly relieves the ties of home, also to meet new friends.'[129] A housewife, 33, from Peckham commented: 'I quite look forward to my night out and it bucks me up for the rest of the week and keeps me feeling young.'[130] Another married woman from East Dulwich argued: 'I get a lot out of this dance because I am on my own all day and it gives me a chance to meet a few people, also it gives me a break from the ordinary day life and great enjoyment.'[131] Among married middle-class women, the restraints were often even less numerous, and many couples continued to dance after marriage. Afternoon tea dances were a popular pastime in upmarket hotels and restaurants in London and throughout the country. Moreover, with more income available and a tendency not to have children until a later age, middle-class married couples would carry on dancing to a greater extent than working-class ones. The private functions and regular dances of sports associations, employers, social groups etc. outlined earlier in the chapter extended the dancing lives of the middle class in this period.

[125] See C. Langhamer, *Women's Leisure in England, 1920–60* (Manchester: Manchester University Press, 2000).

[126] M. Spring Rice, *Working Class Wives* (Harmondsworth: Penguin, 1939).

[127] M-O A, MJD: 38/1/E, 'Peckham Pavilion: V6', 7 February 1939, 2.

[128] M-O A, MJD: 38/1/G, 'Peckham Pavilion Questionnaire Survey Results: 39', March/April 1939, 1–2.

[129] Ibid., 1. [130] Ibid. [131] Ibid.

Finally, the other main determinant of the dancing audience's profile, as hinted at previously, was age. During the interwar period, the most habitual dancers were young people of both sexes. This was the group that made visits to the dance hall up to three, four, or even six times a week. The only limit to their attendance was the amount of money and the amount of leisure time that they had. As the manager of the Empress Hall in Bolton stated in 1938: 'They would come to dances every night if they could afford it, they love it...'[132] Indeed, the majority of Mass Observation studies of dancing undertaken between 1937 and 1939 point to a preponderance of young people in the halls. The following report from 1938 is typical: 'The patrons of the hall are all young—boys ranging from 14 in isolated cases to about 25 at the other end of the scale. But the majority are between 18 and 21. Girls range from 16 to 25 with the majority between about 17 and 21.'[133] In Mass Observation studies of dancing in Blackpool, Aldershot, Brighton, Ipswich, Canterbury, Liverpool, Portsmouth, Glasgow, Southend, Streatham, and Wandsworth, the evidence was that dances were packed with those in the 18–25-year-old age group. As Cameron and Lush noted:

> Many young men pass through a phase which has often been described by their parents and friends, and sometimes even by themselves, as 'dancing mad.' The only limitation to the number of dances they attend is the amount of pocket-money available.[134]

Harrisson's survey of Bolton dance halls identified and analysed the impact on the community of these young dancing enthusiasts, something which will be explored in more detail later:

> In a typical room in a cotton mill, fifteen of the forty-two female workers were dance-hall regulars, all the ones under twenty-five. In churches, pubs, political organizations and all other groups with social and co-operative interests, young people are to-day conspicuously absent in Worktown; the elder folk continuously complain about it. In six main dance-halls on Saturday evening there are nearly as many young men as on Sunday evening in all the town's 170 churches.[135]

Outside urban areas too, the young were the keenest on dancing. A 1938 survey of rural Lincolnshire highlighted how they were the most prolific dancers in the various village-run dances held in the area. It went on to note their willingness to travel further afield to find dancing too: 'Young people are energetic; the whole district can roughly be included in a ten-mile radius from Grantham; all the young people invariably possess bicycles; and there are few steep hills in the neighbourhood. One schoolmaster of a small village wrote that, despite the very low agricultural wages paid, no distance or cost was great enough to deter the young folk from attending dances.'[136]

132 M-O A, TC: MJD, 38/5/F, 'Interview: Manager and Lessee of the "Empress Hall" XXXV', 15 July 1938, 2.

133 M-O A, TC: Worktown, 48/C, 'Shall We Dance?', 1938, 2.

134 C. Cameron, A. J. Lush, and G. Meara (eds), *Disinherited Youth* (Edinburgh: Carnegie United Kingdom Trust, 1943), 105.

135 T. Harrisson, 'Whistle While You Work', 50.

136 Bevington, *Leisure*, 113.

CONCLUSION

By 1939, dancing played an increasingly important part in the leisure time of working- and lower-middle-class people. The facilities provided for dancing had improved immensely in little over twenty years, with purpose-built dance halls providing cheap, regular, and well-run dances in virtually every town and city in Britain. These new facilities, combined with less permanent provision, in church halls and assembly halls, meant that the opportunities for dancing in working-class communities were greater than they had ever been. Even allowing for the fluctuations in attendance by periods of 'dance booms', going to dance halls was a leisure time activity engaged in by a large proportion of the population.

Chapter 2

Wartime Boom

Dancing and the Dance Hall Industry at War, 1939–45

INTRODUCTION

The coming of war in 1939 presented new challenges to the dance hall industry but the conflict was to see a further growth in the popularity of dancing in Britain. Indeed, dancing boomed during the Second World War and it played a vital role in the war effort at home, for both civilians and military personnel. This chapter will examine the expansion in the dancing population and the impact of the war on where people danced, together with an investigation of the resilience of the businesses involved in the dancing industry.

THE WARTIME AUDIENCE FOR DANCING

How popular was dancing during the war? Although statistical evidence of the popularity of dancing during the Second World War is hard to come by, there is plenty of other evidence to suggest that the period was one of unprecedented success. Contemporary surveys suggest that despite the problems of war, dance halls were doing better business than ever before, and that the conflict brought a huge boom for dancing.

However, when war was declared in September 1939, the dancing business faced considerable uncertainty. Indeed, the declaration of war caused a collapse in dancing, as dance halls, dance teachers, and dancers were caught up in the early confusion of the conflict. The government, expecting an immediate and prolonged aerial bombardment of Britain's major towns and cities, closed down all places of public entertainment. As a result, dancing in major urban areas stopped overnight. Confidence in the dance business slumped. Carl Heimann, for example, thought that he 'was finished' and a feeling of despair spread throughout the rest of the industry. The manager of one of the biggest and most popular West End dance halls told Mass Observation:

> We closed on September 3rd. In the morning we listened to the broadcast, and I called in what members of the staff there were to hear it. After the speech we realised we couldn't keep on. I told them the situation, and we all went into the ballroom and

> started taking the glass tops off the tables and clearing the room, making it ready as an air raid shelter.[1]

Other sections of the dance business also suffered. Dance demonstrating collapsed and, more seriously, so did business amongst dance bands. As *Melody Maker* remarked on 9 September 1939:

> No one bothered about their gigs or their jobs. The few theatre bands played to practically empty houses... no-one was wanted and everyone knew it... The date books of everyone were wiped clean, as with a sponge. To pass the time one wandered to Archer Street. Only a handful of boys at the best, and for a good part of the time not a soul could be seen.[2]

Thus, the start of the war brought an almost total collapse in business. However, the impact of such harsh government restrictions on morale was so great that the press launched a campaign to persuade the government to relax them. As the predicted air war did not materialize, the government relented and from mid-September 1939 places of public entertainment started to re-open. Yet, whilst dance halls were back in business, the war brought important changes to the way that they operated and this influenced attendance levels and patterns. Opening times were restricted as a result of blackouts, and as we shall see, these opening hours were extended and curtailed numerous times by local authorities over the coming years of the war. The huge local variations in opening and closing times could often be confusing for dancers.

There were other problems for the dance hall business. The blackout had a serious impact on leisure patterns during these first months of the war. Mass Observation even claimed that it had 'reversed the whole trend of leisure' with a new focus on staying at home, rather than going out.[3] Certainly, amongst Mass Observation's national panel of volunteers, visiting dance halls was one thing that had decreased as a result of the blackout: 2 per cent of men and 6 per cent of women said they were visiting dance halls less for this reason.[4] Yet, compared with other leisure activities, dancing was relatively unaffected. Cinema-going had decreased 20 per cent with men and 17 per cent with women; theatre-going 18 per cent and 15 per cent; visiting friends, 13 per cent and 32 per cent; and going for walks, 20 per cent and 13 per cent. Only the pub had declined less in popularity than dance halls. This was an early indication that the popularity of dancing was to prove more resilient to wartime changes than other leisure activities, though cinema attendance was also to recover strongly. As Mass Observation concluded: 'All of this correctly reflects the strong influence and interest of dancing on those who like it, and the way that this strength is almost strong enough to overcome the blackout.'[5]

1 M-O A, TC 38/6/E, 'Jazz and Dancing—article draft', 4.
2 M-O A, TC 38/6/E, 'Jazz and Dancing—article draft', 17.
3 M-O A, FR20, 'Recording the War', January 1940, 2.
4 M-O A, FR11A, 'Jazz and Dancing', November 1939, 1.
5 M-O A, FR11A, 'Jazz and Dancing' November 1939, 1.

In fact, in some cases the blackout actually increased the popularity of dancing. As one manager of a large dance hall in London stated to Mass Observation, the blackout boosted business as it eliminated most outdoor leisure activities: 'Boys and girls who go dancing, before the war used to go dancing some nights, to the pictures on others, and on other nights would parade round and look at the shops. But now every night they have to go inside somewhere.'[6]

Certainly by the end of 1939 Mass Observation was able to note that business was starting to return to normal in London following the initial collapse. At the Streatham Locarno in November 1939 there were over 1,000 people dancing on a Saturday night, 'well up to pre-war average' and a Jitterbug Marathon held at the Paramount dance hall Tottenham Court Road attracted some 1,400 people, described as 'phenomenal for a Monday evening'.[7] The same month, *Modern Dance and Dancer* also observed that dancers in London were defying the blackout and '[d]espite the rigid adherence to the lighting regulations . . . dancers in ever increasing numbers are filling, in many instance to overflowing, the Palais and dance halls'.[8] In the rest of the country too, there were signs that dancing was rapidly regaining its popularity. In Leeds good business was reported, and it was noted that 'most of the halls are in full swing again, a welcome relief from those early black out days of "closed ballrooms"'.[9] In Derby, too, some halls were reporting a return to normality, whilst in Scotland it was indicated that '[a]lthough "business as usual" is hardly an accurate description of the activities in Scottish dance halls at the moment, things seem to be settling down quite nicely'.[10] Business was good enough for a new dance hall, the Berkeley, to open in Glasgow that month, an indication that confidence was returning to the industry.

Throughout 1940, the popularity of dancing continued to increase, and by the end of the year there were the first indications not only that the initial slump had been overcome, but that dancing was becoming more popular than it had been in peacetime. In London Josephine Bradley noted: 'Restaurants are packed to capacity . . . Dance halls are flourishing. Nightclubs that had, pre-war to close down, are opening again. Tea dances that previously had flagged and failed, now draw a large public.'[11] By February 1940 Irene Raines was able to report that business in London's West End was thriving and that 'fresh places open every week'.[12] Mecca was confident enough of business in the capital that it took out a lease on the Royal Opera House Covent Garden, turning it into one of London's largest dance halls for the duration of the conflict[13] (see Fig. 2.1). In Manchester too a new hall opened, the Palais de Danse Newton Heath.[14] Elsewhere there were clear signs of a new increase in business. In County Durham, dance entrepreneur Robert Hindmarsh reported confidently that 'there are more people dancing in the

[6] T. Harrisson and C. Madge (ed), *War Begins at Home by Mass Observation* (London: Chatto & Windus, 1940), 225.

[7] M-O A, TC 38/6/E, 'Jazz and Dancing—article draft', 5.

[8] *MDD*, November 1939, 4.

[9] *MDD*, December 1939, 4.

[10] *MDD*, December 1939, 8.

[11] *DT*, February 1940, 292.

[12] *DT*, February 1940, 29.

[13] *MDD*, January 1940, 19.

[14] Ibid.

county than ever before'. In nearby Newcastle it was reported that in spite of air raids, the summer business had been 'excellent'. In Cheltenham it was reported that dancing business was 'particularly good', the receipts for the summer season dances being more than double those of the previous year. In Derby too the manager of the Plaza stated that dancing was 'more popular' than before the war.[15] In Liverpool it was argued that the only period when audiences had been larger pre-war was in the 1924–5 season.[16] From Bristol, news came that there were 'larger crowds' than in pre-war days and that 'hundreds of people had to be turned away' from dances both there and in Bath.[17] The same situation was true in Birmingham, where at the West End dance hall, 'House Full' signs had to be erected and queues formed outside the 2,000 capacity hall—for the first time in its history.[18]

Such evidence is made even more remarkable by the fact that during 1940 and into 1941 there was sustained bombing of Britain, with major towns and cities suffering considerable damage (including dance halls) and large numbers of casualties. The impact of the Blitz on dancing, and the way in which dance halls coped with the challenges it presented are examined later in the chapter. Whilst in some areas the Blitz seriously disrupted dancing attendances, in other areas it boosted them. Indeed, by 1941 the increase in the popularity of all forms of dancing was being reported as a 'boom' by those in the dancing business. For example, one of the country's leading dance teachers, Frank Spencer, commented: 'Ballroom dancing for the masses is booming; dance promotion—normally a precarious business—is at present a gilt edged security.'[19] This was confirmed by reports from dance hall owners throughout the country. From northern England a correspondent for the *Dancing Times* stated: 'There is definitely a boom in Ballroom dancing in Manchester . . . All halls report unusually good business,' concluding that 'attendances at the Ritz are little short of marvellous at the present time . . . and dancing in Manchester is now *the* most popular entertainment.'[20] A sign of unprecedented demand, in November 1941 Manchester's Plaza reopened and extended its dance provision from once or twice a week, to dancing twice daily.[21] Suburban halls in Manchester were also doing well, and the Levenshulme Palais, the Plymouth Grove, and the Palais de Danse Newton Heath claimed 'record business'. Indeed, so good was business that in order to cope with the huge demand for dancing, a further spate of new halls was opening up in Manchester, particularly in the suburbs where 'innumerable little halls' were doing 'a roaring business', according to the *Dancing Times*.

As the war progressed, the unprecedented demand for dancing continued. The end of the worst of the Blitz certainly acted as a further catalyst to growth, but by 1942 the boom had proved enduring enough for those in the dancing business to recognize that dancing's new-found popularity was not just fleeting. In Liverpool in early 1942, attendances at the two largest dance halls, the Rialto and the Grafton,

[15] *DT*, October 1940, 21.
[16] *DT*, February 1940, 315.
[17] *DT*, February 1940, 321.
[18] *MDD*, November 1940, 11.
[19] *DT*, December 1941, 153.
[20] *DT*, April 1941, 413.
[21] *DN*, 15 November 1941, 1.

The Dance Hall That Has Become a Mecca for Half the Men and Girls on Leave in Central London: Fifteen "Mecca Dancing at the Royal Opera House, Covent Garden," is the official name. There are two dances every day. Both of them are crowded The boxes are filled with lookers-on. And the band—Blanche Coleman's—plays on a revolving platform that takes the place

WAR-TIME DANCE HALL

The Dance halls are booming everywhere. These pictures were taken at Covent Garden, Hammersmith Palais and Green's Playhouse Ballroom, Glasgow.

ROYAL Opera House, Covent Garden (Mecca Dancing), the Astoria, Charing Cross Road, the Hammersmith Palais, Green's Playhouse Ballroom, Glasgow, Sherry's, Brighton, the Tower Ballroom, Blackpool—these are some of the dance halls of Britain, the good-pull-ups for dancers, the heaven on a subway for the Smiths, the Jones, the Kellys and the Cohens, and a very large number of democracy's other sons and daughters. At the Astoria Charing Cross Road, you pay 2s. 6d. entrance and walk straight in. At Green's Playhouse, Glasgow, you pay 3s. 6d. week-days, and 6s. on Saturdays, and they let you in through a turnstile. In Glasgow, the pubs close at 9.30, so Green's starts crowding up about 10. In the West End of London, the pubs close at 11 and so does the Astoria. In the Astoria, you go down two flights of stairs to reach the dance floor. In Green's you go up 95 feet in a lift to reach the dance floor. But when you get to either you might be at the other—you might be at Sherry's for that matter, or at Hammersmith or the Tower or any one of the Meccas—the general scheme or lack of scheme is the same. The same bran-tub crowd. The same tunes from what looks at first like the same band. The same plump woman in a white satin blouse and gold shoes. The same A.T.S. with her tunic buttons undone

The British Sailor in the Balcony
He sits in the balcony, an empty bottle in front of him and looks wistful. At Green's Playhouse Ballroom, Glasgow.

The English Girl at the Buffet
A dance hall is a good place to eat as well as dance. This buffet is immediately off the dance floor at Covent Garden Royal Opera House.

14

Fig. 2.1. Wartime dance hall: *Picture Post*, 22 February 1944
Source: Getty Images.

broke twenty-year records, with four-figure crowds at both evening and afternoon sessions. Their managers claimed that 'this was no flash in the pan over a holiday interval. Very large attendances have been sustained.'[22] Indeed, by the end of the

[22] *DT*, February 1942, 279.

Hundred Dancers Crowd the Converted Covent Garden Opera House Twice Daily
and raucous, but orderly and decorous. The men who dance are mostly on leave, many of them Americans.
of a stage where the greatest opera singers and ballet dancers in the world used to appear.

because of the heat. The same man with a tight pin-striped suit feather-stepping professionally with a woman who would make two of him.

Look down from a balcony, when the main lights are lowered, and the floor is lit with revolving coloured spotlights and one of those revolving reflectors that hang from the ceiling and shower bilious light spots over a smoky ballroom. Hear the muted sax taking a second chorus and catch sight of the tipped-over glass and the spilled drink. It all seems just the same everywhere.

Of course, the opinion prevalent among aunts and clergymen and birds of their feather is that dance

Continued overleaf

The U.S. Naval Policeman
In the balcony, his truncheon stops swinging for a few minutes. At Green's, Glasgow.

The R.A.F. Man On Leave
Dancing is serious and conventional at Covent Garden. Most dance halls forbid jitterbugging.

The Crooner
Lind Joyce sings with Henry Hall's band at Green's Playhouse Ballroom, Glasgow. 15

Fig. 2.1. Continued

year it was claimed that '[d]uring 1942 all records were broken in the Liverpool dance halls'.[23] In Belfast observers noted that dancing was so popular that 'at times the floor is too crowded to be comfortable'.[24] Tom Harrisson made similar points to a North American audience in a BBC broadcast that year, stating that dance halls were 'booming exceptionally'. He continued:

[23] *DT*, February 1943, 245. [24] *MDD*, February 1942, 14.

> In a number of our big cities the biggest dance halls are packed completely to capacity, and the other evening in Glasgow I simply couldn't get in when I arrived at ten o'clock hoping to see the local finals of a Jitterbug competition. Hundreds were being turned away from the doors.[25]

There is some evidence of the overall size of the dancing audience by this point too. In 1942 Mecca estimated that in one large provincial hall they ran, average attendance was 1,000 per session, for eight four-hour sessions per week, with a total weekly attendance of 8,000. If this was replicated in 500 dance halls across Britain we can presume weekly attendances of four million—double that estimated in 1938.[26]

Furthermore, even though dance halls and dancing were already enjoying sustained and unprecedented popularity by 1942, a further fillip to the industry came with the arrival of the first American troops. By 1945 three million US soldiers, sailors, and airmen had passed through Britain.[27] American servicemen were keen, and often expert, dancers. With their relative affluence, their presence caused an already booming dance business to reach unprecedented levels of success. It is fairly clear then that by 1942 dancing was more popular than it had been before the war.

Such was this success, that by 1943 it was recognized that there was not enough space in dance halls to cater for demand. In September *Danceland* stated: 'So many people want to dance these days that queues are frequently seen outside dancehalls and often people have to be turned away. Inside, the halls are filled to capacity . . . "I've never seen anything like it," a veteran dance organiser told me. "If we had elastic walls we could not find room for everybody who wants to dance."'[28] By April 1943, London County Council had issued eighteen new licences for dancing and was encouraging existing dance halls to extend their accommodation. In Manchester it was reported that '[a]ll halls are filled to capacity at every session'.[29] So popular was dancing in Aberdeen, that in 1943 the Town Council decided to auction off the lease of the city's Music Hall for Saturday night dancing to the highest bidder. Six different parties bid.[30] By this point in the war, Mecca estimated that its chain of halls attracted 8.6 million customers, with its directors earning £1,000 a year.[31] Inevitably, the huge profits that seemed to be possible from dancing created problems. The prosperity of the dancing business was causing greed amongst some. According to the *Modern Dance and Dancer* dance demonstrators were exploiting the situation to demand fees of almost 'blackmarket dimensions'. The journal cautioned: 'the tendency now is to become over-optimistic as there is plenty of work for everyone . . . Good times do not last forever . . . and it is advisable to exercise some caution before the wave of prosperity

[25] M-O A, FR634, 'Broadcast for North American Service, 20.4.41', 7.
[26] *DN*, 14 November 1942, 5.
[27] J. Gardiner, *Over Here: The GIs in Wartime Britain* (London: Collins & Brown, 1992), 158.
[28] *Danceland*, September 1943, 1, 3.
[29] *DT*, February 1943, 247.
[30] *Danceland*, December 1943, 9.
[31] *Daily Mail*, 27 September 1943, 2.

carries one to a giddy height.'[32] Concern at this kind of greed and the rise of the casual dance promoter was reflected in the energetic activities of the dance halls' professional associations. The Association of Ballrooms, for example, was running a full schedule of meetings in 1943, with six bi-monthly meetings in Manchester, Leicester, London, Liverpool, Birmingham, and Derby.[33]

Despite such problems, and only dented temporarily by the new blitz by the V1 and V2s in 1944, the confidence of those in the dance hall industry was maintained throughout the rest of the war. Despite the shaky start, the popularity of dancing had not only endured during the war, it had increased to levels above those of the pre-war boom. Indeed, during the war, the only limit to dancing's popularity was the availability of venues for dancing and the musicians to provide music. Dancing had never been more popular.

So why was there such a boom for the dance business? One important explanation lies in the wider social and economic context of wartime Britain. As we shall see later, the increasing affluence of large sections of the population, and particularly those sections of society most likely to go dancing—the working class, the young, and women—meant that economic barriers to leisure activities were removed. Yet, whilst there was more money around to spend there were fewer things to spend it on. The wartime contraction of non-essential industries meant that there were few consumer goods available. In addition, whilst the cinema and some spectator sports were still available, many other alternative leisure forms had disappeared (for example, hundreds of amateur theatre and sports groups closed as members were called up, whilst many crafts and hobbies were stopped by a lack of materials). This meant that remaining leisure outlets were patronized to a greater degree. So to some extent then, dancing boomed because there was little else to do. As a regular female patron of the Streatham Locarno said: 'Yes, I used to come on Tuesdays. But I come two or three nights now. It's the only thing to do, isn't it? There's nothing else to do these nights.'[34]

This is not to say that dancing did not face any competition from other leisure activities during the war. Even though the variety of alternatives had been reduced, the cinema, for example, retained and even extended its popularity. But these two leisure forms served different needs. As well as providing escapism, the dance hall was popular because it offered communal entertainment, and sociability. At a time of conflict, and often intense danger, the desire to come together was a natural one—and this gave the dance hall an advantage. Whereas the cinema might be a communal experience in the sense that it was enjoyed by everyone, the dance hall involved a much greater degree of communal interaction. As *Modern Dance and Dancer* noted in 1941, the difference between the dance hall and cinema was quite marked. Of the cinema it stated: 'the conversation there must be furtive and is soon rebuked, but the dance halls offer an easy, inexpensive and pleasing solution.'[35] Group and party dances accentuated the sense of community enjoyment, but even during normal dance programmes, the ability to form and break away from groups

[32] *MDD*, November 1943, 7. [33] *MDD*, February 1943, 21.
[34] Harrisson and Madge, *War Begins*, 225. [35] *MDD*, June 1941, 20.

of people gave the dance hall a vital element of sociability. Dance halls helped people to form friendships with strangers more easily than many other activities, as there were prescribed conventions that made introductions easier. This was particularly important during the disruption of war.

Another important reason why dancing boomed was that it provided much needed escapism from the tensions and horrors of war. This coincided with a 'live for today' atmosphere that pervaded much of wartime life, particularly amongst the young. Max Turner writing in the *Modern Dance and Dancer* in 1942 saw this as an important part of its appeal. 'It is a complete avenue of escape from the ordinary routine of life,' he argued, 'taking one into a happy atmosphere where one may forget one's work and worries for a while.'[36]

Dance halls also proved attractive to wartime audiences because they offered light and colour in a country darkened by the blackout. Even more than in peacetime, the way that dance halls looked was an important part of their appeal. Lighting was especially important. The contrast between the dark and often bleak wartime urban landscape and the bright, colourful, loud, vibrant atmosphere of the dance hall was marked. Carl Heimann argued: 'Dancing... has attained national popularity in our halls because they are so brilliantly lit. They are today a sharp, appealing contrast to the blackout.'[37] A dance hall manager in the north-east of England agreed, arguing that his dancers were 'like the butterflies, they like to be where the bright lights are'.[38] Colour was also important, and Mecca spent £10,000 during the war on making their dance halls more colourful. As Heimann explained: 'Khaki is a protective colour; it is not... a gay one. We were quick to realise that we must provide colour in contrast; we have done it in various ways, lighting, costumes, decoration.'[39] The dance hall then, was entertainment par excellence for wartime audiences—offering them escape, social interaction, colour, and gaiety at a time of extreme stress.

WHO WENT DANCING IN WARTIME?

The war created a new dancing public in Britain. Whilst in key respects the profile of those who went dancing remained essentially the same as before the war, the huge increase in the popularity of dancing drew thousands of first-time dancers into dance places. As Eve Tynegate Smith noted in April 1940, drawing parallels with the First World War: 'As was the case twenty five years ago hundreds are attending dances for the first time in their lives.'[40] Mass Observation noted a sharp decline in standards amongst those dancing in London's dance halls following the outbreak of the war, concluding that this suggested 'an influx of new dancers'.[41] Indeed, these lowered standards acted as a catalyst to the growth in attendances recorded earlier,

[36] *MDD*, February 1942, 19.
[37] *Danceland 1941 Souvenir* (Danceland Publications, 1942), 4–6.
[38] *The Observer*, 19 July 1942, 6. [39] *Danceland 1941 Souvenir*, 4–6.
[40] *DT*, April 1940, 418. [41] M-O A, TC 38/1/A, 'Locarno AH 4.11.39', 3.

because they made people less self-conscious on the dance floor. Glasgow dance teacher Alex Warren made this point in 1941. He argued:

> More and more people are dancing who never before gave it a thought, and with the general standard so deteriorating, nobody feels out of it if they have the slightest knowledge of the art.[42]

Certainly, sections of the dance hall industry were keen to target the new dancers. As before the war, Mecca in particular tried hard to cater for those who did not wish to take dancing seriously. A list of the events being run by Mecca in one fortnight in May 1941 shows the range of novelty events being laid on, with a clear emphasis on creating a light-hearted atmosphere to appeal to the new dancing public. At the Locarno Glasgow there was a 'Twins and Doubles' night, followed by a Gents Singing Night. At the Ritz Manchester, women were being celebrated with 'Our Girls at Work and Play' night featuring Toni and Her Orchestra. At the Mecca-Locarno Leeds, there was a 'Search for Miss Leeds 1941' competition followed by 'Novelty Musical Week'. At the Paramount London there were two competitions every Tuesday, one 'straight' and one 'novelty'; 'Continental Night' every Friday; and Empire Day celebrations on Saturday. At the Palais Croydon there was the first heat of a national singing competition, a quickstep competition, and a waltz competition. At Sherry's, Brighton, there was 'Can you Take it?' with 'new gags, new stunts', a staff cabaret, and 'Pot Pourri' dance competitions.[43]

The shift in the type of people dancing and the lowered standard of dancing in wartime served to increase the split between 'serious dancers' and 'social dancers'. One keen dancer, for example, on visiting a dance hall in 1944 after many years' absence, complained that he was 'disgusted with the standard. I don't think there were two couples dancing alike and that, I may say, is the case all over England. If people can't learn to dance properly, why bother at all?'[44] Serious dancers often criticized the new crowd for their lack of manners. In 1941 the *Modern Dance and Dancer* complained: 'Out of time, on they go, the selfish dancers of today, barging into everybody, kicking their feet about, laddering stockings and bruising the legs and feet of other couples.'[45]

So who were these dancers? At first sight, the age and gender profile of those who went dancing during the war seems little different than before the war—it was largely young and female. However, the war accentuated and extended the dominance of these two groups. In gender terms, even more women went dancing during the war, and they outnumbered men to an extent not seen before. Whilst conscription of men into the armed forces did not necessarily mean that they were denied opportunities to dance, as we shall see later, at key points in the war it did mean that there were fewer men in dance halls than women.[46] At the same time, the war saw the mobilization of young, single, and later married women, and gave

[42] *DT*, April 1941, 399.
[43] *Danceland*, May 1941, 4.
[44] *Danceland*, July 1944, 8.
[45] *MDD*, May 1941, 10.
[46] See p. 164.

them increasing spending power. For both reasons, women flocked to dance halls in their leisure time.[47]

The other notable change to the dancing audience in wartime was its age. Whilst it is true that even before the war, those who went dancing most frequently were young, the war brought greater numbers of young people, and even younger dancers, into the dance halls than before. For example, in November 1944, the Liverpool correspondent of *Danceland* reported an influx of under-fourteen-year-olds, mostly girls, especially during the afternoons in the city's ballrooms. Indeed, in some areas the appearance of children in dance halls, against byelaws, began to be an issue.[48] The war had provided numerous new opportunities for leisure for young people, and given them a new sense of independence—either as a result of the dislocation of family life, or through their improved economic position resulting from the scarcity of labour in key sections of the economy. As will be discussed more fully later, these younger dancers increasingly separated themselves from the other dancers, preferring different dances, and even colonizing separate parts of the dance floor.[49]

So what about the class profile of the wartime audiences for dancing? Like the pre-war period, dancing appealed to people of all classes. As we shall see, the range of venues available for dancing meant that dancers of all social backgrounds remained well catered for during the war. However, the war brought about significant improvements in the economic well-being of the working class. During the war, those sections of the working class who had previously been unable to afford to go dancing now had the money to do so.

Indeed, for most of the working class, the war brought huge improvements in income. Unemployment virtually disappeared, falling back to 0.5 per cent by 1943. For the rest of the war, full employment was maintained. At the same time, wages rose by an average of 80 per cent when the cost of living rose by only 30 per cent, with the prices of food, rent, and other essentials kept down by government subsidies. Mass Observation commented on the growing affluence of the working class and its impact on pleasure-seeking. In an investigation of Chatham in 1940 it noted:

> The people of Chatham are earning more money than ever before . . . There is a new spirit of alertness and cheerfulness—as if a boom had set in . . . they pour into the main street on Friday and Saturday evening in search of entertainment more gaily than in pre-war days.[50]

In 1942 *The Observer* found the same sort of affluence in Ashington, Northumberland, a pit town of 30,000: 'The town is alive with the virile energy of the mining community. There is . . . uniform prosperity . . . the main street on a Saturday evening is crowded.'[51] For the first time in a generation this was a population enjoying full employment and decent wages. It is likely then, that the

[47] See pp. 163–4. [48] See pp. 137–8.
[49] See pp. 149–58. [50] M-O A FR877 'Chatham, September 1941', 1–2.
[51] *The Observer*, 19 July 1942, 6.

greater part of the new dancing public during the war came from this newly affluent working class.

Did the war bring about any greater class mixing? At the extremes, the upper class continued to dominate dancing in the top hotels, restaurants, and nightclubs of London and other cities. Similarly, many seedier dance halls continued to be frequented by those at the lower ends of society. However, in public dance halls and numerous other dancing venues, where the majority danced, there was a greater potential for cross-class mixing. The war brought numerous dislocations to normal patterns of work, home, and leisure, uprooting thousands from their normal surroundings. Two apparently contradictory features of the war in particular had an impact on the class composition of dance hall audiences. The first was the blackout and the Blitz. These both encouraged a tendency to dance locally. Mass Observation noted that people were shifting from travelling to their preferred hall to staying close to home and dancing in their nearest local dance hall. It noted that the war 'has produced a change in patronage which is now more localised'[52] and that '[t]ransport difficulties sent up the proportion of "locals" in dance halls'.[53] This trend continued for much of the war. In 1943, for example, Mass Observation noted: 'With local bus services stopping about 9pm in many areas and work going on later in many jobs, people's leisure is increasingly confined within walking distance of home.'[54] Private transport facilities were also affected by the widespread rationing of petrol—only the very richest were able to continue to use their cars for such non-essential tasks as driving to dances. This meant that many middle-class dancers went along to their local dance halls for the first time (as opposed to travelling to more exclusive city or town centre ballrooms) and a new degree of class mixing, as people of different backgrounds were thrown together. The extent to which the classes mixed depended on the proximity to different class-based neighbourhoods—in some areas class danced with class, but in those areas on the 'margins' there was greater class mixing.

The other, more dramatic, change to the composition of audiences in dance halls came from the impacts of evacuation and mobilization, together with the presence of large numbers of military personnel in some towns. This huge increase in the number of 'outsiders' in many parts of the country made many dance hall audiences incredibly cosmopolitan. In such circumstances, particularly in areas with limited facilities for dancing, the variety of people dancing in any one venue could be much greater than in peacetime. People from different parts of the country, different nationalities, different colours, and different classes were often thrown together. Whilst many may have chosen to remain within their own cliques in such circumstances, it is likely that for some, the wartime dance hall offered an opportunity for social mixing that was unprecedented, as we shall discuss further later. Certainly, the issue of class mixing at service dances was one that caused concern for the military. For example, Army officers were banned from dancing in the

52 M-O A, TC 38/5/D, 'Jazz since the war began AH 13.11.39', 1.
53 Harrisson and Madge, *War Begins*, 225.
54 M-O A, FR1632, 'Some Notes on the Uses of Leisure in Wartime', March 1943, 2.

Bournemouth Pavilion Ballroom in 1941 because, according to the Southern Command Public Relations Officer 'in some dances, such as the "Paul Jones" an officer might have to take his partner back to the table occupied by NCOs and men'.[55] By August this ban had been lifted however, with the exception of Friday and Saturday evening when the ballroom was reserved for WOs, NCOs, and 'men'.[56] The RAF was less accommodating, however, seeing dances where all ranks mixed as 'contrary to the custom of the Service'. In 1944 it therefore designated the ultimate decision on whether or not to allow such mixing to the Group Commander of each Station.[57]

Indeed, this military example highlights the fact that no account of the audience for dancing during wartime would be complete without an examination of the popularity of the pastime amongst the armed forces. Even though a large section of the population was conscripted into the armed forces during the war, this did not necessarily mean that they were denied the opportunity to dance. Indeed, men and women in uniform dancing became a key feature of wartime British life, either in public places or in dances arranged in military establishments.

Many military bases had facilities for dancing as part of their entertainment facilities. At Donnington Army Depot in Cheshire, for example, a large Nissen hut was used as a theatre capable of accommodating 1,000, and the men voluntarily laid a dance floor so that they could dance. Dances were held once a week, run by a dance committee, and there were additional dances run by the YMCA and NAAFI, who also had facilities on the base.[58] Similar arrangements were made at bases throughout the country. As Lance Corporal A. H. Franks told *Dancing Times* in January 1942:

> In most army camps ballroom dancing is indisputably the chief form of amusement all the year round. Gymnasia are large and plentiful; the floors, although not sprung are usually of well laid blocks . . . The bands are as a rule first rate . . . In any garrison area there are many thousands of men, and every dance (one is held almost every night) collects a full house.

In order to provide dancing partners for the men, 'coach loads of girls from various branches of the Services are brought in; and civilians from nearby villages are sometimes invited'.[59]

Dancing offsite was aided by transport provided by the military. Dances could be specially laid on for those serving. For example, the Entertainments and Welfare Officer of a unit would often organize dances in nearby dance venues specifically for their men. When dances were not laid on especially for them, servicemen would go to local public dances instead. One solider remarked: 'When . . . I've been thoroughly "browned off" . . . I have decided that there's only one thing to do—trot

[55] *DN*, 19 July 1941, 3. [56] *DN*, 16 August 1941, 1.
[57] PRO AIR 2/8865, 'RAF Dances for All Ranks—Policy', 31 January 1944.
[58] M-O A, FR1105, 'Morale in Donnington', February 1942, 13–14, 23.
[59] *DT*, January 1942, 213.

along to a dance. And more often than not . . . I've taken myself off to the nearest Palais or barn . . . and returned feeling happier . . . for my visit.'[60]

Dance halls were eager to offer preferential treatment to those serving in the armed forces, as a sign of their gratitude and an indication of their patriotism. Reduced entrance prices for servicemen were thus a regular feature of wartime dance halls, and in some cases, even free entrance was offered. In the larger dance halls, special concerts and other attractions were provided for troops. In July 1941, for example, in the Hammersmith Palais the same month HM Forces were admitted free of charge to a variety show featuring some of the biggest names in the entertainment word. The one-and-a-half-hour show featured Noel Coward, Lupino Lane, and Mantovani and attracted thousands.[61] Some dance halls even provided special gifts for servicemen. At the Plaza Ballroom, Derby in January 1942, for example, the management secured the attendance of nine local sailors from the 'Ark Royal' who were each given one hundred cigarettes, a wrist watch, and a shaving outfit. All other sailors were admitted free and given free refreshments throughout the evening.[62]

Opportunities for dancing could also be found in the numerous Services clubs established in major towns and cities in Britain. Such places offered a range of facilities for service men and women, with bars, lounges, sleeping accommodation, and often dancing facilities. In South Shields, for example, the United Merchant Navy Club was equipped with a dance hall, where dances were run three times a week.[63] Another indication of the popularity of dancing with those in the armed services was the success of dance competitions run for the Services. Malcolm Munro of the Grafton, Liverpool, for example, declared that 'the Forces are very keen competition dancers'.[64] Local and national competitions were held throughout the country, and the many professional and semi-pro dancers who had been conscripted were able to continue their passion for dancing. In August 1941 a 'Star' All Services Amateur Ballroom Championship was announced with heats in the Royal Opera House, Streatham Locarno, Tottenham Royal, Croydon Palais, and in Sherry's Brighton and Grand Casino Birmingham. The Grand Final was held in the Royal Opera House on 10 December.[65]

Having briefly outlined where members of the armed forces went dancing, it would be useful to consider the range of opportunities for dancing for the wider population.

VENUES FOR DANCING DURING THE WAR

Where did people go dancing during the war? Continuity, rather than change, characterized the range and type of venues available for dancing during the war. Whilst some buildings used for dancing were requisitioned by the government for

60 *MDD*, April 1942, 11. 61 *DN*, 26 July 1941, 4. 62 *MDD*, January 1942, 19.
63 *Sunday Sun*, 23 April 1944, 3. 64 *DT*, October 1940, 20.
65 *DN*, 23 August 1941, 1.

the war effort, and bombing destroyed buildings and shortages caused closure, on the whole, towns and cities remained well catered for. Indeed, dancing even moved into new areas of life during wartime, and several new venues were created. In rural areas too, the provision of facilities for dancing often increased considerably.

Undoubtedly though, requisitioning did have some impact. On the outbreak of war, and for the duration, the government commandeered a large number of public buildings for the war effort. Hundreds of church halls, assembly rooms, village halls, scout halls, and other venues formerly used for dancing were taken over, considerably reducing the facilities for dancing in many areas. Many permanent dance halls were also closed down in this way, as they were often very large buildings, with significant floor space that could be put to alternative use. In Leeds, for example, several of the largest dance halls in the city were used as first aid posts or for storing military equipment.[66] In Birmingham too, the Palais de Danse was requisitioned by the Ministry of Food to store sugar.[67] A dance teacher in London who had only months earlier installed a new dance floor in his studio soon lost it, as Government officials commandeered the teacher's premises, tore up the newly-laid floor and installed Home Defence workers in it.[68] The requisitioning policy was often met with resistance from local populations. For example, a 20,000-signature petition was sent to the authorities to ask for the Ilford Palais to be reopened after it was commandeered by the government for storing furniture.[69]

As might be expected, dance halls, a common feature of inner city and town centre landscapes, were regularly hit and destroyed by enemy action. In 1941, for example, Mecca was periodically forced to close the Royal Opera House and the Royal, Tottenham, through war damage. They also had to evacuate their Head Offices, whilst twelve members of staff from one hall had their homes destroyed by bombing.[70] Even after the end of the worst of the Blitz, German bombers continued to harass London and other cities with occasional raids. In November 1943, for example, six consecutive night raids on London saw a crowded dance hall hit, and several dancers killed or injured. With alternative buildings often in short supply, this could have the effect of removing the dancing venues in some localities altogether. For example, in 1940 Mass Observation noted that bomb damage in Bermondsey and Paddington had seriously affected dancing provision there, and its investigators were unable to locate any public dance in either area during the week or at the weekend.[71] Elsewhere, those in the dance industry were more resourceful—the Blitz meant that dance hall owners had to be adaptable and at the height of the bombing, dance halls shifted around a variety of temporary venues. As *Dancing Times* reported in November 1940, 'bomb hopping' had become a way of life: 'you may have your lesson in Regent Street one day and be asked to turn up for the next one in Timbuctoo.'[72] During the worst of the

66 *DT*, January 1945, 175.
67 *Birmingham Evening Dispatch*, 14 October 1948, 6.
68 *MDD*, December 1939, 1.
69 *DN*, 9 August 1941, 1.
70 *Danceland 1941 Souvenir* (1942), 9.
71 M-O A FR533, 'Young People: A Social Survey in London', January 1941, 31.
72 *DT*, November 1940, 76.

bombing, dance teachers and dance promoters often co-operated with each other to provide temporary accommodation for those bombed out.

Yet, whilst requisitioning and bombing reduced the number of venues in some areas, in most towns and cities, the variety and range of opportunity for dancing remained large. In Newcastle in 1943, for example, 250 licences were issued for public dancing, including occasional ones.[73] In Birmingham that year 153 places were licensed for dancing, and a further 1,812 occasional licences were granted for dancing in council schools alone.[74] In Glasgow in 1943 there were still some ninety-six venues permanently licensed for dancing. These included twenty dance halls, twenty corporation-owned halls, seven masonic halls, four Co-op halls, six church halls, two dance schools, and six sports clubs:[75] a very similar range of venues to that found in the city before the war.

One other traditional dancing venue not adversely affected by the war, perhaps surprisingly, was seaside resorts. Although it is often presumed that holidays stopped during the war, they did not. Although the work day lengthened, pre-war legislation to introduce annual paid vacation to all workers continued to apply. Indeed, the government encouraged this as a way of maintaining morale. As Minister of Labour, Ernest Bevin, one of the chief supporters of the 1938 Act and a member of the Holidays With Pay committee, also supported the introduction of a three-day weekend in the spring for war workers. In effect, as John Walton has pointed out, the Minister of Labour actually extended the number of annual paid holiday days throughout the war years.[76] Whilst the number of seaside resorts open was reduced, with coastal towns in the east and south of England officially off limits, many northern, Welsh, and Scottish seaside venues remained open for business. Indeed, even after requisitioning for war use, three-quarters of all resort accommodation remained available to holidaymakers.[77] Demand for holidays increased. Indeed, the pent-up demand of affluent and over-worked industrial workers meant that many holiday resorts boomed during the war. Despite the shortage of trains, and government requests not to travel, workers flocked to the seaside during bank holiday and summer periods.

Dancing remained a key attraction for holidaymakers; indeed the curtailing of many alternative amusements in holiday resorts meant that it was often one of the few remaining leisure activities available to them. Mass Observation, for example, reported in the summer of 1940 that seaside towns in Lancashire were 'packing their dance halls'.[78] In Dunoon, a popular holiday destination for Glasgow workers, summer dances at the Dunoon Pavilion proved so successful that the Dunoon

73 TWA: MG.Nc. 7/5, 'Licensing Minutes 1936–45'.

74 CBA, *Twenty-Ninth Annual Report of the Public Entertainments Committee of Justices*, 4 January 1944, 3 and 5.

75 GCA: E7/4/1, 'Register of Music Halls etc, 1934–52'.

76 J. Walton, *The British Seaside: Holidays and Resorts in the Twentieth Century* (Manchester: Manchester University Press, 2000), 62.

77 Unpublished thesis, S. Dawson, Islands of Leisure: British Holiday Camps in War and Peace, PhD, University of California Santa Barbara (2007), 222.

78 M-O A: FR295 'On Jazz 1940', 5.

Development Association was able to pay the Town Council £1,000, £400 more than the previous year, when it bought the right to run dancing for summer 1943 season.[79] In summer 1944 *Danceland* similarly reported: 'Thousands upon thousands make their way to the dancehalls, for Blackpool caters for dancers probably more than any other place in the country. Admission is cheap, but the bands and floors are good.'[80]

Even outside the main holidaying periods, dancing in seaside resorts boomed, due to the influx of outsiders brought about by the war. Many government departments were relocated to northern seaside resorts to avoid the danger of the Blitz. In Blackpool, for example, the town was chosen as a base for relocation because of the huge numbers of boarding houses and hotels. Over 37,000 evacuees were housed in former holiday accommodation, paid for by the government, and 1,700 civil servants were also billeted in the town. In addition, the RAF Blackpool Station was established in October 1939 and over the course of the war nearly 770,000 RAF personnel were given initial training there, together with 31,000 WAAFS. It was estimated that there were around 45,000 RAF personnel in the town at any one time, with much of their preliminary training conducted in the huge Winter Garden and Empress ballrooms. Both venues were returned to civilian use each evening. In 1940 a further influx of workers came to the town when the Vickers Armstrong Factory was built to make Wellington Bombers. Blackpool's population also took on an increasingly cosmopolitan air, as foreign servicemen arrived in large numbers. The Polish Air Force Headquarters was based there, and around 18,000 Polish personnel were billeted in Blackpool during the war. In 1942 the first of 20,000 Americans arrived in the town.

To cater for all of these new residents, the winter depression disappeared from Blackpool. The Pleasure Beach opened throughout the winter, and the Tower Ballroom and the ballroom at the Winter Gardens were packed out nightly. In January 1940, for example, the *Daily Mirror* reported that 'Blackpool finds money circulating in stores, shops, restaurants and cafes and places of entertainment', noting that the town's dance halls were 'crowded with Civil Servants of all grades', and that there were 'hundreds of pretty girls . . . at Blackpool Winter Gardens . . . dancing, drinking coffee and obviously enjoying themselves'.[81] In December 1941 *Modern Dance and Dancer* pointed to the 'nightly influx' of HM Forces of both sexes and members of the civil services to its 'huge' ballrooms.[82] Although Blackpool's war was a particularly good one, similar situations could be found at other seaside resorts, such as Rhyl, Llandudno, and Southport—where a newly enlarged patronage swelled the dance halls of the holiday towns.

In addition to traditional holiday venues, dancing also became a major attraction of the wartime 'Holidays at Home' scheme, and in many towns and cities throughout Britain new, albeit temporary, venues were created for dancing. In order to discourage people from travelling during holiday periods, and using up vital railway stock and scarce coal and petrol resources, the government introduced the Holidays

[79] *DT*, April 1943, 345.
[80] *Danceland*, September 1944, 1.
[81] *DM*, 8 January 1940, 15.
[82] *MDD*, December 1941, 19.

at Home scheme from 1941. It encouraged local authorities to provide programmes of holiday entertainment to coincide with local holiday periods. Whilst existing dance halls did their best to provide holiday entertainments, new dancing venues were opened by councils, some of them with enormous capacity, and sometimes free. Some of the schemes were extremely ambitious.

Huddersfield was one of the first towns in the country to take the scheme seriously. 20,000 workers stayed at home over a six-week staggered holiday period in summer 1941. Special shows were put on at the theatres and cinemas, open air concerts and games organized in the parks, and dances were run 'for young and old' in a number of locations.[83] In Leeds in 1942, the Holidays at Home scheme attracted two and a half million people and included ballroom dancing demonstrations given by local professionals, and the construction of a marquee for dancing with a tiled wooden dance floor.[84] Glasgow's 1943 scheme also involved the construction of a 100 ft by 80 ft dance floor of compressed asbestos cement costing £700 and capable of accommodating up to 1,000 dancers in Kelvingrove Park.[85] The *Daily Record* and *Glasgow Evening News* ran a week-long series of open air dance competitions, with average attendances of 4,000 dancers and spectators per night.[86] Dancing was also central to the Holidays at Home scheme in Edinburgh in 1943. Indeed, so popular was the open air dancing in Princes Street Gardens—it attracted over 200,000 dancers—that the city council was able to use the profits from it to fund the entire holiday scheme in the city.[87] The dancers included large numbers of soldiers on leave and women on night shift who could not get to a normal night's dancing. In summer 1944 in Liverpool, three new ballrooms were created in the city's parks. Two were fairly rudimentary marquees with sectional board floors which were waxed to improve dancing. The third had a fully sprung maple floor and was remarkably elaborate. The *Dancing Times* commented that 'the green and red canvas, tubular lighting, and general spaciousness makes it an ideal spot for holiday dancing'.[88] The authorities in Leeds also expanded their provision for dancing that year, with three 'big tops' for dancers provided at Roundhay Park, Cross Gates, and Woodhouse, and some free dancing lessons as part of a £21,000 Holidays at Home scheme.[89]

The Holidays at Home scheme was not the only new venue for dancing brought about by the war. The war improved the availability of dances in some areas, as the influx of outsiders created new demand. For example, Ipswich had no regular dances before the war, but by 1941 there were at least two regular dances per week, something Mass Observation put down to the large number of soldiers based in the area.[90] M. Haylock, manager of Leicester's £40,000 Palais de Danse, put the boom in dancing down to the number of evacuees and other new residents in the city.[91]

[83] *DM*, 28 July 1941, 6. [84] *DT*, November 1942, 83. [85] *DT*, April 1943, 345.
[86] *DT*, September 1943, 583. [87] *Danceland*, December 1943, 5.
[88] *DT*, July 1944, 477. [89] *DT*, April 1944, 331.
[90] M-O A, FR884, 'Report on Ipswich Morale,' September 1941, 3–4.
[91] *DN*, 6 September 1941, 4.

During the war factories and other workplaces also became new venues for dancing. The provision of dancing facilities in the workplace varied widely, from informal dances around the radio to formal provision of ballroom facilities for workers. Dancing's incursion into the workplace on a large scale during the war was part of a wider move to improve working conditions in order to raise morale and to increase productivity. As Minister of Labour, Ernest Bevin encouraged employers to improve workplace facilities for those in the vital war industries. New canteens, washing facilities, and the provision of welfare officers were ways of combating absenteeism, especially following the influx of women into industry. Entertainment was also seen as important. Concerts were organized for shift workers by ENSA and CEMA, and most famously the BBC, encouraged by the Ministry of Labour, produced 'Music While You Work', a programme of background music broadcast into factories to relieve the boredom of munitions work. By 1943 over 3,000 factories had loudspeakers to broadcast these programmes, reaching nearly four million workers.

What is less well known is that dancing went into Britain's factories too, sometimes encouraged directly by the Ministry of Labour, but more often on the initiative of factory managements and sometimes on the initiative of the workforce themselves. Thus, according to the *Dancing Times*, in canteens and factories, informal dancing to the radio during recreation hours was a very popular pastime.[92] Such dances often provided relief from the demands of war work. Mass Observation noted this:

> If the wireless is put on . . . there are general shouts and shrieks of delight as women . . . prance round to the music. The fattest are the nimblest on the whole, and certainly the most popular spectacle. There are no inhibitions or fears of being ridiculous on this floor. The works police on the door and stray odd job man are an appreciative audience.[93]

Elsewhere, arrangements for dancing were more formal and more substantial. In 1941, several war factories in Coventry were providing dance bands and facilities for dancing, some holding two midday concerts per week, and one even running dances from midnight to 1 am, in response to demands from younger workers.[94] In Edinburgh similar demands led the management of one large munitions factory to open a dance club for their employees:

> We have decided to open the hall at 4 o'clock in the afternoon so that those on night-shift may have a few hours dancing before going to work . . . Talk of absenteeism through amusement at night is utter rot. We are certain that by bringing the workers together like this they will get to know one another better and will look forward to meeting at their benches in the morning.[95]

[92] *DT*, March 1941, 340.
[93] M-O A, FR1496, 'Tube Investigation November 1942', 20. The factory was in Birmingham.
[94] *DM*, 19 March 1941, 1.
[95] *DN*, 29 November 1941, 3.

At an RAF factory in northern England, the popularity of dancing as a recreation for workers was reflected in the provision of a 'magnificent ballroom' and a number of dance clubs where tuition was given.[96] As with the BBC's 'Music While You Work', it was argued that the provision of dancing facilities during breaks increased productivity. Thus, in August 1941 *Dance News* reported:

> More and more war factories are to have schemes for holding dances for their employees. This is because reports show that wherever dances have been arranged, they are popular, benefit the health of the employees, keep them 'smiling'—and improve work output.[97]

Following on from the example set by many managers, the government increasingly became interested in the provision of dancing facilities in the workplace. Many Royal Ordnance factories, for example, started to provide dances for their workers. In 1941, the Central Ordnance Depot in south-east England started to give workers lunchtime dances and the Ministry of Labour also promoted dances for women war workers in an effort to aid recruitment, something discussed in more detail in Chapter 6.[98] In 1942, the government even sponsored the provision of a dancing master, a retired ballroom champion, in engineering factories in the north-west of England to give dance lessons and physical training instruction to the workforce.[99]

In addition to new venues in towns and cities, rural areas often saw an increase in the size and number of dances being run. Like their urban counterparts, rural communities were often transformed by the war as the influx of large numbers of outsiders swelled local populations, and altered their profile considerably. The stationing of members of the armed forces, evacuees, war workers, or Land Girls in an area could dramatically alter the dynamics of the local population. With very little else to occupy them, and with often poor transport facilities made worse by the war, the local dance became a key focus of social activity. In 1941 *Dance News* observed, 'So great has been the demand for dancing facilities in small villages that many dancers have been turned away from local halls, which are frequently too small to accommodate everyone who wants admission.'[100] As Elizabeth Cross described in 1941, the dance was an important feature of rural life: 'Everyone . . . comes to these dances. They come to dance, to listen to the efforts of the band, to see each other's clothes, and they all have the glorious reason of supporting the Spitfire Fund.'[101] In early 1942 *Dance News* was able to report the huge popularity of dancing in tiny villages and small towns all over Scotland's country districts, from Inverness in the north to Dumfries in the south: 'Everywhere I went I found young folk and old thronging to their local town or village hall in the evenings for a night's dancing and relaxation from war work. Saturday night dances were especially popular.' It concluded: 'Dances like these are doing a lot to brighten up the Scottish countryside through the long winter nights of blackout. Many a lonely

96 *DT*, February 1945, 214.
97 *DN*, 2 August 1941, 1.
98 *DN*, 30 August 1941, 1.
99 *DM*, 4 March 1942, 5.
100 *DN*, 15 November 1941, 2.
101 *DT*, January 1941, 220.

country road north of the Tweed will echo tonight to the happy laughter of dancers wending their way home to village, farm and cottage.'[102]

WARTIME CHALLENGES TO THE DANCE HALL INDUSTRY

Despite the increased popularity and economic prosperity of the dance business, the war brought new challenges to the industry. Staffing was a key problem. Whilst recognizing the importance of entertainment to morale, the government was reluctant to give reserved occupation status to those who worked in the leisure industry. As a result, the start of the war brought about serious challenges to dance hall owners. The manager of the Streatham Locarno, for example, told Mass Observation that he had lost many of his staff to war reserve police, ambulance units, AFS, and so on.[103] Similar difficulties led Mecca to complain in December 1941:

> There is no doubt that the Government realise the need for entertainment, but daily the staff problem in dancehalls becomes a most serious matter. Managers, staff and musicians are being conscripted. Entertainment including dancing, should be considered as one of the national services, almost as important as war work in the factories.[104]

However, although Equity arranged with the Ministry of Labour to make a small number of largely female entertainers exempt from war work, dance hall staff were never included in any reserved occupation groups. As a result, dance halls had to show considerable ingenuity in staffing matters. Women and those either too old or too young to be conscripted were given jobs and dancing work had to be fitted around war work. For example, the leading dance teacher Charles Thiebault became a war reserve policeman, and then took on eight-hour shifts in a war factory before giving lessons at his Normandie School in London.[105]

Getting musicians during the war was also hugely problematic. The outbreak of the war saw a near collapse of work for semi-professional musicians, as pessimism and uncertainty caused the cancellation of most private appointments, and as many venues were closed down.[106] Even though professional dance bands saw a boom in business following the resumption of normal leisure activities, widespread conscription subsequently saw large number of musicians removed from the business. This often happened with considerable speed. Whilst in February 1940 *Dancing Times* could claim that in Bristol 'there are still plenty of musicians in the city who have come from other parts of the country to get work', it warned that conscription would soon alter this, particularly for 'the outfits which are mainly composed of the younger generation'.[107] Only a few months later, by December 1940, conscription

[102] *DN*, 14 March 1942, 12.
[103] M-O A, TC 38/1/A, 'Chaperlin 1.11.39', 2.
[104] *DN*, 6 December 1941, 2.
[105] *DT*, July 1942, 509.
[106] See M-O A, TC 38/6/F, 'Jazz and Dancing, Draft', 17–21.
[107] *DT*, February 1940, 321.

of dance musicians caused considerable difficulty for local dance halls. *Dancing Times* now reported that there were 'very few outfits functioning'.[108] Mass Observation noted the impact elsewhere:

> [T]he war situation is playing havoc... Since the jazz world is essentially youthful in basis, most of the bands have been affected, and the supply of good musicians drastically reduced. The effect in Bolton itself is just beginning to be seriously felt. Nearly all the Palais bands are affected by the latest conscript groupings. About 80% of the Musicians Union membership is similarly affected.[109]

The shortage of musicians meant adaptations had to be made to the usual musical arrangements. There were several solutions. In a small number of venues, live music was replaced altogether by gramophone records, experiments being made along this line in some Liverpool halls in December 1940, but this was not popular.[110] More popular was the use of all-women dance bands. Mecca engaged several female bands to play in its circuit of dance halls in order to fill the gaps left by conscription of men.[111] In its Locarno dance hall in Leeds, for example, in December 1940 it started to engage Pauline Gray and her female band.[112] Numerous other female bands played throughout the country, and by July 1942 Irene Raines was commenting: 'One of the most outstanding features of war-time dancing is the way ladies' bands have come to the front and made a genuine success.'[113] The most famous of the all-female bands was that of Ivy Benson, who achieved considerable success.

Another solution was to use military bands. All of the main services had their own traditional military bands, but one novel feature of the Second World War was the appearance of dance bands provided by the armed forces. The most famous of these was the Squadronnaires, the leading dance band of the RAF, composed of the former personnel of such famous bands as those of Ambrose, Oscar Rabin, Eddie Carroll, and Jack Harris. In addition to these headline military bands, even the smallest of military units put together dance band outfits made up of professional and semi-professional dance band musicians. For example, an all-soldiers dance band known as the 'Hot Shots of Rhythm' was started in December 1941 at a gun site in south-east Scotland. It broadcast in the BBC Forces programme and provided music for local dances.[114] Furthermore, individual musicians who were serving in the forces could be allowed to play in local dance bands when they were on leave or if given special permission to do so by their commanding officer.[115]

Finally, men in reserved occupations could also play in dance bands. Many who before the war had supplemented their day jobs with semi-professional musical work remained in Britain during the war as part of the workforce. However, as the war progressed and wages and working hours increased, it became less attractive for semi-professionals working in war industries to play in dance bands. In February

[108] *DT*, December 1940, 169.
[109] M-O A, FR301A, 'First Weekly Morale Report 1940', 46.
[110] *DT*, December 1940, 165.
[111] *Danceland*, 22 May 1941, 1.
[112] *MDD*, December 1940, 10.
[113] *DT*, July 1942, 509.
[114] *DN*, 13 December 1941, 2.
[115] *Danceland*, July 1944, 4.

1942, for example, a Yorkshire association of dance teachers debated the issue, complaining that 'those who at work are getting such good wages that the money earned for playing is reduced by half for income tax. It is known that musicians are fighting shy of playing regularly and prefer Gig jobs where the money is not so likely to be taxed.'[116]

In addition to staffing difficulties, dance halls were faced with other practical problems. Curfews were one major problem. The government, local authorities, and the police were all given the power to impose curfews. There were wide variations in their severity, which some dance hall owners thought acted to their disadvantage. In Yorkshire, for example, whilst Harrogate Town Council allowed dancing until midnight in the Royal Hall, in Halifax and Huddersfield dance halls closed at 11 pm and in Bradford licensed dance halls had to close at 10 pm and those with occasional licences at 9.30 pm.[117] Restrictions in Birmingham were particularly harsh, a continuation of the city's traditional hostility to public entertainments. From 1 September 1941 dance halls and other places of entertainment in Birmingham had to close at 9 pm.[118] The following month the Chief Constable of Glasgow consulted managers of cinemas and dance halls in the city with a view to a possible 9.30 pm curfew.[119] Such fluctuations in opening times clearly had implications for the ability of dance halls to survive.

Another impact of the war which affected dancing was the reduced transport facilities available in both urban and rural centres. Public transport facilities were often curtailed as local authorities faced shortages of both personnel and petrol. Services finished much earlier, partially in order to ensure that populations were at home during bombing raids. Such restrictions also meant that larger dancing events and special occasions needed considerable forward planning. Local authorities had to be consulted in holiday periods, and during extensions to dancing hours at Christmas and New Year.

As well as these challenges to the dance hall industry, perhaps the biggest threat to their existence was that provided by the Blitz. How did the Blitz affect dancing and the dance hall industry? As we have seen, at the outbreak of the war places of entertainment were closed down by government order in anticipation of widespread bombing. Whilst this did not materialize in 1939, once the bombing began in earnest in 1940, the government had to reconsider its policy. The Blitz began on 7 September 1940 and lasted until 21 May 1941, some 267 days or nearly thirty-seven weeks. Various cities throughout Britain were targeted, sixteen of them heavily, including London, Liverpool, Manchester, Birmingham, Plymouth, Bristol, Southampton, Cardiff, and Glasgow. As a result, 43,000 civilians were killed, almost half of them in London. In addition to these deaths a further 71,000 were seriously injured, and over one million houses were destroyed in London alone. In March 1941, following the bombing of several dance halls, the Ministry of Home Security considered the question of whether dancing in public halls should be allowed during air raids. Herbert Morrison decided that there would not be any

[116] *DT*, February 1942, 281.
[117] *MDD*, December 1940, 4.
[118] *DN*, 23 August 1941, 1.
[119] *DN*, 18 October 1941, 1.

official prohibitions on night sessions at London dance halls. Having got the issue wrong at the outbreak of the war, the government had to weigh any public safety considerations against the impact on morale of closing entertainments. It appeared to officials that the risk to public safety was less than had been anticipated before bombing began. That month, for example, a direct hit on a London dance hall had seen three casualties out of 200 present.[120] This had clearly influenced Morrison, who, according to the national press, had 'reached this decision after considering the recent air-raid casualties among dancers as well as the national demand for facilities for recreation'.[121] Instead, government advice was that the public themselves had to decide what action they took in the event of air raids. Thus, dancers were to be informed of an alert and then left to make their own decision whether or not to go to the nearest shelter. However, the ultimate decision as to whether to keep dance halls open during the Blitz lay with local government, not central government. Many towns and cities were to be far more prescriptive and restrictive than Herbert Morrison wanted them to be.

Clearly, the destruction wrought by the Blitz created major challenges for the dance hall industry and threatened to undermine its popularity. One response of those in the dancing business to the very real prospect of bomb damage was to emphasize the range of measures taken to ensure dancers' safety. In line with government preparations for the war, managers of places of public entertainment had been given ARP training even before war was declared. Dance halls also provided firespotters from their staff, to keep watch on their roofs during the Blitz. Frequently they would have to extinguish incendiaries before they could cause damage and dance hall staff would carry out minor repairs so that the dancehall could open as usual.[122] Premises for dancing were adapted, and attempts made to make dance halls bomb-proof. Some dance halls even doubled as public air raid shelters, the Ritz dance hall Manchester and the Paramount, Tottenham Court Road, London, being two examples. Mecca's Paramount had a nine-foot wall of sandbags constructed around its entrance, and the manager doubled as the official air raid warden.[123] After the evening dancing session the public were permitted to stay all night, and could rent a bunk for a shilling. Up to a thousand people regularly stayed overnight.[124] Elsewhere, dancing went underground, as a number of dance venues opened premises in their basements. For example, in December the 'Below Ground Club' was open on Charing Cross Road, with dancing from 6–11 pm and facilities for sleeping over for those who wished.[125] Most of London's top hotels also provided this facility. At the Mayfair Hotel the underground ballroom was decorated to look like an eighteenth-century garden and was also an official air raid shelter. Like the Paramount, dancers were provided with a mattress and blankets if they wanted to stay overnight.[126] The Piccadilly Hotel had similar facilities and at Grosvenor House, too, dancing was provided in a subterranean

[120] *Manchester Guardian*, 17 March 1941, 5. [121] *Manchester Guardian*, 22 March 1941, 7.
[122] *DN*, 6 September 1941, 1. [123] *MDD*, November 1939, 17.
[124] *Danceland 1941 Souvenir* (1942), 5. [125] *MDD*, December 1940, 2.
[126] *DT*, November 1940, 76.

ballroom. The Café de Paris was already largely an underground venue, and it capitalized on this, advertising itself as the 'safest nightspot in London' (although it too received a direct hit in March 1941, causing thirty-four casualties). At the Dorchester Hotel there was not an underground ballroom, but dancing was relocated to the Gold Room on the ground floor in the centre of the building, which was under eight floors of reinforced concrete.[127] Mecca was keen to emphasize the safety of dancing compared with other entertainments. In October 1940, Byron Davies argued that dancing was the safest of amusements:

> The space needed for movement, the fact that people are all on one level adjacent to all 'emergency exits' gives a great advantage during air raids—there are not the closely-packed seats the narrow stairways and gangways, the balcony or gallery of the usual theatre or cinema. Additionally, practically all the time a dance hall is fully lighted. Dancing is safer than other forms of entertainment during air raids.[128]

The Blitz and blackout, together with the widespread introduction of shift work, led to a shift in the hours most dance halls operated. Afternoon dances became increasingly popular, for both men and women. Evening dances started and ended earlier, with dancers filling up the dance floors much earlier than in pre-war days. Dancers soon adapted, as Mecca's Carl Heimann noted as early as December 1939:

> It is surprising how quickly the public have disciplined themselves to the earlier hours. The tendency pre-war was for the public to become later and later in arrival. But today there are as many people in a public dance hall at 6.30, as there used to be at 8 or 8.30.[129]

Yet, once dancers had started to drift back to town and city centre venues, they stayed later, and a resilient spirit of 'carrying on' was reported in the press, as dance halls became symbols of normality, and a sign of resistance. At the Grafton Rooms in Liverpool, the management advertised itself as 'Liverpool's Bombproof Ballroom' and it had a policy of carrying on dancing during alerts and barrages, with Mrs Wilf Hamer conducting the orchestra wearing her tin hat during air raids.[130] In November 1941 dancers in the West End carried on dancing despite a heavy calibre bomb dropping next to them. The event was being broadcast on the BBC, since Jack White and his Orchestra were performing. The press reported the event with a keen eye on its propaganda value:

> Two hundred couples were dancing on the crowded floor. Suddenly a heavy thud shuddered through the sprung maple floor. Crashing of glass followed. Clouds of choking brick dust covered the dancers. On the music dais the pianist shot off his stool. The trombone player's silver instrument flew from his hand across the room. 'Carry on, boys, keep playing,' said the band leader—and prevented what might have been panic... Brushing plaster and brick dust from their clothes, the dancers began the 'Lambeth Walk'.[131]

127 Ibid. 128 *DT*, October 1940, 22. 129 *DT*, December 1939, 142.
130 *DT*, December 1940, 165. 131 *MDD*, November 1940, 17.

CONCLUSION

Not only surviving the challenges of wartime, dancing blossomed. Indeed, it is no exaggeration to claim that it was vital to the maintenance of morale on the home front. The huge growth in business was testament to this, and the Second World War thus cemented the place of dancing in Britain's social and cultural life.

Chapter 3

Rise and Fall

The Golden Age of the Dance Hall, 1945–60

INTRODUCTION

After the war the popularity of social dancing in Britain soared to new heights, before rapidly declining. The golden age of the dance hall was the 1950s. Buoyed up by an era of full employment and rising prosperity, dancing became Britain's pre-eminent national leisure activity. As Maurice Jay observed in 1951, dancing was 'an activity which is indulged in by more people than any sport, pastime or art . . . and that includes the great National sport, Football . . . More people go dancing on a Saturday evening than attend all the other weekend sports put together!'[1] But the prosperity that had created the boom was also responsible for the bust. Despite appearing entrenched in Britain's social and cultural life, the dance hall disappeared with surprising speed. By the end of the 1960s, superceded by nightclubs, and later discos, the palais was no more. Dancing was still popular, but in a form and at venues much altered. A cultural and social phenomenon that had survived for around four decades was gone. These developments were shaped by the rapid economic and social change witnessed in the era, as Britain went through first an age of austerity and then an age of affluence.

DANCING IN AN AGE OF AUSTERITY, 1945–53

The end of the Second World War brought a potential crossroads for dancing. Those in the dance industry wondered whether the buoyant levels of business seen during the conflict could be maintained, or whether they were just a temporary boom caused by wartime conditions. It was suggested by some in the industry that dancing would decline in popularity as rival attractions in a revived leisure industry took patrons away from the ballroom. Thus, the shrewder businessmen involved in the dancing industry recognized that the return to peacetime conditions would create a new set of challenges as well as opportunities. As one, P. Rocks, wrote in 1946: 'I am . . . concerned with whether dancing will retain its popularity. A little organising and planning in advance might well make all the difference . . . directors of leading dance halls will be well advised to study every possible angle to retain a

[1] *Danceland*, May 1951, 8.

virile and ever increasing interest in the ballroom.'[2] Whatever the long-term future of dancing, however, both pessimists and optimists were agreed that there was likely to be an immediate post-war 'craze' for dancing, as there had been following the First World War. In this respect they were right, and the immediate aftermath of war did see dancing 'boom'. This boom was unlike the 1918/19 boom, however, in that it was tempered by material and labour shortages, yet boosted by an unprecedented period of full employment.

Although the years immediately after the war were to be fraught with difficulties for those in the dancing business, as with so much of life in post-war Britain, there were also reasons to be hopeful. In many respects, the return to peacetime conditions offered improved prospects for dancing. Dancing was boosted by the gradual return of properties requisitioned by the government during the war. In Liverpool in December 1945 for example, it was reported: 'In the past month about a dozen dance centres opened in this district, in the centre and the suburbs, several in halls and buildings now derequisitioned by the government.'[3] 1946 saw a spate of de-requisitioning. In April, Agincourt Hall, in Camberley, Surrey, which had been used as a military store, re-opened for dancing.[4] In August, the Trentham Gardens Ballroom near Stoke-on-Trent, wartime home of the Banks Clearance House, was de-requisitioned together with the Greyfriars dance hall in Nottingham, which had been occupied by a section of the Army Post.[5] The re-opening of dance halls closed during the war was taken as an indication of some kind of 'return to normalcy' after the conflict. As *Lancashire Dance News* observed in April 1946, the 'gradual return to peacetime conditions in Lancashire is shown by the constant additions to the list of new dance halls opening, and the extensions and redecorations which are going on everywhere'.[6] Certainly, in the drab climate of austerity Britain, the attraction of dance halls was boosted by the fact that they were a rare spot of colour in the public and social life of the nation, as they had been during the war. Redecoration of halls was crucial to this process. As one 1946 report commented: 'After seven years of "make-do-and-patch-up," Manchester dance hall managements are making every effort to brighten things up.'[7] This impressed patrons who, dance teacher Cyril St John argued, had eyes 'jaundiced by city smoke, bomb sites and unpainted houses and shop fronts'.[8]

The demobilization of men and women from the services, and war work, also served to boost the popularity of dancing. This happened in a number of ways. Firstly, returning soldiers were keen to re-start a pastime that had eluded many of them in the later stages of the war. More men entered dance halls and this in turn increased the number of women attracted to the pastime as a result. Dancing was particularly popular among returning servicemen for a number of other reasons too. As one dance teacher remarked: 'a lot of the boys who had been overseas had found themselves out of touch mentally and socially on their return . . . Dancing is helping

2 *LDN*, 13 July 1946, 1.
3 *DT*, December 1945, 149.
4 *Danceland*, April 1946, 1.
5 *LDN*, 3 August 1946, 4 and 17 August 1946, 1.
6 *LDN*, 27 April 1946, 1.
7 *LDN*, 25 May 1946, 3.
8 *Danceland*, July 1948, 7.

them to recover their poise and at the same time they are making social contacts in a world that was lost to them for several years.'[9] In Liverpool, the gradual relaxation of wartime working conditions also acted as an impetus to dancing. In July 1946 for example, in Liverpool it was reported: 'With more regular spells of leave from the Services, and the release of many war workers from factories, plus shorter working hours, the ballrooms in this area report increased business.'[10]

The return of servicemen and women helped in other ways too. One of the factors limiting the growth of dancing at the war's end had been a shortage of musicians. In Liverpool in February 1945, for example, it was reported that despite more venues becoming available, 'the frequency of sessions at these halls is only curtailed by the difficulty of providing bands'.[11] With many professional and semi-professional dance band musicians released from service, the dance band scene was revived again. Indeed, the dance band scene in these early days was a lucrative one, as dance promoters and dance hall owners queued up to hire their services.

As the emergency situation receded from memory, dancing began to secure a new position in post-war Britain. It was given a considerable boost by the new spirit of planning and welfare ushered in by the Labour government of 1945 to 1951. The establishment of the welfare state, with its concern for the well-being of working-class men, women, and children, saw an expanded role for the state, both locally and centrally. Building on the experience of wartime 'Holidays at Home' schemes, many local authorities became involved in the provision of dancing facilities. Seeing dancing as a popular and established feature of Britain's social and cultural life, councils up and down the country decided either to offer dancing facilities directly themselves or to lease out their properties for dance promoters. In Glasgow, for example, in 1946 the City Corporation provided open-air dancing facilities at the Kelvingrove Park.[12] That year in Blackburn the Prime Minister's wife, Violet Attlee, opened a £15,000 community centre, which included a dance hall as one of its key features.[13] Perhaps equally importantly, dancing was recognized as a ready source of revenue generation for local authorities, and at a time of straightened resources and grand plans, this money was significant. Thus in Birmingham, the local council decided to run its own 'healthy and attractive dances' with the Labour leader of the Council, W. S. Lewis, stating that private proprietors had been making money out of running dances in the baths and it was 'only fair that such profits should revert to the taxpayers'.[14] The amount of money to be made was often considerable. In Sandbach, Cheshire, dancing run by the Council raised so much money that in 1946 it was able to fund a 3d rebate on the local rates for all of the town's residents.[15]

Local authorities were also keen to try and put colour back into their towns and cities following the war and many of them made extensions to the opening hours of dance halls in the early post-war period. In Birmingham, for example, in April 1946 *Danceland* reported that civic authorities were 'discussing ways to brighten up the

[9] *LDN*, 31 August 1946, 2.
[10] *DT*, July 1945, 469.
[11] *DT*, February 1945, 227.
[12] *Danceland*, May 1946, 2.
[13] *DM*, 7 November 1946, 6.
[14] *Daily Mail*, 8 January 1947, 3.
[15] *DM*, 18 April 1946, 3.

city's night life' and there appeared to be a new attitude towards granting licences for music and dancing in a city previously notorious for its tough stance on entertainment.[16] Thus, emergency regulations concerning dance hall opening hours, and ARP precautions were relaxed immediately on the cessation of war in Europe. Hours were extended for dance halls, now allowed to stay open until 10.30 pm, and special provision was made to extend the hours of late night bus services to the suburbs.[17] The city's authorities also encouraged and supported the owners of the West End dance hall in their application to the Ministry of Works for licences to cover necessary repairs and renovations.[18] In 1947 the Licensing Committee met with a delegation calling for a 'Brighter Birmingham' to discuss the shortage of dancing, theatre, and music hall facilities, their opening hours and also the extension still further of transport services. 'The parties were assured... of the hearty support of the Public Entertainments Committee in any proposals which were designed to bring more and better entertainment to the City' and also agreed that tax was too high for such entertainments. A further conference followed.[19]

In 1947 the Musicians' Union, in an attempt to promote greater provision of music by local councils, undertook a wide ranging investigation into the topic. It clearly wished to give greater control of dancing to local government and reduce the dependency of its members on employment in the often cut-throat free market. This was in line with the extension of state control of the economy and cultural life taking place more generally under the Labour government. Its report, *Music and the Borough Councillor*, argued that '[n]o Council should allow local dances to become the hunting ground for commercial adventures', and it advised that councils should employ only the 'finest dance bands available' thus 'raising the standard of such events'. A particularly go-ahead council in this respect was Kingston Council in London. It was used by the Musicians' Union as a model for other councils to follow. In Kingston it had been the practice to let the Coronation Baths Hall to private promoters on Saturday nights at a fee of 20 guineas. During the 1946/7 season, however, the entertainments committee of the Council started running the Saturday dances itself. They consistently showed a profit on the ventures. In Wembley too a series of twenty-six dances run by the Council in 1946 over three months showed an overall profit of £1,117 or about £45 each.[20] A British Institute of Public Opinion (Gallup Poll) survey of the attitude of the public throughout Greater London towards municipally sponsored concerts and dances found that two-thirds wanted to see their councils arranging dances.

Council provision of dancing proved particularly important during the immediate post-war period of severe shortages, which limited the private sector's ability to provide dancing facilities. In doing this, councils ensured that a need was met,

[16] *Danceland*, April 1946, 1.

[17] CBA, PS/B 4/1/1/5, *Twenty-Ninth Annual Report of the Public Entertainments Committee of Justices*, 4 January 1946, 6.

[18] CBA, PS/B 4/1/1/5, *Thirtieth Annual Report of the Public Entertainments Committee of Justices*, 3 January 1947, 3.

[19] Ibid., 8.

[20] Musicians' Union, *Music and the Borough Councillor* (London: Musicians' Union, 1947), 8.

and that interest in dancing was maintained. Thus, local authorities provided dancing facilities in parks, in former air raid shelters, and even built mobile dance halls in some areas experiencing the worst shortages, or most damaged by bombing. In Hull, for example, dancers had been 'suffering for severe lack of ballroom space due to so many of the halls being blitzed'. Recognizing the need for dancing accommodation, the chairman of the Corporation Parks Committee, Councillor H. Kneeshaw, arranged for a 'portable' dance hall to be erected in the East Park. The ballroom had a maple floor and accommodation for 500 dancers. Alderman A. Stark commented that it would 'take the dances to the people, instead of the people having to go a long way to them'.[21]

In addition, dancing was boosted by new legislation regarding town planning. In 1946 the New Towns Act was passed as part of the process of rebuilding Britain's war-damaged towns and cities. It allowed for the creation of new towns under the direction of Development Corporations controlled by central government. A new department, The Ministry of Town and Country Planning, was created, promising that Britain's new towns were to be 'brighter, gayer and more beautiful' than ever before. An indication of how significant dancing had become to daily life in Britain, the government, encouraged by the dance hall industry, sought to include dancing facilities in these schemes for New Towns and other town planning developments. The Minister of Town and Country Planning, Lewis Silkin, visualized towns with an array of entertainment and leisure facilities such as theatres, concert halls, sports grounds, etc. The dance industry also got the following promise from him, when he failed to specifically mention the provision of dance halls in the House of Commons debate concerning the Bill in May 1946: 'Dancers need have no fear that they have been forgotten . . . Provision is being made for all forms of social activity, and dancing, being the foremost of them, will be well provided for.'[22]

Related to this new spirit of welfare and planning, and in part an extension of wartime experiments, some employers looked to provide dancing facilities in their factories (see Fig. 3.1). In 1946 Mullard's Electronics at Mitcham, Surrey, one of the largest factories in the south of England, introduced half an hour's dancing for their employees during the lunch interval. Music was provided by a radiogram and part of the canteen floor was sectioned off for the purpose.[23] It was believed that dancing would help to improve productivity and there is some evidence to support this claim. In a worsted factory in Wakefield, Yorkshire, for example, productivity increased 7 per cent after lunch hour dancing was introduced. The factory welfare officer reported:

> Since the girls became boppers, production has soared . . . The management are very keen on the idea. They believe that if the girls are given the opportunity of dancing in their dinner hour, they are happier at their work and that increases production. Another thing, the exercise they get in this really energetic dancing helps to keep them fit.[24]

[21] *Hull Daily Mail*, 27 June 1946, 1. [22] *LDN*, 18 May 1946, 1.
[23] *LDN*, 15 June 1946, 4. [24] *DM*, 20 April 1951, 7.

Fig. 3.1. Dancing at work: Female ICI employees enjoy a dance, South Yorkshire, 1957
Source: Getty Images.

As well as increasing productivity, providing dancing facilities was seen as a way of attracting employees in an era of labour shortages. This was particularly important as female workers were used to plug the gaps in Britain's labour force, and dancing had a particular appeal for women. Night shift workers were also catered for. To sweeten the pill of working late hours, the Manor Mills works of the Hercules Cycle Company in Birmingham, for example, provided dancing between 1 and 2 am every night in 'an effort to make night workers feel they are not missing all the fun that day workers can have'.[25] Employers were keen to present themselves as 'enlightened' and in touch with the new mood in industrial relations and government. That dancing took its place alongside the provision of clean working

[25] *PP*, 29 March 1947, 10.

environments, proper washing and toilet facilities, canteens, and so on, as a way of attracting employees, is testament to its popularity.

There were other ways in which the gradual return to peacetime conditions helped dancing too. Building on their wartime success, seaside resorts also started to improve their dance facilities; indeed, considerable investment was made by seaside towns in their provisions for dancers. Confident of a more prosperous future than before the war, many local authorities drew up ambitious plans. As early as 1946 in Margate, for example, £40,000 was earmarked to rebuild the Winter Gardens for dancing, after they were heavily damaged during the Blitz.[26] Even within the existing seaside dance facilities, the immediate post-war period saw huge crowds of dancers and numerous re-openings. In June 1946 it was reported that 'new dance halls are opening, and old ones, closed since the early days of the war, are re-opening in large numbers on the South East Coast'. At Brighton, a former air raid shelter was turned into a dance club, the Brighton Casino, opened by the town's mayor. It had 'modernistic decoration', a first class band, and an organ costing £2,000. Two other new dance clubs also opened in the town, the Rhythm Club and the Young People's dance club. At the Aquarium, the Princess Hall was available for dancing and another new dance floor was being constructed in the former Imperial Theatre, being re-opened as a big dance restaurant.[27] Holiday camps also grew in popularity and most of them had excellent dancing facilities for their guests. The Butlin's camps in particular did much to encourage dancing. Butlin and Mecca's Carl Heimann had become acquainted prior to the war, and this cross-fertilization of business ideas led Butlin to invest heavily in his camps' dancing facilities. Some of the biggest ballrooms in the country were provided by Butlin's. At their Filey camp, the two ballrooms were very large and very well appointed, each taking 3,000 dancers plus 2,000 seated at tables. Butlin offered a touch of glamour to Britons used to austerity and shortages. Filey's Regency Ballroom, for example, was decorated in soft pastel shades and lit by six huge chandeliers, which once lit the reception rooms of the German Embassy in London. The other hall, the Viennese Ballroom, was decorated with gabled balconies and made to look like a Viennese market square. Flowers trailed from special troughs in the ceiling.[28] First-rate bands were also employed. At Skegness, Alan Green and Ivy Benson and Her Girls provided the music, at Ayr there was Ronnie Munro and His Orchestra.[29] In order to encourage dancing Butlin arranged for Victor Silvester to develop a programme of ballroom dancing lessons for the campers, with a simple step taught each day by specially trained 'red coats'. So great was the demand for these lessons that it was necessary to relay the instructions to the camps' skating rinks which acted as overflows to the ballrooms. It was estimated that this was bringing about 2,000 new dancers each week.[30] At Skegness alone 50,000 campers used the ballroom in the summer of 1946.[31] Butlin also encouraged dancing by arranging a huge dancing event at Earl's Court in 1948,

[26] *Danceland*, April 1946, 3.
[27] *Danceland*, June 1946, 3.
[28] *LDN*, 31 August 1946, 3.
[29] *Danceland*, July 1948, 7.
[30] *Danceland*, August 1948, 3.
[31] *DT*, March 1947, 315.

where he put on a five-week-long 'Health and Holiday Exhibition' at which he provided a ballroom of 26,000 square feet, providing dancing for 3,000. Twenty-five broadcasting bands and ten guest conductors provided the music, with competitions, guest dance teachers, and events held for a 'People's National Dancing Club'.[32]

Yet despite the apparent resumption of 'normality' in the years immediately after the end of the war, it must be remembered that this process was often a very protracted one. The end of the conflict did not in fact signal an immediate return to pre-war conditions in the dance industry. Many former dance halls were not returned to public use for several years after the end of the war. In Birmingham, for example, the West End dance hall was not returned to dance hall use until September 1947, and Tony's Ballroom in the city did not re-open until June 1950.[33] Similarly the Admiralty did not de-requisition dance venue Mount Wise Hall in Plymouth until June 1950.[34] Some dance halls were lost forever. The second palais de danse in the country, in Monument Road, Birmingham, never returned to its former use. Requisitioned as a sugar store by the Ministry of Food during the war, it was bought by compulsory purchase by the Birmingham Corporation in 1948 and then sold in 1950 as a warehouse—the building had been badly damaged by neglect and hooliganism in the interim, and was no longer suitable for dancing.[35]

There were other problems too. A variety of restrictions—legal, economic, and material—meant that even though the dance hall industry was extremely buoyant, there were limits to the extent to which it could expand. Building materials were in short supply—homes, factories, and other infrastructure projects were given priority for timber, steel, and other materials ahead of dance halls. Furthermore, the Home Department had to issue work permits for any large-scale building work. The prospects for anyone wanting to build new premises were not good. In March 1946 in Tredegar, Wales, for example, plans for a municipal dance hall were deferred until the local housing programme had been arranged.[36] In Bath, the Bathavon Rural District Council went so far as requisitioning a dance hall to use for housing in February 1948.[37] The only way for the dance halls to expand was to convert existing premises, but they were extremely restricted in their access to materials, and thus in their options for conversion. In 1946, for example, of the re-opening of a dance hall in Nottingham, it was reported: 'Shortage of labour and material, together with official restrictions, have delayed even the most vital of repairs, and will for some time inhibit the complete restoration of the hall.'[38] Similarly in 1946 the press reported that Aberdeen Beach's dance hall would only re-open 'if materials can be secured for the necessary reflooring'.[39] Paint, timber, furniture, and a host of furnishings and fittings were all in very short supply in the

32 *DT*, February 1948, 258.
33 *DT*, August 1947, 609; June 1950, 581.
34 *Western Morning News* (Plymouth), 16 June 1950, 5.
35 *Birmingham Mail*, 7 August 1950, 4.
36 *Danceland*, March 1946, 4.
37 *Bath Weekly Chronicle and Herald*, 28 February 1948, 4.
38 *LDN*, 17 August 1946, 1.
39 *The Press and Journal* (Aberdeen), 16 February 1946, 4.

early post-war period. The more enterprising dance hall owners did manage to find ways to overcome such conditions, however. With typical business acumen and foresight, Mecca's Carl Heimann had ripped up and purchased hundreds of carpets at the outbreak of war in 1939, which he stored over the wartime period. Once the war was over he brought them back and installed them at a time when new carpeting was virtually impossible to find. Thus he was able to give the Mecca dance halls a fresh new look and offer a luxury feel to his dance halls that marked them out from their rivals.[40] He also created a central stores facility for his company, where all materials were sent to be repaired and recycled. The situation was helped in some areas if they had enlightened councils. Some authorities recognized the importance of dancing as a social and cultural activity and made efforts to allocate raw materials to dance halls, though often with criticism from some quarters. Thus, in 1945 the government agreed to the conversion of the Lyceum Theatre on the Strand, London, to a dance hall, following the return of Covent Garden Opera House to its original functions. The cost was £3,450, of which only £390 was spent on general building work. The Minister of Works, George Tomlinson, had to justify this to the House of Commons, arguing that '[d]ance halls fill a great need, especially for leave troops'.[41] That the authorities allowed this work in such straightened circumstances is an indication of just how important dancing had become to British national life. Not everyone was happy, however. In Perth, for example, the local Education Committee complained when a dance hall in the town was given timber for re-flooring, but school buildings remained un-renovated due to shortages. Ex-Bailie J. R. Christie complained: 'if they can provide timber for pleasure then we need it more desperately for schools.'[42]

Getting money was also a problem for dance hall owners who wanted to expand or even redecorate. In the hard economic times of the immediate post-war period, loans were hard to come by due to severe lending restrictions from the banks, dictated by the government. As Mecca's Carl Heimann recalled:

> We were going all out to expand, bearing in mind we would be coping with difficult periods. Don't forget that . . . things were very much in short supply—yet the public was demanding much more. . . . shortages lasted for years after the war—also . . . there were restrictions on the amount of money you could borrow.[43]

Transport was another problem. Whereas during the war, the Blitz and curfews had curtailed transport facilities, in the immediate aftermath, it was shortages that caused problems. Fuel shortages, lack of vehicles and parts, and a transport system pushed to breaking point by the demands of war, meant that public transport in many towns and cities was not back up to pre-war levels of coverage in the first year or so after the end of the war. In particular, the kinds of late night services of especial importance to the success of the dance hall industry were not a priority for

40 R. Fairley, *Come Dancing, Miss World* (London: Neamme, 1966), 123.
41 *Daily Mail*, 7 November 1945, 4. 42 *DET*, 24 January 1946, 4.
43 Fairley, *Come Dancing*, 121.

overworked councils desperate to rehouse the population and repair their cities. Sometimes, businesses took the initiative in order to cope. In Oldham, for example, in April 1946, transport problems were so great that the Plaza Ballroom, which drew dancers from Rochdale, Shaw, Royton, and Newhey districts, introduced a special coach service of its own direct to and from the dance hall, charging inclusive rates which covered hall admissions as well as transport.[44]

Even musical instruments were hard to come by. Not a priority for the domestic market, the use of precious metal resources for instrument manufacture meant that musicians had to make do with their old instruments or trade in second hand instruments. Imports were also restricted. As *Danceland* observed in 1946, demand for instruments exceeded supply, stating that 'after six years of war restricted imports, musicians are looking in vain for new instruments'.[45] This meant there were a finite number of dance bands that could exist in the country. With so many shortages, increased costs were also a concern for dance hall owners. A Liverpool dance hall owner complained in 1946: 'Bands cost far more, catering is a constant headache, printing and advertisement charges are up, prizes for competitions, "spots" and the like are difficult to obtain, in addition to being subject to luxury tax.'[46] On average dance band musicians were costing about £10 10s a week in 1946, which was double the pre-war figure.[47] Moreover, dancers, it seemed, were unwilling to pay more for dancing, thus reducing the profitability of some businesses. As one Liverpool manager observed, despite dancing being one of the cheapest forms of entertainment 'the dancing public refuse to pay increased admission charges, unless the attraction is a most expensive one, which automatically cancels out, from the promoter's point of view, the extra charge.'[48]

In spite of all of these problems, the immediate post-war period saw dancing maintain and extend the levels of popularity attained during the war, which were already unprecedentedly high. As early as 1946, managers of dance halls throughout the country were able to report new levels of interest in dancing. That August bank holiday saw 'record business' recorded in dance halls in Manchester, for example, with about 10,000 dancers at the Coronation Ballroom, Belle Vue alone.[49] By this stage it was estimated that there were three million regular dancers in Britain a week, a rise of 50 per cent on pre-war figures.[50] Such was its popularity, the national press were able to pick up on the economic importance of the dance business. L. C. Henshaw, writing in the *Daily Mirror* in October 1946, claimed: 'Not since the early twenties has ballroom dancing been so popular. Palais promoters with a well developed box office sense are looking forward to a good winter.'[51] He estimated that at Mecca alone, they were expecting eight million patrons and that takings would be worth over £1 million. Altogether it was estimated that about thirty million tickets would be sold in Britain's 400 dance halls.[52] Similarly, Ralph Howins of the *Daily Mail* reported in November 1946

[44] *LDN*, 27 April 1946, 1.
[45] *Danceland*, May 1946, 2.
[46] *Danceland*, December 1946, 5.
[47] *DM*, 15 October 1946, 2.
[48] *Danceland*, December 1946, 5.
[49] *DT*, September 1946, 655.
[50] *Danceland*, October 1946, 3.
[51] *DM*, 15 October 1946, 2.
[52] Ibid.

that dancing had moved up 'to the big business class' and described its 'Formula for a Fortune': 'Painstaking organisation and clever finance have turned dancing into a thriving new industry and earned a handful of far-sighted individuals a fortune.'[53] Estimating the attendance at the thirty biggest dance halls in Britain to be around fifteen million per year, it pointed to the profits of Mecca as a 'six figure mark'.[54] Indeed, the profitability of dancing is best exemplified by the development of Mecca at this time, as the original firm of Mecca Cafes agreed to a merger with Heimann and Fairley's dance hall offshoot in November 1946, after four years of profits averaging £100,000. Profits were £132,378 in 1945–6, and £53,644 for the first twenty-four weeks of 1946–7.[55] The deal was worth £450,000 for Fairley and Heimann and they were left in charge of the whole organization.[56] The prospects, despite the problems discussed so far, looked good. Leonard Well, chairman of Ye Mecca, observed: 'under the aegis of the present government, the public have ample time and money to spend, and a long era of prosperity in dancing lies ahead.'[57] His confidence was well founded, and a year after the merger Mecca reported unprecedentedly high profits, with a dividend for shareholders of 50 per cent for the year.[58]

Mecca's success was not isolated. Throughout the country the signs were of considerable buoyancy in the dance business. In April 1946, the Hammersmith Palais celebrated its twenty-five millionth dancer by offering them free dancing for the next twenty-five years.[59] By 1949 it was getting three-quarters of a million dancers each year.[60] In Glasgow, by April 1946 there were some fifty major dance halls operating in the city, with attendances of 20,000 per night on a busy night. The estimated cash paid by these Glasgow dancers was £600,000 per year, and it was thought that around four to five hundred musicians were employed in the dance halls.[61] Businesses were becoming valuable investments too. In Birmingham in June 1946 a dance hall at the corner of Dudley and Chiswell Roads sold for £7,500. That same month two new ballrooms opened in Halifax.[62] In Bristol by late 1946, the demand for dancing was so great that the city's dance halls could not cope, *Dancing Times*' Bristol correspondent noting: 'The need for a hall suitable for a large ballroom event—one capable of holding about 1,000 people—has once again been raised in Bristol as the result of the boom which is taking place in the city.'[63] Bristol was not alone. In Leeds too by January 1947 it was reported that the largest ballrooms, Armley Hall and the Town Hall, were 'typical of all other ballrooms' in the area in that there were 'record attendances'.[64]

The boom in dancing was so great that it was putting the existing dance industry under severe strain throughout the country. With the demand for dancing far

[53] *Daily Mail*, 26 November 1946, 4. [54] Ibid. [55] *Daily Mail*, 9 November 1946, 3.
[56] *Daily Mail*, 5 November 1946, 4. [57] *Daily Mail*, 9 November 1946, 3.
[58] *Daily Mail*, 5 April 1948, 4. [59] *Danceland*, April 1946, 3.
[60] *Danceland*, August 1949, 12. [61] *Danceland*, April 1946, 2.
[62] *Danceland*, June 1946, 8. [63] *DT*, September 1946, 651.
[64] *DT*, January 1947, 219.

exceeding the supply, overcrowding in dance halls became a problem. As *Danceland* remarked in April 1947:

> Dancing today is more popular than it has ever been and hundreds of thousands of extra dancers have to be accommodated in the same number of halls that were available before the war—in fact, less, for many were damaged or completely ruined during the blitz and are now closed. Due to Governmental restrictions, promoters are forbidden to either repair the damaged halls or build new ones, and the dancer therefore has to put up with crowded conditions.[65]

By 1948 then, it was clear that there was yet another 'boom' in dancing. C. Williamson reported that the ballrooms in the North of England had 'if anything, boomed even more than before during the past year'.[66] At the Beach Ballroom, Aberdeen attendances were also up. In June 1948 there were 15,655 admissions, compared with 13,133 for the same month in 1947. In July 1948 the total was 33,954 compared with 33,377 in 1947.[67] Rowntree's survey of *English Life and Leisure* undertaken at this time estimated that there were some 450 dance halls in Britain used exclusively for dancing by this point and Mark Abrams estimated that there were three million admissions per week to these halls.[68]

So why was there yet another boom in dancing? Economic conditions are vital to explaining this first post-war boom in dancing. The immediate post-war period combined full employment and rising wages, with austerity measures—increased rationing and restrictions on production for domestic needs. Full employment, together with wartime savings, meant that most people had a new level of economic security and well-being. This particularly benefitted the working class. Unemployment was virtually eradicated and in 1949 the average earnings of a manual worker were 241 per cent of their 1937 level.[69] Yet, with an economy geared towards regaining Britain's export markets, there were few consumer goods on which to spend this new-found wealth. Furthermore, the leisure industry could not yet diversify sufficiently to take advantage of this new wealth, due to controls on building and shortages of materials. As a result, money poured instead into the existing leisure forms. In the period 1946–8, football and other sports recorded record crowds and the cinema reached the zenith of its appeal, as Ross McKibbin has noted.[70] As another entrenched leisure habit, dancing also benefitted accordingly. This view is also supported by Ferdynand Zweig's 1948 study of working-class life, which argued that 'habit' was a crucial factor in the demand for certain leisure activities.[71] Thus, already used to dancing as a pastime, people fell back into this leisure habit, albeit with renewed vigour. Yet Zweig also argued that the boom conditions for dancing (as well as cinema and sport) were also partially a

[65] *Danceland*, April 1947, 3. [66] *Ballroom Dancing Annual 1948* (1949), 76.

[67] *The Press and Journal* (Aberdeen), 15 August 1950, 6.

[68] B. Seebohm Rowntree and G. Lavers, *English Life and Leisure. A Social Study* (London: Longmans, Green & Co., 1951), 279.

[69] R. McKibbin, *Classes and Cultures* (Oxford: Oxford University Press, 1998), 118.

[70] See McKibbin, *Classes*, 332–77.

[71] F. Zweig, *Labour, Life and Poverty* (London: Victor Gollancz, 1948), 47.

psychological response to the ending of the war. As he put it: 'The six or seven years of austerity and restriction, and often self-denial and sacrifice, have produced a relapse and reversion of the trend in a hunger for pleasure.'[72] Moreover, many who had gained a sense of purpose during the war were restless and seeking compensation. As he put it: 'The restlessness and disillusionment of man in the post-war world finds expression in the boom conditions in all exciting recreations.'[73] Dancing was incredibly popular because it offered an outlet for those increasingly fed up and frustrated at the drabness of austerity Britain. Rather than a new-found affluence prompting a boom in demand for dancing, it was the survival of older patterns of work and behaviour that drove it. In addition, Zweig argued that despite the arrival of full employment, old feelings of insecurity were responsible for the big demand for entertainment: 'a strong sense of the insecurity of life—the living in the present—make the worker the best customer for all sorts of service industries which cater for his amusement.'[74] Thus, the traditional working-class fear of the future meant that a 'live for the moment' attitude was adopted—even when economic affluence was increasing and economic security had arrived. Perhaps doubtful that such improved economic conditions would last, and bound also by experience and habit, working-class people in the late 1940s were inclined to spend what they had, rather than saving it. Much of this money went on 'having a good time'. The excitement offered by the palais de danse was one of the best ways of achieving this. This conclusion was also reached by a study of the coal mining community of Ashton, Yorkshire, *Coal is Our Life*, which cited insecurity as one of the main reasons for the prevalence of 'frivolous' leisure activities, although physical danger as well as economic insecurity were included in this definition.[75] All of these arguments were neatly summarized in 1953 when *The Economist* asked: 'Why should this country be the only one in the world to possess hundreds of big dance halls?' It went on to explain: 'A curious outcome, this, of three unrelated factors: a working-class living standard considerably below that of America; an attitude towards alcoholic refreshment considerably stricter than that prevailing in Europe; and a national disposition, which defies all comparison, to take pleasures seriously.'[76]

DANCING IN AN AGE OF AFFLUENCE, 1953–60

Economic hardship and uncertainty appeared to be waning in Britain by the mid-1950s. If dancing could boom in an age of austerity, once Britain entered the 'age of affluence' the potential for growth was even greater. The gradual ending of rationing and other economic restrictions at the beginning of the 1950s laid the foundations for a period of sustained growth in the dance industry and in the popularity of dancing and dance halls. An era of unprecedented economic

[72] Zweig, *Labour*, 49. [73] Zweig, *Labour*, 50–1. [74] Zweig, *Labour*, 44.
[75] N. Dennis, F. Henriques, and C. Slaughter, *Coal is Our Life: An analysis of a Yorkshire mining community* (London: Eyre & Spottiswoode, 1956), 130.
[76] *The Economist*, 14 February 1953, 402.

well-being underpinned this new boom. Real wages rose by 20 per cent between 1951 and 1959. Average weekly earnings for industrial workers grew by 34 per cent between 1955 and 1960 and by 130 per cent between 1955 and 1969. Furthermore, home ownership amongst manual workers reached 40 per cent by 1962.[77]

The Conservative government elected in 1951 came to power partially as a result of its promise to end the prolonged restrictions that had been necessary at the end of the war. Whilst the restrictions did not end overnight—food rationing continued until 1954, for example—more material resources gradually became available. Now the dancing infrastructure could expand.

With the gradual relaxation of building restrictions and the easing of material shortages, the number of places for dancing began to increase again in the early 1950s. One estimate of the number of permanent dance halls during the 1950s put the figure at around 500.[78] The numbers in Britain's larger cities were substantial. In Manchester, for example, there were eighteen dance halls in 1954.[79] Glasgow had fourteen permanent dance halls in 1952 and three dance schools. Moreover, the city boasted some of the largest dance halls in the country, with seven having capacity for 1,000 or above, the largest, the Palais de Danse, accommodating 1,800.[80] In Birmingham there were some eight public dance halls.[81] As we know, however, permanent dance halls were not the only place for dancing. In addition, therefore, Rowntree estimated that there were another 2,000 locations where dancing took place regularly.[82] We can get a sense of the dancing provision within major cities from a number of sources. In 1955 the *Dancing Times* conducted a series of informal surveys of dancing provision in some key British towns and cities. It found that in Nottingham and Derby, with a combined population of around half a million, there were seven public dance halls open daily, and fifty schools of dancing, together with dances run by the local Corporation at the Kings Hall and the Assembly Rooms in Derby.[83] In Bristol, with a population of half a million, there were forty-five schools of dancing but a surprising lack of decent public dance hall facilities. Various dance halls existed, and hotels and other public places offered dancing facilities, but apart from one or two larger halls (one of them a Mecca hall), dance halls were too small to cater for their audience.[84] There were, however, about 900 youth clubs that, according to *The Times* in 1960 provided 'ample dancing facilities'.[85]

An investigation of licensing statistics in key cities reveals more accurately the wide opportunities for dancing. In Birmingham there were some 239 places permanently licensed for dancing in 1950. This included 101 institutes and church

[77] A. Marwick, *British Society Since 1945* (Harmondsworth: Penguin, 1990), 114.
[78] *Daily Mail*, 17 October 1956, 8.
[79] GCA: M117/218, 'Applications for Music Exemptions: 1954'.
[80] GCA: E7/4/2, 'Register of Music Halls etc, 1934–52'.
[81] B. H. Reed, *Eighty Thousand Adolescents. A study of young people in the city of Birmingham, by the staff and students of Westhill Training College, for the Edward Cadbury Charitable Trust* (London: George Allen and Unwin Ltd, 1950), 21.
[82] Rowntree and Lavers, *English Life*, 284.
[83] *DT*, June 1955, 551.
[84] *DT*, November 1955, 95.
[85] *The Times*, 14 March 1960, 8.

rooms, twelve public baths, and 123 hotels and licensed premises. There was also provision for dancing in thirteen public parks and occasional licences were granted for dancing in 126 schools.[86] By 1955, it was found that there were around eighty dance schools, about half of which taught ballroom dancing. It found that the public dance halls open six days a week only had accommodation for about 4,000 dancers at one time.[87] Newcastle had fewer venues, at eighty-five in 1950, but a similar variety, with twenty church halls permanently licensed for dancing, twenty-one public halls, twelve hotels and restaurants, seven swimming baths, nine assembly rooms, and ten social clubs. Together these eighty-five venues had a capacity for 25,099 dancers.[88] In Glasgow in 1952, there were ninety-eight venues permanently licensed for dancing, including twenty-one corporation-owned halls, seven masonic halls, five church halls, seven sports clubs, and four works clubs permanently licensed. In total, the city had capacity for 32,107 dancers in these venues.[89] In addition, dancers could dance for longer as the number of 'extensions' granted to allow late night dancing was also increasing by this time. In Manchester, for example, the number of extensions granted by the city magistrates grew from 716 in 1945 to 1,768 by 1950. They were granted to just thirty-nine and forty-five venues respectively, with the majority being taken by normal dance halls.[90]

The expansion in dancing also saw a growth in demand for dance bands. In 1953 the Musicians' Union estimated that there were 50,000 dance musicians in the job market. The semi-pro local band was the key growth area, as Keith Waterhouse wrote in 1953: 'There's a big boom in the dance band industry. But not for the big names with the big bands. It's in the Saturday night bop halls . . . that business is booming. And its booming for the part-time boys who change into dinner suits after work and play at the local half-crown hops.'[91] Such bands worked up to four nights a week, and played long hours, and heavy schedules—on average they played about eighty tunes a night.

Councils also continued to play their part in providing dancing facilities, encouraged by experiments in the 1940s, municipal participation increased in the 1950s. As the *Dancing Times* remarked: 'Borough Councils seem to be becoming more and more involved in the running of dances, and in the improvement of conditions for dancing.'[92] They took this responsibility seriously too. In 1954 in Sheffield the Borough Council sent representatives to dance halls in various large cities throughout Britain to inspect equipment and other arrangements, in preparation for making its own provision. Great Yarmouth Council was considering a plan for the erection of a £125,000 ballroom in the town centre that year. Hemel Hempstead Development Corporation built a £20,000 hall towards the end of 1953 and started to run weekly dances. In seven months these dances attracted 5,000 patrons. The Camberwell Council in South London were also providing

86 Reed, *Eighty Thousand*, 21. 87 *DT*, April 1956, 395.
88 TWA: MG/NC/11, 'Register of Music, Singing and Dancing Licenses 1908–1964'.
89 GCA: E7/4/2, 'Register of Music Halls etc, 1934–52'.
90 MCA: M117/216–218, 'Applications for Music Exemptions'.
91 *DM*, 7 February 1953, 2. 92 *DT*, October 1954, 37.

'Old Time' dances. Worthing's Saturday night dances made over £2,300 profit per year.[93]

So how many were dancing in Britain in the 1950s? By this point, dancing had entrenched itself as a key feature of daily life in Britain and there was far more interest in estimating the numbers who went dancing than before the war. Many of these estimates were guesswork, however, and figures vary widely. In 1951 one survey found a staggering 95 per cent of those asked who said that they danced. Only 3 per cent said they did not and the other 2 per cent were 'vague'. In terms of frequency, this survey found that 25 per cent went once a week, 15 per cent twice, 14 per cent three times, and 6 per cent went every night. Twenty-five per cent said occasionally, 10 per cent once a month, and 5 per cent once a year.[94] In 1953 a 'conservative' estimate was that there were four million weekly dancers, which had risen to five million by 1955. This did not take account of dancing classes nor afternoon dancing sessions.[95] Other statistics suggested that the five-million-a-week mark was not reached until 1959. In 1960 the *Daily Mail*, for example, reported that '[s]ince the war the number of people going dancing every week has nearly trebled'. It gave the following figures: 1955, 3.2 million weekly dancers; 1956: 3.6 million; 1957: 4.1 million; 1958: 4.5 million; 1959: 5 million; estimating an annual audience in 1959 of 250 million.[96] There were some more reliable surveys undertaken, however. In February 1953, the *Economist* surveyed the dance business, naming it 'the second biggest entertainment industry' after cinema (and soon to overtake the cinema). It estimated that weekly audiences were around four million and annual audiences were around 200 million, compared with only eighty to ninety million for football, and that these generated revenue of £25 million (a 'conservative estimate') compared with only about £15 million from broadcasting.[97]

Despite the variations, what is clear from these estimates is that the numbers dancing in the 1950s were higher than ever before (see Figs. 3.2, 3.3, and 3.4). Moreover, dancing was more resilient than the other well-established leisure activities that had also thrived in the immediate post-war period. By the mid-1950s, other traditional entertainments were beginning to witness falling attendances. Even cinema started to fall behind in popularity. Admissions nearly halved between 1956 and 1960. As Marshall Pugh wrote in the *Daily Mail* in 1956: 'Rank is closing 79 cinemas, football suffers from TV, the variety theatre is running down. But, in or out of season, the palais waltzes in wealth.'[98] By 1958, *The Times* could write: 'more and more people are taking up dancing, fewer and fewer are going to the cinema . . . Apart from television, other entertainments have gained ground since the war, notably those in which young people have a chance to do things for themselves. Dancing is predominant among these.'[99] Dancing thus appeared to be weathering the storm of changing leisure habits following the war.

[93] Ibid. [94] *Danceland*, July 1951, 5. [95] *Daily Mail*, 15 October 1956, 4.
[96] *Daily Mail*, 1 June 1960, 2. [97] *Economist*, 14 February 1953, 401.
[98] *Daily Mail*, 15 October 1956, 4. [99] *The Times*, 13 January 1958, 6.

Fig. 3.2. Dance hall facilities: queuing for soft drinks, Dennistoun Palais, Glasgow, April 1954
Source: Herald and Times Group.

MECCA AND THE FURTHER COMMERCIALIZATION OF DANCING, 1945–60

A further indication of the popularity of dancing was the huge amount of money to be made from it. As the *Economist* observed of the palais in 1953: 'Since the war they have been making handsome profits.'[100] Marshall Pugh, writing in the *Daily Mail* in 1956, claimed that the big names in dancing, such as Carl Heimann and Victor Silvester, were millionaires in charge of a vastly profitable industry. Talking of his visits to ballrooms he wrote:

> I was mesmerised by money. For at least 5,000,000 others, the palais was a little kingdom complete in itself... But, unknown to them, the reigning monarch was King Midas and everything he touched became gold. No one knows the total wealth of the

[100] *Economist*, 14 February 1953, 401.

Fig. 3.3. Dancers on the floor, Glasgow, July 1959
Source: Herald and Times Group.

industry . . . It is often said that dancing grosses £25,000,000 or £30,000,000 or £40,000,000 a year.[101]

As in previous decades, big business had moved in to capitalize on the success of dancing. In fact, they were largely responsible for this success, and should be admired for their ability to capture and extend a market for dancing. By the end of the 1950s two large cartels dominated dancing, Mecca and the newcomer Rank.

Mecca, already well established by 1945, grew to new heights of success following the war. Mecca became one of the leading leisure companies in the country, gaining a notable stock market presence and becoming a trusted investment opportunity. As Roma Fairley put it:

> The achievement from large thoughts on shoestring facts to being considered an important service to the country, brought the City well into the picture. Now many people wanted to invest their money in the company and the faces behind the figures were beginning to focus into big business.[102]

[101] *Daily Mail*, 17 October 1956, 8. [102] Fairley, *Come Dancing*, 156.

Fig. 3.4. Crowded dancefloor 1958—Edinburgh Palais de Danse
Source: Scotsman Publications Ltd.

Mecca had started the post-war period on a very good footing—the war years had secured its place as the dominant business in the dance hall industry. Profits for the war years had been good. Not complacent, however, Fairley and Heimmann worked hard to capitalize on their strong position. Recognizing the importance of a prominent presence in the centre of London's entertainment world, the West End, they secured the Lyceum Theatre on the Strand when the State bought up Covent Garden Opera House in 1945, spending £3,450 on its conversion to dancing.[103] They also consolidated and expanded their control of their business, as they effectively 'bought out' the original parent company Ye Mecca.

Mecca continued to expand in the 1950s. In 1956 it took over another dance hall company, and issued another one million shares.[104] By this stage, the company was able to make huge investments and spent heavily to acquire and build new properties. In 1956 alone four new dance halls were acquired, and a freehold site in Bradford also purchased for the building of a new dance hall.[105] In August 1958

[103] *Daily Mail*, 7 November 1945, 4.
[104] *Daily Mail*, 26 November 1956, 2.
[105] *Economist*, 18 May 1957, 636.

they spent £100,000 erecting a dance hall in the new town of Stevenage and also purchased the Palais de Danse, Dennistoun, Glasgow.[106] In December 1960 Mecca made a £600,000 bid for the Hammersmith Palais.[107] Most substantial of all, in 1959 Mecca agreed to a deal to buy the Empire Theatre, Leicester Square, from cinema moguls MGM at a cost of £1 million. It aimed to build a combined luxury cinema and dance hall—and as a sign of the relative importance of these two long-time rivals, the dance hall was to have a capacity for 3,000 but the cinema only 1,325.[108] The conversion was completed by 1963.[109] It also continued to add to its portfolio of dance halls. Business was extremely buoyant. In 1955 and 1956 trading profits were £380,652 and £494,540 respectively, with after-tax profits of £151,788 and £194,361.[110] By 1957 these figures had risen to £555,464 and £199,358 respectively. By 1958 they were £659,571 and £277,199.[111] Turnover was £4.5 million in 1959 and £5.25 million in 1960.[112] The future looked bright. In 1960 Mecca reported that '[t]he boom at the Palais is fantastic. Our business increases by 10 per cent every year.' It planned to spend £3 million over the next three years expanding.[113] In 1961 it therefore opened several new halls throughout the country—the Locarno Bradford; the Locarno Hull; The Mayfair Newcastle; the Locarno Basildon; the Crystal Ballroom Newcastle-under-Lyne; the Palais Ashton-under-Lyne; and the Orchid Ballroom Coventry.[114] In 1962 Mecca announced plans to raise about £3.75 million for expansion into even more dance halls and ice rinks. Shares had trebled in value between 1958 and 1962,[115] by which time nine months' profits were up by £337,000 and the dividends were at 22 per cent.[116] Such was the success of Mecca that in 1963 it announced that it would be expanding into Europe. First stop was Germany. Mecca formed Mecca Germany with an initial capital of £1 million. It had plans to build a combined entertainments centre, with dance hall and ice rink, in a major German city, probably Dusseldorf. Others were to follow in Hamburg and Cologne. Trading profits that year were up almost £600,000 to £1,672,000.[117] The number of dance halls Mecca owned rose from twelve in 1951 to forty-four by 1966, by which time it employed some 7,000 staff.[118]

Another large firm which entered the dance business in the post-war period was the Rank Organisation. Rank was keen to diversify into the non-cinema side of the entertainment business. With a decline in cinema-going estimated at 20 per cent in 1957 alone, the company saw its profits fall significantly, from £5.8 million in 1957, to around £3 million in June 1958.[119] Thus it converted many of its cinemas into dance halls. As early as 1959, the *Economist* reported that the dance halls and dance studios that Rank was running were already making a profit, unlike its

106 *Daily Mail*, 29 August 1958, 5.
107 *Daily Mail*, 20 December 1960, 5 and *Economist*, 30 May 1959, 902.
108 *Daily Mail*, 26 September 1959, 5.
109 *Economist*, 22 June 1963, 1295.
110 *Economist*, 18 May 1957, 636.
111 *Economist*, 30 May 1959, 902.
112 Fairley, *Come Dancing*, 164.
113 *DM*, 12 February 1960, 23.
114 *Daily Mail*, 2 January 1962, 3.
115 *Daily Mail*, 1 October 1962, 15.
116 *Daily Mail*, 6 November 1962, 13.
117 *Daily Mail*, 18 May 1963, 13.
118 Fairley, *Come Dancing*, 160.
119 *Economist*, 20 September 1958, 971.

venture into gramophone records.[120] By 1961 Rank also had twenty-four dance halls and planned to spend more than £2 million during 1961–3 building twenty more, mainly in the north of England.[121] Symbolic of the cartelization of the leisure industry which had been present ever since the days of music hall, Mecca and Rank domination of the dance industry shows how significant a pastime dancing was. They also prove that dancing was a lucrative business.

Mecca's success was so great that it became the subject of takeover bids. In late 1961 talks were held to consider the possibility of a merger between Mecca and the catering group Forte. This was enough to increase ordinary shares from 44s 6d to 67s in a short space of time.[122] The business was estimated to be worth £17 million by this point.[123] Even when Forte's bids had fallen through, Mecca was subject to the interest of other large businesses interested in taking it over. Most significantly, Rank became interested in Mecca. Though overall about five times as big as Mecca, Rank's ballrooms business was second to Mecca's. Rank's chief John Davies wanted the merger to 'cut out the present murderous competition for bands, halls, big names, etc.'[124] As the *Economist* put it, Mecca's 'growth has stemmed from its ability to transform down at heel dance halls into highly profitable palaces. Clearly this expertise would be of immense value to Rank.'[125] In June 1964, however, Mecca rejected the £30 million share swap offer by Rank but then tried to enter into negotiations to buy their thirty dance halls.[126] Explaining their refusal to accept merger, Alan Fairley said:

> Mecca felt that it was not being offered its fair value . . . If we'd sold out Carl and I would be very rich . . . Money has a great use, but if . . . you've built up and achieved what you set out to do, and are running a good business with a contented staff and believe that money isn't everything—why give it up?[127]

THE DECLINE OF THE PALAIS

Such confidence makes it all the more surprising then that within a few years, dance halls were in decline. Although Mecca was still opening up more dance halls in the early 1960s, elsewhere there were indications that dancing was declining. As early as 1964, despite expansion in this field, rumours spread that Rank's dance halls were not doing very well.[128] By January 1965, Mecca's profits also began to fall as dancers stayed away. Hit by a particularly long summer of good weather, the *Daily Mail's* City correspondent reported: 'Last year's long, dry summer helped to make it the worst in ballroom memory. Dancers stayed away in droves, spending heavily on drink and petrol. Now leisure executives, smiling through their losses, ask anxiously: "Will ye no come back again?" The answer is still only maybe.' Mecca's Alan

[120] *Economist*, 19 September 1959, 966.
[121] *Daily Mail*, 9 December 1961, 11.
[122] *Daily Mail*, 27 October 1961, 17.
[123] *Daily Mail*, 12 September 1962, 13.
[124] *Daily Mail*, 8 June 1964, 11.
[125] *Economist*, 13 June 1964, 1276.
[126] *Daily Mail*, 11 June 1964, 1.
[127] Fairley, *Come Dancing*, 169–70.
[128] *Daily Mail*, 16 September 1964, 16.

Fairley argued that the City was wrong to predict a decline in dancing. Shares, however, fell, from 33s 3d at the start of summer 1964, to only 19s 4.5d by January 1965.[129] Profits too were down £18,000 on the previous year.[130] The expansion of the previous years started to look more like the consolidation of a larger share of a shrinking market by Mecca. Not that dancing disappeared—it continued to play an important role in daily life and leisure for some time to come, and is, indeed, still a significant feature of Britain's cultural life. Nightclubs took over from dance halls, then evolving by the 1970s to discos. Typical of developments was the 1960 conversion of a disused sausage factory near Birmingham's Meat Market into a three-floor and basement nightclub at the cost of £60,000.[131] In Newcastle-upon-Tyne too six nightclubs opened up between 1962–4, including the Cavendish Club, La Dolce Vita, the Flamingo Club, and Club 69.[132] By 1965, Mecca was advertising the fact that it ran 'Discotheques' as well as dance halls.[133] Discotheques first started as intimate private clubs in Paris, with expensive drinks, dancing to recorded music, and an exclusive membership. By the early 1960s they had spread to New York and, with traditional night clubs and live music venues becoming unfashionable and too expensive, as the *Economist* explained, the 'discotheques arrived just when economics and fashion had conspired to create a gap in the city's night life'. It went on: 'not only do the dancers want to dance to records but they want also to dance at the "in" place.'[134] Mecca rushed to imitate the new trend by providing 'discos' in Britain's towns and cities. As it reported in 1970:

> A few years back we operated only ballrooms. Today, we still have ballrooms . . . but the need for smaller, more intimate establishments is being met as quickly as possible. 'Tiffanys' now appears in several provincial towns and cities, and 1969 saw the launching of the Cats Whiskers branches in others. The latter feature a little cabaret as extra entertainment. The Heart Beat and Bali Hai branches also blended Mecca Dancing and Mecca Catering to provide something for all tastes and practically all ages.[135]

Many dance halls were closed. The fate of those in Glasgow was typical. In the 1960s the Locarno changed its name to Tiffany's but dancing finished when the building was converted into a casino in the 1970s.[136] The Dennistoun Palais continued to provide dancing until 1962, after which the building was converted into a supermarket.[137] The F & F Palais was converted into a bingo hall not long afterwards.[138] Some of the old dance halls tried to update themselves and remained open for a considerable amount of time, however. The most famous dance halls proved particularly resilient. One of the most resilient was the Grafton in Liverpool, which hosted the Beatles and later became a nightclub operating well into the 1980s and 1990s before closing down in 2008. Barrowland's Ballroom in Glasgow,

129 *Daily Mail*, 16 January 1965, 15.
130 *Daily Mail*, 4 May 1965, 15.
131 *Birmingham Mail*, 11 March 1960.
132 TWA: MG.NC.11, 'Register of Music, Singing and Dancing Licenses 1908–1964'.
133 *Economist*, 19 June 1965, 1452.
134 *Economist*, 28 August 1965, 786.
135 *Economist*, 27 June 1970, 92.
136 GCA: D-CA 8/2930.
137 GCA: D-CA 8/2636.
138 GCA: D-CA 8/988.

built in 1934 then rebuilt in 1960 following a fire, survived as a dance venue into the 1970s, briefly becoming a roller disco, but by the 1980s it had become a rock venue hosting some of the biggest names in rock and pop. The Hammersmith Palais also endured in a similar way, being a dance venue up until the late 1980s, after which time it hosted concerts, dance nights, and private events. Despite its importance to Britain's cultural history, it was demolished in 2012. The Nottingham Palais de Danse also survived as a dance venue well into the 1980s, after which time it became a nightclub. It continued to provide dancing as Ritzy's nightclub and was refurbished in 2004 as Oceana Nightclub, still in operation. Yet, despite the survival of these venues, and the persistence of some others as dance halls, it was clear that by the end of the 1960s, the 'dance hall' as a social venue was more or less dead. It had been superseded by the nightclub and the disco. It was the relic of another age. Therefore, whilst in 1977 Mecca still had 101 dance venues throughout Britain, they were no longer 'dance halls' in the traditional mould. Barely a handful retained even their former dance hall names—only four 'Locarnos' and four 'Palais' were still in existence. The company did not change the name of the iconic Manchester Ritz; Nottingham Palais; London's Lyceum and Empire Rooms; nor the Café De Paris. But they now had fifty-one 'Tiffany's' nightclubs, six 'Cat's Whiskers', together with 'Raquel's', 'Samantha's', 'Annabella's'—the new names hinting at a new atmosphere for the new times. In Stoke-on-Trent, the group even had the 'Adulte Ballroom'. A rather seedy end to a grand tradition.[139]

So why did the dance hall decline? There were a variety of reasons. Perhaps the most important was the long-term economic environment. Dancing was the victim of long-term economic security amongst the working class. With full employment and the welfare state lifting people out of poverty and giving them increasing affluence, working-class people started to demand more. Rising affluence brought about growing consumerism—Britons increasingly turned towards the home. Outside the home, they wanted more and more leisure pursuits and interests. Such trends were picked up in Ferdynand Zweig's 1961 study *The Worker in an Affluent Society* where he identified a 'new mode of life' and a 'new ethos'. Both had a negative influence on the popularity of dancing. Zweig observed how a rising sense of economic security was leading to an erosion of the 'live for the moment' mentality that had been behind much of the previous growth in demand for recreation. Increasingly, working-class people were thinking about the future. With newly developed 'rising expectations' and a rise in 'acquisitive instincts', the working-class Briton was increasingly concerned with spending money on consumer durables and housing. Linked to this, Zweig saw a turn towards family-mindedness and domesticity: 'He seeks his pleasures and comforts at home more than ever . . . Family life stands, in his mind, for happiness, enjoyment and relaxation. As he sits by his fireside and watches TV he feels free and happy . . . the worker is moving away from his mates . . . social contacts with neighbours suffer the same fate.'[140] Whilst the impact of television on dancing may have been minimal,

[139] Anon., *Mecca Limited: Manager's Handbook, 1977* (London: Mecca Publications, 1977), 25–7.
[140] F. Zweig, *The Worker in an Affluent Society* (London: Heinemann, 1961), 208.

the effect of a working-class culture centred on consumption and family life was considerable. Furthermore, even when the 'new worker' went outside the home for leisure, this was also different than before. Family-centred leisure, or the 'multi-purpose' leisure facility was growing in popularity. People were prepared to spend more and wanted somewhere where they could eat, drink, and relax at the same time.

The diversification of leisure interests and its impact on dancing is nowhere better illustrated than in the later development of Mecca. Although still providing dancing in the late 1960s, it was dancing in a different kind of atmosphere. Many of Mecca's dance halls saw increasing turnover from the provision of catering—especially 'banqueting' facilities that could be hired out for private events. As a result, the company converted existing ballrooms to provide the necessary facilities and ensured that all newly built halls were able to cater for this growing 'eating out' market.[141] In 1964 work started on an all round 'Entertainment Centre' in Bristol consisting of a dance hall, a banqueting suite, ice rink, cinema, bowling alley, and car parks.[142] Mecca looked elsewhere for profits too. By the early 1960s Mecca had moved into bingo, which as *Daily Mail* put it in 1961 was 'the greatest arouser of middle-aged female passions since Ivor Novello'.[143] The 1960 Betting and Gaming Act had made it legal for bingo to be played in any club for money. Mecca were one of the first to move into this area, first setting up their own bingo club which operated two nights a week in some of its dance halls in London and Lancashire. Reporting on its 1961 AGM, Mecca made the following telling announcement: 'We have started Bingo as a means of recreation, in many of our Dance Halls, at times when these Halls were not in full use, but this does not affect our Policy of Mecca dancing which has proved so highly successful for so many years.'[144]

Always abreast of changes in customer preferences, Mecca was diversifying. By 1962, Mecca had bingo interests in its 'Mecca Casinos' offshoot, which purchased many failed cinemas and theatres. It had the Rialto York; Theatre Royal Hanley; Pullman, Seven Kings, Essex; Pavilion Liverpool; the Hippodrome Derby, and the famous Empire Hackney.[145] It also had another new venture, joining with Silver Blades Ice Rinks to provide skating in Birmingham, Streatham, Liverpool, and Leeds, with plans to build 'luxury ice rinks throughout the country'. In addition Mecca Catering was still running, along with the Mecca Agency Ltd providing dance bands, and *Dance News* the publishing arm, and Danceland Records was also still going.[146] By the mid-1960s Mecca was also expanding into motorway catering.[147] In 1965 it ventured into billiard halls, mail order, holiday travel, and personal insurance.[148] The diversification was such that by 1961 only about half of Mecca's profits were coming from dancing.[149] Only a quarter of the estimated sixty million people who came through Mecca's doors that year were dancers

[141] *Economist*, 22 June 1963, 1295.
[142] *Economist*, 20 June 1964, 1418.
[143] *Daily Mail*, 8 February 1961, 8.
[144] *Economist*, 3 June 1961, 1038.
[145] *Daily Mail*, 2 January 1962, 3.
[146] Ibid.
[147] *Daily Mail*, 27 April 1964, 13.
[148] *Economist*, 9 July 1965, 188.
[149] *Daily Mail*, 9 December 1961, 11.

(300,000 a week), the rest coming from their other interests.[150] Rank too had diversified. Recognizing the changing leisure industry they continued to rationalize their film interests and closed cinemas. By 1960 Lord Rank had pushed his organization into investing in television, motels, motorway service stations, bowling alleys, and manufacturing—Xerox and Bush Radio being two of the companies it owned. Moreover, he pushed the company into the retailing of consumer durables, an obvious symbol of the new affluence of the working classes.[151] Like Mecca, Rank also went into bingo—with over sixty bingo centres by 1962, by which time it was estimated that bingo was attracting more than two million people a week.[152] A sign of how rapidly leisure tastes and business policies were changing, by 1963 the proportion of the organization's profits from non-film activities was 51 per cent, compared to 34 per cent in 1962.[153]

The liberalization of licensing laws also served to undermine the popularity of the dance hall. Multi-purpose entertainment venues became fashionable as people increasingly demanded somewhere to drink, eat, and be entertained. Mecca had long wanted licensed dance halls and in 1962 it put in applications for fifty full liquor licences for its dance halls. Eight had already been approved, and Mecca negotiated with licensing authorities so that only those who had paid to come and dance could drink and that it would take precautions to prevent underage drinking.[154] Dancing became less and less integral to the proceedings. Indeed, businesses found that they could make far greater profits from food and drink, something which prolonged periods of dancing could actually undermine. Where dancing did survive, new dancing experiences evolved. The group behind Angus Steak Houses—Golden Egg—moved into 'the young swinging market' in the mid-1960s opening a chain of 'dine and dance' Italian restaurants called 'La Dolce Notte'.[155]

There were several changes to popular music and dancing which also caused dance halls to decline. The 1950s saw the triumph of the solo artist and the small group over dance bands and music for dancing. The gradual emergence of a pop industry focused on selling music for teenagers, or for listeners, rather than dancers, meant that 'dance music' became increasingly seen as out of date. The new music was also considered by some less easy to dance to. The frustration of dance hall owners and teachers of dancing at such changes was revealed in a tribunal concerning copyright laws, where a representative of the North British Ballroom Association, Mr J. F. Stewart, claimed that modern hit tunes were 'tripe that people can't dance to'. He said ballrooms did not regard it as important for bands to play the latest hits because they were 'absolutely useless for a ballroom'.[156] Stewart went on to blame television, the radiogram, and youth clubs for a decline in dance hall attendances. He said that some halls were lucky to get even 50 per cent capacity, even on a Saturday night. Furthermore, the dance halls' subsequent fight to

[150] *Economist*, 10 June 1961, 1153.
[151] *Economist*, 17 September 1960, 1127.
[152] *Daily Mail*, 5 March 1962, 13.
[153] *Economist*, 19 October 1963, 314.
[154] *Daily Mail*, 16 March 1962, 15.
[155] *Economist*, 6 May 1967, 602.
[156] *The Times*, 6 November 1958, 7.

liberalize the copyright laws so as to allow the performance of records in their halls and thus attract young people backfired. Although it provided a temporary fillip to dancing it was eventually to increase competition for dancers.

Dancing also changed considerably and there was an increasing diversification in tastes and styles. Of particular importance for the decline of the dance hall, there was a move by the mid-1960s towards solo dancing, outlined towards the end of this chapter. Ballroom dancing was increasingly regarded as 'old fashioned', and dance halls suffered as a result. A 1962 commentary on the BBC's 'Come Dancing' television programmes reveals the generation gap that was emerging in regard to dance fashions: 'for those who do not belong to the cult they have a decidedly musty flavour. The men, their hair slickened down and their teeth bared into rigid smiles, look like junior clerks or waiters of a vanished era; and the girls . . . aspire to the bloodless perfection of the fairy on the Christmas tree.'[157] The palais appeared to be the preserve of the older generation. As we shall see shortly, dancers increasingly segregated themselves according to age. If younger dancers wished to express themselves more freely and openly they also had a wide range of other venues where they could do this away from the dance hall. The liberalization of copyright/royalty laws was one reason for this change, underpinned by a huge growth in the recording industry. The British record industry was worth £6 million in 1953, rising to £27 million by 1958. Sales of single records were huge—peaking at 64.5 million in 1958.[158] The increased performance of recorded music in public increased the number of venues where young people could go and dance. In the 1950s, two of the most popular of these were the coffee bar and the milk bar. Moreover, young people especially wanted to hear the music of their favourite groups, rather than 'pale' local imitations of them at their local palais. The wider availability of juke boxes—there were some three thousand in the country by 1955, rising to ten to thirteen thousand by 1959—meant that those wishing to dance needed only a small venue in which to dance solo together, rather than a palatial hall with live orchestra.[159] In such venues, the young also had total control over what was being played and when.

Finally, a change in social mores was also behind the decline of the dance hall. As we shall see, one of the chief social functions of the dance hall was the opportunity that it provided for members of the opposite sex to meet. Particularly for men, this was a key attraction. For decades the dance hall served the purpose of a 'marriage bureau' providing an acceptable place where boys and girls could meet up in public, in a world where their working and private lives could be quite different and separate. This was recognized and encouraged by those in the dance industry itself, who realized that this was perhaps the dance hall's chief attraction. As Carl Heimann prophetically noted in 1960, when asked if his business would last: 'As long as our dance halls are the only places where nice young girls can meet nice

157 *The Times*, 15 September 1962, 4.

158 S. Frith, *The Sociology of Rock* (London: Constable, 1978), 99 and 102.

159 A. Horn, *Juke Box Britain* (Manchester: Manchester University Press, 2009), 50.

young men without an introduction.'[160] Increasingly, they were not. Although equality had not been achieved by the mid-1960s, many barriers to interaction between the sexes had been broken down. As Zweig observed in 1961: 'The segregation of the sexes, which used to be a marked feature of the worker's life, is on the decline.'[161] This, together with changing attitudes towards sexuality and relationships between men and women, meant that the role of the dance hall had been superseded. There were far more public places where men and women could meet on equal terms than in the past, and leisure in particular was becoming much more mixed-sex. Even the traditional gender-separated pub was being transformed, as distinctions between lounge and public bar began to disappear. The changing position of women in society also had an impact on dancing in the traditional dance hall style. Many younger women were no longer prepared to conform to a pastime which utilized a set of rules on introductions little altered since the 1920s. What had seemed groundbreaking and modern then was, by the 1960s, anachronistic to many women. They no longer wished to wait to be asked to dance, they wished to dance when they wanted, and how they wanted. In February 1959, for example, one woman had complained about this dance partnership ritual thus: 'I would like to see one brave female when addressed as "chick" strut out on the floor, clucking merrily with her arms flapping.' Similarly, the men noted a more assertive attitude amongst some of the women: 'In a West End dance hall I escorted a girl back to her seat and, as it was near the end of the evening, I asked her politely if I could have the last dance. Her curt reply was: "You've just had it, mate!"'[162] Thus, the social dances of the new era were not partner dances but solo dances.

CONCLUSION

By the mid-1960s, an important chapter in Britain's social and cultural history had come to an end. In the space of little over twenty years the palais had gone from boom to bust. No longer in tune with the times, the dance hall seemed increasingly anachronistic in a society with apparently rapidly changing values. Not that social dancing had lost its appeal amongst the British population—as a recreation it was to outlive the venue that had given birth to it at the centre of Britain's civic culture. The palais, however, was lost forever and Britain's social and cultural life was the poorer for it.

160 *Daily Mail*, 25 April 1960, 2.
161 Zweig, *Worker*, 208.
162 *DM*, 28 February 1959, 2.

Chapter 4

The Development of Dancing in Britain, 1918–60

INTRODUCTION

Having outlined the development of the dance hall, the growth of the dance business, and the emergence of a mass audience for dancing in Britain, it is now necessary to focus on dancing. What was danced in Britain's dance halls in the decades between 1918 and 1960? How was dancing transformed and what styles of dancing dominated dancing experiences? In addition to looking at particular dances, this chapter will examine how people learned to dance and whether they bothered to learn at all. Moreover, we will examine whether there was a national dance culture, or if there were significant differences in dancing preferences according to class, geography, and other socio-economic factors. We start with an examination of how people learned to dance and chart the development of dance teaching in Britain.

LEARNING TO DANCE

The most obvious way to learn dancing was to take dance lessons. The number of dance schools and dance teachers grew rapidly in conjunction with the growth in popularity of dancing in the twentieth century. The availability of dance teachers varied throughout the country, but in most large towns and cities it was considerable. In Birmingham, for example, *Kelly's Directory* listed six teachers of dancing in 1920, rising to twenty by 1925, forty-two in 1935, and sixty by 1939.[1] In Glasgow in 1937 *Kelly's* listed five dance schools licensed for dancing, one with capacity for 722 dancers.[2] The number of Glasgow dance teachers listed in the *Post Office Directory* for the city was larger, however. In 1920 there were ten, rising to sixteen in 1925, before falling back to thirteen in 1930 and eleven in 1935.[3] Such figures undoubtedly underestimate the number of dance teachers in these two cities however, as not everyone paid to be included in these directories. There were numerous dance

[1] Anon., *Kelly's Directory of Birmingham* (1920, 1925, 1935, 1939).
[2] GCA: E7/4/1, 'Register of Music Halls etc, 1934–52'.
[3] Anon., *Post Office Directory of Glasgow* (1920–35).

schools, ranging in size from the large, well-run businesses with sizeable and often luxurious premises, to the humbler dancing 'academies' set up in the front rooms of teachers' homes. During the 1920s and 1930s we can estimate that there were several thousand dance teachers in Britain, not all of whom were recognized by the approved associations of dancing. The popularity of dancing lessons was particularly large in some parts of the country, where dance classes were sometimes conducted on a mass scale. In 1938 in the north-east of England, for example, R. V. Hindmarsh held classes at Spennymoor, Consett, and Crook with regular class sizes of between 650 and 2,000.[4] Such mass teachings were unusual, however. Mostly dance classes were smaller and they catered for every section of society and every pocket, though the majority had a middle- and lower-middle-class clientele. Typically enterprising, Mecca opened up its own dance school headed by Adele England in 1937. The Locarno School of Dancing was located over their Locarno dance hall in Streatham. It had three dance studios where it gave lessons. Its prospectus advertised its aim: 'We teach you quickly, well and cheaply—we are pioneers in "classes for the masses."' Private lessons were also available, though at 16 shillings for a course of five or 3s 6d each, they were relatively expensive.[5] However, despite these costs the public lessons were popular, with about 1,000 pupils attending the school.

As a group, dance teachers did much to try and enhance their profession's status and that of dancing. No one could become a 'recognized' teacher of dancing without passing one of the examinations set by the leading dance teaching organizations, the Imperial Society of Teachers of Dancing (ISTD) being the largest. This took a minimum of six months' intensive training. The theory of balance and deportment, as well as the techniques of the various dances, was taught. As the number of dance teachers grew so did the number of dance associations. The sheer number of organizations and the desire to form them are indications that there were very many dance teachers in business in Britain. The ISTD, for example, was founded in 1904 and formed a separate Ballroom Branch in 1924. By 1930 membership of the Imperial Society was 2,000, about half of which were in the Ballroom Branch[6] and by 1939 the ISTD had 5,000 members, the largest dancing teacher society in the world.[7] The National Association of Teachers of Dancing was also an important group founded in 1906. They helped to spread dance-teaching standards by forming District Councils, sending lecturers to monthly meetings throughout the country, and holding annual conferences. They also instituted 'Amateur Ballroom Tests', with the award of medals, developing a rigorous syllabus and examination for keen amateurs who wished to develop their skills to a high standard.[8] The British Association of Teachers of Dancing was formed in 1892, and held numerous conferences and was a particularly keen supporter of using competitions to encourage high standards of dancing. By 1933 it was awarding

[4] *MDD*, March 1938, 13.
[5] Anon., *Locarno School of Dancing Prospectus*, nd 1930s, 2.
[6] *DT*, September 1930, 583.
[7] *PP*, 19 August 1939, 21.
[8] *DT*, December 1933, 341.

sixteen trophies annually, a number that grew as the decade progressed.[9] There was also the Allied Dancing Association (1921); the International Dancing Masters' Association (1930); and regional dance groups such as the Midlands Association of Dance Teachers (1920) based in Birmingham; the Northern Counties Dance Teachers' Association (1925) based in Manchester; and the Scottish Dance Teachers' Alliance (1934) based in Glasgow. Another sign of the capacity of dance teachers to organize themselves at a local level can be seen in the establishment of so-called 'Dancers' Circles' in towns and cities throughout Britain from the late 1920s onwards. These were groups formed by any amateur or professional interested in dancing, holding regular meetings and lectures.[10]

Such was the success of some dance teachers that they became celebrities in their own right. The most successful was Victor Silvester. The son of a Wembley vicar, he started his dancing career as a paid 'dancing partner' for women at the Empress Rooms, Kensington in 1919. His proficiency was such that by 1922, with Phyllis Clarke, he won the world's ballroom dancing championship at the Queen's Hall, London. He opened his first dance school, at Rector's Club, in 1923. The following year Silvester was to play an important role in the codification of ballroom dancing via the ISTD, and he achieved fame with numerous dance competitions, publications (most notably his *Modern Ballroom Dancing* (1927)), and radio broadcasts. He went on to lead the biggest selling dance orchestra on record, after recording first for Parlophone, setting up a 'strict tempo orchestra' in 1935.[11] Another household name from the world of dancing at this time was Santos Casani. Born in South Africa and of Italian heritage he moved to England during the First World War. He gained early fame by featuring in a British Pathe newsreel dancing the flat Charleston on the top of a taxi whilst driving through the streets of London. It has become an iconic image. Casani was the proprietor of 'the largest dancing school in England' and he too published widely in the specialist and national press, and wrote his own guidebooks for teaching dancing. His influence was such that in 1932 W. Abbot and Sons Ltd produced the 'Santos Casani Dance Shoe' specially designed in co-operation with Casani for men who danced.[12] In 1933 Casani opened his own exclusive dance club in the heart of London's West End on Regent Street, with two dance floors and dancing every night from 9.30 pm to 3 am.[13] Leading female teachers also became famous, Josephine Bradley being an important example. She won numerous competitions in the early 1920s, most notably the *Daily Sketch* foxtrot competition and the World Championship at the Queen's Hall in 1924. That year she opened her first dance school and joined Silvester on the invitation of the ISTD to codify dancing. She also chaired the Ballroom Branch from its foundation in 1924 to 1947. Like Silvester she led a dance band, providing records and broadcasts suited to dancing, recording for

[9] Ibid., 343. [10] *DT*, October 1928, 2.

[11] Derek B. Scott, 'Silvester, Victor Marlborough (1900–1978)', *Oxford Dictionary of National Biography* (Oxford: Oxford University Press, 2004); online edn, January 2011 [http://www.oxforddnb.com/view/article/31685, accessed 8 July 2014].

[12] *DT*, December 1932, 285. [13] *DT*, January 1933, 329.

Decca from 1935.[14] By the end of the 1930s, often inspired by these success stories, the number of dance teachers in Britain was probably higher than it had ever been. The coming of the war in 1939, however, was to create new challenges.

What impact did the war have on dance teaching? It had initially seemed as if dance teaching would fall away once the war began. As in the First World War it was presumed that many men and women on leave from fighting and war work would not have the time to learn complex steps. In addition, there was a new emphasis on sociability in the dance hall that pushed serious dancing to the side and made the need for lessons less obvious. Moreover, the early confusion about opening places of public entertainment, the uncertainty caused by the blackout, and the general disruption to social life and infrastructure caused a collapse in demand for dance lessons. Dance teaching therefore halted at the outbreak of the war. Most dance schools closed down because they saw no future in the business, and large numbers of staff were dismissed. For example, Mecca's Locarno School of Dancing dismissed everyone apart from the principal, Adele England. She described the war's initial impact:

> For a week there was not a soul in. It was awful . . . I used to get up and get my coat, lock the place up, and leave a note, 'BACK IN AN HOUR.' I would walk down the road and back. I felt better then; anything to get out of the place a bit.[15]

However, this collapse, like the early wartime collapse of dance halls, proved very shortlived. Once people became accustomed to the new wartime conditions, teaching revived. Even as early as October 1939, dance teachers in the reception areas to which thousands had been evacuated, reported being 'overwhelmingly busy'.[16] By the end of 1941, things had picked up everywhere, one leading dance teacher stating that '[t]eachers in reception and neutral areas report very good and in many cases record business, and even in evacuation areas the dance halls and schools seem to keep going'.[17] By March 1942, *Dancing Times* estimated that many dance teachers throughout the country were getting five and six times the business of pre-war days.[18] The large number of people taking exams also suggests that despite initial fears, dance teaching was thriving. The Imperial Society of Dancing, for example, held nearly 5,000 examinations and tests in 1941.[19] Dance schools held on too despite the challenges. The *Post Office Directory* for Glasgow named ten dance schools in 1940, rising to twelve in 1945.[20] In Birmingham there were more dance teachers. *Kelly's Directory* for the city listed forty-two teachers of dancing in 1935, rising to sixty in 1940 before falling back to forty-three in 1945, still above the pre-war level.[21]

Further evidence that 'business as usual' had returned to the attainment of dancing skills, was the continued interest in dance competitions during the war.

[14] J. Bradley, *Dancing Through Life* (London: Hollis & Carter, 1947).
[15] M-O A: TC 38/6/E, 'Jazz and Dancing – article draft', 2.
[16] *DT*, October 1939, 37. [17] *DT*, December 1941, 153. [18] *DT*, March 1942, 311.
[19] *DT*, January 1942, 215. [20] *Post Office Directory, Glasgow* (1940–45).
[21] *Kelly's Directory, Birmingham* (1935–45).

The number of competitions held inevitably declined, as professional and serious amateur dancers were conscripted or took up war work. However, surprisingly given the difficulty of travelling long distance, and the Blitz, a substantial number of local and national competitions continued to be run for the duration. A survey of competitions being run in 1940 shows this was the case. *Dancing Times* was able to report that the Star Championships would take place that year in London, together with the 'Gaumont British Trophy' held at the Astoria, Tottenham Court Road, and the 'Lonsdale Cup' at the Hammersmith Palais. Elsewhere the 'Allied North of England Championships' were to be held with a final in Liverpool; the Ulster Amateur and Open Championships organized by the Northern Ireland Society of Dance Teachers were running in Belfast; the Midlands Championship ran at Wolverhampton and there were other competitions being held in Warwickshire, Lancashire, and Somerset.[22]

Having survived the war, dance teachers emerged into peace with considerable confidence about their future business prospects. There were numerous reasons for this. With dancing booming in popularity and a new economic security, the prospects were good. Out of practice and out of touch with the latest steps, the return of servicemen too led to a boom in demand for dance teachers and dance lessons. In Bristol in 1946 it was reported: 'teachers are finding it as much as they can cope with to keep up with the demand for lessons, either private or class.'[23] Commenting on the business on his return from war service in 1946, dance teacher Charles Scrimshaw noted: 'there seem to be far more now learning to dance. I have been so amazed at attendances I have seen and heard of at school dances.'[24] An indication of the demand for dancing lessons came from Bob Garganico, President of the NASTD, who claimed that 'generally speaking, members of the teaching profession have been run off their feet in coping with the unprecedented demand for instruction'. He also noted that there had been over 5,000 test examinations in the NAST in the year 1945–6.[25] This trend in growth continued throughout the 1940s and into the 1950s. In 1956 *The Times* estimated that there were something between four and five thousand recognized schools of ballroom dancing in Britain, with around 30,000 medal tests held by the big associations of ballroom dancing, who organized around 200 dancing championships each year. The top three national ballroom championships attracted 8,000 entrants each per year. As it commented: 'Britain . . . is pre-eminent in ballroom dancing. No other nation has such style, so many entrants for the annual ballroom events or such support from its public.'[26]

That there was a sizeable market for dance teaching in Britain by the early 1950s is evidenced by the fact that an American chain of dance schools, the Arthur Murray dance schools, invaded Britain in 1954. Murray had over 300 dance schools in the United States, run on franchise lines. These dance schools took in £17 million in fees a year on average, and had some 7.5 million pupils in the

[22] *DT*, February 1940, 291; May 1940, 485. [23] *DT*, December 1946, 161.
[24] *DT*, February 1946, 261. [25] *Ballroom Dancing Annual 1947*, 44.
[26] *The Times*, 6 August 1956, 10.

United States.[27] The chain introduced 'high pressure American methods of publicity and salesmanship' to Britain with a syllabus focused on social dancing and 'fun'.[28] Its first schools opened in London in 1955. The *Dancing Times* speculated that this incursion into Britain would bring about a revolution in dance teaching, as other dance teachers would have to respond by adopting similarly modern business techniques to attract customers. Dance lessons were only available as whole courses, no single lessons were taught. These courses were, however, tailor-made for the individual. The number of dance styles taught was also very limited, starting at two initially, though later increasing. Cost was relatively modest with a discount for upfront payment, or the option to pay by instalments.[29] Murray targeted a mass audience, with very large dance schools, the ones in London having a staff of around fifty each. Certainly the Murray approach to teaching dancing inspired the creation of a British chain of dance teachers. The Rank Organisation soon adopted a similar business strategy. Thus, between 1958 and 1960 Rank converted twenty-one cinema-restaurants into dance studios, and managed to attract about 75,000 dance pupils.[30]

Yet beneath this apparent success story, it must be noted that the popularity of dancing lessons, and the number of dance teachers and dance schools, started to fall by the end of the 1950s. Like the decline of the dance hall, this fall was rapid. Taking a look at the numbers of teachers in two key cities, we can see when and by how far this collapse occurred. In 1950 the *Post Office Directory* named eleven dance teachers in Glasgow, falling to eight by 1960 and just five by 1965.[31] *Kelly's* found forty-two dance teachers in Birmingham in 1950, more or less maintained, at forty-one, in 1960 before falling to twenty-eight teachers in 1965.[32] The decline in take-up of dance lessons had been noted some time before this, however. Increasingly the mainstream dance hall dancer and the dance teachers were becoming estranged. This was caused by a number of factors. Explaining why fewer and fewer people seemed to be taking dance lessons from teachers, the *Ballroom Dancing Annual* surmised in 1949 that dance teachers had become obsessed with 'masses of technicalities'. It went on: 'Many of them . . . are living in a small world all by themselves. The solution, I believe, is for them to get among the public, and find out what *they* want.'[33] Dance hall manager E. W. Bourne made the same point, arguing 'most dancers consider ballroom dancing a pastime and not an art. This is no bad thing, for a hall crammed full of foxtrotting experts does not bear contemplation. Cede this point, teachers, and you will agree that you should concentrate on the learner and social dancer.'[34] Few did, however, and the long-term developments in dancing which will be outlined in this chapter were making dancing lessons less necessary.

In addition to taking dance lessons, there were a host of other ways in which knowledge of the new dance steps was disseminated, indicating the ever-increasing

[27] *DT*, November 1955, 101. [28] *DT*, November 1954, 103.
[29] *DT*, December 1955, 203. [30] *DM*, 12 February 1960, 23.
[31] *Post Office Directory, Glasgow* (1950–65). [32] *Kelly's Directory, Birmingham* (1950–65).
[33] *Ballroom Dancing Annual 1949*, 69. [34] *Ballroom Dancing Annual 1947*, 23.

cultural presence of dancing in national life. Dancing could be learned via a variety of media, old and new. Indeed, as dancing's popularity coincided with the growth of new mass media forms, it is unsurprising that they were utilized in order to teach dancing and to spread dancing trends and fashions. Let's start, however, by examining the use of traditional media.

The press was one way of spreading dance instruction and it was utilized by dance teachers from an early stage. During the 1920s and 1930s a specialized dancing press emerged, the most important journal being the *Dancing Times*, which had started in 1894 and began to devote increasing attention to ballroom dancing following the First World War. The *Dancing Times* printed articles and photographs of the key social dance forms and provided a host of dancing instruction tips from top dance teachers including Victor Silvester, Josephine Bradley, Maxwell Stewart, and others. It had a wide readership with sales in October 1929, for example, of 9,494.[35] Other journals followed in its wake, notably *Popular Music and Dancing Weekly* from 1924, the *Modern Ballroom Dance Instructor* from 1926, and *Modern Dance and Dancer* and *Ballroom and Band* both from 1934 onwards. The general press also catered for dancers and by the end of the 1920s most popular national newspapers contained a regular column on dancing, which illustrated how the 'professionals dance' and gave news and instruction on dancing. The *Daily Express*, *Daily Mail*, and *Daily Mirror* all had dancing correspondents, for example. Regional newspapers also supported the efforts of the dance teachers, with regular columns often written by local members of the dance teachers associations, the *Liverpool Echo*, *Manchester Evening News* and *Glasgow Herald* being good examples. In addition to newspapers and magazines, a myriad of different guides and handbooks to dancing were also produced, the most influential coming in 1927 when Victor Silvester wrote *Modern Ballroom Dancing: History and Practice*—it has never been out of print since. It spawned many imitations: Santos Casani's *Self Tutor of Ballroom Dancing* (1927), John Warren's *Modern Ballroom Dancing* (1931), Eve Tynegate Smith's *Textbook of Modern Ballroom Dancing* (1933), and Henri Jacques' *Modern Ballroom Dancing* (1939) were joined by dozens of others as well as being re-issued several times during the period.

In addition, the new mass media were an important source of dance instruction. Radio, for example, was an important impetus to dancing in the 1920s and 1930s. Radio's popularity in the interwar period was rapid. From 35,000 radio licences in 1926, by 1939 over nine million licences had been sold, representing about three-quarters of British households.[36] The BBC did much to sponsor the development of dance music. Certainly, dance music had been an important feature of BBC broadcasts since its inception. The first dance music programme went out in early 1923 and live outside broadcasts from ballrooms in London's top hotels and restaurants were the mainstay of the BBC's dance music output in this period. In 1928 it formed its own resident dance band and Jack Payne was appointed musical

[35] *DT*, October 1929, 2.

[36] A. Briggs, *The History of Broadcasting in the United Kingdom*, rev. edn (5 vols., Oxford: Oxford University Press, 1995), i. 17 and ii. 6.

director. The band broadcast every weekday afternoon for four years, in addition to numerous evening shows. Later in 1932, Henry Hall was appointed the new orchestra director, by which time the BBC was providing a diet of dance music that proved incredibly popular. In regular later afternoon and late night slots, programmes were broadcast every day of the week but Sunday.[37] Once commercial radio began broadcasting in 1934, dance music fans were given even more exposure to their music. Radio was thus central to the ubiquitous presence of dance music in Britain from the interwar period onwards. It also offered the chance for dancing at home. Rolling up the carpet and taking to the dance floor at home became a popular domestic leisure pursuit. In 1926, for example, it was estimated that some 2,000 private dances took place every evening to broadcast music.[38] Formal dance lessons via the radio also emerged later in the period, as in 1937 Victor Silvester and his Ballroom Orchestra made their radio debut on the National Programme in May.[39] This influence continued throughout the war, when liberalization of the BBC's output, particularly on the Forces Programme led to a significant increase in airtime for dance music. Radio also had some part to play in the post-war popularity of dancing. As before the war, the BBC provided a regular supply of dance music, together with a number of programmes dedicated to the technique of ballroom dancing. Old Time Dancing, for example, was well catered for. 'Those Were The Days' with Harry Davidson and His Orchestra had first been broadcast in November 1943 and by 1953 there had been 482 broadcasts. In July 1954 on the Light Programme, Sydney Thompson and his Orchestra were running 'Take Your Partners' and 'May I Have the Pleasure?' The reintroduction of commercial radio in 1946 also served to increase the popularity of dance music and popular dance crazes. Radio Luxembourg was much more inclined to play popular dance music than the BBC.

Film was also utilized to instruct people how to dance, with the obvious benefits that the medium could bring. Famous dance teachers lined up to offer guidance. Santos Casani started giving dance steps from 1927 in the weekly film magazine *Eve's Film Review*.[40] These films briefly showed dances in full formation and then took each of the fundamental steps and filmed them, showing the dancers' feet from underneath a glass floor, in slow motion.[41] As the *Dancing Times* remarked: 'Properly executed ballroom dances, carefully filmed and explained in detail, can show a vast public a high standard of dancing at which to aim . . . as a means of showing the multitude how graceful ballroom dancing is *when correctly danced*, the cinema is unsurpassed.'[42]

In the post-war period, film and radio were joined by television which was also utilized to teach people how to dance. Although it was initially feared that television would keep dancers at home, during the 1950s this did not happen and at first

[37] See J. J. Nott, *Music for the People: Popular Music and Dance in Interwar Britain* (Oxford University Press, 2002), 58–85.
[38] *PMDW*, 30 January 1926, 2.
[39] *DT*, May 1937, 204. [40] *DT*, April 1930, 43. [41] *DT*, December 1927, 349.
[42] Ibid.

dancing was actually boosted by television's popularity. The take up of television was rapid. In 1950 only 4 per cent of the adult population owned a television set; by 1955 this had risen to 40 per cent and by 1960 it had doubled to 80 per cent.[43] There were several television programmes catering for dancing, and they were some of the most popular items in early television broadcasting in Britain. First was Victor Silvester's 'Television Dancing Club' that began in 1948 and ran for seventeen years. This programme included demonstrations of the four key dances of the English style by leading professional dancing couples, a dance lesson from Silvester, and a background of amateur dancers who took to the floor. There were also two dance competitions judged by the viewers. Next Mecca organized 'Come Dancing', first broadcast in 1949, which was to become one of the most successful programmes in television history, ending only in 1995. 'Come Dancing' had demonstrations of top dancing by professionals, but also gave lessons in party dances and entertainment from formation teams. They included competitions filmed in Mecca's ballrooms.[44] The BBC also provided several other programmes with dancing, including the Six-Five Special in 1957. Once commercial television started in 1955, there were further opportunities for television dance programmes. The first dance teacher to appear on Independent Television was Josphine Bradley. In December 1956 she started a series of short instructional programmes, designed for young dancers home for the Christmas holidays, broadcast twice a week for a fortnight.[45] ITV also introduced 'Palais Party' in 1956 which was broadcast from the Hammersmith Palais and featured dance competitions, quizzes, and demonstrations.[46] This was followed by 'Oh Boy!' (1958), 'Thank Your Lucky Stars' (1961–66) and 'Ready, Steady Go!' (1963–66) all of which featured dance demonstrations and dancing. So how did these programmes help dancing? Those in the dancing industry speculated that such programmes inspired people who had never been dancing before to take it up and also encouraged those who had only a basic grasp of the steps to seek improvement. Moreover, some thought that they had reduced 'antagonism' towards dancing from some quarters, by showing it as a wholesome, ordered, and respectable pastime.[47]

Records had also helped to popularize dance steps, though the record, unlike television, was ultimately to damage dance teaching in Britain. The new medium of the gramophone had been helpful to dancing when it first appeared. Although not as ubiquitous as the radio, the gramophone nevertheless spread rapidly in Britain from the interwar period onwards. In 1930, for example, there were over three times as many gramophones sold (778,492) as the number of houses built that year (200,900) and there was more than one record sold for every single person in Britain (sixty million records sold, population 45,685,000).[48] As with radio, the gramophone promoted interest in dance music and offered the opportunity to practise dance steps at home. The gramophone was used frequently for domestic

[43] J. Bourke, *Working Class Cultures in Britain: Gender, class and ethnicity* (London: Routledge, 1994), 188.

[44] *Danceland*, July 1953, 5.

[45] *DT*, January 1956, 261.

[46] *DT*, July 1956, 603.

[47] *Ballroom Dancing Annual 1951* (1952), 16.

[48] Nott, *Music*, 1.

parties and home entertainment. In addition, portable gramophones allowed dancing to take place on picnics and group outings. For day-trippers and holiday-makers, dance music could be taken with them wherever and whenever they wanted.[49] As well as providing the occasion for dances, dance steps could also be learned from the gramophone. In 1927, the *Daily Mail* observed the suitability of using the gramophone for learning to dance: 'The gramophone is excellent to provide the music for the novice because the speed can be set slow, and as progress with the steps improves the speed can be increased in stages.'[50] Record companies produced special records to aid dancers and provide instruction. Some were recordings of dance teachers reading out instructions, referring to specially produced accompanying dance manuals, followed by snatches of music with the tempo marked out strongly by a drum, during which record owners were supposed to practise their steps. In addition, the record industry, encouraged by the leading dance teachers issued more straightforward musical records that had been specially recorded at the 'official' tempo necessary for dancing to. By the post-war period, however, the availability of cheaper record players and the 45rpm single specially targeted at youth was to erode the need for dance lessons. As we have seen, the more relaxed and expressive dancing style that accompanied new musical developments of the 1950s and 1960s meant that many young people were content to practise dancing in their own homes to the sound of their favourite bands and singers. Together with cheap transistor radios, young people were forging a dance culture of their own away from dance schools.

DANCES AND DANCE FASHIONS, 1910–39

So what did people dance? The popular history of dancing in Britain is one dominated by concentration on particular 'dance crazes', the Charleston and the Jitterbug being two notable examples. Whilst recognizing the popularity of such dances, we need to take a more nuanced approach, noting especially the varying audiences and variety of dance styles popular at any one time. In order to give a sense of what was being danced throughout this period, we will thus examine three distinctive periods and what was danced during them rather than looking at the separate evolution of particular dance styles. It is not intended to provide a descriptive outline of the key dance forms, though where this is relevant this will be done.

Three major developments dominated dance in Britain in the period 1910–39. First was the arrival of a number of new social dances just before the First World War and after it, which were to transform traditional dancing habits. Second, the development of the 'English style' which formalized, simplified, and tried to 'tame' these new dances. Finally, 'novelty dances' and a move towards simple 'party

[49] See Nott, *Music*, 33–55.

[50] *Daily Mail*, 14 January 1927, 15.

dances', most notably the Lambeth Walk, which were popular throughout the whole period.

We start with an examination of the new social dances. Between 1910 and 1920, dancing and dance music in Britain were transformed by the widespread popularity of revolutionary new styles of music and dance which had arrived from the United States, as first 'ragtime' then 'jazz', and the numerous new social dances that developed alongside them, took hold of and captured the public imagination.[51] The Cakewalk, Bunny Hug, Turkey Trot and, most importantly, the foxtrot, transformed the dancing scene in Britain, and ushered in a new era of social dancing. The new dances overturned existing rules and practices. They transformed social dance from sequence dances where everyone performed the same steps, to dances deliberately formulated for couples, with freer and more fluid movements. These new dances arrived in Britain around 1912, coming from New York via Paris, where British dance trends had traditionally been set. The first big hit of this period, however, was of South American origin—the tango. The tango was first mentioned in the British press in 1911 and in 1912 it was featured on the London stage in 'Sunshine Girl', danced by George Grossmith and Phyllis Dare. By 1913 there was a tango craze in Britain, the first great dance craze of the twentieth century, so great that as one dance teacher recalled: 'it affected almost everyone and everything in England even outside the dancing world.'[52] Its life was short however, and by 1914 the dance's popularity had started to ebb. This was a pivotal year for dancing in Britain. This was when the most significant of the new American dances arrived—the foxtrot. This dance had been popularized in the United States by a vaudeville entertainer, Harry Fox, drawing on dance steps and traditions from African-Americans. It first came to Britain in the summer of 1914 where it was demonstrated at London's '400 Club' on Bond Street and at the fashionable tea dances held at Harewood Place. The first British teacher to show it was D. G. MacLennan in Edinburgh. After the First World War broke out, the dance increased in popularity, especially amongst men on leave who had no time to learn more complex steps. The simplicity of the foxtrot gave it wide appeal. As P. J. S. Richardson noted: 'when home for short leave either from France or the training camp a dance was the favoured form of amusement. They had not the time to learn the Valse . . . but the then more or less go as you please steps of the Foxtrot . . . offered few difficulties.'[53] The new dance was soon being featured in the top London dance places and in May 1915 a Foxtrot Ball and Competition was held and many West End shows featured the dance in their productions. Had it not been for the arrival of large numbers of American troops in 1917 the dance would probably have faded away, but this, together with the new 'jazz' music gave the foxtrot an enormous fillip.[54] The new music fitted the dance form extremely well,

[51] As has been well documented, ragtime, jazz, and the associated dances evolved from America's South and Midwest, part of the legacy of slavery. Forced into 'juke joints' and 'honky tonks', black Americans evolved unique musical and dancing styles incorporating African and white European traditions. See for example, K. J. Ogren, *The Jazz Revolution: Twenties America and the Meaning of Jazz* (Oxford: Oxford University Press, 1989).

[52] *DT*, October 1935, 52. [53] Ibid. [54] *DT*, October 1930, 28.

and the rush of songs published in the new idiom helped secure the foxtrot in the dancing public's favour. Once the war was over, the dance spread rapidly through the newly emerging network of dance halls. The dance's form also changed, undergoing numerous transitions, with steps and tempo altered to bring about a smoother dance. Foxtrot competitions helped further cement the dance in the public's consciousness, one of the first, and most important, being held at the Embassy Club in London in 1920. In 1921 a generously supported competition from the *Daily Sketch*, which offered £1,500 in cash prizes, spread the vogue for the dance even further. By this date, the foxtrot had established itself as one of the most popular dances in British ballrooms, and was to retain that position for the next three decades. It was joined in the mid-1920s by the quickstep which was in essence a faster foxtrot. It was developed in England as a response to the snappy, fast paced dance music of the early 1920s. It was an energetic and light-hearted dance that took elements of the Charleston and involved a lot of movement on the dance floor, with various hops, runs, and rotating steps. In addition to these new dances, this period also saw the transformation of an old favourite, the waltz. During the war, the waltz had nearly disappeared, overtaken by the new dances and forsaken because of its complexity. In 1922 Victor Silvester and Phyllis Clarke developed the modern waltz in preparation for the World Championships, with the help of Bernard Carrington, an important exhibition dancer. They simplified the dance, removing complex variations, and introduced a 'natural turn' to make it more graceful and also easier to dance.[55] This process of simplification and the ironing out of dance steps was part of a movement gathering pace by the early 1920s that was to bring about the next great change to dancing in Britain, the development of the English style.

The reasons for the development of the English style, and the influence of the dance profession over it, will be discussed in detail later in the chapter. Here we provide a precursory overview. We should note that this was a development being directed by dance teachers in an attempt to wrest control of dancing back from foreign and commercial interests. It was also an attempt to create more order from the improvised and often energetic flourishes that dancers were adding to dances like the foxtrot. As the *Dancing Times* noted:

> With the signing of the Armistice there came a great dancing boom, but our ballrooms were in a very chaotic state. Freak steps were much in evidence, many of them totally unsuited for a ballroom and people complained that no two couples danced alike. In an attempt to reduce order out of chaos The *Dancing Times* invited all ballroom teachers to attend an 'Informal Conference' . . .[56]

As we have already noted, the growth of the dance business during the 1920s had been accompanied by a rapid growth in the number of professional dancing instructors and associations. Via a series of informal conferences in the 1920s, these groups demanded action to improve the reputation of dancing and they led a national campaign against 'objectionable dancing'. Moreover, they decided that the

[55] *DT*, October 1935, 53. [56] *DT*, October 1935, 81.

Fig. 4.1. Shaping the dance: 'You may dance according to the rules', W. K. Haselden, *Daily Mirror*, 31 October 1918
Source: © Mirrorpix.

basic steps of the foxtrot, one-step, and waltz should be standardized (see Fig. 4.1). These decisions manifested themselves at a local level through the numerous dancing schools that had opened in many towns and cities. As the 1920s progressed they began to develop a distinct style of dancing, known as 'the English style' which eventually became associated exclusively with 'ballroom dancing'. Little by little dance instructors were regulating and standardizing a pastime that many had found initially attractive because it allowed a means of expression and freedom of movement. Dancing was becoming a serious business.

In sharp contrast to this development, one other notable trend during the 1920s was the emergence of novelty dances, and periodic dance crazes, the most famous being the Charleston in 1925/6. Introduced to Britain in 1925, the Charleston caught on like no other dance had done since the tango. Energetic, wild, and defiantly youthful in its appeal, it was a huge success, as Victor Silvester later recalled: 'Wherever you went people seemed to be practising the Charleston—in bus queues, in Tube stations waiting for a train, at street corners, in shops; even policemen on point duty were seen doing the steps—because in practically every ballroom in London every second dance was the Charleston.'[57] It had first been introduced to Britain on the stage by the 'Midnight Follies' at the Hotel Metropole but it took a promotion by two well-known exhibition dancers before the dance really gained favour. In July 1925 Annette Mills (sister of actor John Mills and later to gain fame on early BBC television hosting Muffin The Mule) and Robert Sielle, who had just returned from the USA, put on a 'Charleston Tea' at the Carnival Club, Dean Street in conjunction with the *Dancing Times*. Their demonstrations attracted considerable interest and by the autumn the dance was making major headway in Britian's dance halls, first as a variation on the foxtrot and then, due to demands for encores by the public, as a separate dance.[58] This craze for the Charleston reached its zenith on 15 December 1926, when the theatre impresario C. B. Cochran organized a 'Charleston Ball' at the Royal Albert Hall attended by nearly 10,000 people and with competitions judged by, among others, Fred Astaire. Although it remained in vogue for only six months longer, it provided a vivid image for contemporary commentators who were focusing their attention on a minority of 'bright young things' and their supposedly Bohemian lifestyles.

The success of the Charleston prompted dance teachers and businessmen to try and come up with a new 'dance sensation' and numerous attempts were made to introduce a rival. The frequency with which novelty dances were introduced during the 1920s can be illustrated by reference to the *Dancing Times* which in March 1928 listed recently invented dances, most of which rapidly slipped into obscurity. There was the Baltimore, Heebie-Jeebies, Kinkajou, Mayfair, Rhythm Step, Slip Step, Sugar Step, Trebla, Yale, and Stop Time foxtrot. These had been originated by dance teachers both in the United States and Britain, including Santos Casani, Maxwell Stewart, Cecil Taylor, and 'Monsieur Pierre'.[59] Mecca's introduction of party dances from the mid-1930s onwards was related to this trend, but with a keener appreciation of the dancers' needs. Mecca helped develop a series of simple, easy to dance, group dances starting with the 'Palais Glide' and the 'St Bernards Waltz' in 1935, followed by 'the Lambeth Walk' and 'the Chestnut Tree' novelty dances in 1938—a series of dances that lifted the fortunes of the dance business by countering the hesitation of potential dancers concerned about their ability to dance. All of the dances involved dancers getting into group formations, following a handful of easy movements and changing partners numerous times during the dance. They also involved novelty moves such as the jerking of the thumb and the shouting 'Oi' in the Lambeth Walk; or simple exercise like the stretches used to recreate a developing tree in the Chestnut Tree. Such dances changed the way in which dancers interacted in the dance hall, as Tom Harrisson writing for the *Picture Post* in 1938 observed:

[57] V. Silvester, *Dancing is My Life. An Autobiography* (London: Heinemann, 1958). 88.
[58] *DT*, September 1950, 755. [59] *DT*, March 1928, 807.

> ... [they] marked an important breakaway from the post-war norm, of couple dancing to highly conventionalised movements. The Palais Glide stimulated freer open dancing, everyone in the ballroom joining in together.[60]

This development is particularly interesting as it illustrates the immense influence that Mecca exerted over dancing by the late 1930s. The Lambeth Walk was their biggest success. With massive exposure on the radio, successful gramophone recordings, large sheet music sales and an enormous dancing public, it distinguished itself as no dance since the Charleston had done. Indeed, the success of the Lambeth Walk had increased the popularity of dancing so much that Heimann and Davies planned to release new dances at least twice a year, every few months if possible. In 1938/9 they promoted the Park Parade and the Chestnut Tree. Mecca's example spawned a dozen imitators and in the wake of the Lambeth Walk numerous other party dances emerged. The Blackpool Walk was perhaps the most cheekily named, the music created by Lawrence Wright and recorded by some of the biggest bands of the day in 1938. Even Gracie Fields and Victor Silvester tried to cash in on the fashion, together bringing out The Trek in December 1938, described as a 'Christmas Party Dance'.[61]

Why did these party dances become so popular at this time? Mass Observation in their pioneering work on the Lambeth Walk considered that part of their appeal was in response to the growing sense of crisis developing in Britain as war grew increasingly likely. This was backed up by others too. 'Sitter Out' writing in the *Dancing Times* in 1940 opined that their popularity 'may have been due indirectly to the crises through which we were passing and the consequent craving for a spirit of light-heartedness in our ballrooms as an antidote'.[62]

Despite the revolution in dancing styles represented by the emergence of the new social dances just prior to and during the First World War, and the various dance crazes and party dances, the older sequence dances never quite died away. In some venues the older style of dancing clung on and in the late 1920s and early 1930s, there was a nationwide revival of interest in so called 'Old Time' dancing. In the Isle of Man in the summer of 1928, for example, half of the programme in dance halls was given over to Old Time dances, with the Veleta being the most popular dance. Both young and old seemed attracted to these dances, with the *Dancing Times* describing their popularity as 'nothing short of astounding'. It was observed: 'Elderly folk discover new life in the dances of the past, and the younger people find, much to their surprise, that the dances and dance music of the past years have been singularly lacking in grace and sentiment—and even gaiety.'[63] One of the pioneers of this revival was Malcolm Munro, manager of the Grafton in Liverpool. The Grafton regularly held 'Old Tyme Nights' from 1929 onwards, attracting large numbers. Elsewhere there was evidence of the new popularity of Old Time dances too. In Birmingham in 1930 Tony's Ballroom held both old and new dances with

[60] Draft version of T. Harrisson, 'A Dance is Born' for *Picture Post*, 12 December 1938, 6.
[61] *DT*, December 1938, 335.
[62] *DT*, January 1940, 217.
[63] *DT*, October 1928, 59.

modern and old time orchestras in two daily sessions.[64] Dance halls in other cities followed their lead. In Nottingham in 1932 the Palais de Danse held Old Time nights every Tuesday with an average of 1,000 dancers, and hundreds more turned away, a sign of their popularity.[65] In 1932 a survey of dance halls throughout Britain found that over 70 per cent featured Old Time dances in their regular dance programmes with some reporting them as their most popular evenings. In particular the military two-step, Veleta, and old-fashioned waltz, were favoured by dancers. This popularity proved enduring too and, as we shall see, this revival was to survive into the war and beyond.

WARTIME DANCE FASHIONS, 1939–45

The start of the war caused those in the dancing world to wonder whether there would be momentous changes to dancing as there had been during the First World War. The transition from sequence to non-sequence dancing had been cemented by the conditions of that conflict, and some went out of their way to look for evidence of a similar revolution. The impact of the Second World War on dancing in Britain was not, however, anywhere near as great as the First had been.

Inevitably when dealing with dances of the Second World War in Britain, one must start with the Jitterbug. There is no doubt that it became iconic both during the war itself and afterwards, most notably associated with a rapid Americanization of British dance halls and dance culture. Certainly the Jitterbug was popular and countless competitions and Jitterbug sessions were held in dance places up and down the country. However, there is a considerable folk history surrounding this dance and a more nuanced approach to it needs to be taken. There are several popular assumptions concerning the Jitterbug that are erroneous. First, it did not arrive in Britain with the flood of GIs from America from 1942 onwards. The Jitterbug arrived in Britain even before the war had started in 1939. Talk of Jitterbug dancing predates even that. Some of the first references to the Jitterbug in Britain were made in 1938, when the press picked up on the popularity of the dance in some circles in the United States. Illustrations and sensationalist descriptions of the dance were numerous. In November 1938, for example, *Picture Post* reported on 'Dance Madness in the USA', highlighting the wildness of 'Jitter-bug' dances, 'compared to which the wildest Charlestons and Black Bottoms of a few years back seem as sober and stately as minuets'.[66] The dance arrived in Britain soon after this and appeared to have caught on quickly in some dance halls. By September of 1939, for example, complaints were made that Jitterbugs with their 'ungraceful, un-English, and sometime vulgar gyrations' were not acceptable in Blackpool's ballrooms.[67] We also see a pastiche of the dance performed by Gracie Fields in her pre-war 1939 film *Shipyard Sally*, in a scene where she dances to 'I've Got the Jitterbugs' whilst affecting an American accent. Second, the Jitterbug,

[64] *DT*, October 1930, 85.
[65] *DT*, June 1932, 303.
[66] *PP*, 5 November 1938, 23.
[67] *DT*, October 1939, 37.

though it certainly grabbed the headlines, did not represent such a revolutionary departure from dancing styles as has been previously assumed. Its key elements had been in evidence in British ballrooms since the late 1930s, when 'swing' dancing interrupted the established pattern of dancing. Many of the dance steps and dance moves seen in the Jitterbug built on swing steps like Truckin' and the Susie Q, seen in British ballrooms from around 1937. These two dances involved breaking up the partner dancing and allowing energetic solo performance, with much kicking and shaking of hands and hips. As early as September 1937, Victor Silvester had been advising dancers how to do the swing step.[68] Moreover, the closest dance to the Jitterbug, the Lindy Hop, had also been talked about and danced in Britain long before 1939. This dance with its 'swing out' moves, where dancers remained holding hands but swung away from their partner, was a key feature of the Jitterbug. The Jitterbug then, was the extension of an ongoing trend in dancing in Britain, not a revolution. Another myth that needs to be exploded, is the huge popularity of the dance. The Jitterbug was not universally popular and did not necessarily take British dance halls by storm. There were ebbs and flows in the popularity of the dance in Britain and it started to fall out of favour in 1941, only to be revived by the arrival of American troops in 1942. If we look at the first point in the war when the Jitterbug took off, 1940, we can see that even then the dance was not a success everywhere in Britain. In Newcastle in March the Oxford Galleries held a demonstration of the Jitterbug followed by a Jitterbug championship and there were dozens of similar events held up and down the country. But in February in the Grafton Rooms, Liverpool, a similar attempt to introduce Jitterbugs had met with failure as only four couples were willing to try it. As the *Dancing Times* put it: 'They provided plenty of amusement, but it was apparent that this style of dancing is still in its infancy as far as the provinces are concerned.'[69] Similarly in April it was reported that 'this craze does not appear to have taken hold on Manchester dancers.'[70] This was not merely a case of time lag between a dance craze in London and the rest of the country either. Even in March 1942, a 'northern dance teacher' writing in the *Dancing Times* noted that the Jitterbug's 'efforts to gate-crash our English ballrooms have not met . . . [with] success'.[71] The dance was given a boost by the arrival of American troops however and the presence of these Americans allowed the dance to reach areas previously immune to it. Thus, although it was by no means new in Britain, as late as January 1943, the *Cheltenham Chronicle* was describing a display of Jitterbugging by locally stationed American troops as 'an entirely new form of entertainment'.[72] The American presence also stimulated a more energetic interpretation of the dance. Yet, even this new-found popularity was narrow, as we shall see later. At the heats of a Jitterbug championship held at the Plaza, Manchester in April 1941, for example, it was observed that 'the patrons are merely content to watch these affairs rather than to participate in them'.[73] Whilst exponents of the Jitterbug were certainly avid about the dance, they represented a

[68] *DT*, September 1937, 674. [69] *DT*, April 1940, 449. [70] *DT*, May 1940, 505.
[71] *DT*, March 1942, 313. [72] *Cheltenham Chronicle*, 2 January 1943, 3.
[73] *DT*, April 1941, 413.

small minority of, mostly, young people. Not all young people liked to Jitterbug and not all dancers were young. Moreover, whilst certainly shaking up the world of dancing, the Jitterbug did not oust the standard dances from wartime British dance halls. The foxtrot, waltz, and quickstep remained firm favourites in wartime dance programmes. Thus, in November 1941, dance teacher John Wells could note: 'So far the war has brought no sweeping changes in our ballrooms. The Waltz, Foxtrot, Quickstep and Tango remain firm favourites.'[74] Whilst we must recognize that dance teachers were in general opposed to the Jitterbug and it was therefore in their interests to underestimate its impact, it is still clear that the dance programmes of most dance halls were not substantially altered during the war. As we shall see shortly, the Jitterbug did cause a backlash from both moralists and those concerned with dance steps and order in the dance hall however. One result was an attempt to tame the dance into a more 'refined version' and this led to the development of Jive, which will be considered in detail later.

Aside from the Jitterbug and Jive, which other dances were popular with wartime dancers? In line with the pre-war trend towards party dances, the war saw attempts to introduce a number of war related group dances. One of the first, introduced in November 1939, was The Blackout Stroll, devised by T. Connor and recorded by Joe Loss amongst others. It briefly became popular in 1940. The main idea of this dance was to get people mixing, and the lights would be periodically turned out and dancers would swap with one another. The slightly chaotic partner swapping in the dark was taken in good spirit and it enlivened the atmosphere in the dance hall considerably. Various other dances proved less successful, however, the RAF Patrol devised by Maxwell Stewart in 1940 and the Tuscana devised by Adele England in 1941 being two flops. More enduring was Knees Up Mother Brown. The song dates from the First World War and was re-popularized in 1938. The dance however, was devised by Adele England and popularized first in Mecca's dance halls and then spread more widely at the start of the war. It rapidly caught on and became a mainstay of wartime dances. Equally popular was the Hokey Cokey, whose origins are more interesting than many of the other party dances. The song was written by British songwriter Jimmy Kennedy and it was thought to be based on a traditional Canadian song and to have been brought over to Britain by Canadian soldiers.[75] Kennedy saw these Canadians dancing and singing it in a nightclub and devised his own version. It became incredibly popular. Despite the dubious reference to drug taking (it is thought that the 'Cokey' referred to cocaine), it was an innocent and light-hearted dance. With its group participation, wartime dancers took to it with gusto, and it is still widely known in Britain, more often now amongst children. As with the popularity of such dances during the crises of the period 1938–9, part of their attraction to wartime dancers was their group involvement. The desire of people to join together in common efforts, to socialize and have as much fun as possible, was understandably great at a time of intense stress.

[74] *DT*, November 1941, 82. [75] *DT*, September 1943, 570.

Another pre-war dance trend continued into the war was Old Time, the *Daily Mirror* claiming in 1944 that '[l]ancers and quadrilles and waltz cotillions are displacing the Jitterbug all over England'.[76] Malcolm Munro at the Grafton, Liverpool had led the revival, in 1941, where Wilf Hamer and his Band featured a regular 'Melodious Memories' spot of Old Time dances that mushroomed in popularity.[77] The return of older dancers to dance halls towards the end of the war also gave Old Time a fillip. The Liverpool correspondent of the *Dancing Times* reported in July 1945: 'The old-time "boom" owes something to returning servicemen and factory workers . . . Apparently these jolly sequence dances were prime favourites wherever service men and women gathered abroad, and they were also in great demand at factory canteen and hostel dances.'[78] The Grafton Rooms saw a huge attendance, with 1,500 dancers on the floor at one time, when it introduced an Old Time gala with Harry Davidson's Old-Time Orchestra that month.

DANCE FASHIONS, 1945–60

The immediate post-war period was seen as a crossroads by many in the dancing world. Would dancing return to the pre-war patterns and standards of the English style, or would some of the experiments of the war period, such as Jitterbugging and Jiving, begin to gain ground at their expense? In fact what happened is that neither of these two styles prevailed; instead there was an increasing diversification of dancing styles. Three main developments stand out. First, the standard dances of the English style never went out of favour, they remained the backbone of most dancers' dancing repertoire throughout the period 1945–60. Secondly, however, Jiving (which we consider later) also never went out of style—though in modified form, and despite opposition from some, the Jive was a mainstay of dancing programmes throughout the post-war period. Increasingly the two styles become associated with different age groups, with Jive becoming the preferred dancing style of the young, but a complete 'split' does not occur until nearly the end of the dance hall days, in the mid-1960s. Third, as the period progresses, these two mainstays are joined by an ever-increasing number of dancing trends, which supplemented and extended the appeal of dancing and also increasingly fragmented what was being danced. By the end of the period under investigation, it was not possible to talk of one single national dancing culture, rather a large number of different overlapping ones, catering for different groups.

One of the earliest dance trends of the post-war period was the so-called 'Old Time Dancing' craze, which developed towards the end of the war, and was very popular from 1946 onwards. In December 1945 the *Dancing Times* was able to write: 'The greatest boom in Old-time Dancing that the present generation has ever witnessed, is spreading through the Dance Halls of Northern England and the Midland Counties.'[79] However, whereas previously the interest in Old Time had

[76] *DM*, 6 January 1944, 5. [77] *MDD*, November 1941, 28.
[78] *DT*, July 1945, 471. [79] *DT*, December 1945, 133.

been strongest in the north of England, by 1947 there was growing evidence of its popularity in London too. Several Old Time clubs emerged in the capital to cater for the demand. The London and Home Counties Old Time Dance Club ran dances at Wembley, Acton, and Hammersmith Town Halls, amongst other places. The Universal Old Time Club ran dances at Lewisham Town Hall, St Pancras Assembly Rooms and elsewhere in south-east London. The Olympic Old Time Club held dances every Thursday in Acton and Fulham, and an Old Time Circle was active in Watford. There were also Old Time dances run regularly in Ilford, Woodford, Wanstead, and Wandsworth.[80] An International Sequence Old Time Dance Circle established in 1946 had 3,000 members by 1947.[81] It was estimated that there were approximately 25,000 Old Time nights taking place in Britain by the end of 1946, with around 100,000 regular Old Time patrons by 1949.[82]

Why was it so popular? One dance teacher, Tony Hemming, suggested it was because the dances were easy to perform, and because they were social: 'Many people find a grateful release from the endless succession of churned-out Quicksteps and Foxtrots in the participation in Old Time dancing.'[83] His analysis was supported by Major Cecil Taylor, President of the ISTD. Interestingly, and probably accurately, he considered the success of Old Time dancing to be a continuation of the demand for party dances. Rather than dancing 'authentic' versions of the older dances, Taylor labelled the post-war Old Time dances as 'novelty sequence dances' and saw these new versions more as heirs to the Lambeth Walk, rather than being a continuation of the original dances of the Victorian era and before. One other reason for the popularity of the Old Time dances was that they offered greater variety than the standard dance programme. As Leonard Hayes, a dance band leader specializing in Old Time, remarked in 1949: 'There are literally hundreds of different dances. All with their own set steps in regular sequence, with their own individual music.'[84] Some speculated that the success of Old Time was due to it bringing back 'colour and courtesy to British ballrooms' and believed that it was helping the country through 'days of stress and difficulty'.[85] As a dance trend, it remained remarkably resilient. Even when the leading dance halls reduced their provision of Old Time dances, by the late 1940s, the opportunities for dancing to this dance style were still numerous. In December 1948 in Liverpool, for example, it was noted 'Old Time and sequence dancing has maintained its hold in the district despite the fact that it is no longer regularly featured at the leading ballrooms . . . In the suburbs, however, there is a big following for old-time dancing.'[86] Similarly in 1951 Walter Whitman, writing about the continuing popularity of Old Time, argued: 'Many of the most flourishing clubs, which draw large attendances weekly, are rarely in the news, because they run no competitions or other events . . . they just go on and on, quietly, and are strong local institutions.'[87]

[80] *DT*, May 1947, 429.
[81] *Ballroom Dancing Annual 1947*, 61.
[82] *Ballroom Dancing Annual 1949*, 60, 65.
[83] *Ballroom Dancing Annual 1947*, 47.
[84] *Danceland*, September 1949, 14.
[85] *Danceland*, March 1951, 12.
[86] *Danceland*, December 1948, 16.
[87] *Danceland*, July 1951, 12.

Perhaps the most enduring non 'standard dance' of the post-war period in Britain's dance halls was the Jive. Jiving evolved naturally out of the Jitterbug style of dancing that had been emerging since the late 1930s. One feature of the dance was, like the Jitterbug, its freer form. Many people danced it without learning it, they let the spirit of the music take them over and the steps followed. As Barbara Nott (b. 1942) dancing in Crewe in the late 1950s remarked: 'we just did it, everyone had their own style, it didn't matter how you did it.'[88] Its spread was gradual and steady, it did not create the hysteria associated with Jitterbug, but Jive was to prove much more enduring. A 1946 survey of the managers of the five main dance halls in Edinburgh regarding the popularity of Jive elicited some interesting results. Two thought it would die out, but three predicted that it was 'here to stay', one of the managers indicating that he was perplexed by its continued success: 'I'm puzzled. I thought that as soon as the Yanks went we would begin to see a gradual return to straight dancing. But the opposite seems to be the case.'[89] In 1947 Margaret Cadman, writing about dancing in northern English dance halls explained: 'like most other parts of the country the dancing in the palais de danse, especially among the younger element has been greatly influenced by Jive.'[90] Indeed, as we shall see, the most avid fans of Jive were the young. Unlike the Jitterbug, however, the more sedate Jive attracted a majority of young people, not a minority. Jive caused considerable division within dance halls however, with camps for and against dead set in opposition to each other. The regularity with which those in the dancing world predicted the demise of Jive indicates that many of them wanted to see it disappear. In December 1948, for example, the Liverpool correspondent of *Danceland* posited the idea that Jive was on its way out, arguing that 'the biggest decline has been in jive which is now only favoured by the few experts whose gyrations are a joy to watch, but who are not tolerated in many ballrooms'.[91] That year dance teacher Alex Moore stated: 'Jive as an amusing interlude will last for some time. Jive as a craze is already dead.'[92] Despite these apparent lulls, however, Jive was to maintain its hold on the dancing public's imagination.

A more traditional trend from the USA also took hold in Britain in the post-war period. From about 1952 square dancing became popular up and down the country. This form of dancing had been introduced into Britain prior to this, however. One little known aspect of the wartime American influence on British dancing, obscured by the mythology of the Jitterbug, was the introduction of traditional American square dances. In January 1944, for example, the *Daily Mirror* remarked: 'when the Yanks came over here they brought their square dances with them. Quite a number of the US Red Cross clubs regularly run evenings of square dances, and English girls just "eat them up."'[93] As early as 1945, the *Dancing Times* was talking about 'experiments' in square dancing that had been taking place among some British dance teachers.[94] It wasn't until 1952 that square dancing

[88] Cheshire Dance Hall Interview (CDHI): Barbara Nott (b. 1942), 30 June 2014.
[89] *Danceland*, March 1946, 3. [90] *Ballroom Dancing Annual 1947*, 49.
[91] *Danceland*, December 1948, 16. [92] *Ballroom Dancing Annual 1948*, 35.
[93] *DM*, 6 January 1944, 5. [94] *DT*, December 1945, 125.

took off in Britain in a big way, however. That year in Liverpool it was reported: 'After languishing in some of the smaller ballrooms and only introduced casually as a social diversion in a few schools, Square Dancing has suddenly been taken up with great gusto in this area by most of the leading ballrooms.' At the Grafton, Malcolm Munro held two full square dancing sessions a week, and at the Tower Ballroom, New Brighton Ali Barber and his Corn Cob Quartet played to packed weekly square dance sessions. There was also a new square dance club formed in that town and several local dance teachers were featuring special classes.[95] Similar square dance clubs opened up throughout the country. Television also played a role in popularizing the dance style when in August 1952 a thirty-minute programme of square dancing was broadcast by David Miller. The first of a series, it had teams from several dance schools demonstrating the steps, with music provided by Phil Cardew and his Happy Hoedowners.[96] Also cashing in on the craze, square dance recordings were issued, two examples being recorded by the Butlin's Orchestra, 'Up Town Down Town' and 'Ragtime Annie'.[97] Radio too frequently broadcast music for square dancing, with Phil Cardew appearing regularly on the BBC from 1951 onwards. One of the attractions of square dancing was that it was easy to do. As dance teacher Bob Franks remarked in 1951 'the square dancers do not have to remember every dance. The "memory work" is left to one person who can be heard clearly by everyone in the hall. This person is the "Caller."'[98] The American square dances had no special order for their dance steps either and the caller could change the pattern of the dance at his will, thus adding novelty and variety to the evening's dancing. The approach taken to these dances was lighthearted and it was seen as an opportunity for amusement rather than the attainment of any dancing skill. It was for these reasons that Butlin's introduced square dancing to their holiday camps thus helping promote it further.[99] Instruction books were also issued, with *Square Dancing at Sight* by Nina Wilde and *Square Dancing* by Arthur King being two examples published in 1952.[100]

Beneath all of these various dance trends, the English style remained the mainstay of dance hall dancing programmes, at least in the period up to 1960. Indeed, the desire of many dance teachers and dance hall owners to re-assert the dominance of the English style was strong at the end of the war. In January 1946, for example, commenting on the appointment of a new manager to Mecca's Streatham Locarno, *Dancing Times* wrote: 'Mr Pritchard is good news for lovers of the British style, for he is determined to revert to pre-war policy and make Locarno a centre for the classic style. He really admires the "standard four," and the jitterbug is firmly crushed; incidentally this is to be the 1946 policy for all "Mecca" halls.'[101] Similarly, E. W. Bourne, manager of London's Astoria Dance Salon, complained:

> In the war years dancing became, as far as the public dance halls were concerned, an escapist type of entertainment: dance partners disappeared... bands played more to amuse themselves than the dancers; neglect fell upon strict tempo; and interest in

[95] *DT*, February 1952, 381. [96] *DT*, September 1952, 753. [97] Ibid.
[98] *Danceland*, October 1951, 7. [99] *Danceland*, February 1952, 16.
[100] *DT*, October 1952, 41. [101] *DT*, January 1946, 189.

> competitions dwindled almost to vanishing point. Thus, the public dance hall became a temple of gaiety and irresponsibility in which the true worshippers of the Turn and Contrary Body Movement could no longer practice their rites.[102]

He encouraged teachers and dance hall managements to promote the English style again, with renewed vigour. Mecca also tried to encourage this quieter form of dancing, arguing that after six years of war and 'living on our nerves' people wanted 'something to soothe them'.[103] By the early 1950s some in the dancing world were suggesting that the English style was stagnating, however. Fabian White, writing in 1952, blamed demonstrators and dance teachers, stating: 'It's been standing still or marking time, for quite a number of years. The English style . . . is now being challenged abroad as never before? What should be done about it?'[104] This process of increasing diversification in dancing styles, and the gradual erosion of the dominance of the English style in public dance halls, continued apace until the mid-1960s. Perhaps the biggest development in dancing by this stage, was the emergence of solo dancing, and the gradual disappearance of partner dancing in Britain.

Episodes of 'solo' dancing had been seen in Britain long before the 1960s. The swing dances of the 1930s, such as Truckin', and the Jitterbug and Jive of the 1940s, all contained elements of solo dance moves—where couples broke away from each other and stepped out on their own, usually in an energetic way. This trend re-emerged in the mid-1950s and reached a new direction by the early 1960s, when purely 'solo' dances began to emerge (see Fig. 4.2). These dances, the most notable being the Twist, were not formulated for couples. Indeed, the attraction of these dances was that they allowed dancers a very large degree of individual freedom. Freedom of expression, by now a popular concept in political and cultural circles, became the new driving force behind dances. It must be remembered, however, that there was still an attraction too in dancing the same dance steps as everyone else. Being fashionable meant being able to dance the current dance craze like everyone else. What was different from before was that dancing was no longer partner dancing. In tune with the newly liberated times, dancers could move about the dance floor, interacting with various 'partners', or just 'do their own thing', rather than stay with one dancing partner for the duration of a dance. This mixed things up considerably, and changed the atmosphere of dancing forever. It was also, as we have seen, part of the reason for the gradual decline of the 'dance hall'.

A 'NATIONAL' DANCE CULTURE?

Our discussion of dance trends shows that beneath the headline popularity and craze for particular dances, there was in fact considerable variety in the dancing programmes of Britain's dance halls. There were also numerous dancing publics all

[102] *Ballroom Dancing Annual 1947*, 22.
[103] *Danceland*, October 1945, 1.
[104] *Danceland*, December 1952, 16.

Fig. 4.2. New solo dancing—Glasgow Locarno, 1964
Source: Scotsman Publications Ltd.

with their own tastes and preferences. Let's examine the extent to which Britain's dancers were engaging in a 'national' dance culture.

There was a national dance culture in the sense that the standard dances (and later the party dances) were danced in a network of dance halls and other dance venues that was spread throughout the country. These dances had nationwide appeal and popularity. However, there were some important differences in the way in which these dances were danced and this varied according to class and geography, as well as gender and age (as we shall see in later chapters.) In reality there were a series of overlapping dance cultures, all drawing on a common stock of dances, but executed in different ways. Perhaps most significant was the broad divide between 'social dancers' and 'keen dancers' which first emerged during the interwar period.

The 'social dancer' was described in 1928 to readers of the *Dancing Times*: 'They don't want to take dancing seriously or to bother to learn steps . . . this sort of dancing is only a background for the more important social amenities.'[105] As the 1920s progressed there was an increasing gulf between them and the 'keen dancing

[105] *DT*, October 1928, 20.

enthusiast'. The *Oxford Magazine* noted in 1929: 'Ballroom dancing appeals to thousands upon thousands . . . its followers form two great camps, those who learn to dance, and that quite appreciable number who dance without learning.'[106] With just the minimum of dancing knowledge sizeable numbers of dancers went to dance halls who were content to more or less 'walk' around the dance floor. For these dancers, the attraction of the dance hall was not so much the execution of dance steps, but the opportunities it provided for meeting friends, socializing, and romantic encounters. Dance hall managers knew that they were a lucrative market and it was this group which inspired Mecca to create its party dances. The split between the keen dancer and the social dancer had become even more pronounced by the mid-1930s. Social dancers would often irritate the keen dancer. One Londoner complaining about the poor standard of dancing in Bristol in 1935, for example, wrote: 'Ninety per cent of Bristol dancers, both male and female, are keen on "having a good time" and "we must get tight together." The true art of Ballroom Dancing is sadly neglected and 75 per cent of dances in the district are glorified "booze-ups." . . . There is not a "palais" in the City worthy of the name and the population is nearly half a million.'[107] By the end of the 1930s, those interested in 'ballroom dancing' as a sport, split from the average dancer—and the ballroom, although still influenced by the standard dances, began to be transformed into a more convivial social space. The split between serious and social dancers was perhaps even more evident in the post-war period. Dance teacher Alex Moore claimed in 1948 that there were about one hundred thousand people who were keenly interested in ballroom dancing 'as a recreation and a sport'.[108] Whilst this compares well to the numbers active in other sports, compared to the total number who went dancing in Britain, it was small. As before the war, social dancers were looked down upon by most dance teachers however. Dance teacher Phyllis Haylor, observed in 1947 that a visit to any ballroom in Britain's big cities would alarm most dance teachers because 'there is little grace, less rhythm and an almost unbelievable monotony'.[109] Accoreding to one view expressed in 1952: 'The masses are content to shuffle. All they want is to get round tolerably comfortably.'[110] Clearly then, the social and the keen dancers represented two completely different approaches to dancing and offer a clear demarcation in the emergence of a national dancing culture. Whilst superficially these two groups were dancing the same dances, their conflicting attitudes towards dancing created distinctive and separate dance cultures.

There were differences too in how well people could dance depending on where in the country one was and in which venues. These differing skill levels added a further dimension of difference to the national dance culture, and there was a socio-economic dimension to this. By the late 1920s and early 1930s, majority opinion was that the 'best' dancers were to be found in the palais de danse that were spread throughout the country. As H. St John Rumsey noted: 'As a general rule the better

106 *Oxford Magazine*, 28 February 1929, 453.
107 *MDD*, January 1935, 25.
108 *Ballroom Dancing Annual 1948*, 34.
109 *DT*, October 1947, 24.
110 *Danceland*, December 1952, 16.

the dancing the less it costs.'[111] *Dancing Times* noted in 1927, for example, 'the provincial "Palais" are doing wonderfully good work, and in many towns attract all the best people in the neighbourhood.'[112] In particular, dancers at the palais were seen to be keener and more expert than in other venues. By comparison, the smart hotels and restaurants of London and other major cities, frequented by the upper and upper-middle classes, were seen to have fallen behind. Victor Silvester complained in 1927: 'The majority of people who dance at all the best hotels and clubs where the most exclusive bands are engaged, 90 per cent of them are bad dancers, they have no balance and do not require any when they just walk and shuffle around the floor to quick music.'[113] Josephine Bradley concurred in 1930: 'teachers of dancing . . . have long bewailed the fact that we cannot induce . . . the people who are found habitually at these West End restaurants to take their dancing seriously.'[114] This continued to be the case after the war, one dance teacher noting in 1953: 'Social dancing seen on the small floors of the West End remains deplorable . . . It is the Dance Halls which keep dancing alive.'[115] Aside from a lack of willingness to learn, two further issues contrived to make dancing less skillful here. First, was the lack of space—small, overcrowded dance floors meant a lack of room to perform the correct steps or to adopt the correct posture. This led to the development of so-called 'crush dancing' whereby dance steps and movements were abbreviated to cope with the lack of space. The hold was also more compact than normal, and steps were kept as flat footed as possible.[116] Second, in these top venues the music was provided by the leading national dance bands that developed a style of playing best suited to listening rather than dancing. In a sense, they had become 'show bands'. With a much faster tempo, they were not playing at speeds most suitable for dancing, and they were prone to elaborate solo instrumentals that interrupted the main melodies and rhythms.

As well as class, geography played a role in differing dance standards. Debate raged as to where in the country the best dancers could be found. Several candidates were suggested, the two chief contenders being London and Scotland, specifically Glasgow. In March 1925, for example, Odette Myrtil claimed:

> The finest dancing in the world is to be found . . . in London . . . in no town, in our own country or in any other in the world, can one find such a high standard of dancing . . . Londoners . . . have the cream of the world's bands to dance to, the most perfect of floors, and the finest dancers to teach them.[117]

London might have been the centre of dance trends and barometer of dancing standards before the First World War and, due to its better dancing facilities, it retained this position into the early 1920s. However, the growth of palais de danse in the mid-1920s eroded London's lead in dance proficiency. In August 1928 leading dance teachers who had judged a national professional competition drew

[111] H. St. John Rumsey, *Ball-Room Dancing* (London: Methuen, 1925), 2.
[112] *DT*, April 1927, 21.
[113] *DT*, September 1927, 649.
[114] *DT*, February 1930, 581.
[115] *DT*, August 1953, 687.
[116] *DT*, April 1933, 35.
[117] *PMDW*, 7 March 1925, 132.

attention to the improved standards outside of London. Victor Silvester commented: 'The provincial professional used to be under the handicap of having no really first class dancing hall, but now with the erection of all the palais de danse . . . it is just a matter of time before the standard is equivalent to here.' Eve Tynegate Smith remarked: 'In Birmingham I was amazed . . . at the high standard'; Monsieur Pierre described witnessing at regional heats 'excellent dancing, well up to West End standard'.[118] If some thought the provinces were catching up with London, others thought they had overtaken it. In 1928 'Sitter Out', a regular columnist in the *Dancing Times*, claimed Glasgow had the greatest dancers, taking the crown formerly held by Liverpool.[119] Similarly D. Wellesley Smith, the dancing partner of Josephine Bradley, noted after a visit to the Star Dancing Championships in 1930, when Scotland filled two of the first three places in the final: 'Certainly an eye opener for anyone from the south to make a tour of the dancing places there. The general standard of dancers is higher than that in London.'[120] Many of the top competition dancers in Britain came from Glasgow and the city's inhabitants certainly seemed to be crazy for dancing. We have already noted the above average provision of dancing facilities in the city, a sign of its popularity. Moreover, Glasgow dancers were extremely keen. In 1935, for example, the *Dancing Times* noted: 'One only has to be in Glasgow for a few hours to realize that in the second city of the Empire the enthusiasm for dancing has reached a high pitch.'[121] Dancing standards were encouraged by regular local dance competitions, one of the most popular being the *Daily Record* and Glasgow *Evening News* 'Scottish Professional and Amateur Championships' which were started in 1924. The West of Scotland Championships also started that year, with standards described as 'excellent' by the dancing press.[122] Glasgow was still considered to be the home of Britain's best dancers after the war too. In 1948 Alex Warren claimed: 'it is my conviction that Glasgow is without doubt the most dance-minded city in Great Britain.'[123] He pointed to the fact that all major dance championships in Scotland were held there, that the city had produced the vast majority of amateur and professional champions in Scotland, and some of the best in Britain.

Geography also played a further role in the creation of distinctive dance cultures. Whilst the four standard dances were popular throughout Britain, there were differences in the popularity of particular dances in different parts of the country. *Dancing Times* regularly surveyed the managers of leading dance halls throughout the country asking which dances were most popular in their halls. One such survey published in October 1934 reveals the variety in popularity of the main dances. A total of twenty-one dance halls were surveyed, in Aberdeen, Birmingham, Blackpool, Brighton, Edinburgh, Glasgow, Liverpool, London, Manchester, Newcastle, and Nottingham. They were asked to rank the five key 'modern dances' (including the rumba which was in vogue that year) in order of popularity. Nationally, the order of popularity was the foxtrot first, the waltz second, quickstep

[118] *DT*, August 1928, 496. [119] *DT*, November 1928, 300. [120] *DT*, April 1930, 25.
[121] *DT*, April 1935, 36. [122] *DT*, February 1929, 640.
[123] *Ballroom Dancing Annual 1948*, 61.

third, and then quite a way behind, the rumba and tango in fourth and fifth place. When we disaggregate these results we can note some important regional differences. London's tastes were different than those of the rest of the country. In the eight halls surveyed there, the foxtrot was favourite, followed by the quickstep, the waltz third, the tango fourth, and rumba fifth. In Scotland and the Midlands/North of England, however, the Waltz was more popular. In the eight Midlands/Northern Halls the foxtrot was most popular with the waltz very close behind, and the quickstep third. In the four Scottish halls surveyed, the waltz was even more popular, with the foxtrot and waltz both joint favourite, with the quickstep in third place. In England outside of London the tango was more popular than the rumba, and in Scotland the rumba was more popular than the tango.[124] So whilst it is true that the standard dances established themselves and were popular throughout Britain, their relative popularity varied according to where one was.

This variation continued to be present after the war. Indeed, in the post-war period there was an increasing diversification of Britain's dance culture. In August 1947 *Dancing Times* conducted another survey of the popularity of certain dances in Britain's main dance halls. This time it found that the nation's most popular dance was the quickstep, followed by the waltz and then the foxtrot. The tango was barely mentioned. Interestingly, the pre-war north–south divide over the waltz seemed to have reversed. In London and Surrey, the waltz was named most popular dance in 60 per cent of the halls, yet in the Midlands, North, and Scotland it was only most popular in 22 per cent of halls. The quickstep was favoured in 88 per cent of halls outside London and Surrey, and in only 20 per cent of halls in London and Surrey. As for Jive and Old Time, Old Time was catered for in just over 50 per cent of the halls surveyed, mostly for a keen but minority audience and Jive was played for a different but similar crowd in exactly 50 per cent of the halls.[125] Further evidence of increased diversification can be found by increasing hall and night-specific specialization in certain dances. In December 1947 in Liverpool, for example, some halls decided to specialize in particular dance styles. The Rialto, Marmaduke, and Burton Chambers Ballrooms, for example, all devoted themselves to Old Time, whilst the Grafton and the Marionette Ballroom, in Lime Street, favoured Jive. Elsewhere in the city, managements hedged their bets, dividing time equally between the two: 'Neither side has yet made up its mind who is winning, but when I questioned some of the promoters they all admitted it was a question of £ s d.'[126]

There were some other subtle differences in this 'standard' programme of dancing too. Each band playing the main dances played them slightly differently. Despite the efforts of the dance teachers to standardize, the tempo at which the so-called standard dances were played also varied according to both venue and geographical area. In London for example, a 1934 survey revealed that the foxtrot was played at anything from 32 to 38 bars per minute, the quickstep from 48 to 58,

[124] Calculated from *DT*, October 1934, 41–53.
[125] Calculated from *DT*, October 1947, 588–90.
[126] *Danceland*, December 1947, 16.

the tango from 28 to 32, and the waltz at 34 to 36.[127] It would appear that even within the same dance hall, different skilled dancers demanded different tempos, and many were influenced by the dance music they heard on the radio and on gramophone records. This led them to demand different speeds than those played by the average palais band. As the manager of a Hull dance hall stated: 'All our foxtrots are played at 48 bars per minute, and this speed is favoured by the majority of my patrons. One or two who are particularly keen would like me to drop to about 44–46, but this would not be an easy tempo for the ordinary dancer here.' He went on: 'My personal opinion is that the variance of opinion on tempo amongst the dancing public is entirely due to the bad example set by the big show bands who play dance numbers at speeds entirely unsuited to dancing, for the purpose of obtaining special effects.'[128] Complaints about the variation in the tempo of supposedly 'standard dances' were still being made in the post-war period. In 1946, for example, it was reported that in Manchester 'band leaders have been called to account by floor managers who have been spurred to make protests by the complaints of the patrons of the hall'. It was argued: 'No dancer who knows his tempo appreciates the antics of a band who sacrifice timing in order to present some of the weird and wonderful arrangements which are being perpetrated in the name of "swing."'[129]

Different approaches to and styles of dancing up and down the country were also noted. In 1925, for example it was observed 'Londoners . . . have a style all their own. Their dancing is smooth, dignified and graceful, their steps easy and effortless. It is a style also that allows the dancer to express his own individuality.'[130] Such differences in the way the same dances were danced in different parts of the country were also in evidence beyond this. In 1942 the President of the National Association of Teachers of Dancing, Bob Garganico, noted the divide between the north of England and London when it came to performing the standard dances.[131] For the waltz, Garganico argued that the key difference was speed, the northerners preferring a much slower tempo than in London. Similarly, for the foxtrot, the north preferred a slower tempo too. In addition, Garganico noted that northern dancers were more apt to add in numerous 'variations' in contrast to those in London who preferred a simpler style of foxtrot. With the tango, again, there were more variations in the north and dancers there performed it with more vivacity. As he put it: '[M]y goodness! They certainly capture the atmosphere of this rhythm, and dance with far more expression than the southerners . . . Northerners have a flair for expressing their movement and seem to live their dances.' In contrast, he noted, approvingly, that the quickstep tended to be danced more 'sanely' in the north, without the 'dancebatics' frequently found in London.

In addition to these differences, it should be noted that individuals would dance dances differently too. As one dance teacher admitted in 1928: 'you cannot control

127 *Danceland*, December 1947, 16.

128 *DT*, November 1927, 154.

129 *Danceland*, December 1946, 5.

130 *PMDW*, 7 March 1925, 132.

131 *DT*, May 1942, 408.

people's dance steps any more than you can control dress fashions'. They continued: 'half the charm of modern dancing would disappear if individual expression were eliminated and no control board could *force* the dancing public to dance only its recognised steps.'[132] One of the most significant features of dancing was that the dancer had the ultimate sanction as to the exact execution of dance steps, rhythm, poise, and tempo in any given dance once on the dancefloor. Clearly, most dancers would not try to dance waltz steps to the music of a foxtrot, nor could they get away with creating completely novel steps without meeting the condemnation of their fellow dancers. However, there was still room for individual expression (one of the key attractions of the new social dances when they first arrived), and no number of decrees from dancing professionals could eliminate this. Some dance teachers even chose to encourage it. E. Scott Atkinson, a professional dance champion advised in 1927:

> Don't be a dancing robot with 'mechanised' movements. Be a human being and express something of yourself when you dance. You can maintain the rhythm and you can perform the recognised steps, but you can still put something into the dance that will make it distinctive of you.[133]

It is likely that some dancers did indeed adopt this attitude, creating their own flourishes and embellishments, and even creating distinctive 'dancing personalities' for themselves. In addition, throughout the 1920s and 1930s, dozens of 'variations' were added to the standardized dances thus creating a large number of different ways to dance the same steps. Variations were little side steps or moves that were devised by dance teachers or dancers in order to add a little originality and individuality to their dancing. This process was total counter to the standardizing process which the development of the English style represented. However, not only did their introduction water down the standardization process, variations themselves were the cause of controversy amongst dance teachers. A split emerged between London and the rest of the country on this matter. Leading London dance teachers were particularly keen on introducing these steps regularly, as they could be profitable—they charged large amounts to teach dance teachers the new variations and these were then passed on to dancers. Dance teachers in the rest of Britain were very keen to keep up to date with the latest steps, but many resented what they saw as fashion for fashion's sake. Responding to a Victor Silvester article promoting 'variations' in 1927, one 'provincial' dance teacher complained: 'are the leading London dance teachers aware of the confusion and controversy they have caused by introducing so many new variations before the public have really properly seen the original . . . ?'[134]

The limits of the dancing profession over the dancing public were shown in its failure to get them to dance particular dances which it promoted and in their failure to quell the public's appetite for dances which it condemned, most notably the Charleston, Jive, and Jitterbug.

[132] *DT*, May 1928, 143. [133] *DT*, May 1927, 153.
[134] *DT*, December 1927, 324.

As we have seen, the dance profession was largely successful in promoting what it considered to be the 'standard modern dances' that came to dominate the dance floors of Britain during the 1920—the foxtrot, waltz, and quickstep. However, there was one notable exception—the tango. This had enjoyed a brief craze in Britain in 1912–13, and the leading dance professionals wanted to see it revived in the post-war period. Indeed, the tango was one of the first three dances whose steps were standardized as a result of the first informal conferences of teachers of ballroom dancing of 1920, and promoted by them as one of the key planks of the dance programme. So keen were the profession to get people dancing it, that at the third conference in 1921 it was suggested that 'bands be encouraged to play occasionally a short Tango as an encore to a foxtrot so as to catch the dancers whilst they are on the floor'.[135] Huge efforts were made to promote the dance. In May 1922 the *Dancing Times* organized an informal Tango Conference at the Grafton Galleries, where hundreds of dance teachers came together to try and establish new tango steps, with a Tango Ball held that year and the next. Moreover, a fourth conference, in October 1924, was devoted entirely to the tango, and attended by nearly 300 dance teachers and musicians. Here a 'new tango' was outlined, with a tempo of 30 bars to the minute, and it was agreed to anglicize the names of its component steps. But the conference came to no agreement about the whether it should adopt the old or new tango. Despite this, it was clear that enthusiasm for the tango was widespread amongst professional dance teachers. Throughout the 1920s the dance teachers continued to plug the tango at every opportunity. However, that is was suggesting methods of 'sneaking in' tangos to dance programmes as early as the 1921 conference indicates that it was aware of resistance from the dancing public to this dance. Indeed, the tango never took off with the majority of the British dancing public. Despite repeated attempts to make it one of the key dances, it never joined the ranks of the 'standard modern dances' as danced in popular ballrooms. Dance teachers resolutely continued to try and teach its steps. Dance bands continued to feature it in their programmes, and dance hall managers tried to encourage it with competitions. Yet the dancing public remained immune to these efforts. As the *Manchester Guardian* observed in 1925: 'During the last few years so many efforts have been made to force this shy creature into prominence, none of them with success, that public interest has degenerated into indifference.'[136] Why? Some dance teachers blamed dance musicians—the very poor rendering of tangos and the lack of enthusiasm for featuring tangos amongst British dance bands was seen as a reason for its failure. The idea that the dance was not to suited to the English temperament was another reason given.[137] In 1922, for example, W. De Moray, in charge of dancing at the Savoy Hotel, pointed to the difference in temperament between the 'more reserved and unemotional Englishman' and 'volatile' Frenchman, the French having taken to the tango much more willingly than in England. He continued:

[135] *DT*, December 1929, 302. [136] *Manchester Guardian*, 2 October 1925, 8.
[137] *DT*, February 1938, 61.

> The Englishman dances to please himself and has no eye for the admiration of the gallery. The tango lends itself to display, and for that reason the Englishman remains a 'wallflower' while the Frenchman takes the floor in pleasurable anticipation of admiring eyes.[138]

There was probably some truth in his observations. Whatever the reason, the failure of the tango demonstrates that dancers had to be willing partners in the development of dancing programmes; they could not be persuaded to dance dances, for a sustained period, which they did not take to their hearts.

Not only could the dancing public not be made to like certain dances against its will, it could not easily be dissuaded from dancing dances which it loved, but which were condemned by the experts. Further evidence of the limited power of the dance profession over the dancing public comes from their handling of Charleston, Jitterbug, and Jive. As we have already seen, keen to maintain the respectability of their profession, the dance industry strove to distance themselves from the Charleston and there was also a sustained press campaign against it. Despite all of this pressure, the dancing public refused to give up their obsession for the Charleston. As the *Melody Maker* reported in August 1926, 'Those dance halls foolish enough to have this dance banned are having their bans openly defied.'[139] Indeed, in November 1926, dancers at a dance hall in Stoke Newington, north London felt so strongly that they had even knocked the MC unconscious after his fifth attempt to stop them dancing the Charleston.[140] Dancers jumped to defend the dance. In February 1927, for example, Rev J. L. White, Vicar of Nuneaton, had banned the Charleston from his parish church dances on the grounds that 'they would get all the riff raff of the cheap halls of the town' if it were danced there. Local dancers objected strongly, saying that the Charleston was a 'perfectly legitimate dance which is popular with all classes of people'.[141] Moreover, they resisted the attempts to stop them dancing the dance. As one local newspaper reported: 'Attempts to restrain people from "Charlestoning" at a dance . . . during the weekend were unsuccessful, dancers ignoring the MC's requests to desist. In the end the dancers had their own way . . . '[142]

The same disregard for the proclamations of dance hall managers and dance teachers can be seen in the response of some dancers to the Jitterbug. In 1943, for example, the *Derby Evening Telegraph* reported: 'Despite notices posted at the Plaza Ballroom, Derby, and announcements made in the ballroom itself forbidding jitterbugging . . . visitors persist in performing the banned steps.'[143] The Jive was to prove even more resilient to the periodic bans and condemnations it faced, as dancers refused to give it up. Moreover, the transformation of this dance was regarded by some as something which had come from below rather than above. In Liverpool, for example, it was claimed that the dancers themselves had tamed the Jive, with one local dancer stating in 1945: 'Here we still enjoy it—and have tamed

[138] *The Times*, 29 March 1922, 5. [139] *Melody Maker*, August 1926, 7.
[140] *Manchester Guardian*, 14 November 1926, 19.
[141] *Sunday Sun*, 13 February 1927, 6. [142] *Tamworth Herald*, 19 February 1927, 3.
[143] *Derby Evening Telegraph*, 22 October 1943, 4.

it! But the taming has really been done by the dancers themselves rather than managerial repression.'[144]

CONCLUSION

Britain's dance culture was characterized by its diversity as much as its uniformity, and the idea that the twentieth century saw certain key dances such as the Charleston and the Jitterbug sweep all before them and transform ballrooms, is too simplistic. Whilst these dances were momentarily popular, beneath the headlines were a range of overlapping dance styles drawing from an increasingly common cultural stock, but performed in a variety of ways.

[144] *Danceland*, December 1945, 8.

PART II

DANCING AND BRITISH SOCIETY, 1918–60

Chapter 5

Youth and the Dance Hall, 1918–60

INTRODUCTION

Having examined the development of a mass audience for dancing and the dance culture associated with it, this section will now examine the impact of the dance hall on British society. We start with an examination of youth. In recent years, the idea that youth culture was invented with the arrival of the 'teenager' in the period after 1945 has been challenged. Historians such as David Fowler and Bill Osgerby have argued that the origins of a distinctive youth culture can be traced back as far as the late Victorian period and that by the 1920s and 1930s young people were the major beneficiaries of changing leisure patterns.[1] The evidence from the dance hall confirms this. As the following chapter will show, by the interwar period, youths were amongst the most prolific of dancers and via dance halls they were starting to shape a distinctive dance culture of their own. This relationship between dancing and youth was maintained and developed in the following decades. Indeed, dancing and dance halls became key features in the development and social life of young people in Britain during the twentieth century.

DANCING'S POPULARITY AMONGST THE YOUNG, 1918–60

We have already noted that the young were the most prolific dancers.[2] Let's examine their attachment to dancing in more detail, starting with an examination of the period 1918–39. When did young people start to dance? This depended on gender. Most girls started dancing before they left school, from the age of twelve or thirteen onwards, but quite often even younger than this. Boys usually started to dance later, at about fifteen or sixteen. Explanations for these different starting ages are fairly straightforward. Boys had greater alternative physical activities available to them than girls and there was also social stigma attached to dancing amongst

[1] See D. Fowler, *The First Teenagers* (London: Woburn Press, 1995) and *Youth Culture in Modern Britain c1920–c1970* (Basingstoke: Palgrave Macmillan, 2008) and B. Osgerby, 'From the Roaring Twenties to the Swinging Sixties: Continuity and Change in British Youth Culture 1929–1959' in B. Brivati and H. Jones (eds), *What Difference Did the War Make?* (Leicester: Leicester University Press, 1995).

[2] See Chapters 1, 2, and 3.

younger boys, who thought it was somewhat 'sissy'. Once started however, dancing rapidly became habitual and developed into a 'craze' amongst the young of both sexes. This intense phase usually started in the late teens, lasting only a few years until marriage or work commitments reduced the opportunities for dancing. There is evidence, too, of the dance halls deliberately targeting this group, a sign of their significance. Carl Heimann, the co-director of the Mecca chain of dance halls, was shrewd enough to see the potential of the youth market and the changes he brought to dancing, including the introduction of 'group' dances such as the Lambeth Walk, were made to appeal directly to their sense of fun. He advised others in the dance hall business to 'Encourage the patronage of young people'[3] and in some of his dance halls, Heimann employed very young managers in order to keep abreast of the demands of youth. For example, at the Paramount Tottenham Court Road, a hall specializing in the latest dance styles, in 1939 the assistant manager was only 18 years old and the manager was only 30.[4]

One reason that the surveys found so many young people attending dances was that although their leisure time was limited, it was relatively greater than the time available to adults. In 1939, it was found that those young people of working age (14–21) in Hulme, Manchester, had between four and five hours of leisure time each weekday evening, with half a day on Saturday and all of Sunday free. Tom Harrisson's survey of Bolton dance halls identified and analysed the impact on the community of these young dancing enthusiasts:

> In a typical room in a cotton mill, fifteen of the forty two female workers were dance-hall regulars, all the ones under twenty-five. In churches, pubs, political organizations and all other groups with social and co-operative interests, young people are to-day conspicuously absent in Worktown; the elder folk continuously complain about it. In six main dance-halls on Saturday evening there are nearly as many young men as on Sunday evening in all the town's 170 churches.[5]

Harrisson concluded that although the dance halls played a vital part in the life of all of Bolton's 180,000 inhabitants, their greatest significance was confined to unmarried youths of both sexes.

Importantly, economic factors meant that many youths were in a better position than many other sections of society too. Even though we have seen it suggested in earlier chapters that attendance might have been even greater with additional income, David Fowler highlights how demographic and economic developments in interwar Britain had given some young wage earners an unprecedented degree of independence and influence.[6] Whilst youth unemployment, averaging 10 per cent for the period, was a serious problem, Fowler argues that those in employment had considerable bargaining power due to a shortage of juvenile labour and its relative

[3] Heimann, 'Dancing after the War', in Anon., *Stepping Out* (London: Danceland Publications, 1940), 54.

[4] M-O A: TC: MJD, 38/1/B, 'Paramount AH', 20 March 1939, 15.

[5] T. Harrisson, 'Whistle While You Work' (1938) (Winter) *New Writing* 50.

[6] D. Fowler, *The First Teenagers: The lifestyle of young wage-earners in Interwar Britain* (1995), Table 1.1, 172.

cheapness compared with adult labour. The teenage wage-earner was thus in an advantageous economic position, being less likely to experience poverty than at any other stage in his or her life.[7]

Several contemporary social surveys indicate that the level of disposable income available to young wage earners was high. Although it was common for the majority of younger wage earners to hand their whole wage packet over to the family and receive a set amount of pocket money each week, Rowntree found that this practice stopped after the age of 16. At 16 the young workers would pay sufficient to cover 'board and lodgings' and retain an average of 50 per cent of their own wage packet, sometimes a higher proportion, the amount increasing with age. This gave them a degree of economic freedom that few young people previously, or their elders at that time, could enjoy. The young then were amongst the major beneficiaries of the expansion of leisure facilities and opportunities in the interwar period.

During the war, the young continued to hold their position as some of the most frequent attendees at dance halls. As a 1943 Carnegie Report found: 'Many young men pass through a phase which has often been described by their parents and friends, and sometimes even by themselves, as "dancing mad."'[8] Indeed, that same year, a report of the Youth Advisory Council appointed by the Board of Education, found that dancing was the second most popular leisure activity amongst youths, behind only the cinema.[9] As we have seen in Chapter 2, however, there were two notable developments in attendance patterns for the young during the war that mark it out as different from the interwar period. First, young dancers' dominance of the dance hall actually seemed to increase during the war, at least in the perception of contemporary observers. For example, early in the war, in 1940, a local newspaper argued that 'young Sheffield' had gone 'crazy dancing'. It explained:

> Sheffield is starting dancing young, and many more 16 year olds are going to public dances than ever before . . . Many of the married and middle aged people are engaged in war work of one kind or another, or have decided to give up dancing 'for the duration,' but the youngsters are living for the day, and for them the day starts round about half past seven, when they get on to the dance floor.[10]

In 1941 Frank Spencer writing in the *Dancing Times* noted the same trend: 'One cannot help noticing that our ballrooms are now invaded by a preponderance of very young people, girls and boys in their teens who are earning more money, enjoying more freedom and growing up very suddenly.'[11] Indeed, the second key change in attendance patterns during the war was a tendency to attend at ever younger ages. In some city ballrooms large numbers of under-14-year-olds, especially girls, were trying to gain entrance to dances. Such was the pressure that in one or two places notices asking such children to be accompanied by an adult had to be

[7] Fowler, *The First Teenagers*, 94–5.

[8] C. Cameron, A. J. Lush, and G. Meara (eds), *Disinherited Youth* (Edinburgh: Carnegie United Kingdom Trust, 1943), 105.

[9] *DT*, December 1943, 98.

[10] *The Star*, 31 July 1940, 3.

[11] *DT*, December 1941, 153.

exhibited.[12] Similarly, in Durham, in March 1945, children under 16 were banned from attending public dances following a decision of the local magistrates.[13]

We should consider which factors affected youth attendance at dance halls during the war. As we have seen, the war presented considerable challenges to the dance industry, and wartime circumstances might easily have reduced the popularity of dancing among the young. As might be expected, in the face of heightened dangers, parental concern about their children was increased, and this acted as a restriction on the ability of young people to attend dances. As one wartime teenager recalled: 'Naturally, my parents dreaded hearing me say that I was going out any evening; they were so worried for me. An air raid could start at any time, anywhere, so each day was lived precariously.'[14]

Yet, as we have also seen, the Blitz acted in several ways on leisure patterns: for some sections of the population there was a tendency to retreat indoors at night, avoiding outdoor leisure pursuits, whilst for others it encouraged a 'live for today' attitude. Young dancers tended to fit into the latter group and Home Intelligence and Mass Observation both noted the greater resilience of young people in the face of the disruptions of the Blitz. Talking of capacity filled dances in 1943, the manager of the dances at the Opera House Covent Garden concluded: 'The dancing public is a young public—and you can't frighten them.'[15] Determined not to miss out on their youth, the war encouraged many young people to live for the moment. As one wartime teenager from Stockton-on-Tees commented: 'The lights, the music and the company let you forget the misery, austerity and danger of war for a few short hours. You could live your dreams in a make-believe world on a par with a Hollywood film.'[16] Dances thus became even more attractive because they offered youths release from the pressures of war.

In addition, as before the war, financial considerations were important in determining whether youths could go dancing. During the war, the affluence of young workers grew, in line with the general economic improvements of most working-class people. Full employment and longer working hours meant that young people were better off than ever before, yet there were fewer things to spend money on. As the government's wartime social survey noted, the young were most likely to spend their increased income on leisure activities, particularly commercialized leisure activities such as the dance hall. With more money in their pockets, yet fewer alternatives on which to spend them, young people's spending on dancing increased to unprecedented levels.

Once the war was over, as we have seen, there was a boom in the popularity of dancing, as pent-up demand and renewed opportunity led to a surge in the numbers dancing. The particular appeal of dancing to youths was retained in this early post-war boom. In 1947, for example, Mass Observation noted:

[12] *Danceland*, November 1944, 5. [13] *Danceland*, April 1945, 1.
[14] PWA, Patricia McGowan, Article A2869770, 27 July 2004.
[15] *DM*, 15 November 1943, 2.
[16] PWA, Frank Mee, Article A2553761, 23 April 2004.

> The large dance-halls which exist today in most sizeable towns and cities draw a very high proportion of their clientele from youth. In many cases it is the exception to see a middle aged couple, and often only a very small minority are over the age of about twenty five. Organised large scale dance hall dancing is particularly a youth, and often an almost entirely youth, activity.[17]

This conclusion was supported by numerous other surveys of the time. A 1946 survey of 6,000 teenage girls by the National Association of Girls' Clubs, for example, found that dancing was their favourite hobby, more popular even than cinema.[18] A Musicians' Union survey of music and dancing habits in London carried out for borough councils in the Greater London Area in 1947 also confirmed that the popularity of dancing declined as age rose. Among those under 30, nearly two in three stated that they had been to a dance in the last three months, in the 30–49 age group one in three had been to a dance, but only a very small minority, 8 per cent, of people over 50 had been to dances.[19] The following year, Mass Observation found a similar pattern in its survey of work and leisure habits throughout Britain. It found that dancing was four times as popular with the under-25s as with the over-25s, with 24 per cent as opposed to 6 per cent mentioning it as a regular activity. For those over 45, Mass Observation noted that there was 'practically no interest in dancing'.[20]

The same was true during the 1950s. The University of Birmingham's 1953 study of *Living in Towns* found that for the people of Coseley in the West Midlands, dancing was 'exclusive to' the young, with adult males preferring the pub and the cinema respectively.[21] John Barron Mays' 1954 study of a poor district of Liverpool commented that it was 'the younger folk' who went to the large commercial dance halls and the 'frequent' smaller dances and socials organized in church halls and clubs in the area, naming dancing as the most popular pastime amongst adolescent girls.[22] Similarly a 1956 study of the Yorkshire mining community of Ashton, found that it was those aged 15 to 22 that packed the weekly Saturday dance at the Miners' Welfare Institute, with the 'great majority' of them being between the ages of 17 and 20.[23] The study noted that in 1951 the total Ashton population of those aged 15–22 was 716, yet the Saturday dance regularly attracted 400–500—a very high proportion of local youngsters very clearly loved to dance.[24]

17 M-O A, FR2473, *Report on Juvenile Delinquency* (1947), 47.
18 *DM*, 15 October 1946, 2.
19 Music Development Committee, Musicians' Union, *Music and the Borough Councillor: A Report addressed to Borough Councillors in the Greater London Area* (1947), 19.
20 M-O A, FR3067, Work and Leisure, (1948), 11–12.
21 L. Kuper (ed), *Living in Towns. Selected Research Papers in Urban Sociology of the Faculty of Commerce and Social Science, University of Birmingham* (London: Cresset Press, 1953), 358.
22 J. Barron Mays, *Growing up in the City: A Study of Juvenile Delinquency in an Urban Neighbourhood* (Liverpool: Liverpool University Press, 1954), 71.
23 Dennis, F. Henriques, C. Slaughter, *Coal is Our Life: An analysis of a Yorkshire mining community* (London: Eyre & Spottiswoode, 1956), 125.
24 Dennis, Henriques, and Slaughter, *Coal*, 126.

As previously, part of the popularity of dancing amongst young people can be put down to their relative and growing affluence. As John Barron May commented in his 1954 study of Liverpool adolescents: 'Leisure is no good without money . . . Money confers status . . . Money brings friends and allows a boy to mix more freely in social life, to go to dances and meet girls and treat his friends.'[25] Even at the beginning of the post-war period, youths remained amongst the most privileged workers in terms of time and money available to them. In 1948, Mass Observation calculated that most people worked between 41 and 44 hours weekly, with people aged 25–44 having the longest working week—25 per cent of people in that age group working more than 48 hours per week, compared to only 8 per cent of those under 25 and 19 per cent of those over 45.[26] By 1950, a survey of over 80,000 adolescents in Birmingham found that the average amount of pocket money for 16-year-olds was 11 shillings a week; at the age of 19 boys were averaging 38 shillings a week spending money and girls 26s 10d.[27] Wages also grew considerably. The Albemarle Report found that in 1938 males aged 15–20 earned 26s 0d a week on average, this had risen to £5 12s 0d a week on average by 1958.[28]

There were still clear differences in popularity between boys and girls, however. In 1950 the Edward Cadbury Charitable Trust surveyed 500 teenage boys and 504 teenage girls as part of their investigation of youth leisure activities in Birmingham. Amongst boys, it found that nearly 60 per cent enjoyed dancing—with just under a third (32 per cent) going dancing at least once a week (including nearly 11 per cent who went more than once a week), 4 per cent who went once a month, and 23.4 per cent who went occasionally. Amongst girls, it found that over 75 per cent enjoyed dancing—with 38.5 per cent going dancing at least once a week (including 17.5 per cent who went more than once a week), just over 3 per cent who went once a month, and 34 per cent who went occasionally.[29]

DANCING AND TRANSITIONS TO ADULTHOOD

'Dances' allowed young people their first taste of independence, where they could learn to socialize with their peer group and be introduced to the codes of behaviour expected of their sex. Dances also gave young people familiarity with the opposite sex, offering a controlled environment in which to observe and interact with them. Indeed, it was at dances that most young people had their first experience of finding 'dates' and 'dating'. In addition, dances often introduced young people to the 'adult' pleasures of drinking and smoking. Let's look at these important roles in three periods, interwar, wartime, and post-war, starting with the interwar period.

[25] Barron Mays, *Growing up*, 99–100.

[26] M-O A: FR3067, Work and Leisure, (1948), 2.

[27] B. H. Reed, *Eighty Thousand Adolescent. A study of young people in the city of Birmingham, by the staff and students of Westhill Training College, for the Edward Cadbury Charitable Trust* (London: George Allen and Unwin Ltd, 1950), 38.

[28] Albemarle Report, *Youth Service in England and Wales*, HMSO, 1960, 23.

[29] Reed, *Eighty Thousand*, 28–9.

Dancing and going to dance halls were social skills and practices that were a key element in the transition from childhood to adulthood for working-class youths of both sexes in interwar Britain. As Tom Harrisson noted in 1938:

> It is now an essential part of any youth's social equipment, that he or she be able to go through two variations of these movements (waltz and fox-trot) with sufficient grace to avoid treading on a partner's toe. When you leave school you learn to work, to smoke, to bet and to dance.[30]

Initially, virtually all young people attended dances in groups of their peers and for the youngest, attendance in mixed sex groups was rare. Groups were made up of school friends, groups of workers from the same mill or factory, and sometimes mixed with family members and those of different ages. Most people learning to dance in the 1920s and 1930s first went to dances in school rooms, church halls, assembly rooms and so on, held close to where they lived. These venues offered the opportunity to perfect dancing skills and learn social skills. Some smaller suburban dance halls also opened up in the daytime to provide young learners with practice time. As George Taylor, a teenager when dancing in Dundee in the 1920s recollects: 'Nearly all the [suburban] halls were open every Saturday afternoon to prepare first steppers before going to the larger halls. Each district in Dundee and Lochee were open from 2pm until 4pm.'[31]

Sometimes attendance at dances would not involve any dancing on the part of the youngest. For example, Mary O'Neill, who was 13 in 1933, recalled: 'Occasionally older girls would go to the Masonic Ballroom and I would go with my friends when I was 13 or 14 to just watch them go in wearing their satin dresses and we would love to see them.'[32] Familiarity with the etiquette and atmosphere of dances could be gained in such a way. Significantly, trips to dances allowed younger boys and girls to learn from their peers and elders. Often dance steps would be picked up from friends or work mates and social groups of friends would be formed easily. Liverpool dancer Jane Campbell (b. 1922), who had been taught by her older brother, recalls 'I was quite good at dancing . . . when I was working like . . . and the girls I went out with, we'd all arrange that we'd go to such and such a dance and I could always take them and teach them what my brother was teaching me, I was showing them . . . '[33]

In addition to picking up dancing skills, trips to dances gave young people an important arena in which to socialize more generally. As Mass Observation noted in 1938: 'The dance hall is used as a centre where the patron can discuss his personal affairs with friends; or where he can make new friends.'[34] Indeed, the importance of dances as meeting places for social interaction amongst young people is shown by the large numbers not dancing. In most dance venues frequented by the young a large proportion of those present were chatting, joking, and laughing, rather than

30 Harrisson, 'Whistle While You Work', 50.
31 Taylor, *Round*, 1.
32 GDHI, Mary O'Neill, b. 1920, 8 June 2011.
33 LDHI, Jane Campbell, b. 1922, 23 June 2009.
34 M-O A: TC: Worktown, 48/C, 'Shall We Dance?', *c* 1938, 7.

actually dancing. As Mass Observation noted of a dance in a church hall in Bolton in 1937: 'A great deal of floor space was obviously wasted by the crowding forward of non dancers towards the middle of the hall . . . Only about half the people were dancing. There were people sitting around, courting couples and the crowd who obstructed the other people who were not dancing.'[35] Groups of same sex friends watching the dancing, commenting and gossiping about the personalities present, were a key part of the experience.

Dancing also provided a clear structure for progressing from one age group to another. In larger towns and cities, growing up was accompanied by progression through a series of dance venues in a locality, moving from hall to hall, each one catering for a particular age group. In Dundee in the 1920s for example, there were thirty-one different halls for dancing, each appealing to youths at various stages of their dancing career.[36] A converted church on Lindsay Street, Kidd's Dancing Rooms, catered for the early teens: 'This was where the younger generation frequented . . . if you were eighteen years old here you were considered too old and had great difficulty getting a partner . . . you were "past it" at Kidd's at nearing nineteen.'[37] Moving on to the next hall could sometimes come as a shock: 'After months at the Blackie we decided it was time to move to the centre halls but we were not prepared for the shock of the big time. Dancing wasn't so easy as Birsie [the dance teacher] had made it out to be . . . the tempo was quick and moving round wasn't so easy . . . '[38]

As well as moving from place to place, as youngsters grew older they started to attend dances for reasons other than socialization with their friends. Meeting the opposite sex became important. Going to dances in groups meant that these early encounters with the opposite sex could take place in a supportive atmosphere. Groups of boys and girls standing or sitting together would give each other encouragement and offer advice on dating. A Liverpool teen of the 1930s remembers: 'we'd know so-and-so was going to be there and so-and-so was. So you knew someone was going to be there to sit with while you waited for someone to get you up for a dance.'[39] A Glasgow dancer argued that this gave her courage: 'we always went two or three of us together. I was worried to go at night. With fear we would go . . . '[40] Once they were older, some attended dances alone. Marjorie Hooley (b. 1917) from Liverpool recalls her first experiences of dancing at 14: 'I went with my sister and a couple of friends, cousin mostly. But then . . . when I got older, I used to just go on my own.'[41] That dating became the chief reason for attending dances amongst older teens is confirmed by a survey of middle-class adolescent boys taken in 1939. The most popular single reason given for going to dances was 'on account of female companionship' (24 per cent), the next stated reason being the dance steps (14 per cent), and the rhythm (14 per cent). Some comments from those

[35] M-O A: TC: Worktown, 48/C, 'Observations of Saturday Night', 3 April 1937, 2–3.
[36] Taylor, *Round*, 11. [37] Taylor, *Round*, 5. [38] Taylor, *Round*, 2.
[39] LDHI, Jane Campbell, b. 1922, 23 June 2009.
[40] GDHI, Mary O'Neill, b.1920, 8 June 2011.
[41] LDHI, Marjorie Hooley, b.1917, 23 June 2009.

surveyed: 'I go to dances to enjoy myself and to make friends with as many girls as possible. I seldom leave without at least one kiss'; 'I go to enjoy myself and to have a good time with various girl friends.'[42] Indeed, as we will see in Chapter 7 dances were to become a key venue for dating and they had many advantages over other locations for romantic liasons. Moreover, dancing accustomed the young to socializing with members of the opposite sex on more or less equal terms. This was a new development. The manager of the Empress Hall, Bolton noted how young people were more familiar with each other, less embarrassed to be around one another, especially in the 'learner halls', than in previous times: 'the young people who come here dancing nowadays are more real than they used to be. You take the young men here now, they are not afraid to cross the floor in between dances . . . it's because they get used to one another, they are all young folks from 15 and 16 to 25.'[43]

Altogether, dances allowed youths of both sexes a familiar, safe environment to progress from peer and mixed socializing to the first stages of dating and romance. As one Mass Observer put it in 1937: 'My impressions is that dancers are mostly adolescents, going to meet opposite sex, but quite innocently, young men waiting to get confidence by dancing with a lot of girls, perhaps wanting love, but very vaguely.'[44]

During the war, the key social functions of the dance hall for young people described earlier endured and dancing remained a key part of the transition from childhood to adulthood. Due to the pressures of wartime, however, the period saw an accelerated progression towards adulthood and the dance hall's chief social function for young people increasingly became that of a venue for finding a date. The period of same sex socialization became shorter and less important.

During the war, there were several important changes that increased the pace at which some young people sought to become 'adult'. Perhaps most importantly, conscription hastened childhood transitions. For men, this meant being conscripted into the army, or service in a reserved occupation or, later, as a 'Bevin Boy' in Britain's mines at 18. This usually brought dislocation from normal surroundings, removal from peer groups, and an absence of parental influence. The ever-present possibility of death also hung heavily over this generation of youths. Predictably, this accentuated the desire to have a good time. The manager of the Aspin Hall, one of Bolton's main dance halls, noted in 1940 the effect of the war on young men's attendance:

> [N]ow we have noticed that there are more boys than girls some nights, which is very unusual. Though a lot have been called up those left behind are having a damned good time before they go. It is making boys come out a bit sooner. When they have to be grown up at 20 to fight they might as well be grown up at 16 to enjoy themselves.[45]

[42] M-O A: Directive Reply: 'Jazz 2, July 1939', 'G. L. Wallace'.

[43] M-O A: TC: MJD, 38/5/F, 'Interview: Manager and Lessee of the "Empress Hall" XXXV', 15 July 1938, 3.

[44] M-O A: TC: Worktown, 57/D, 'Worktown Notes', 4 September 1937.

[45] M-O A: TC: Worktown, 48/D, 'Manager, Aspin Hall, Bolton, AH', 8 Jan 1940, 7.

So despite a general shortage of men in wartime dance halls, younger men seemed more likely to dance before they got called up.

Learning the skills of adulthood had to come quicker too. Dancing remained the ideal way of doing this and attending dances in same sex peer groups helped boys get over their initial shyness. As one wartime Liverpool youth recalls: 'I used to knock around with about five, six or seven people and you were in like a little group, so you'd go to the dancing and you'd be alright.'[46] Moreover, friends were there to initiate their mates into the rituals involved. As a wartime teenager from Stockton-on-Tees recalls:

> [T]hey took me aside and introduced me to the rules of going dancing. You must first get tanked up before asking girls to dance. You never go into the hall before the interval, it was unmanly. I then got a lecture on the various stratagems for getting a girl and dancing was only low on the list. They also told me I had to learn to smoke so I could offer girls a cigarette as an introduction.[47]

As before the war, dancing could offer young boys their first brushes with the opposite sex, a function confirmed by Pearl Jephcott, who wrote in 1943:

> Dancing is one of the recognised ways, particularly now that churchgoing has so declined, in which boys and girls expect to find their future partner. Magazines advise their readers that this is so. 'If you want a boy friend, learn to dance,' they say: and many mothers are perfectly willing to let their girls of fourteen and fifteen go off anywhere to dance.[48]

As before the war, dancing offered some of the first experiences of physical proximity with the opposite sex. Such encounters made a big impact on some of those concerned, as one Liverpool dancer recalls of his dancing lessons sixty-five years earlier aged 15:

> I used to go to this dance school—Campbell's—and he had this daughter that used to teach. She had the most enormous knockers! And of course, she used to get us up to teach, and when you put your hand on their shoulder they'd take you round the floor on a Waltz or Quickstep . . . she was a taller girl and her breasts were just opposite your eyes, you know! [laughs][49]

It was the promise of such proximity to girls, together with peer pressure, which acted as an incentive for many boys to start attending dances. A wartime Liverpool youth, for example, explained why he first took up dancing:

> I was fourteen . . . working at the docks and . . . we were going obviously, looking for girls, you know, and the best place to find the girls was the dance places.'[50]

For girls and young women, conscription also involved being uprooted from normal surroundings, and whilst the threat of death was not as great as with men, the war

[46] LDHI, Bert Smith, b. 1926, 23 June 2009.
[47] PWA, Frank Mee, Article A2553761, 23 April 2004.
[48] Jephcott, *Girls Growing Up*, p. 123.
[49] LDHI, George Cauldwell, b. 1929, 21 June 2009.
[50] Ibid.

brought about new dangers. Conscription of women was introduced in stages, with full conscription in 1943. This meant that the period between leaving school and doing war work became a golden age of freedom, and dancing's importance in the transition to adulthood was increased. As before the war, girls started to go dancing with their peers, in groups with their elder sisters, or friends. They did so earlier than boys. This mixing with slightly older girls offered role models and access to the adult world. Sometimes, eager to prove their adulthood, girls would try to 'jump ahead' and dance at venues usually reserved for those older than themselves, much to their parents consternation. A Liverpool dancer remembers:

> [M]y father used to make sure that I went to the right places at the right age. I remember sneaking into Reese's in school . . . And I saw my father and he went [gestures]. Oh, I'll never forget that . . . 'Don't you dare go into these places until you're old enough!' I was about fourteen . . . I went with school friends of course . . . thought we were being very big.[51]

For many young girls during the war, dancing and romance went hand in hand—they occupied an important place in teenage imaginations, imaginations often fired up by the conflict. A wartime Rotherham teenager commented:

> We were mad about uniforms. Even at fifteen, but not considered old enough for boyfriends, we would imagine ourselves dancing with some handsome military partner but had to make do 'bust to bust' with our girlfriends instead . . . Growing older I was allowed to attend dances at the Rotherham Town Hall . . . Tapping our feet and swaying to the rhythms we longed for and hoped some lovely airman would swing us into action on the dance floor. We . . . prepared to be carried away on cloud nine.[52]

Following the Second World War, and certainly by the later 1950s, 'youth' became a more distinctive and protracted life stage than in previous decades. Now, the transition to adulthood slowed and the dance hall's social functions subtly shifted to allow greater exploration of youth identity. The emergence of a more protracted period of youth manifested itself in several ways in the dance hall. First, young people were dancing for longer—now they continued to dance into their mid-twenties. Second, young people remained in same sex peer groups for longer, enjoying the company of their peers for its own sake, and allowing themselves to develop identities before pairing up for dating. Indeed, the dance hall's role as a place to explore identity was accentuated in the post-war world—as ritualistic aspects of display became more pronounced. Finally, the dance hall's role as a venue for making dates remained undiminished, but there was a return to the more leisurely dating patterns of the pre-war era, and an even greater emphasis on gaining dating experience with many partners rather than settling down straight away.

Turning first to the length of time young people spent dancing. Now girls could start dancing at 13 or 14 and continue into their mid- to late 20s. For boys too,

[51] LDHI, Bettina Silverstone, b. 1929, 22 July 2009.
[52] PWA, Audrey Lewis, Article A3346823, 30 November 2004.

dancing could take place for longer, starting at 15 or 16 and carrying on to a similar stage, the mid- to late 20s.

The dance hall had always been a space for young people to develop identity, but following the Second World War, it was more clearly used as a space for showing off and posing, as greater affluence allowed more young people to develop distinctive dress patterns and personal styles. Madeline Kerr's Liverpool study of 1958 found that even in the poorest areas, adolescents were increasingly concerned with their looks. In one family, debts of £16 had been incurred by the three sons, aged 16, 18, and 20 who were 'always buying new clothes'. Kerr commented: 'Adolescent boys become particularly interested in their hair and it is common to hear a young girl explain her attachment to a particular boy with the exclamation, "Ah, he has lovely wavy hair."'[53] She went on to observe: 'with this awakened interest in clothes and looks, it is not uncommon to hear an adolescent express a wish for a wardrobe.'[54] Moreover, she noted that dancing made teenage girls particularly concerned about matters of cleanliness:

> As soon as girls start going to public dances, great stress is placed upon cleanliness and personal hygiene. Two girls aged 16 used to visit us frequently on a Saturday night on their way to a dance-hall. They had both just had baths and washed and curled their hair. They had on clean underclothes and full skirts with elaborate blouses. They had washed their blouses the night before and had ironed them just before putting them on. Both girls work in factories. They had cleaned, manicured and painted their nails.[55]

The dance hall was a key venue for the public display of 'style' amongst teenagers. A 1947 report on juvenile delinquency, for example, highlighted how some youth came to the dance hall to 'pose', show off their clothes, and make their presence known:

> The single males coming in at the moment are of a slightly older age—eighteen, nineteen and twenty. They are dressed in the American film star style—zoot suits, with heavily padded shoulders and collar attached shirts with the large knotted tie, usually in a plain colour. They are in groups of three or four and keep together most of the time. They spend the majority of the time swaggering up and down the gangway between the rows of chairs and tables.[56]

As well as a place to show off, dancing's function as place for young people to gain experience with the opposite sex was vastly expanded after the war. However, there were some important shifts in the type and frequency of dates involved, depending on which part of the post-war period we are examining. In the period from the end of the war up until the early 1950s, the main focus of young people attending dances still remained finding dates for longer term relationships. Young people went to dances to find 'the one'. As Millicent Thorp (b. 1937) from Manchester recalled: 'We went out with a crowd of girls but hopefully found a boy to walk you

[53] M. Kerr, *The People of Ship Street* (London: Routledge, 1958/1998), 69.
[54] Kerr, *Ship Street*, 70. [55] Kerr, *Ship Street*, 71.
[56] M-O A, FR2473, *Report on Juvenile Delinquency* (1947), 50–1.

home from the dance. The boys would be eyeing up the girls and vice versa.'[57] Pat Spencer (b. 1933) agreed, remembering that 'we went there to catch a fella, really. You're not saying you're going to marry them, but you go there. That's how you meet them, girls and fellas.'[58] Boys often remained far shyer than girls when it came to dating. In one Southport dance hall in 1950 teenage girls asked the management to introduce more 'ladies invitation' dances because many of the boys were too scared to ask them to dance. Diana Miller, 18, complained: 'Occasionally a boy will scuttle across like a scared rabbit and, blushing all over, mumble something under his breath about dancing. But most of them huddle in a corner and just stare all the evening.'[59]

However, by the late 1950s, whilst dating remained the key reason for going to dance halls, the emphasis shifted to less serious dating. Dating itself became the focus rather than finding someone to settle down with. Youths thus began to acquire more experience with larger numbers of dates before settling down. The dance hall was particularly well suited for this rapid turnover of potential partners. As one 1956 study in Yorkshire observed, at a dance:

> the breaking of ties between individuals of opposite sex is facilitated. If the partners do not suit one another then the man simply does not ask for another dance, or the woman declines the invitation. The importance of this lies in the greater freedom it affords. Generally speaking, strangers will enter more readily into relations with each other if they feel that they are not committed to anything by doing so.[60]

Further evidence from Madeline Kerr's 1958 study of a Liverpool slum supported the view that dancing was allowing non-serious contacts to be made. It observed of girls: 'They go to dances with a friend of the same sex whom they call "mate" and then dance with any boy they meet at the dance hall who comes up and asks them to dance. They say they do not feel so tied to the same partner in this way.'[61] The evidence of this new sociability between the sexes is confirmed by the dancers themselves. As Kath Hogan (b. 1936) from Dundee stated: 'If you went to the Palais at that time you really got to know everyone, the boys and girls stood and chatted to one another and you really got to know everyone'[62] (see Fig. 5.1).

Dancing was used by some youths to allow them to playfully engage with the opposite sex, without thinking about serious dating. As Stewart Murray (b. 1940) from Glasgow recalls of the later 1950s:

> We used to play games. We used to say you'll have to ask the first girl who comes off the floor to dance, you'll have to ask the second girl to dance, no matter what they looked like . . . It was more an enjoyment, we didn't ridicule the girls or anything, we were just enjoying ourselves, have fun rather than going to meet a girl. At that

57 NWSA Oral History: 2001.0417, Millicent Thorp, b. 1937, Manchester, 2001.
58 LDHI, Pat Spencer, b. 1933, 21 July 2009.
59 *DM*, 21 September 1950, 7.
60 Dennis, Henriques, and Slaughter, *Coal*, 127.
61 Kerr, *Ship Street*, 32.
62 DDHI, Kath Hogan, b. 1936, 11 March 2011.

Fig. 5.1. Youth and dance: watching the dance, Lyceum Theatre, London, *Picture Post*, 1 July 1954
Source: Getty Images.

> stage we always went together, we never took girls home. It was just a night out for a bit of fun.[63]

He continued:

> We went in a group of 10 or 12 boys, we all got on well . . . you got to know all the girls that went there . . . you got to dance with the same girls every week . . . We used to chat about all the girls we had met when we were going home on the tram—this was when I was about 18 and we never had any serious girlfriends then, we went and came back together.[64]

Talking of the deep sense of solidarity which shared leisure time created between groups of youths in mining towns in Yorkshire in the 1950s, *Coal is Our Life* also

[63] GDHI, Stewart Murray, b. 1940, 19 July 2011. [64] Ibid.

noted how those aged 15 to 18 were not interested in serious dates. It quoted one youth, who stated 'I don't bother with girls. Sometimes I'll pick one up on Sunday, and never see her again.' It went on to comment 'At this stage youths will be anxious for any sexual experience... but... they are trying hard to be men; any display of tenderness or affection seems to be regarded as "soft."'[65]

Such innocent pleasure provided young people the opportunity to familiarize themselves with the opposite sex in a safe and usually well conducted environment. Although many of its detractors were to claim otherwise, dancing and the emerging youth culture of the 1950s were, on the whole, neither dangerous nor rebellious.[66] Neither did most young people want them to be. By 1956 one survey of cultural life in a Yorkshire mining town was able to talk approvingly of this aspect of dancing. 'The main function of these weekly dances,' it noted, 'appears to be that of bringing young people together in a manner which facilitates the approach of the two sexes. Judged in this light... it seems to be not inappropriate.'[67]

DANCING AND THE EMERGENCE OF YOUTH CULTURE, 1918–60

In addition to performing these social functions, dancing and dance halls were central to the emergence of a distinctive youth culture in the period from 1918 to 1960. Increasingly, they allowed youths to inhabit distinctive physical spaces from their elders and to adopt distinctive dances and dancing styles. Moreover, these functions of the dance hall did not just arrive with the supposed birth of the teenager after 1945. An embryonic youth culture was clearly discernable in the dance hall as early as the 1920s.

Following the First World War, their dominant presence in the dance halls was testimony to the emergence of newly prosperous and increasingly independent working-class youth. Importantly, these 'new' youths were shaping a distinctive culture of their own. Their increased leisure time and spending power were transforming the way in which youths chose to relax and find entertainment. Rowntree's York Survey, for example, pointed to a marked move away from the public house and 'hanging about on street corners' towards more 'ready-made' commercialized leisure forms, such as the cinema and dance hall. Teenagers were now willing, and for the most part able, to pay to be entertained. Indeed they were developing sophisticated tastes and making distinctive choices in the way in which they spent their leisure time. We can see the beginnings of a 'separate' youth culture emerging in the numerous age specific dance venues catering for young people that were common in most towns and cities throughout Britain by the 1920s. As we have seen, youths progressed from age-specific dance venue to age-specific dance venue as they grew up. This allowed them to develop a peer group identity that

[65] Dennis, Henriques, and Slaughter, *Coal*, 221–2.
[66] See Chapter 10 for a discussion of the 'problem' of young people dancing.
[67] Dennis, Henriques, and Slaughter, *Coal*, 126.

separated them from their elders. In the 1920s and 1930s there were a number of other ways in which dance halls were 'made their own' by the younger crowd too. One of the most significant was the 'adoption' of certain key dances along age lines. Throughout the interwar period, there were dances and music which, although available to all, were most popular with younger dancers. Most of these dances were ones that 'shook up' the established musical and dance styles and caused some kind of 'sensation'. Indeed, this was part of their appeal to youth. This established a pattern that was to survive into the wartime and post-war period.

One of the first dances that proved to be particularly popular amongst the young was the Charleston. Energetic and 'wild' this dance was well suited to young dancers (see Figure 5.2). Indeed, the Charleston was seen as symbolic of the new post-war generation by contemporaries. For example, in 1926 it was observed that the Charleston was 'essentially unsuitable for any but quite young people . . . only the very young were supple enough to accomplish the "waggle" which was considered to be *sine quo non*'.[68] In 1927 it was also noted that although 'all sorts and all ages' of people danced it, 'it is really the young peoples' dance'.[69] Via imagery and debates about 'Flappers' and the new woman, the Charleston became a symbol of a new, hedonistic generation intent on living their lives to the full in the 1920s. Although this image was exaggerated for numerous reasons, not least a sense of moral panic at the social change brought about by the war, it was a dance that many youths made their own. Even outside the ballroom, young people seemed addicted to the Charleston. In 1927 one press report observed that 'girls, shivering as they wait for the tram or 'bus, twist about their feet in the most ridiculous fashion . . . In the big offices of the city typists indulge in impromptu steps the moment their employer turns his back.'[70]

Perhaps equally significantly, in the later 1930s the appearance of a number of swing dances laid the foundations for the distinctive youth dance culture that was to emerge over the next twenty years. It could be argued that to a great extent, dance music and 'jazz' were the music of the younger generation during the 1930s. For example, Mass Observation in its 1939 panel survey of attitudes towards jazz and dancing distinguished a noticeable drop in enthusiasm for 'jazz' (by which it meant all modern dance music and popular songs) after the age of about 20–25, with 'jazz fanaticism' noticeable as a distinctive adolescent 'stage' that many went through.[71] As Tom Harrisson noted: 'Jazz has become or is becoming the religious ritual of post-war youth, and these songs of hope and happiness . . . are the hymns of young England.'[72] More significantly, in the 1930s, swing music and 'free form' dances such as 'Truckin'' found some of their most ardent supporters amongst the young. As we have seen, in the late 1930s 'Swing' brought a new energy to popular music and heralded the arrival of a new type of dancing in Britain's dance halls, the

[68] *Aberdeen Press and Journal*, 22 November 1926, 3.
[69] *Aberdeen Press and Journal*, 24 January 1927, 3.
[70] *Aberdeen Press and Journal*, 28 February 1927, 3.
[71] See M-O A: Directive Reply: 'Jazz (January 1939)'.
[72] Harrisson, 'Whistle While You Work', 66.

Fig. 5.2. Youth and dance: 'Modern Youth and Self-Expression in Dancing', W. K. Haselden, *Daily Mirror*, 2 January 1920

Source: © Mirrorpix.

first notable swing dance being Truckin'. Truckin' derived from 1920s Lindy Hop dances and was an interruption to normal dancing patterns. It was an expression of happiness and joy taking the form of a strut, where the shoulders would rise and fall as dancers moved towards one another, with fingers pointing up and wiggling back and forth like a windscreen wiper. There were several features of this dance style that made it particularly popular with youth. The formalized, standardized, controlled environment typified by the 'English style' was one that left little room for self-expression or for spontaneity in the ballroom. Truckin' allowed a marked departure from this norm, with its freestyle movements and space for individual interpretation. One account of the dance from 1938 illustrates how it shook up the staid dancing of the ballroom:

> [M]any 'truck', walk arm in arm, strut, wag forefingers relentlessly, shake hips; sometimes groups of couples doing this come together, form a little procession . . . Others,

> Truckin', leave go, walk away from each other, turn backs, come together again . . . The idea of swing music is that you make it up as you go along; these people are doing swing with their feet, freelance shufflings and jiggings; its all a long way from the formalised foxtrotting steps.[73]

Younger dancers especially found this spontaneity appealing, and took to it naturally. For example, one 20-year-old 'Trucker' in Peckham, London remarked: 'It's easy . . . you just waggle your feet, shake your stomach, and wave your arms.'[74] Mass Observation noted that those who swung were 'pronounced in their movements—hips shaken with marked emphasis, feet stamped, legs kicked out, trunk sinuated, heads shaken, arms waved with a trembling motion.'[75] Such movements were amusing and allowed dancers to 'let themselves go'—to rebel against the physical conformity of ballrooms, offices, and factories. The informality and exhibitionism which the dance permitted clearly made it appealing to younger dancers too, as this report from a Peckham dance hall in 1939 reveals:

> [T]wo girls . . . introduced a new variation by dancing along the row of seats sitting down alternately by holding in truckin' fashion and one sitting down whilst still holding the other. As she got up she turned and the other sat on the next seat. They did this right down the empty seats on the left side . . . roaring with laughter.[76]

Truckin' thus involved an element of display, something else that appealed to some young dancers who were eager to impress their friends and members of the opposite sex. Being seen, being popular, and being fashionable were particularly important to young people discovering and developing their identities.

Dancing and dance halls then were helping some young people to carve out a distinctive identity for themselves and we can see the beginnings of a distinctive youth culture emerging by the 1930s. Several important qualifications must be made, however. This was an embryonic youth culture. Only a minority of young dancers were interested in swing dancing and Truckin', the majority preferring more conventional dance styles. Most youngsters were more interested in 'fitting in' rather than 'standing out' in the ballroom, and elsewhere. In addition, the room for youngsters to separate themselves off from their elders in the interwar period was limited and was not necessarily indicative of a desire to be different. There was clearly not enough demand from younger dancers to make providing permanent commercial dance halls aimed at them a going concern. For the most part, age distinctive 'learner's halls' were rather small and amateur affairs, conducted in church halls and assembly halls, and they appealed mostly to teens who were just learning to dance. Moreover, such halls were a 'stage' which youngsters wished to 'grow out of' and progress away from. The aspiration of most young dancers was to be like their elders and to move on quickly to the adult world, which was seen as 'superior'. In addition, once in that adult world of professionally run dance halls,

[73] M-O A, TC: MJD, 38/1/A, 'Streatham Locarno', 17 November 1938, 1.
[74] M-O A, TC: MJD, 38/1/E, 'Peckham Pavilion, V14, AH', 1 April 1939, 1.
[75] M-O A, TC: MJD, 38/1/B, 'Paramount AH', 20 March 1939, 15.
[76] M-O A, TC: MJD, 38/1/I, 'Stones, Rye Lane, IX2, AH', 6 March 1939, 8.

there *was* a mixing of ages, as Horace Richards observed in his 1934 study of dancing throughout Britain.[77]

Despite this, during the war we see the further development of an embryonic 'youth culture' in dance halls, most significantly in some young people's enthusiastic adoption of the Jitterbug. Whilst not all fans of the Jitterbug were young, the largest proportion was. As a Sheffield newspaper, *The Star*, noted in 1940: '16 year olds have taken to it like a duck takes to water and put up some really hot exhibitions up and down the city ballrooms.'[78] In Liverpool too, Malcolm Munro of the Grafton Rooms noted its youthful appeal, remarking: 'Jitterbug dancing is certainly making headway, especially with the younger generation.'[79] Why did the Jitterbug appeal so much to the young and how did it help in the creation of a distinctive youth culture? There were several reasons. First, was its energy—the Jitterbug was extremely energetic, requiring considerable physical dexterity, as one newspaper commented: 'It calls for far more energy, abandon, rhythm, and lack of self-consciousness than anyone beyond the teens possesses.'[80] John Robb (b. 1927) a teenager of the time, agreed, commenting: 'it was quite energetic to perform these things. It was more for the younger element, it was just being out for a good time and a bit of exercise.'[81] This combined with a youthful desire for something different, something new. As one reader of *Danceland* commented in 1944: 'the younger generation needs something more exciting and thrilling than the ordinary routine.'[82] Another reason for the appeal of the Jitterbug amongst the young was that, like Truckin' from which it came, it allowed greater chances for self-expression than the standard ballroom dances. As dance newspaper *Top Spin* put it: 'The youth of 1940 expresses itself in Jitterbug. It is a reaction from the strain of living under war-time conditions.'[83] Liverpool dancer George Cauldwell, 16 years old at the time, recalled the attraction: 'that was what we wanted to do as youngsters, because you're wired, you know . . . it was wild, you know. You made your own steps up . . . It was letting yourself go, you know.'[84] The link between the dance and feelings of 'abandon' was cemented by the fact that the Jitterbug allowed dancers to become completely absorbed in the frenetic swing music which accompanied it. Contemporary dance and music critics commented on how the Jitterbug was one of the first dances where people reacted directly, and physically, to the accompanying music. A London Jitterbug explained: 'We listen to the music and it tells your body what to do . . . we just trust to luck and the music to lift us. If it's a good band it gets you.'[85] Moreover, the Jitterbug involved a degree of exhibitionism that was even greater than that of

[77] H. Richards, 'Dancing Throughout Britain', a series of six reports in *PMDW,* November to December 1934.

[78] *The Star,* 31 July 1940, 3.

[79] *DT,* March 1940, 357.

[80] *The Star,* 31 July 1940, 3.

[81] GDHI, John Robb, b. 1927, 20 June 2011.

[82] *Danceland,* January 1944, 1.

[83] *Top Spin: a periodical devoted to the interests of north London dancers,* 1 April 1940, 1.

[84] LDHI, George Cauldwell, b. 1929, 21 June 2009.

[85] M-O A, TC: MJD, 38/1/A, 'Locarno–Jitterbuggs', 1 July 1939, 1.

Truckin'. A report of a Jitterbug contest held in London in 1942 indicates the element of showmanship involved:

> [D]ance candidates vied with each other for the plaudits of stomping patrons . . . Public applause was the decisive factor . . . it was rendered painfully obvious from the start that an impression was the 'big idea', and from just high stepping capers the competitors tried everything including somersaults.[86]

To increase its appeal to the young even more, the Jitterbug created a chorus of disapproval from the older generation. One critic writing in the *Modern Dance and Dancer*, for example, described it as 'adolescent madness which masquerades under the title of dancing'.[87] As we shall see, many dance halls banned the dance.

Significantly, Jitterbugging allowed the young to claim the dance as part of an emerging and 'separate' culture. This 'separateness' was physically manifested within the dance hall itself, as young people Jitterbugging occupied distinct areas of the dance floor, either crowding around the bandstand, or marking out a space in the middle of the ballroom. Dress and speech were another important feature of the Jitterbugs, which also allowed young dancers to mark themselves out as different. Young dancers copied a distinctive American High School style. A report of Jitterbug dancers from 1939 describes their outfits:

> Two girls come on in white pleated skirts, red gym slips type tops with white silk blouses underneath and white shoes. They wear no stockings and their full skirts fly up when they are dancing to reveal short white knickers.[88]

Jitterbug culture also came with its own language derived from black American urban slang. This was much parodied in the British press. The *Daily Express*, for example, alerted its readers to this new vocabulary via a report of the Fifth Annual Jazz Jamboree at the Stoll Theatre, London in 1943, even including a glossary of terms at the end:

> Four thousand killer diller gams, hepped to the Jive but unable to strut their stuff, had just to tap time as the cats frisked and boogie woogied in town yesterday. The cats were all in the groove. Jitterbuggs and Scobo Queens one an' all pronounced the jam session not off the cob.[89]

However, the emphasis on this emerging youth culture should not detract from the fact that most youths did not adopt distinctive styles of dress, nor take to the wilder dancing forms represented by the Jitterbug. Nor were the young able to forge a separate physical space away from their elders, by dancing in different and separate venues. In fact, the circumstances of war actually made age mixing at dances more

[86] *DN*, 28 February 1942, 1.

[87] *MDD*, March 1944, 23.

[88] M-O A, TC: MJD, 38/1/A, 'Locarno–Jitterbuggs', 1 July 1939, 1.

[89] *Daily Express*, 23 October, 1943, 3. (Glossary: 'Killer diller': a Jitterbug; 'Gams': Legs; 'Hepped': warmed up, prepared; 'Jive and Strut your stuff': dance; 'Cats': swing musicians; 'Frisk': play; 'boogie woogie': highly syncopated piano music, with a rhythmic roll on the bass; 'In the groove': going smoothly, with perfomers in form; 'Scobo Queens': girl Jitterbuggs; 'Jam session': a swing music performance; 'Off the Cob': 'Corny' or second rate.)

common. Many of the small 'learner halls' previously frequented by teenage dancers, were closed and requisitioned during the war. This forced younger dancers straight into the mainstream ballrooms, one reason for the supposed influx of younger dancers noted by some contemporaries. Wartime dance halls were therefore less age stratified than before the war. As a Glasgow dancer explained: 'this cut off that there is with young people wasn't there then. There was a mixture of age groups at the Albert Hall. From young to approaching middle age.'[90] Indeed, at some dance halls in wartime, older dancers taught younger ones to dance, a sign of the closing down of many learner venues. Another Glasgow woman recalls: 'There was a good range of boys and girls from 16 to in their thirties. The older dancers taught the younger ones to dance, that was how you learnt. They would take them up and put them through the paces.'[91]

Let's finally turn to the post-war relationship between youth culture and dancing. Discussion of a distinctive post-war youth culture has traditionally centred around the Teddy Boy and Teddy Girl who emerged in the 1950s. As we shall see in Chapter 10, their association with dance halls and trouble was certainly a key development of the decade and one that created a moral panic amongst many elder contemporaries. However, the Teds, important though they were, were not representative of the great majority of young people in the 1950s. The most significant youth culture of the 1950s was the 'Jive culture' found in most dance halls throughout Britain. In Jive, as in Jitterbug and Truckin' before it, youths found real opportunities for self-expression and were able to carve out a space for themselves in the dance hall. Unlike earlier dance crazes however, Jive was not a minority youth dance, it was, by the late 1950s, the dance preference of the majority of young people. Indeed, by the mid-1950s dancing was starting to fragment much more clearly along age lines than in any period before. Now when various age groups started to prefer distinctive dance styles they began to go to different venues for dancing. It was in the 1950s that the trends of the previous two decades come to fruition and we see far greater evidence of a distinctive and separate youth culture in the dance hall than at any point before.

It is true that Teddy Boys were associated with Jiving. As Leonard Sims, a Ted invited in 1953 by the *Daily Mirror* to explain his lifestyle to its readers described: 'I am eighteen. I wear Edwardian suits. I love bop music and Jive dancing.' He went on: 'Our idea of a good night out is to dance at the jazz clubs . . . I don't need a drink to put me in the right mood for a good time. The music does that. That real gone-noisy bop is what we love better than anything. We like our music loud and hot, and I find the old boxing routine gives me good footwork for Jive dancing.'[92]

Yet whilst the Teddy Boys were the most visible development in post-war youth culture, the majority of teenagers and young people in post-war Britain were developing their own distinctive culture from within, and alongside, the dominant adult culture. In the dance hall, this meant that at the beginning of the post-war period, virtually all youths of both sexes were still wedded to the standard dances

[90] GDHI, Rae Birch, b. 1922, 8 August 2011.

[91] GDHI, Jean Meehan, b. 1921, 14 June 2011.

[92] *DM*, 13 November 1953, 7.

created two decades before. Even the wartime Jitterbugs had not shaken the grip of the English style on British ballrooms. The majority of youngsters were equipped to dance the foxtrot, quickstep, waltz, and tango, with varying degrees of success, as had been their parents before them. Indeed, this remained the case until the start of the 1960s, when new dance developments, notably the Twist, marked a completely new direction, and the emergence of non-partner dancing finally ended the long rule of ballroom dancing in public dance places. In the intervening period, 'Jive' emerged as the dance of choice for most young people.

So what was the attraction of Jive for youngsters? Like the Jitterbug before it, one of the key attractions of Jive was the room it left for individual expression. The regimented nature of the standard dances was unattractive to a great many teenagers, some of whom wished to break free of the constraints of adult rules and regulations, and also yearned for an outlet for self-expression. As Jack Hogan (b. 1934) stated:

> The energy—if you did the waltz, you all did the same thing, the same with the foxtrot. When it came to Jiving it was completely different, you did your own thing, your own way, different twirls, different moves. You weren't curtailed by convention, you did your own steps.[93]

The beauty of Jive was that the individual dancers could develop their own distinctive dancing personalities. Jiving allowed young people to 'let go of themselves' and let their bodies move to the beat of the music. As Frank Borrows, giving a definition of 'Jive' in 1949 wrote: 'It is the response in movement to modern swing music.'[94] A Mass Observation account from 1947 describes the exuberance of young Jivers: 'They yell and throw themselves about. Their whole body shakes . . . '[95] Older dancers often found themselves too inhibited to really let themselves go in this way. Youngsters picked it up naturally; as early as 1944, for example, *Dancing Times* remarked: 'It has been noted that the most persistent Jivers are youngsters between 14 and 17 who have the rhythm so much in their system that they Jive everything—even their walk into the ballroom!'[96] Yet Jive did have a wide appeal amongst the young. Unlike 'Jitterbug' one did not have to be quite so extrovert nor energetic to 'Jive'. This widened the appeal of the dance to include the majority of young people.

Underlying this change was a gradual weakening of formal adult control over dancing. For example, the more freestyle nature of the dancing that was starting to evolve in the 1950s meant that youths' reliance on formal dance training was lessened and this led to a weakening of adult control of their dancing. As already noted, it became increasingly common not to attend dance lessons and instead to pick up steps from friends. This added a further element of socialization to Jive. Whilst peer group dance lessons had been a feature of youth dancing since the 1920s, then the impromptu lessons were likely to be an addition to formal dance

93 DDHI, Jack Hogan, b. 1936, 11 March 2011.

94 *MDD*, April 1949, 33.

95 M-O A, FR2473, *Report on Juvenile Delinquency* (1947), 51.

96 *DT*, August 1944, 523.

lessons, and were concerned with teaching the standard dances. By the 1950s peer group lessons were increasingly replacing formal dance lessons altogether, and were helping to develop a different and separate style from the adult dancers.

Changes in technology also weakened the control of adults over youths dancing. The availability of increasingly cheaper radios and record players meant that youths could take control of dancing at an earlier age. With the availability of 6 inch 45 rpm records aimed deliberately at the youth market, teenagers could start their dancing earlier, and often without the supervision of parents. Informal 'get togethers', dancing in the street, or in each other's houses, was fairly common. Even the poorest could do this, if by somewhat unconventional means. A Liverpool dancer from a poor background remembers:

> It all started in the street, on the street corners. We were all about twelve, thirteen . . . in the teens . . . we used to sing, you know, and dance. We were lucky if we got in someone's house, you know, because we would put the records on then. And, you know, if there was no-one in, we'd go in. [laughs] If the mother was out, we'd be able to sneak in . . . and get out before they came back . . . and they'd all say: 'You heard that record,' you know. And you'd go 'oh yeah' and you'd say 'how would you dance to that?' We'd all get together and you'd do that and you'd do that and you'd do that [shows dance steps], you know. That's how it came about.[97]

The growth of youth oriented cafés and milk bars with jukeboxes in the 1950s, outlined in Chapter 3, also allowed youths to develop and practice dancing styles away from the watch of their elders.

This fragmentation of dancing along taste and age lines was echoed in increasing fragmentation in terms of physical space. In one dance hall in Crewe, for example, a row of chairs was used to designate distinctive areas of the dance floor to be used for Jiving and non-Jiving. As Barbara Nott (b. 1942) recalled: 'if you wanted to Jive . . . you had to go behind the chairs.'[98] Moreover, during the 1950s, certain dance venues became associated with certain dance styles and certain age groups to an extent not seen before. This occurred in a number of ways. For a start, the post-war period saw the return of age-delineated 'learner's halls' in most towns and cities. As the number of dance venues increased again after the wartime contraction, the post-war period started to see the re-emergence of numerous dance studios, church halls, assembly rooms and so on, each catering for a certain section of the young, as in the interwar period.[99] However, unlike the 1920s and 1930s, in the 1950s we start to see an age fragmentation both within and between the main commercial dance halls as well. First came age differentiation within individual dance halls. Younger people would gather in a specific area of the hall, older people in another. In Glasgow's Barrowlands in the later 1940s, for example, one part of the dance hall was nicknamed 'Jiver's corner', as one dancer recalls: 'everyone used to crowd round there to see the really good Jivers dancing.'[100] Throughout the

[97] LDHI, Marie Kernan, b. 1942, 21 July 2009.
[98] CDHI, Barbara Nott, b. 1942, 30 June 2014.
[99] DDHI, Dolores Brown, b. 1939, 22 April 2011.
[100] GDHI, Margaret Taylor, b. 1938, 31 June 2011.

course of an evening, young dancers laid claim to certain sections of the dance floor. As Kath Hogan (b. 1934) of Dundee explains, dancers took their own spot on the dance floor 'with the Jiving... you picked your spot and that's where you stayed.'[101] Indeed, so noticeable were the different tastes of dancers by this stage, that dance halls had to introduce '50/50' programmes of dancing—half 'old time' (ie ballroom) and half 'modern' (ie Jive). By the 1950s, mainstream commercial dance halls were also catering for specific age groups, each hall specializing in putting on dance programmes that appealed to their specific patronage. In Dundee, for example, the 'JM' Ballroom opened in 1953, deliberately aiming to appeal to the youth market, providing music for Jiving and later the twist.[102] Certainly in the minds of many young dancers, particular dance halls in the locality were designated as 'ours', whilst others were associated as 'theirs'. As Jack Hogan (b. 1934) commented: 'When you were 16 or 17 or 17 you stuck to your own dance halls.'[103] One teenager remembers that at Dundee's Star ballroom 'they began to get an older crowd and they were too old for us so we went to the Palais'.[104] Similarly, in Glasgow, Margaret Taylor (b. 1938), recalls: 'I never went to the Locarno... It just wasn't my scene, a lot of older people went there.'[105] Stewart Murray (b. 1940) recalls similar age and taste divisions in Glasgow: 'The Plaza and the Albert and the Astoria were more for older people who were ballroom dancers.'[106] Age was becoming a defining factor in choosing which halls to dance in.

CONCLUSION

Dancing and dance halls were vital features of the expanding experiences of young people in the twentieth century. They allowed a relatively ordered, safe, and ritualistic environment in which to grow up, offering tastes of independence and first encounters with the opposite sex. The emergence of a distinctive youth culture in twentieth-century Britain is also inextricably linked with dancing, as key dance styles were taken over by young people and dance halls became central to the display of increasingly distinctive styles and patterns of behaviour.

[101] DDHI, Kath Hogan, b. 1936, 11 March 2011.
[102] DDHI, Jack Hogan, b. 1936, 11 March 2011.
[103] DDHI, Jack Hogan, b. 1936, 11 March 2011.
[104] DDHI, Dolores Brown, b. 1939, 24 April 2011.
[105] GDHI, Margaret Taylor, b. 1938, 31 June 2011.
[106] GDHI, Stewart Murray, b. 1940, 19 July 2011.

Chapter 6

Women, Dancing, and Dance Halls, 1918–60

INTRODUCTION

Altogether the dance hall was young, modern, and exhilarating. It had a particular significance for women, however. The dance hall allowed women opportunities and a freedom of expression often denied them at work and home, allowing them to mix with the opposite sex and to socialize with their peers. It helped to carve out an influential female public space that was vital in their social and cultural emancipation in the twentieth century.

CREATING A 'FEMALE' PUBLIC SPACE

One of the key significances of the dance hall for women was that it carved out a 'female' public space that allowed them to explore their public and personal identities. The dance hall both reflected and helped create changing gender boundaries, as women were able to enter this part of the public sphere ostensibly as 'equals', in an environment where they often outnumbered men. Moreover, women were taking part in an activity in which they were frequently more skilled and experienced than men and in a setting that was particularly attractive to them. As we shall see in Chapter 8, this was not without controversy. However, despite the protestations of critics, the dance hall allowed women to expand their social and cultural horizons.

The dance hall was symbolic of new relations between men and women in the twentieth century. Britain's traditional and rigid gender structure was beginning to loosen from 1918 onwards, as the First World War saw women taking on the role of men in the public sphere; while in the post-war period women's employment opportunities expanded due to the growth of clerical and service jobs and the development of 'light industries'.[1] This meant that women were becoming economically more independent and enjoying a greater presence in public. That being said, the public sphere was still dominated and defined by men, and regarding leisure, there were few pursuits that were either appealing or socially acceptable for

[1] J. Stevenson, *British Society, 1914–45* (Harmondsworth: Penguin, 1984), 159.

young women to enjoy. However, from the 1920s onwards, the dance hall (together with the cinema) rapidly developed to fill this void. Dance halls became a key feature of an expanded female social space. They were 'female' because women dominated these spaces numerically and also because they were reflective of and helped shape a growing 'feminization' of culture and social life in Britain after 1918.

Dancing was more popular with women than with men, and in a literal sense the dance hall was a predominantly 'female' space. The female 'obsession' with dancing was observed soon after the end of the First World War. Guy Thorne, writing in 1919, commented:

> All over the country . . . dancing halls have sprung up like mushrooms, and are thronged by girls of every class. Two out of three girls one meets will talk of nothing but the jazz, the Turkey-Trot, and the rest of the passionate gymnastics we have borrowed from the negroes of America. Dancing . . . has become an obsession. It is ousting everything else in the mind of the modern girl.[2]

In most dance halls women far outnumbered men. This proportion could be as much as two to one. In Blackpool in 1938 for example, Mass Observation noted that 67 per cent of dancers at the Winter Gardens on a sampled evening were women.[3] There were various factors that influenced such proportions. Women dominated the dance hall to a greater extent at certain times of the evening, particularly early on. This was because many men went to the pub before coming to the dance hall. During this part of the evening's proceedings, the dance hall was essentially a social club for women. Women used this time to practise their dance moves with each other (and thus one of the dancing pair had to assume the lead role of the 'man'). They also chatted and gossiped with their friends and could make adjustments to their appearance.

In towns and cities with particularly good employment prospects for women, the disproportion between men and women could be larger than normal too. In interwar Nottingham, for example, where textile industries were strong, the local dance halls were so full of women that attempts were made to solve the 'wall-flower' problem by offering men free dancing lessons.[4] This experiment was repeated in 1937 by the Mecca dance halls, in order to try and get more men to dance. As Carl Heimann argued: 'If we dance hall proprietors can once get the males dance minded and enthused, it will be an enormous fillip to the dancing business . . . surely this business of ours should attract both sexes.'[5] The fact that special measures had to be taken in some places to attract more men shows how dominant women could be in the dance hall. Some even regarded the greater keenness of women as a social problem. In 1929 for example, the *Daily Express* 'dance expert' complained: 'The modern masculine aversion from dancing is one

[2] *Sunday Sun* (Newcastle upon Tyne), 21 September 1919, 5.
[3] M-O A, Worktown: W60 File D, 'Dancing' 1938, 13.
[4] *DT*, August 1931, 447. [5] *DT*, November 1937, 195.

of those irritating problems which the average woman of today is trying to solve.'[6]

There were other ways in which dancing and the dance hall were 'female' too. As we have seen, working-class girls took an interest in dancing several years younger than boys did—as schoolgirls of thirteen and fourteen they attended dances in public dance halls with their elder sisters or friends. This alliance of elder and younger sisters, together with groups of friends, provided a controlled means of independence for girls, giving them support while largely unsupervised by adults. Socializing with their own sex was a vital part of a girl's development. Moreover, their earlier involvement in dancing meant that women were usually more skilled in dancing and its social conventions than boys were. Here was one of the few social spaces and leisure activities where women started off with a potential 'head start' over their male counterparts. Furthermore, women tended to maintain this keener interest in dancing throughout their lives. As the *Daily Express* remarked in 1929: 'The failure of many men in the ballroom can be attributed to the fact that, compared with women, they do not take dancing seriously. Too many are content to master the simplest steps and some do no more than walk. Women are prepared to learn and practice.'[7] Women dancers themselves reflected on this. Liverpool dancer Jane Campbell commenting on her husband's dancing skills observed: 'He would get up, and just shuffle round with me. He could shuffle around, that was all.'[8]

The atmosphere in the dance hall was also much more conducive to female patronage than many other public places of leisure and in this respect it marked a change from older traditional forms of leisure. Because behaviour was closely monitored and because dance halls were 'dry', serving no alcohol, it was usually much more orderly than in other public spheres. The pub, for example, although it admitted women in segregated areas, could be very traditionally 'masculine'. Bravado, arguing, and fighting were common features of traditional working-class pub culture. Moreover, the presence of women in pubs, whilst tolerated, was often resented by men and seen as an incursion into a male world. Whilst women were also admitted to music halls, the other mainstay of pre-First World War working-class leisure, here the atmosphere also could be rowdy and volatile, especially in their earlier manifestations. Women who attended alone were also considered to be morally dubious. Dance halls, on the other hand, were much more welcoming to women, indeed women were crucial to the central activity of heterosexual couple dancing. Furthermore, dance halls were less obviously 'masculine' than pubs. Although fighting did occur at some dance places, much of this was squeezed out by firmer management action as time progressed, especially in the larger palais de danse.[9] This search for respectability amongst the dance hall owners helped create a safe public environment. Strict rules of conduct were usually enforced at dance halls too. Overly pushy men who mistreated or manhandled women would be censored by MCs, aggression would result in expulsion, and drunkenness was not tolerated.

[6] *Daily Express*, 18 November 1929, 10. [7] Ibid.
[8] LDHI, Jane Campbell, b. 1922, 23 June 2009. [9] See pp. 289–92.

In most dance places such rules would be accepted without fuss. As Mass Observation noted in 1938: 'Every large ballroom has its MC in evening dress who rules the dancefloor and no observer records any occasion on which he was challenged.'[10] In addition, the whole range of conventions on dancing that we will discuss later also gave a ritualistic element to the dance experience that left less room for spontaneous and potentially volatile behaviour. Thus, dances usually proceeded in an orderly, controlled way, something that also made them attractive to women as they knew what to expect and when.

The physical spaces in which dances were conducted also contributed to their appeal to women. The best dance halls were decorated and designed in a way that emphasized comfort and luxury. These attributes lent themselves to more 'refined' behaviour from their patrons, most of whom chose to 'live up' to the standards of their surroundings. Smart uniformed staff, slick professional managers, and high standards of service lent an air of refinement. Moreover, many dance halls were deliberately decorated in ways that emphasized a newly 'feminized' leisure world. Thus, flowers, fresh table linen, colourful evocations of exotic scenes painted on the walls, and expensive lighting schemes all lent themselves to the creation of an atmosphere of sophistication and romance—also something seen to appeal to women. Whereas pubs could often be shoddy, smelly, and dirty, the best dance halls were 'palaces' for the people.

The dance hall was not just a female space because there were more women interested in, and better at, dancing than men however. There were other features of dancing which made it an activity where women could find a sense of self-worth. Perhaps most fundamental, in the dance hall men and women were not segregated and this meant that they entered a single public space as equals. Although men and women tended to occupy their own distinct areas of the dance hall, this was done as a matter of choice and habit, rather than something that was prescribed by managements or dictated by architecture. Indeed, it was an indication of a pronounced gender-based identity association. There was no forced physical separation of men and women in the dance hall—separate rooms or areas were not necessary. Together with the cinema, dance halls then were allowing women to enter the public sphere on an unprecedented scale.

What impact did the war have on this new 'female public space'? At the beginning of the war, the increasingly 'public' leisure patterns of the previous decade were in danger of being reversed. Women were affected much more by the blackout than men, and this lead to a widespread unwillingness to go out at night. Home-based leisure activities became increasingly popular, thus threatening the centrality of dancing to women's lives. In the early months of the war, Mass Observation argued that 'all the indications now are that the blackout has had a major effect, and a much stronger deeper effect on women'.[11] In December 1939, for example, Mass Observation found that 43 per cent of women stated that they

[10] M-O A: Worktown: W60 File D, 'Dancing' 1938, 12.

[11] T. Harrisson, 'Working Women in this War', *Industrial and Personnel Management*, December 1939, 4.

had reacted to the blackout with feelings of 'hate, fear, resentment and distinct depression'.[12] It put this down to a 'female fear of the dark' that it described as a 'powerful female neurosis'.[13] Anxiety about the dark was thus forcing women to stay inside—with 43 per cent of women as compared to only 11 per cent of men staying in on a sampled Saturday evening in December 1939, and 55 per cent of women but only 38 per cent of men the following Tuesday.[14] Mass Observation later concluded: 'A very large number of women spent the first weeks, or even months, of the war with no outside leisure activities.'[15] For young women in particular, parental pressure to remain inside was strong. As one woman from Neilston, Scotland who was 18 at the time and a regular dancer, recalled: 'Once the war began mother would not let us go out. She was too scared and the blackout was scary.'[16] Certainly, safety fears were a significant factor in the desire to stay indoors. There were other issues that explain these shifting leisure patterns too. For many women, there was much less time available to spend on leisure. In 1941, for example, Mass Observation noted that its largely middle-class female diarists were noting that increased voluntary service, civil defence, and fire-watching meant that many women had 'very much less leisure, and less entertainment'.[17] The collapse of organizations running theatre groups, tennis clubs, etc. also changed women's habits. As a result, when women did get free time, they seemed less likely to want to leave their home and Mass Observation noted that home-based activities such as sewing and knitting, reading, and listening to the radio, became increasingly popular in the first months of the war.

However, important though these early changes in wartime leisure were, we must be careful to note their short-lived nature together with significant differences amongst certain groups of women. After an initial collapse in non-domestic leisure seeking, young women proved much more resilient to wartime changes such as the blackout than the middle-aged. As Mass Observation noted, young women were soon returning to dance halls in big numbers:

> Dancing was perhaps the first to regain its public...The dance-hall public is of course predominantly youthful, and the blackout, rather than make many girls stay at home as their mothers preferred to do, encouraged then to go more to the cinema or the dancehall because there was nothing else to do.[18]

Indeed, as more women were recruited for war work, there were important changes in their socio-economic status. For these women, there was a greater ability to spend time and money on leisure than ever before. In the West End of London, for example, it was observed that suburban girls were frequenting central dance halls and other places of entertainment in large numbers for the first time. One publican noted that they were '[m]ostly factory girls . . . and fairly young, about 17–20. Before the war they wouldn't have come to the West End because they wouldn't

12 Harrisson, 'Working Women', 4. 13 Ibid. 14 Ibid.
15 M-O A, FR290, 'Women in Wartime', June 1940, 162.
16 GDHI, Jean Meehan, b. 1921, 14 June 2011.
17 M-O A, FR733, 'The War in M.O. Diaries, Comparative Report', July 1941, 2.
18 M-O A, FR290, 'Women in Wartime', June 1940, 171–2.

have had the clothes to wear, but now they've got more money and they like to show themselves off a bit.'[19] Elsewhere too these mobile women flocked to dancing. As *Dance News* observed in 1941: 'Dancing is . . . the most popular recreation with girl workers in war factories in town and village dancehalls outside Edinburgh.'[20]

Moreover, the war actually accentuated the dance hall's role as a key 'female' public space. The dance hall became even more 'female' in a literal sense as the proportion of women to men increased during the war—as men were called up to fight in the forces in large numbers. The National Service (Armed Forces) Act of 1939 conscripted all men aged 18 to 41, and this was extended to 51 in 1942. Even in those areas of the country where men remained fighting on the Home Front in reserved occupations, the influx of mobilized women from all parts of the country often altered the gender mix substantially. National Conscription of women aged 20 to 30 had begun in 1942 and was subsequently extended to those aged 19 to 43. In many coastal towns away from possible invasion areas, for example, there were large numbers of women who were employees of government departments which had been evacuated out of the reach of bombers. In such areas, it was estimated that there were five and six women to one man.[21] Dance halls also became more 'female' as women began to take over important public roles in the running of them. Women stepped into various roles, from security to providing music. For example, at the Belle Vue Ballroom in Manchester when the MC joined the National Fire Service in 1942 his wife took over his duties. During the weekend she controlled crowds of 3,000, often rising to 6,000 during the summer months.[22]

In the post-war period there were several developments that cemented the female domination of the dance hall and also reinforced its 'feminine' characteristics. As the professionally run palais de danse extended their dominance of the dance hall industry, dance culture became even 'safer' and even more attractive to women. The elimination of rowdyism became a central feature of the larger dance hall's long-term growth strategy after 1945.[23] Even more effort and money was put into monitoring the behaviour of dancers, making the dance hall increasingly orderly and safer. It was found by groups like Mecca that female members of staff were the most effective in diffusing angry situations, thus adding to the female nature of this public space. There was also a continued effort to eliminate drunkenness, with searches of dancers and the eviction of those found to be under the influence of alcohol. As before the war, dance halls were keen to create a sense of luxury too. As greater profits were made in the post-war period, the emphasis on providing glamorous surroundings became even more pronounced. Dance halls competed to provide the best decoration and the most elaborate facilities that they could. This created sophisticated entertainment venues far removed from the hard drinking environments of the past. When licensed ballrooms began to emerge in the 1960s, the environment in which drinking and dancing took place was far removed from

[19] M-O A, FR1835, 'Behaviour of Women in Pubs', June 1943, 4.
[20] *DN*, 15 November 1941, 2.
[21] *Danceland*, November 1943, 9.
[22] *DN*, 18 April 1942, 2.
[23] See pp. 290–2.

the seedy atmosphere of early interwar night clubs. Food was available, the surroundings lent themselves to restraint and 'good' behaviour and increasingly the new leisure facilities became 'family' oriented.

DANCING AND THE DEVELOPMENT OF FEMALE IDENTITY

Of key significance to women, dancing provided the opportunity for them to express themselves and to shape their identity. This could be done in a number of ways, via the dancing itself, via their general behaviour in the dance hall, and via the way they presented themselves to the world—their clothes, their make up, hairstyles and so on.

We start with dancing. Dancing was important to the development of women's identity in a number of ways. The sense of achievement in developing the skills of dancing helped increase women's self-confidence and in this respect, dancing for women was equivalent to sport for men. In addition, via the dance forms themselves, and their interpretation of the dances and music, women could create 'dancing personalities' for themselves. How they chose to perform dance steps and interpret the music was thus vital in women's social development.

Let's start with an examination of dancing and skill. Attaining excellence in the execution of dance steps was very important for women. A Manchester dancer of the 1940s exclaimed: 'I thought I was the bee's knees when I could Jive.'[24] Acquiring dancing skills could also make women more confident. As a 24-year-old girl from New Eltham told Mass Observation in 1939: 'Coming to this hall gives me something to look forward to each week. I once suffered from acute inferiority complex, now I'm completely cured, thanks to Old Time Dancing.'[25] Older women could benefit too, as a 47-year-old married office cleaner from South London explained: 'To me, dancing is the greatest pleasure one could have and is a great factor in helping me to take life with a smile. It keeps both body and mind young, active and alert.'[26] Even attainment of rudimentary steps could be beneficial. One woman from Liverpool dancing in the 1930s remarked: 'you felt good if you could do a little bit of dancing, really. I wasn't a marvellous dancer . . . If you could just do the basics and get around, you know, you felt good, really.'[27] Most women, however, did their utmost to try and perfect their skills. More women took dance lessons than men. Furthermore, women tended to take their dancing more seriously than men and, as we have seen, were more skilled at it. A dance teacher in Peckham, London, for example, told Mass Observation in 1939: 'The girls particularly like to know a thing properly—girls are more serious about good dancing

24 NWSA Oral History: 2006.0179, Maggie Hardy, b. 1931, 2006.

25 M-O A, MJD: 38/1/G, 'Peckham Pavilion Questionnaire Survey Results: 15', March/April 1939, 1.

26 M-O A, MJD: 38/1/G, 'Peckham Pavilion Questionnaire Survey Results: 9', March/April 1939, 1.

27 LDHI, Marjorie Hooley, b. 1917, 23 June 2009.

than gentleman.'[28] Similarly in 1951 the same seriousness was still in evidence, one dance teacher remarking that women were more eager to carry on improving than men were: 'it is something she does not easily forget. She keeps on learning, picking up little tricks that help her toward improvement.'[29]

That women got satisfaction from the act of dancing alone is evidenced by the fact that it was largely the love of dancing that drew them into the dance hall, rather than other social attractions. In 1922 Millicent Lester Jones, writing in the *Daily Mirror*, in seeking to explain why so many women went dancing argued that, unlike men, they were there for the sake of dancing itself, not to flirt: 'Most women go to dances because they like dancing and for no other reason . . . Let it be clearly understood that were are out for dancing—for the exercise and the pleasure of the rhythmic motion to good music, and the pride all human beings take in doing a thing well.'[30] That women got pleasure from dancing for its own sake can also be seen in the large numbers of same sex couples at most dances. Groups of girls dancing together was a common sight in the dance hall. In its observations in Blackpool's dance halls in 1937, for example, Mass Observation found that the number of female couples dancing over the evening was around 25 to 40 per cent of the total. Earlier in the evening the number of female couples was even higher, peaking at 65 per cent.[31] Same sex dancing was not always because there were too few men to dance with either. Some women could relax more when dancing with another woman. As one female dance teacher put it in 1929, women liked same sex dancing because: 'They are not hampered by struggling to make a good impression on their partners, and they are absolutely natural. They dance for the sheer love of the movement to music.'[32]

In addition to providing skills and a sense of self-worth, dancing provided one of the most important means of physical exercise for women. Many working-class and lower-middle-class girls working in factories, shops, or as typists, were required to stand or sit for long periods of time throughout the day. This was as true of jute mill workers in Dundee as it was of those assembling wireless sets in the new industries of the south-east of England. For these girls there was an urgent need for active recreation, no longer available to them in the form of school games and physical drill. Indeed, the dance profession repeatedly targeted the health benefits of dancing in an attempt to attract women. That dancing could aid slimming was one line of argument promoted by dance teachers and dance halls alike. As Josephine Bradley argued in 1931: 'If you wish to become slim, there is no modern exercise as good and as beneficial as ballroom dancing.'[33] Dancers also appreciated this benefit, as one from Bacup recalled: 'We used to weigh ourselves before and after the Jive club and would lose as much as 4lbs because we never sat down all the time we were there.'[34] Mass Observation found that many other women also appreciated the

[28] M-O A, MJD: 38/1/D, 'Peckham Pavilion: Mollie Bourne', 19 August 1939, 2.
[29] *Danceland*, March 1951, 8. [30] *DM*, 22 September 1922, 5.
[31] M-O A, Worktown: W60 File D, 'Dancing' 1938, 15. [32] *DM*, 25 October 1929, 18.
[33] *DM*, 11 December 1931, 25.
[34] NWSA Oral History: 2001.0712, Lorna Macintosh, b. 1940, 2001.

exercise which dancing provided. Some comments from a 1939 survey: 'Leading a sedentary life, I find that three hours of sheer exercise to the rhythm I like, serves to keep me fitter and my tummy flatter.'[35] A single woman from East Dulwich drew comparisons with cinema: 'one gets stiff with sitting for a couple of hours or so, but to dance means to exercise the muscles, and therefore it helps to keep one young.'[36] A housewife, 55, from South London explained that dancing gave 'plenty of exercise [which] enables one to keep fit, [and] keeps rheumatism at bay'.[37] There were seen to be mental health benefits for women from dancing too. A feature in the *Daily Mirror* in 1921, for example, informed readers of the 'tonic effect' of dancing on both body and mind: 'There is no finer sedative to the nerves in all this world than dancing, its immediate action being to sooth and calm and at the same time exhilarate. How all those little everyday worries seem magically to merge and evaporate into the sparkling atmosphere of the . . . ballroom!'[38] It was the focus on getting the steps right which could prove so relaxing, as female dance teacher Marguerite Vacani argued in 1933: 'the necessary concentration on new steps, poise and movement to music rests the brain in an extraordinary fashion.'[39] Indeed, that dancing provided uplift and escape from the monotony and problems of daily life was one benefit cited by women dancers themselves. In 1939 Mecca carried out two surveys into why people went dancing. The following remarks indicate the power it had to provide escape for women. A young woman from Birmingham told them: 'It makes me feel very light hearted and it is something either to look back on or to look forward to with great pleasure.'[40] Another working-class woman from Peckham observed: 'I come because it puts new life in me—makes one feel life is worth living.'[41] Indeed, many women looked forward to their dancing as the highlight of their week. A married woman from South London explained it as '[t]he one evening I long for and am most unhappy when unable to get there.'[42] Another housewife argued that dancing '[r]ejuvenates the spirits, keeps you going. Tuesday and Saturday is something to look forward to.'[43]

Not only did dancing offer women self-worth, exercise, and escape, it also allowed self-expression. That women could express themselves through dance may seem odd however, given that the conventions of the new social dances of the twentieth century meant that men were supposed to take the lead in matters of interpretation and expression. Dance teacher Santos Casani wrote in 1927: '[D]ancing is a correct interpretation of the spirit of music; it is a physical expression of music.' He went on to add that this interpretation applied:

> particularly to the man. It is his function to interpret the music into terms of motion. The lady should be able entirely to ignore the music. She should confine herself to

[35] M-O A, MJD: 38/1/G, 'Peckham Pavilion Questionnaire Survey Results: 31', March/April 1939, 2.

[36] M-O A 'Peckham Pavilion', 1. [37] Ibid.

[38] *DM*, 15 November 1921, 9. [39] *DM*, 26 October 1933, 27.

[40] M-O A, MJD: 38/6/F, 'Danceland Questionnaire Survey Results: 2', April 1939, 1.

[41] M-O A, MJD: 38/1/G, 'Peckham Pavilion Questionnaire Survey Results: 40', March/April 1939, 1.

[42] M-O A 'Peckham Pavilion', 1. [43] Ibid.

> expressing in her individual style the man's interpretation of it. She should aim at becoming a perfect 'follower.' It is obvious, since no two persons have exactly similar temperaments, that nothing but inharmony could arise from a dual interpretation of the same music. That is why the woman should subject herself entirely to her partner. Some women are born with a natural gift for rhythm and an aptitude for 'following.'[44]

Yet as we shall see, there were a number of important ways in which women could take control of dancing, and contemporaries pointed to its role in female expressiveness. As a *Dancing Times* reporter put it in 1927:

> The longing for self-expression which is the characteristic of the age is driving the girls of to-day to seek satisfaction in dancing. In response to this compelling impulse they flock to join the world of rhythm . . .[45]

The link between dancing and 'expression' was well established by the twentieth century and the proliferation of new social dances provided the opportunity for renewed discussion of this association. In 1921, for example, a *Daily Mirror* article observed:

> Dancing . . . is the performance of a beautiful thing in a beautiful manner. It is the natural, age long expression of delight, and when we are happy we are always beautiful . . . the feeling of exhilaration which the body swinging in perfect rhythmic unison gives, sends a becoming flush to the cheeks and a sparkle to the eyes.[46]

Moreover, the new social dances of the early twentieth century were particularly well suited to allowing individual adjustments and interpretations. As we have seen, the new dances overturned existing rules and practices. They transformed social dance from sequence dances where everyone performed the same steps, to dances deliberately formulated for couples that were far freer. There was considerable room for improvization, even once the attempt to regulate dance steps that was typified by the development of the 'English style' had been introduced in the later 1920s. Despite the best efforts of dance teachers, the room for individuals to add their own flourishes was still considerable. Whilst men too could develop dancing in this way, as we have seen large numbers of them were content to equip themselves with only the most basic level of dancing skills. The issue of 'self-expression' then was one that was of most concern to women. This was partially because women were considered to be more 'natural' dancers, somehow better suited than men to dancing. For example, in answering the question of why women liked dancing, Professor D. Fraser-Harris explained in the *Daily Mirror* in 1927 that they had a 'natural instinct for grace of movement'. He proclaimed that women had an 'acuter perception of rhythm' than men 'and since dancing is the emotional expression of the appreciation of rhythm, it should follow that women would make better dancers than men'. He also argued that women had greater 'refinement' and appreciation of beauty than men: 'Dancing is the poetry of motion, it is the

[44] S. Casani, *Casani's Self Tutor of Ballroom Dancing* (London: Cassell & Co., 1927), 102.
[45] *DT*, November 1927, 162–3. [46] *DM*, 15 November 1921, 9.

aesthetic aspect of muscular movement, and therefore women, sympathetic as they are towards all refining influences, find pleasure in dancing.'[47]

That women found an outlet for 'beautiful' expression in dancing can be seen in their justification for dancing in a certain way. Specific dances were attractive to some women because of the beauty they found in the steps. In a survey of why women went to Old Time dancing carried out in Peckham in 1939, the following observations were made of the dance steps. A 36-year-old housewife argued: 'I prefer old time danc[es] because they are more stately and ladylike.'[48] A 23-year-old single clerk: '[T]hey are so spectacular and graceful . . . there are so many different steps . . . one moment it is slow and dreamy, and the next, one is flying around, and yet the dance is still graceful.'[49] One young housewife, 24, concurred: '[Y]ou can throw yourself into it with real interest and learn something new every week and not just keep shuffling around.'[50] One married woman from Lee, South London, concluded: 'I prefer old time dancing because I have found it to be a great deal more graceful in deportment and movement.'[51] An older dancer confirmed this: 'Old time was better because the movements of the body synchronize with the tempo of the music, forming a beautiful mental rhythm. In modern dancing most seem to move where they like and broadly speaking how they like, their steps not at all conforming to the tempo of the music.'[52] A 47-year-old married cleaner was particularly articulate on the topic: 'I prefer Old Time Dancing because it embraces Beauty, Art and Grace to a degree not attainable in modern dancing. The Movements and Figures are far more varied and interesting.'[53]

In addition to finding expression in the dance steps, women could develop their sense of identity by the way they looked when dancing. That clothing formed an important aspect of identity was recognized by contemporaries. Writing in *Danceland* in 1949, for example, Peter Shirley observed:

> Not only do the clothes we wear affect our appearance, they change our mental outlook in a subtle way. Usually, when we are dressed well we feel well. Fashions change our personalities, tending to produce hidden facets in our characters, the way we act, the way we think . . . Any psychologist will agree that styles in dress affect our outlook on life and leisure.[54]

The dance hall was one of the key public spaces where women could display themselves to the world and their choice of clothes, hair style, and make-up formed part of the development of their identities as women and as individuals. In addition, what women wore and how they wore it in the dance hall, was a reflection of greater freedom in dress and public visibility, though it also created a critical reaction.

That clothing had changed sufficiently for women to be able to perform the new social dances of the post-First World War period was a sign of women's growing

47 *DM*, 28 September 1927, 4.

48 M-O A, MJD: 38/1/G, 'Peckham Pavilion Questionnaire Survey Results: 36', March/April 1939, 1.

49 M-O A 'Peckham Pavilion', 1. 50 Ibid. 51 Ibid. 52 Ibid. 53 Ibid.

54 *Danceland*, September 1949, 16.

acceptance in the public sphere and also of a more relaxed attitude towards femininity. In November 1934 a London fashion designer, 'Matita', told readers of *Modern Dance and Dancing* that '[f]ashion says "freedom"' for women. He believed that 'this is just what the dancing woman seeks: she wants to look her best and wear beautiful clothes, but she wants, too, to have that freedom which enables her to move gracefully, easily, and—most importantly of all—confidently.'[55]

Dressing up was an essential part of 'going to the palais' during the 1920s and 1930s and added much to the atmosphere of glamour. Women would wear a variety of outfits but their 'best' clothes were saved for the weekend dances. The working- and lower-middle-class women in the dance halls were skilled in the deployment of devices designed to achieve maximum glamour from restricted resources. As a result, the variety of styles and levels of sophistication in the average palais could be impressive. A Mass Observer in the Streatham Locarno noted:

> The girls mostly wear flashy blouses and tight short skirts—there are quite a lot of flat waved blondes in evening dress—a lot of women have diamante stars and clips in their hair whether in evening dress or not . . . a lot have flower sprays in hair (on top etc.) One . . . has a white frock and dark red tuille streamers flowing back from clips on her shoulders. The dress is low backed and floor length.[56]

Mass Observation were so interested in the dress of women in dance halls that they conducted several surveys into the type and range of outfits worn, noting differences between those worn in the afternoon and the evening. From their evidence it is clear that women's clothing was particularly colourful and varied. In their 1939 observations of women's clothing at the Streatham Locarno they noted maroon, green, pink, yellow, grey, black, and white dresses, often with collars of a different colour, or with edging of lace or small embroidery at afternoon dances. They also noted dresses being worn with 'coatees' (wraps or shawls) as part of an ensemble. Evening dresses were similarly varied and colourful. In the evening there were maroon, red, petunia, cream, blue, green, pink, brown, black, purple, mustard, peach, yellow, and white dresses with gold, flowered, or striped coatees. Some women also chose to wear jumpers and a skirt, also in a whole range of colours and designs. There were also plain, check, striped, and flowered dresses and skirts—some were a single colour, others were two-colour. Shoes were similarly varied, with the most popular colours being black, gold, and silver. Scarves, brooches, and even furs were used as accessories.[57]

Such variety was testament to the advent of mass produced clothing in the interwar period. The proliferation of chain stores throughout the country selling smart clothing meant that the range of affordable dancing outfits available to women had been greatly expanded. No longer was such variety in clothing the preserve of wealthy women. The majority of women in Mass Observation's Bolton survey got their clothing through 'clothing club cheques', which they would pay off

55 *MDD*, November 1934, 17.
56 M-O A, MJD: 1/A, 'Streatham Locarno: Big Apple Ball', 17 January 1939, 5.
57 M-O A, MJD: 38/1/D, 'Clothing, Locarno I14 and I23', 19–21 April 1939, 1–5.

at a shilling per week. Most large shops and department stores provided such a service. Elsewhere, at home or at sewing classes, other women made their own clothes or mended and adapted older styles. Home-made clothing was still common despite the appearance of cheap off-the-peg clothing. To protect their best dresses, many women would wear another dress over the top when going to and leaving the dance halls. In the dance hall, the toilets and make-up rooms provided the amenities for last minute clothing and make-up alterations as well as gossip and advice. Magazines and the cinema were important influences too. It was common for younger women to be stylistically influenced by Hollywood. The hairstyles and clothing of film stars, more often American than British, were followed closely. The results were impressive:

> People from other areas can sometimes scarcely believe that the resulting beauties, divided into some ten main types based on film stars, are girls working, as these are, from 7.45 till 5.30 each day in tropical temperature and humidity and tremendous noises of the cotton mills, for an average wage of thirty shillings a week.[58]

These changes also meant that it became harder to distinguish class on the basis of clothing. As Mrs Victor Silvester remarked in 1933:

> In the dance halls nowadays they challenge comparison with the best. The girls dress smartly and well on limited means, which again says a lot for the inexpensive departments, where they undoubtedly go for their dresses. Speaking generally, I have seen dowdy woman at exclusive restaurants, and smart women at dance halls, so it goes to prove that 'dress sense' has a lot to do with it—not always the price of the gown![59]

Dressing up for the dance hall was not just about looking smart. It was a critical part of the process that took girls out of the drabness of their everyday lives and allowed them to emulate the women they saw in higher society or the glamorous actresses they saw on screen. This emulation transported women into a completely different environment than their own. It also allowed them to experiment with who they were. As one young female dancer from Edinburgh explained in 1939: 'When I feel blue I get dressed up and go along, even the thought of going makes me happy.'[60]

We should remember, however, that whilst dressing up allowed women to explore their identities there were limits to their freedom to experiment. A combination of peer pressure and societal expectations could limit women's ability to dress as they pleased. As a women's advice column in Glasgow's *Evening Times* remarked in 1928: 'It is only natural that every girl should wish to look her best when she goes dancing. The bright lights of the Palais not only reflect beauty but also accentuate any little blemishes that detract from beauty, and it therefore behoves each one of us to see that there are no blemishes for the lights to discover and magnify.'[61] Instruction on what to wear, how to wear it, and how to prepare make-up and hair when at a dance was bountiful. Local and national newspapers,

[58] Harrisson, 'Whistle While You Work', 48. [59] *DT*, March 1933, 685.
[60] M-O A, MJD: 38/6/F, 'Danceland Questionnaire Survey Results: 17', April 1939, 1.
[61] *Glasgow Evening Times*, 17 October 1928, 2.

dancing manuals, and the dance press all targeted women's concerns with their appearance, hoping to control and shape it. In January 1933, for example, A. T. Edger, writing in the *Dancing Times*, advised women to adopt a health and beauty regime in order to improve their skin and figure for dancing. He also advised women to adapt their make-up specifically for the conditions of the dance hall:

> Consider the lighting effects of the dance hall or hotel you visit. You will find that now they usually have a golden colour scheme, and in this case it is unbecoming to use Rachel tinted powder, as your face will look yellow. And as the lights are usually rather subdued it is an error to use a heavy make up. Study the colour of your dress, too, when you consider how to enhance the beauty of your face.[62]

Choice of dresses for dancing was also a potential minefield. Advising women what to wear when dancing, Mrs Victor Silvester described the ideal 'dance frock' as one that combined figure hugging tightness and also freedom of movement below the hips. As she put it: 'although there must be plenty of room for movement . . . the skirt of every dance frock must have that close fitting line which accentuates the effect of slimness—that asset which every woman strives for.' She also advised that the dress's length should come to just below the ankle but no further so as to avoid becoming a danger on the dance floor.[63] Colour, shape of arms, length of sleeves, backless or not, the material used, accompanying shoes, and jewellery were all further considerations that women had to think about before choosing their outfits.

Advice could also try to restrict what women wore. In 1925 a *Popular Music and Dancing Weekly* correspondent cautioned: 'Don't, if you are a girl—and want to attract admiration and not notoriety—wear skirts up to your knees unless you have slim, graceful legs; which, alas, so few girls are blessed with. Remember that silk stockings beautify the beautiful, but only show up the ugly.'[64] In 1929 Santos Casani told women: 'Very long skirts are undoubtedly a handicap to dancers who are not yet expert. I have even seen men holding up the long skirts of their partners in ballrooms recently. When the women wear petal frocks or those with hanging panels, they get entangled and often cause a couple to trip up or come to a complete standstill.'[65]

During the war, the question of dress became even more significant. Largely because the opportunities for women to express their femininity were much more limited during the war and because wartime conditions often suppressed that femininity, the dance hall became one of the most significant venues in which women could assert themselves as 'women'. Despite the problems of wartime rationing and shortages, 'smartness' was something that most women still aspired to in their personal appearance. Coupons, rationing, and shortages did make women's task harder however. Mass Observation noted in 1941 that women's greatest complaint about the impact of clothes rationing was the difficulty of getting new 'dancing clothes or going out things'.[66] However, this did not deter

[62] *DT*, January 1933, 479. [63] *DT*, March 1933, 685.
[64] *PMDW*, 4 April 1925, 202. [65] *DM*, 24 October 1929, 20.
[66] M-O A, FR742, 'Broadcast for the North American Service', June 1941, 8.

women. Indeed, Mass Observation commented that 'quite a number have determined that the more difficult it gets, the smarter and brighter they will look . . . It seems to be the youngest women, the under twenties, who feel most strongly of all about this.'[67] An emphasis on dressing well continued. For example, the appearance of women in the mining town of Ashington, Northumberland, caught the attention of a journalist writing for *The Observer* in 1942. He wrote that the women had 'a smartness comparable with Regent Street' and were 'beautifully permed', noting that there were seventeen women's hair dressers in the small town of 30,000.[68] In particular, most women made a special effort for dances. As one woman who was 18 when the war started noted: '[E]veryone was dressed up . . . your best good dresses that maybe you went to church in. You wore working clothes in the week and wore your better dresses to go out.'[69] To help such women, most national newspapers had a column offering women fashion advice, and tips on how to make do and mend in a period of scarce resources and rationing. The resourcefulness of women in dress matters during the war was considerable. Dancing clothes were made using parachute silk, reworked men's flannel suits and so on. One woman from Coventry used to make clothes with her sister, using whatever they could lay their hands on. She recalls:

> We managed to acquire the lining of a fur coat . . . a most wonderful shiny satin material. This was black and Margaret made me a beautiful skirt on a deep band with pleats all around for dancing, I was the bees knees. But the pleats had to be ironed every time I wore it . . . I remember cycling to a dance . . . and standing on the pedals all the way so as not to crease my lovely skirt.[70]

A Liverpool dancer recalls her wartime clothing improvizations:

> I only had one grey dress, and it was the sort of dress that you could alter the collars and cuffs different colours. I'd put little lace bits on. You could still buy little bits of lace and things, and I made collars and cuffs. And I remember I got that red fluffy stuff, and I sewed that all round the neck. And then I'd do green.[71]

Hair styling was also an area where women would work to create an individual look despite scarce resources. Hairnets taken from munitions factories would be dyed different colours and sequins sewn on. In the absence of proper hair rollers one Liverpool women recalls: 'we used to get pegs and wrap our hair round it and do . . . like Victory V rolls, and we put little bows of ribbon in the back and anything sparkly . . . and we'd have the Veronica Lake and the . . . Rita Hayworth style, all flowing and big bangs.'[72] Sometimes, war work brought some unexpected hair trends in the dance hall. One Glasgow man remembers: 'in the era when the munitions factory was here the girls all appeared with red hair. Something they used

[67] M-O A, 'Broadcast for', 9. [68] *The Observer*, 19 July 1942, 6.
[69] GDHI, Jean Meehan, b. 1921, 14 June 2011.
[70] PWA, Mary Matthews, Article A4055636, 12 May 2005.
[71] LDHI, Vera Jeffers, b. 1926, 22 July 2009. [72] Ibid.

at the factory dyed their hair red and that was a fashion for a short while, they all dyed their hair red.'[73]

It was not just civilian women who retained a key interest in looking good either. Many women serving in the forces were also keenly interested in fashion. One conscripted woman commenting on life in the WAAFs in 1941 observed: 'There is a lively interest in clothes, fashion and general dress matters . . . They take great pride in their uniform; clean their buttons diligently; press their skirts regularly . . . Like all girls, there's a tremendous pride in appearance. When we went to a dance last week, some girls spent the entire afternoon titivating themselves.'[74]

The result of this attention to clothing in the dance hall was to re-assert the femininity of women. We should note however that many men were encouraging women to be 'feminine' in this traditional sense due to their disdain for the challenges to femininity that the war had brought about. Many women became more 'masculine' during the war and dancing was one way of encouraging the femininity of such 'errant' women.[75] Sections of the press were keen to emphasize this. For example, in 1942 the Social Club of the Women's Land Army was opened in Stratford-upon-Avon and *Dance News*' report was predictably patronizing: 'There was no suggestion of the "tough girl" among those present. They might have been able to perform prodigious feats in the course of their daily work but here, attractively dressed and well groomed they were the sort of nice girls you can meet anywhere at this type of function.'[76] Being able to dance well, in the appropriate clothes, was one way of re-asserting the femininity of wartime women. *Dancing Times* made similar comments on the clothing of girls from the 'Factory Front' in Liverpool in 1942, commenting: 'they still retain their peacetime attire despite the call of coupons and the fact that shell-filling or machine jobs have played havoc with their manicured hands.'[77]

Women's ability to express their identity in the dance hall through dress was similarly fraught with difficulties after 1945. Once the war ended, there was not an automatic return to pre-war availability of clothing. Indeed, clothes rationing continued until 1949 and there were severe shortages of cosmetics and other essentials for dressing up that lasted until the mid-1950s. Yet, once the restrictions and shortages ended and a new sense of affluence emerged, the dance hall resumed its place as one of the most important venues for showing off clothes, hairstyles, and personal style. With greater resources available than ever before, the later 1950s became a golden age for women to dress up in the dance hall. For some, it was a highlight. Pat Spencer, dancing in Liverpool in the early 1950s, recalls that this was her favourite part of the evening: 'Getting done up, I love getting ready to go out. You had that buzz. That's it really. I was so confident, you see.'[78] Many women would put considerable time and effort into choosing their outfits. Stella Morrison dancing in the early 1950s in Bolton recalled preparations for monthly trips to

[73] GDHI, John Robb, b. 1927, 20 June 2011.
[74] M-O A, FR757, 'WAAF Life', June 1941, 4.
[75] See pp. 229–30.
[76] *DN*, 10 January 1942, 2.
[77] *DT*, December 1942, 147.
[78] LDHI, Pat Spencer, b. 1933, 21 July 2009.

Blackpool dances: 'We would plan for weeks in between what we were going to wear. We went into Manchester to C&A to find something to wear. We were always style conscious, it was a big part of the trip planning what we were going to wear.'[79] By the end of the 1950s there was greater variety and more income again. For young working- and middle-class women in an era of full employment, dance outfits were one of the most visible outward signs of a new affluence and one of the most important ways of recognizing their new financial independence. The spending power available to choose new clothes could be considerable. Margaret Taylor, dancing in Glasgow at this time, commented:

> Every week you had something new. You didn't want to turn up with something you had worn the week before because all the other girls would have something new. You would go out with your pay on Friday lunchtime and buy yourself a new blouse and wear whatever skirt you had. Another week you would buy a new pair of shoes and a clutch bag... I used to have my hair done as well.[80]

Inspired by images of the new female form, particularly a new emphasis on having a large and pronounced bosom, women became skilled at enhancing their dance hall appearance using all sorts of tricks. Millicent Thorp (b. 1937) from Manchester recalled: 'We used to wear whirlpool bras that we dipped in sugar water to stiffen them. We also put sugar and water on our hair before we put it in pin curls for a couple of hours before we went out.'[81] Increasingly, dance halls improved the facilities available to allow women to adjust and enhance their appearance on site too. As one dancer recollected, it was quite common for women to get ready in the halls: 'You would see girls coming in with their hair in curlers and a headscarf on. They would go into the cloakrooms and do their hair and things, then come out with a glamorous hairstyle.'[82] The range of facilities provided for women could be impressive. In Dundee dance halls, for example, there were automatic perfume machines which allowed women to apply scent: 'In the cloakrooms they could get a squirt of perfume from a machine for 6d—"Evening in Paris" or "Lily of the Valley" or something.'[83] Even for those younger girls still at school and with more restricted incomes, home-made clothes meant that they could remain fashionable. As Barbara Nott (b. 1942) dancing in Crewe at the time recalls: 'we'd buy two and a half yards of material from the market and make ourselves a skirt in the week to go to dances at the weekend... you didn't like to go to the dance in the same things all the time.'[84] It must be remembered too that the emergence of distinctive youth styles of clothing, outlined in Chapter 5, meant that more and more women were expressing themselves in individual ways. With a wider range of clothes and styles available and greater peer acceptance of 'individuality', experimentation in clothing was on the increase.

79 NWSA Oral History: 2006.0145, Stella Morrison, b. 1933, 2006.
80 GDHI, Margaret Taylor, b. 1938, 31 May 2011.
81 NWSA Oral History: 2001.0417, Millicent Thorp, b. 1937, 2001.
82 DDHI, Sandy Melville, b. 1934, 11 March 2011.
83 DDHI, Sandy Melville, b. 1934, 11 March 2011.
84 CDHI, Barbara Nott, b. 1942, 30 June 2014.

However, as before, there were limits to women's freedom to dress as they pleased. Throughout the post-war period there was considerable pressure to push women in certain directions with their clothing. In January 1946, for example, partly dismayed at the new fashion for 'inelegant' short skirts and partly in order to help overcome clothing shortages, Mecca encouraged women to dig out their 'long, pretty frocks' for the dance hall. Moreover, they encouraged women to do this in order to satisfy men. A journalist in their magazine *Danceland* opined: 'hundreds of returned servicemen have complained to me about the drabness of our modern ballroom as far as the ladies' dresses are concerned. Afternoon frocks, blouses and skirts, or tailored suits are OK for an afternoon dance, but in the evening let's go gay.'[85] Similarly in 1948 women were advised to pay particular attention to their faces as this was what would be under most scrutiny by men: 'your partner in a dance *does* have a very "close up" view of you; and, in the way that men have, no doubt indulges in some unspoken observations about your general appearance!'[86] The same magazine also contained a regular column, 'Beauty in the Ballroom' with the strap-line 'Prepare in Advance, for the Night of the Dance'.[87] The female columnists could be scathing about women who dared to be different: 'You will have noticed little Dresdens in pastel shaded dresses, wearing toy solider cheek blobs of rouge; and dark skinned girls attempting to look pale-and-interesting by using none at all. Both equally disastrous.'[88] Women in the dance hall often exerted their own forms of censure over their peers too. One Glasgow dancer remembered:

> In the fifties it was a straight black skirt and a spotted blouse or a taffeta frilled skirt with a white nylon blouse with a little rose at your throat. If you were a little bit gallous you would wear a tight sweater with a little handkerchief tied at the side like a cowboy.[89]

Over-emphasis on appearance might also be condemned, as one woman complained: 'Some girls were never out of the ladies room doing themselves up renewing their make up in the big mirrors.'[90]

Thus, the dance hall was a vital arena for the expression of female identity via clothing throughout the twentieth century. It allowed women to experiment with who they were and how they looked, albeit within the bounds of peer and societal pressure. Nevertheless, the assertions and definitions of femininity worked out and displayed in the dance hall were an important part of women's greater social and cultural emancipation.

THE DANCE HALL AND WOMEN'S INTERACTION WITH MEN

The dance hall provided an arena where young women could explore their sexuality and develop an assertiveness seldom found outside. Although more common

85 *Danceland*, January 1946, 1.
86 *Danceland*, July 1948, 8.
87 *Danceland*, October 1947, 8.
88 *Danceland*, October 1948, 8.
89 GDHI, Margaret Taylor, b. 1938, 31 May 2011.
90 Ibid.

among men, for both men and women one of the most significant functions of the dance hall was the opportunities it offered for meeting members of the opposite sex. We have already dealt with this in some detail previously in reference to the early opportunities for meeting members of the opposite sex amongst the young. We will explore further the way in which women (and men) gained degrees of sexual experience via dancing in the next chapter. Here then we will examine interactions between men and women in regard to the choosing of dance partners. It will be shown that the conventions of the dance hall allowed considerable opportunities for women to exert control and influence over men, and thus were reflective of, and accelerated, changing gender boundaries. The scope for female alteration of the prescribed conventions was not static, however. It changed over time and varied from hall to hall and with different classes of clientele.

We have already seen that during the interwar period the convention of dancing gave agency to men in the choosing of dance partners. It was men's prerogative to approach women and ask them to dance, apart from in the occasional Ladies' Excuse Me dances where roles were reversed. Women particularly looked forward to such occasions as George Taylor dancing in Dundee in the 1920s recalls: 'This was very noticeable when Ladies Choice was announced and they made for the boy of their dreams.'[91] Aside from these occasions, at first sight dance hall conventions seem to reinforce the dominance of men over women in this very public display of ritualistic mating. However, women adopted numerous strategies.

Women's first point of control was the ability to say 'no'. Men could not force women to dance with them if they did not want to and women were at liberty to refuse as many times as they wished. Indeed, the ability to say no was a powerful weapon in women's social armouries. Furthermore the way in which the refusal was carried out allowed women to censure and control men. Not that women were free to be 'rude' to men without condemnation—those who did were usually shunned by peer pressure. It must also be noted that women risked gaining the reputation for being 'frigid' or 'cold' if they continually turned men's advances down. Gossip and name-calling were powerful currency in the closely knit communities from which dancers came. Nevertheless, this cut both ways. Deciding who to refuse was usually a matter of personal preference, but it should be noted that women developed powerful networks to alert one another of men to avoid. Men who were 'too persistent', those who were bad dancers, boring, smelly, too frisky—the list of possible objections was endless—would be made known to and passed around the female dancing community, with men potentially 'blacklisted'. It must be noted, however, that the room for women to exert influence varied considerably. In some dance halls, the etiquette for asking for a dance was particularly draconian. In many interwar dance halls in Liverpool, for example, women had very little opportunity to say no. As one woman dancing in the mid-1930s remembered:

> If a young man came over and asked you for a dance and you refused to get up with him, you were barred from the dance hall . . . Even if you didn't like them . . . Even if

[91] C. F. Taylor, *Round the Dundee Dance Halls from the 1920s* (Dundee: Private, 1987).

you hated the sight of him. And sometimes you did. The way he danced you or the way he held you, even, you didn't like. There was plenty of things you didn't like about them . . . you could get, be asked to leave, if he reported you, or they knew that she'd refused.[92]

However, even if through peer pressure a woman had agreed to dance with a man whom she did not like, she still reserved the right to end the pairing immediately after the dance had come to an end. It was perfectly acceptable to have one dance and then never see each other again. There was no expectation or sense of entitlement created by agreeing to a dance. Women did not have to put up with any 'funny business' either. Men who held too tightly, or whose hands slipped to 'non-approved' places on the woman's body could be reported to the MCs and other dance hall staff. Dance hall managements themselves looked carefully for such behaviour anyway, and tried to eliminate it when they saw it.

In addition to saying no, women could also help influence the choice of partner by careful manoeuvring within the hall. Some women became adept at positioning themselves in places where they were most likely to be 'chosen' by the man they wanted to dance with. Standing across from them on the opposite side of the hall, pretending not to have noticed any glances that might be coming from the men's half of the room, women could also attract the attention of men they wanted to dance with, with glances of their own. One Liverpool dancer, for example, notes how she and other women tried to get their man: 'we'd move up to where he was standing, you see, navigate through the crowd and be nearby and hope that he'd ask you to dance . . . Or you'd smile at them.'[93] Female friends might also be utilized in order to get the chosen man. Particularly attractive female friends might be used as a kind of 'bait' to attract men and then allow the other female members of the group to step in and take the dance at the last moment. Powerful female friendship networks were in operation in the dance hall either consciously or subconsciously acting in a way to maximize the opportunities for finding an eligible dance partner.

Women's control over their interactions with men underwent some important changes during the Second World War however. The wartime shortage of men, together with increasing self-confidence among many young women, led to some experiments with gender boundaries in the dance hall. The most notable of these experiments was the so-called 'Equal Rights' campaign promoted by Mecca dance halls. In December 1941 the Mecca dance hall chain, using its journal *Dance News*, started a campaign to try to oust the pre-war system of choosing a partner. Under the front page headline 'We demand Equal Rights for Women—Pick Your Own Partners in the Dancehalls!' it argued:

It is absurd that in 1941 the rigid rule that ladies must be asked to dance by gentlemen should continue. *Dance News* demands that this antiquated custom should be abolished and that women should have equal rights, and be able to ask the men to dance . . . In this war the women are playing their full part alongside the men. They

[92] LDHI, Jane Campbell, b. 1922, 23 June 2009.
[93] LDHI, Marjorie Hooley, b. 1917, 23 June 2009.

are serving in the ATS, WAAF, WRNS, and other services. They are doing men's jobs in factories . . . We urge girls not to wait until they are asked to dance. Go up to the men and say, 'May I?' or make your request more emphatic if you like.[94]

It was trialled almost immediately at Mecca's own Royal Opera House Covent Garden and declared 'an enormous success'.[95] The campaign soon spread to Scotland, where at the Edinburgh Palais during Christmas week 1941 girls were asked to use the right to choose their partners following an announcement over the microphone. A few weeks later *Dance News* was able to report that '[g]irls in increasing numbers are seizing the opportunity of asking the men to dance, instead of having to wait on their pleasure'. By the end of January 1942 *Dance News* observed that 'equal rights for women in the dance halls is rapidly becoming a definite policy in most halls in the country'.[96] Whether or not this was accurate, the experiment had certainly created debate. The opinions of some of those dancers who wrote to *Dance News* on the issue are worth considering at length, for they give us an interesting insight into wartime thoughts about gender relations, and women's roles. One girl in favour, Miss Rowcroft of Salford, argued: 'we pay our expenses to come in to dance, not to sit there and have the fun of watching the chaps look us over and see them getting up to every dance and with just whom they want. I think "Lady's Privilege Night" a great idea.'[97] It made some men more sympathetic to women too. 'Why Not Equal Rights Every Night?' asked Alan Ross of Edinburgh in 1942. The experiment had made him realize how women must feel to be rejected, when he was not asked to dance at a ladies' choice night: 'Not being a double of Robert Taylor, this is understandable enough,' he wrote, 'but it rather brought it home to me how girls who are seldom asked to dance must feel. If I felt somewhat depressed after two or three dances, what is the effect of a whole evening of the same experience?' It was their contribution to the war effort that meant women should have equal rights, he argued: 'I consider that as ladies are taking on an almost equal share in the prosecution of the war, surely they are entitled to a fuller share in the few enjoyments that are possible under present conditions. It cannot be very amusing for a war worker to come to the Palais for some dancing on her one night off duty, and then have to spend most of the time in kicking her heels.'[98] The campaign even gained support from a surprising quarter—Victor Silvester—who argued: 'I agree that in these wartime days, particularly when many girls find themselves away from home and in strange surroundings, it is a big advantage if they can have the right to ask for dances . . . The right of the man to ask the lady for a dance may be just another of these old-fashioned customs which must give way to modern ideas. It will be very interesting to watch the progress of the new movement.'[99]

Not everyone was in agreement though. Alex Moore, another leading dance teacher, thought that the equal rights scheme would produce more problems than it

94 *DN*, 13 December 1941, 1.
95 *DN*, 20 December 1941, 1.
96 *DN*, 31 January 1942, 3.
97 *DN*, 21 February 1942, 2.
98 *DN*, 28 February 1942, 3.
99 *DN*, 10 January 1942, 1.

solved. The problem of how men could turn down women was a key issue for him. Moore argued: 'To my mind the crux of the whole question lies in the fact that a lady can quite easily and gracefully refuse to dance with a man, but would it sound quite so good if a man pleaded tiredness or a headache when, for some legitimate reason he did not wish to accept an invitation to dance?' He suggested a reversion to three or four 'Lady's Privilege' dances in every programme.[100] P. H. Tapsell, writing in the *Modern Dance and Dancer*, also thought the idea unnecessary, admitting that he was not prepared for this degree of role reversal. He argued: 'the thought of ladies habitually choosing their male partners is somewhat alarming . . . It would appear that however much we admit the necessity of a woman doing a man's work in the factory, in the ballroom we still prefer . . . her to be gracefully feminine rather than a long-trousered she-man.'[101]

Furthermore, despite successes at some dance halls, there is no evidence that the campaign was taken up in the majority of ballrooms. Even when trials were offered in particular halls, not everyone participated. For example, when the 'Ladies' Choice' evening was first introduced in Edinburgh's dance halls, only about half of the women present took advantage of the opportunity to choose their own partners.[102] Some women were unsure about using the new power, one woman expressing her unease thus: 'I feel you ought to publish a book of guidance to us gals "Who To Choose and Why"' wrote Alice Greening of Pendleton.[103] Another female dancer thought that the experiment would cause confusion: 'In my opinion the Ladies Equality idea is not going to be very popular. A large percentage of the male patrons are strangers on leave and they would be rather mystified to be invited to dance, thus making it very embarrassing for the lady who would have to spend the dance explaining her behaviour . . . On the whole, the average dancer has a good time so why cause a minor revolution for the best dancers.'[104] Whilst some of these sentiments could be explained by unfamiliarity with the new system, the fact that the campaign was not sustained nor did it gain the momentum sufficient to alter dance hall etiquette permanently, is important. By 1944, the same questions were being asked about the problem of women 'wallflowers', Eddie Winstone asking in *Modern Dance and Dancer*: 'A keen girl dancer after a hard day's work at factory or office requires the tonic of some dancing and social contact, and risks the dangers of the Blackout and Air Raids in search of the same. Is there any school in London where she can be guaranteed sufficient dances to make her feel that her evening out has not been wasted?'[105]

So, how can we assess the significance of this 'Equal Rights' campaign in the dance hall? First we should consider where the impetus for the campaign came from and why. This move was sponsored largely by the Mecca chain of dance halls, and does not appear to be the result of demands from women themselves to take the initiative. Had the campaign been the result of a groundswell of female assertiveness, it would have been very significant indeed. However, the initial motives seem

[100] *DN*, 17 January 1942, 3.
[101] *MDD*, May 1941, 10.
[102] *DN*, 3 January 1942, 1.
[103] *DN*, 24 January 1942, 4.
[104] *DN*, 21 February 1942, 2.
[105] *MDD*, March 1944, 23.

to have been largely commercial. Clearly Mecca had considerable self-interest in this campaign. The majority of its patrons were women and the company had to consider their enjoyment if it was to make money. With so many men absent it could often be a lonely and unappealing evening for some women to spend in a dance hall if they were not asked to dance by men. Mecca was no doubt concerned then that such women would be deterred from entering its dance halls, and thus they would lose their most profitable section of the audience. It needed to shake things up. It could also be seen to be 'on the side of women' in promoting such a campaign. However, of more significance is the response of women to this campaign. The hesitancy and reluctance of many women to accept the new roles in the dance hall which Mecca was offering them suggest that the move towards equality between men and women was limited. The campaign didn't seem to ignite a great deal of interest either—Mecca's *Dance News* constantly invited readers' opinions on the topic, offering a prize and publication for the best letters, but even this did not result in the expected surge of debate. Traditional gender roles were not easily overturned and there appears to be a natural conservatism on the part of both women and men to altering the rules of courtship. Nevertheless, the dance hall was offering women the ability to experiment with their identities and to push the boundaries of gender relations. This was significant and important. Some women did grasp this opportunity and became more assertive in the process. It allowed them an unprecedented degree of independence and illustrated that convention could be broken if this was desired.

In the post-war period, the brief and largely isolated wartime experiments with changing the rules of choosing a partner were abandoned. Certainly, it was clear that some women seemed to like the arrangement. Marie Kernan, dancing in Liverpool in the late 1950s remarked: 'They were the men, you know. A girl to ask a man? That was awful!'[106] Yet despite a return to pre-war norms, there were some important changes in the later 1950s and early 1960s which were reflective of changing gender boundaries. Despite the return to the convention of men asking women to dance, there was an increased perception amongst women themselves that they were influencing this process. As Pat Spencer from Liverpool put it: 'I always say we picked the man out ourselves, you know what I mean? I still think that women are making the eye contact and that.'[107] Positioning within the hall was still important: 'If you sat against the wall, that was it—you had no chance. You just had to get up and come forward and let them know you were expecting to get taken up on the floor.'[108] Another dancer agreed: 'Sometimes if there was someone you liked or fancied, you would move over to the men's groups.'[109] There were still numerous ways to turn men down too. Marie Kernan recalls: 'you'd say you didn't like the music... "Oh, no I don't like this one," you know, and it was him you

106 LDHI, Marie Kernan, b. 1942, 21 July 2009.
107 LDHI, Pat Spencer, b. 1933, 21 July 2009.
108 GDHI, Margaret Taylor, b. 1938, 31 May 2011.
109 GDHI, Agnes McHugh, b. 1934, 1 June 2011.

didn't like. Cos you had your eye on someone else.'[110] A dancer from Glasgow noted how women would pull together in order to avoid being asked to dance by someone they did not like: 'Sometimes you would get a creepy guy you didn't want to dance with so we would try to keep talking so that he would pass by.'[111] It would appear, however, that by the late 1950s and early 1960s it was increasingly common for women simply to say no, a fact that was reflected on and often resented by men, as we shall discuss later.[112] Neil Foster, a man dancing near Liverpool in the late 1950s and early 1960s, observed: 'All the girls stood in lines around the edge waiting to be asked to dance and if they didn't get asked they didn't dance. On the other hand, the girls could easily turn the boys down when they were asked. That meant they would sheepishly go back to their mates who had been watching their progress.'[113] In some places, women seemed to be getting more assertive. As Stewart Murray recalls: 'You never really got many knock backs in the Majestic but at the Locarno, they weren't as polite when they told you they didn't want to dance... some of them could be quite cheeky, they would say "well, why are you asking me?!"'[114] Another change appeared to be a greater emphasis on women choosing their partner on the basis of looks. Dancing skill was no longer as important as one Liverpool dancer recollects: 'It doesn't matter. If you liked him. If he had nice eyes or... nice hair. But if he was ugly, like you know... If he was [ugly] and he couldn't dance he was on his own!'[115] Related to this increasing self-confidence, by the mid-1960s many women became increasingly dissatisfied with the traditional rituals of partner dancing found in dance halls. As we shall discuss later, by this time the development of solo dancing together with demands for greater equality meant an increasing refusal to allow men to determine who danced with whom. Despite the considerable room for female control of the process already outlined, many women rejected the conventions that had existed for the previous forty years. The etiquette of the ballroom seemed increasingly anachronistic to women of the later 1960s, and this was one of the reasons for the decline of the dance hall as a social and cultural phenomenon.

CONCLUSION

For women then, dancing and the dance hall were pivotal to their identities and their quality of life. As a rare public arena that was geared towards their tastes and interests, where they often outnumbered men, and where they could interact with men with a considerable degree of freedom and equality, the dance hall was also vital to women's growing emancipation. Through dancing, women could express themselves, increase their self-confidence, and boost their physical and mental health. It was wholly liberating.

110 LDHI, Marie Kernan, b. 1942, 21 July 2009.
111 GDHI, Margaret Taylor, b. 1938, 31 May 2011. 112 See pp. 236–7.
113 NWSA Oral History: 2001.0725, Neil Foster, b. 1940, 2001.
114 GDHI, Stewart Murray, b. 1940, 19 July 2011.
115 LDHI, Marie Kernan, b. 1942, 21 July 2009.

Chapter 7
Romance and Intimacy in the Dance Hall

INTRODUCTION

As a result of its requirement for heterosexual coupling, the dance hall soon assumed an important social function as a venue for meeting members of the opposite sex. Indeed, throughout the period under investigation, the dance hall was central to dating and marriage in Britain. In 1953 *The Economist* observed: 'To dress up and mix with a large crowd, to dance with soft lights and sweet music, has an almost universal appeal for young workers. Certainly a well-run dance hall is nowadays as satisfactory an arrangement for boy to meet girl as any social worker could devise.'[1] This role was well established before the 1950s, however. As early as the 1920s the dance hall was regarded as an important meeting place by virtually everybody. By the 1930s, both those who approved and disapproved of the public dance hall were well aware of its function as a place to meet members of the opposite sex. A 32-year-old male civil engineer from Surrey described this role in 1939:

> The chief social function of dance halls is to get young people of both sexes together. It is very often a young boy or girl's first introduction to the opposite sex . . . many men first met their wives at the dance hall.[2]

The Carnegie Trust similarly remarked:

> The main attraction of dancing is the opportunity it gives for the sexes to mix socially. (A number of the married men said they had first met their wives at dances.) In this it meets a real need. Where can young men and women of the industrial classes mingle socially other than in the dance hall?[3]

Let's explore how the dance hall served this vital social function and the extent to which it led to romantic and intimate encounters.

THE DANCE HALL AND THE RULES OF COURTSHIP

First, a study of the conventions used to ask partners to dance during the 1920s and 1930s, and the advantages the dance hall had over other forms of entertainment as a

[1] *The Economist*, 14 February 1953, 401.

[2] M-O A: Directive Reply: 'Jazz 2, July 1939', 'F. H. Milner'.

[3] C. Cameron, A. J. Lush, and G. Meara (eds), *Disinherited Youth* (Edinburgh: Carnegie United Kingdom Trust, 1943), 105.

way of meeting potential romantic partners. One reason why the dance hall was such a popular place to meet members of the opposite sex was that dancing required heterosexual coupling. Because forming a couple was central to proceedings, it made the preliminary introductions between the sexes easier, offering a set of prescribed conventions on the choosing of dancing partners and permitting interaction between strangers. As Tom Harrisson noted:

> The ballroom sanctions the approach without introduction, 'picking-up' and 'getting-off' are accepted as normal behaviour... Here, there is none of the preliminary manoeuvring... The method of approach is more confident, since prescribed by convention, and the chances of success are greater. Once the introduction is made the course of the acquaintanceship is a matter of mutual preference.[4]

In the interwar period, the central convention was that the man asked the woman to dance.[5] Only in special circumstances was this role reversed. The man would approach the female side of the hall, select his partner and usually ask 'May I have this dance', or something similar. George Taylor dancing in Dundee in the 1920s recalls: 'romance started with the words "Do you come here often?" or "You're a smashing dancer", when the answer most often was "You're no so bad yourself."'[6] At the dance hall then, men and women could meet with only the briefest of introductions. Indeed, this was the expectation. This made pairing up with strangers easier than in any other social setting. As the period progressed, the method of introduction became even more informal. In 1938 a Bolton dance hall manager commented of these changes that 'they are not less chivalrous, it's just because they are more direct... they will converge, what has happened is that they have had a nod from the man, they understand, watch the man move up to a girl, he hardly speaks, but the woman turns to him with her arms ready to begin.'[7] For working-class dancers, this kind of informality came naturally, and it was one reason for dancing's popularity.

If the central conventions of public dancing made finding a dancing partner straightforward, then particular dances provided greater opportunities to find romantic partners than others. 'Optional' or 'Excuse-Me' dances were ones where an individual could approach any couple on the dance floor, touch a member of their own sex who would stop and give up their partner. As Mass Observation remarked: 'Such dances... give an opportunity for everyone to dance with the partners they wish. If you see a girl or boy dancing past with whom you wish to dance you walk on to the floor, touch his or her arm, whereupon the partner will break away and you dance off with your prize—until someone else does the same to you.'[8]

There were limits to the sociability of the dance hall however. Cliquishness was one problem. As we have seen, many groups of friends attended dances en masse

[4] M-O A: Worktown: 60/D, 'Dancing', 1938, 9.

[5] Although as we have seen, women could exercise a large degree of control of the proceedings—see Chapter 6.

[6] C. F. Taylor, *Round the Dundee Dance Halls from the 1920s* (Dundee: Private, 1987), 10.

[7] M-O A: MJD: TC38/5/F, 'Alfred Clarke, Empress Hall, Bolton', 15 July 1938, 7.

[8] M-O A: Worktown: 48/C, 'Shall We Dance?', 1939, 2.

and often they remained together throughout the evening. In 1925 Elsie Denham, writing in *Popular Music and Dancing Weekly*, observed:

> The success of the dance depends entirely upon a thoroughly sociable atmosphere . . . no man or girl need be a stranger to his neighbour in the dance room; but with so many dancers forming themselves into separate parties and dancing only among themselves, the difficulties that beset the lonely visitor are hard to overcome.[9]

An observation of a Peckham dance hall in 1939 confirmed how this remained a common problem by the end of the period too: 'Although everyone was natural and jolly, they seemed to collect into almost exclusive small groups and keep together all the time.'[10] A 25-year-old female receptionist from London noted: 'There is . . . an objectionable unwritten rule at large London dance-halls, that the men will only dance with the girls they *know* to be excellent dancers, and will not ask a stranger, however good she may be . . . '[11]

The degree of 'picking up' and 'getting off' also depended on the night of the week and, therefore, the sort of clientele that was in attendance. 'Learners' nights', for those beginning to dance, were the most obvious place to go for introductions and they had a reputation for attracting a sociable crowd. 'Dancers' nights', however, were for the enthusiast. The keenest dancers were totally absorbed in their dancing. The following comments were made about a specialist 'Harlem Night' in a Bolton dance hall:

> One of these girls said to the obs[erver], 'I'm a man-hater . . . I come here for the dancing, not to meet men' and this represents what observers felt about the whole affair—that all the chaps and girls were here because they enjoyed dancing for its own sake, and did not use the dance as an avenue to the process of getting-off with one another.[12]

Such comments should remind us that whilst the majority probably went dancing for both social reasons and for the love of dancing itself, a minority went solely for one or the other reason. Certainly, a minority of dancing enthusiasts had emerged by the early 1920s whose dancing was not motivated by romance. In 1925, Irene Green, a correspondent in Newcastle's *Sunday Sun*, describing these 'serious dancers', lamented the fact that dancing was no longer about romance, but about dancing technique. She argued that in the past:

> dances were always excellent opportunities of meeting new people . . . they were also the scene of the beginning of many a happy love affair . . . All this has changed now. A man chooses his partner because her steps fit in nicely with his, or as he would put it 'she follows well.' As likely as not they will dance together in the evening and enjoy themselves thoroughly, but . . . It is more the exception than the rule that dancing alliances develop into romances. The couples do not seem to combine so well when off the floor.[13]

9 *PMDW*, 17 January 1925, 245.
10 M-O A: MJD: 38/1/I, 'Rye Lane IX6', March 1939, 6.
11 M-O A: DR: 'Jazz 2, July 1939', 'E. Pollock'.
12 M-O A: Worktown: 48/C, 'Harlem Night at the Aspen Hall', 13 July 1938, 6.
13 *Sunday Sun*, 20 December 1925, 2.

She was wrong about the claim that dances were no longer places for romantic liasons, but she correctly identifies the emergence of a section of the dancing patronage who were there to dance for the sake of dancing. Such dancers were more likely to be women rather than men, and this further illustrates that for women dancing performed a multitude of social functions beyond the romantic. Despite these limitations, by the end of the 1930s dancing's role as a venue and opportunity to meet potential dates was well established and well known.

The impact of the war on the dance hall's role as a place for 'picking up' was considerable. During the war, disruptions to daily life intensified the dance hall's function as a key social centre. In addition, the atmosphere in the dance hall altered in important ways which increased its sociability and thus the potential for having romantic encounters. However, whilst these things made finding a partner easier, the war also created new problems, primarily as a result of the shortage of men. This led to interesting innovations in the 'picking up' process.

The crowds in dance halls and other venues became increasingly 'mixed' as mobilization of men and women for war work, conscription, and evacuation, all uprooted people from their normal backgrounds. Making friends in unfamiliar surroundings, away from existing familial and workplace networks could be difficult. Dances thus offered a vital way of meeting new people in a period of extraordinary stress. Accordingly, dancing with strangers became even more common, and even more acceptable, during the war. As one man in the RAF during the war remembers: 'there were many more people moving around in the war, soldiers, sailors and that's how they got to know each other socially . . . You were moving around, so that was how you met people, it was part of the routine.'[14] Indeed, the war saw a marked increase in the number of people attending dances for primarily social reasons. Even more than in peacetime, dancing increasingly became a means to an end—meeting people, on both a platonic and a romantic basis, rather than dancing for its own sake. The number of 'serious dancers' in dance halls was therefore reduced dramatically. Mecca's Carl Heimann was quick to recognize and encourage this, stating in 1941 that the war had brought the dance hall's social side 'prominently to the fore', describing 'dance palaces' as 'a real social centre where they can meet their fellow human beings on equal terms, and without introduction'.[15] In addition, the wartime dancing public introduced greater gaiety to wartime dances, making them less serious, and even more sociable. The manager of the Streatham Locarno, for example, noted that '[p]eople are looking for an atmosphere these days . . . they are concerned with enjoying themselves'.[16] Heimann concurred: 'there is more of a spirit of abandonment, more of a desire to crowd into a few hours a romp, a laugh and something of the "Party" atmosphere.'[17] This 'party atmosphere', especially prevalent during 'party dances' made social interactions easier, as the frequency with which dancers could change partners was increased.

[14] GDHI, John Lang, b. 1921, 3 August 2011.
[15] Anon., *Danceland Souvenir 1941* (1940), 2.
[16] M-O A, TC 38/1/A, 'Chaperlin 1.11.39', 1–2.
[17] *DT*, December 1939, 142.

However, whilst dance halls tended to become more sociable, the war often created a shortage of men. At key points during the war there were more women than men in dance halls, leading to an increasing 'wallflower' problem. In an attempt to alleviate this problem, traditional dance hall etiquette on picking dancing partners was often overturned. For example, in dance halls in Hornsey in 1943, there were so many girls without partners that a 'coupon system' for 'rationing' men was introduced. Every woman on her own was given three coupons and she was able to 'register' with any man she chose—giving a coupon to the three men of her choice who would then promise to dance with her. In order to overcome possible reluctance of men to such a scheme, when the dance was over, the men who had collected most coupons were presented with prizes.[18] A similar scheme was tried in Glasgow's Barrowland dance hall in 1944. Every Tuesday women were given a booklet of ten cards which they signed and handed to their selected partners. Such innovations were helping to alter established practice in the dance hall, and had inevitable consequences for the rules of courtship. As *Danceland* put it: 'It naturally also attracts a lot of girls who appreciate the right to make their own choice.'[19] Indeed, this issue of women's right to choose was reflected in a campaign for 'Equal Rights' in the dance hall during the war, which has already been discussed.[20] This Equal Rights campaign was an experiment held mostly in Mecca dance halls that allowed women to choose their dance partners on equal terms with men, not just for special dances, but for the whole dance programme. That it largely failed to catch on is an indication that the established system of choosing dance partners was well entrenched. Nevertheless, the equal rights campaign shook things up, and the desire of women not to be 'left on the shelf' indicated that romantic coupling was a chief attraction of the dance hall.

There were other developments too. During the war, some contemporaries were alarmed that the 'picking up process' was becoming too easy. Some in the dancing press argued that older notions of etiquette were being eroded and a much more formulaic, almost 'automatic', method of partner selection, with minimum personal interaction, was being seen in dance halls. For example, in Glasgow dance halls, a common wartime call and response was 'Are ye dancing? Are ye asking?'[21] In some dance halls, the introductions were even briefer. For example, some men, especially those aged 18 to 28, no longer bothered to walk up to women and speak to them in order to get them onto the dance floor. Instead, as the *Modern Dance and Dancer* noted in 1941, these men invited the girl to dance by an 'ugly simultaneous movement of jerking the head and flicking the thumb towards the floor'. Another type 'merely raises the eyebrows whilst inclining the head slightly towards the dancers'.[22] The dancing press were out of touch and behind the times, however, as these kinds of 'automatic' methods of securing a partner had been around for some time in public dance halls. The concerns expressed were more

[18] *Danceland*, October 1943, 4. [19] *Danceland*, August 1944, 3.
[20] See Chapter 6. [21] GDHI, William Dewar, b. 1924, 27 June 2011.
[22] *MDD*, July 1941, 15.

likely part of a wider concern about changing social and moral boundaries believed to have been brought about by the war, as we will see later.[23] Despite the numerous attempted innovations, in fact wartime conventions on choosing dance partners changed very little. The dance's role as a venue to meet people became, however, even more central to the lives of most younger Britons.

Following the war, the dance hall continued to fulfil a crucial social function as a place for young men and women to meet. Indeed, in the immediate aftermath of the war, returning soldiers found the dance hall a vital arena in which to become re-integrated into civilian society. Their lack of up-to-date dancing skills did not inhibit the formation of couples. As Mary O'Neill (b. 1920) stated: 'When the boys came back on leave in 1945 they flocked to these dances, they loved it. But they couldn't do the steps—the girls were very willing to teach them.'[24] The re-integration of servicemen into civilian society and their re-introduction to dating was boosted considerably by the dance hall's continuing function as the place to meet. Indeed, by the mid-1950s the dance hall's place as an informal 'marriage bureau' seemed irreplaceable. The opinions of several dancers from the time confirm just how central it was to dating. From Liverpool, Marie Kernan (b. 1942) argues: 'That was the only place . . . You know, the pictures was rubbish . . . You're just sitting quiet, watching the picture. That came later on, the pictures. But dance halls was *the* place to meet, was the only place to meet . . . '[25] In Dundee it was the same—Jack Hogan (b. 1936): 'Basically there were no other places. That was where you met at the dance halls . . . God knows where you met if you didn't like dancing!'[26] In Glasgow too, Margaret Taylor (b. 1938) agreed: 'There were so many who met at the Guild who got engaged and then married . . . It was amazing how many people paired up.'[27]

The reputation of the dance hall as a place to meet potential partners was also discussed widely in the press. In January 1946, for example, Brian Murtough in an article for the *Daily Mirror* on dancing in Britain pointed to 'romance' as one of the key reasons why people attended dance halls. He asked: 'How many friendships, how many romances have been made to the strains of a waltz?'[28] Later, in 1950, Marshall Pugh writing in the same newspaper estimated that 70 per cent of couples first met at a dance hall.[29] As the reputation of the dance hall as a place to meet grew, so the proportion of people attending in order to meet a future partner rose. As Sandy Melville (b. 1934) recalls: 'I think this was conscious or subconscious, but I think you were looking for a mate. I suppose it was a courting ritual . . . It was easier to meet a girl, you needed no introduction.'[30]

The post-war dance hall also saw a clear return to the methods of introduction that had been prevalent before the war. The few wartime experiments with 'equal rights', that had been born out of expediency and were largely unfavoured,

[23] See Chapter 8. [24] GDHI, Mary O'Neill, b. 1920, 8 June 2011.
[25] LDHI, Marie Kernan, b. 1942, 21 July 2009.
[26] DDHI, Jack Hogan, b. 1936, 11 March 2011.
[27] GDHI, Margaret Taylor, b. 1938, 31 May 2011. [28] *DM*, 18 January 1946, 2.
[29] *DM*, 30 November 1950, 4. [30] DDHI, Sandy Melville, b. 1934, 11 March 2011.

completely ended in peacetime. As this report from 1947 illustrates, little had changed:

> As soon as the band begins to play couples make their way on to the floor. Not the slightest reticence is shown by the males—if they want to dance they walk casually around the edge of the floor looking at every girl until they find one of their choosing, they then walk up to the one of their choice and just tap her on the hand or the shoulder. The 'tapped' one, then, without a word, rises, and they go on to the floor and dance, holding each other as if they had known each other for years. They come back the best of pals, sit down and become engrossed in conversation with each other.[31]

By the later 1950s, the convention was the same as it always had been too, with a few concessions: 'The boys asked the girls most of the time, occasionally girls would go and ask a chap to dance. There was always the girls grouped together and the guys grouped together . . . The guys used to have to come across to the girls and ask them to dance.'[32] Indeed, women's growing confidence was to have important repercussions on the popularity of partner dancing, and eventually lead to changes that would usher in solo dancing.

The advantages of the dance hall over other social settings for meeting people remained the same too. The friendly and supportive atmosphere of dance halls aided the pairing-up process. As Jack Hogan (b. 1936) dancing in Dundee in the 1950s recollects: 'There was a camaraderie in the dance hall and the boys would say "Ask her to dance"—you all knew one another. In the Palais you knew everybody.'[33] The strong bonds of community that still existed in Britain during the 1950s were clearly evident in the dance hall, and each town's younger population could enter a dance hall knowing a great number of people already, and more often than not getting to know more as they danced.

However, as before the war, there were some limits to sociability. Shyness, especially on the part of boys, could cause problems, often to the annoyance of girls. Also, despite the friendly atmosphere, some people did not like mixing, as Alistair Brown (b. 1930) dancing in Dundee in the 1950s recalls: 'There would be people who just liked to do certain dances with one person and they wouldn't do those dances with anyone else.'[34] Others would only be available for certain dances, as Dolores Brown (b. 1939) confirmed: 'People did have their favourite dances and they would only want to dance those.'[35] The degree of sociability also depended on the time of the evening. Early on, many men would be in the pub and this was when women would interact with each other. Mixing of the sexes would increase towards the later part of the evening, once men started arriving, often from pubs. As one Dundee dancer recalls: 'it gradually built up, if you went when it first opened at 8 o'clock the girls would tend to congregate down one side and the boys down the

31 M-O A, FR2473, *Report on Juvenile Delinquency* (1947), 48–9.
32 GDHI, Jean Murray, b. 1942, 19 July 2011.
33 DDHI, Jack Hogan, b. 1936, 11 March 2011.
34 DDHI, Alistair Brown, b. 1930, 22 April 2011.
35 DDHI, Dolores Brown, b. 1939, 22 April 2011.

other and then as it warmed up you began to intermingle...'[36] However, many dance halls, particularly Mecca, disapproved of drinking, and could often refuse entry to patrons who had had too much to drink. Thus, the lack of 'Dutch courage' amongst some men could also lend them an air of awkwardness.

The opposite extremes of behaviour were also a factor in reducing the effectiveness of the dance hall as a place to find romance. Some men and women were too intent on trying to 'get off' with one another. In 1953 the *Daily Mirror* described the 'palais pests' who often 'ruined the atmosphere of the dance hall with their selfish behaviour'. It warned girls to look out for the 'boy who reels in from the pub at closing time and wants to breathe down her neck' and the boy who 'gets jealous if a girl he knows dances with anybody else'. Boys were warned to look out for 'the girl who clings round his neck and tries to look as though they are engaged' and the girl 'who uses a dancing partner as a messenger boy to fetch drinks, inquire about last buses', etc.[37]

Despite the presence of 'palais pests' the dance hall occupied an unrivalled position as *the* place to meet members of the opposite sex throughout the whole of the period from the end of the First World War until the early 1960s. The definite requirement of heterosexual coupling gave dancing a prescribed set of conventions for meeting people that could be easily followed, allowing pairing off with the minimum of introductions. The friendly atmosphere also supported the formation of new couples, many of whom were to become romantically involved.

ROMANCE AND THE PALAIS

Aside from the central requirement of partner formation, what was it about dancing and dance halls that led so often to romance? Let's start with an examination of the interwar period where we should consider other features of the dancing experience. The atmosphere of the dance hall, with its soft lighting, partner dancing, and enticing music, certainly provided an adequate backdrop for romance. Lighting was an important feature in creating a romantic ambience in dance halls. Often dance halls were dimly lit, with a mirror ball suspended from the ceiling dispersing 'starlight' over the dancers and the surrounding walls. For slower dances such as the waltz, lights were dimmed further, and coloured filters added, creating a distinctive mood and allowing more discreet intimacy. Added to the generally 'luxurious' surroundings of some of the best dance halls, the emotional impact could be considerable. The music too lent itself to creating a romantic atmosphere, with song titles and their sentiments overwhelmingly focused on love and romance. Indeed, the majority of popular songs written during the period 1918 to 1939 dealt with the universal theme of 'love'. In 1919 for example 42 per cent of the most popular songs in Britain were love songs, rising to 55 per cent by 1935.[38]

[36] DDHI, Sandy Melville, b. 1934, 11 March 2011.

[37] *DM*, 9 October 1953, 10.

[38] J. J. Nott, *Music for the People: Popular Music and Dance in Interwar Britain* (Oxford: Oxford University Press, 2002), 212.

The repertoire of music played by bands in the dance halls would be skewed even more in favour of these romantic numbers. Palais dance bands were skilled at creating programmes designed to appeal to the romantic instincts of dancers, knowing that most of their patrons were young people either on or looking for dates. In Dundee during the 1920s, for example, George Taylor remembers dancing to the 'strains of "Put Your Arms Around Me Honey", "Oh You Beautiful Doll", "Who's Your Lady Friend" . . . I never forgot this hall and dancing the last dance with "Cuddle Up a Little Closer."'[39] The power of this music to move dancers' emotions should not be underestimated. In an age where recorded music dominates, it is difficult to appreciate the power that a well played dance band had in creating 'atmosphere'. Performing songs that its patrons loved, and which everyone knew, and which the dancers could literally 'feel' run through them whilst they held each other on the dance floor, dance bands were integral to the romantic appeal of the palais. The music and low lights could create an intoxicating atmosphere, and were extremely conducive to romance.

Unlike the cinema, dancing also permitted newly formed couples to talk to one another. Jane Campbell dancing in Liverpool in the 1930s recalls: 'more people met in a dance hall than met anywhere else. What can you do in the pictures? You can't meet. You can't. You can go with your friends. But you don't *talk* to anyone. If someone started talking to you, you'd walk away . . . '[40] Finding out about each other, whispering romantic sentiments in each other's ears, or just chatting about the atmosphere were all possible whilst dancing. In addition, there were numerous places to retire to after a dance, where the couples could sit and talk, or dimly lit corners where they might go further.

Although the dancing required heterosexual coupling, there was no sense of obligation on those who had paired up to remain partnered at the end of a dance. Indeed, for many people once the music stopped, the partnership ended. However, having seen their partner close up, listened to their chatter, been held in their arms, caught a glimpse of something in their eye, many dancing couples chose to take things further. So, having decided that they wanted to continue their acquaintance beyond the dance just finished, there were several options available to newly partnered dancers in the dance hall—to carry on dancing, to retire to the balcony or floorside tables and watch, or to have a drink in the bar or café. The bar was often a popular choice. For example, as Mass Observation noted in 1938, the Long Bar, Blackpool Tower Ballroom was: 'occupied almost exclusively by young couples sitting on the long comfortable settees round the back of it, with arms round each other and heads close together'.[41] Similarly, in the Palm Lounge it was 'pretty crowded with people all silent. Love birds twittering, water trickling, subdued lighting. Two embraced couples as the observer enters. Soulful music by orange lit gypsy women. Spooning in corners, even on the auditorium seats listening to

[39] Taylor, *Round*, 6. [40] LDHI, Jane Campbell, b. 1922, 23 June 2009.
[41] M-O A: Worktown: 60/D, 'Dancing', 1938, 27.

music. It is . . . romantic, subdued.'[42] The interwar dance hall then was an ideal venue for romance.

The war brought few changes to the dance hall's social function as a place for couples to find and enjoy romantic encounters. If anything, the circumstances of war made dances even more important as venues for romance. As Mecca noted in 1940 in a typical example of self-promotion, 'they have become meeting places for the youth and middle age of the district . . . Thousands of young folk daily meet their husbands and wives in Britain's better run dance halls.'[43] Indeed, rather than leading to an increase in 'sex', the evidence from the dance hall is that the war brought about an increase in the number of straightforward romantic liasons and an increase in the numbers who then went on to marry.

The difference between dance hall romances in wartime and those in peacetime was the speed with which they progressed. Many people talked of 'love at first sight' in the wartime dance hall. For example one woman from Newhall, Derbyshire, recalling meeting her lifelong love in 1942, remarked: 'I first met him at "The Rink" dance hall in Swadlincote. His name was Frederick . . . and I immediately "liked the look of him" . . . You could say it was love at first sight.'[44] Similarly, one RAF man on meeting a woman at dance in Tisbury, Wiltshire, decided instantly ' "this is the girl I am going to marry" '—which he went on to do shortly afterwards.[45] A soldier in Exeter recalled his first dance with his future wife at the beginning of 1945: 'I saw her across the dance hall and knew she was going to be my girl.'[46] One 17-year-girl attending a dance near Catterick returned from the dance to tell her mother that she 'was in love, love at first sight' after meeting 'the most gorgeous, very handsome blond RAF man'. They married after a three-year courtship.[47] Although such recollections might be coloured by the passing years, emotions certainly could be much heightened during the war. As one Truro man recalls: '[T]his was a time for stolen happiness and the belief of live for today, for there might not be a tomorrow. Each . . . night was precious to lovers . . . There had become a tendency to avoid the reality of this war and to just allow the magic of each moment to happen.'[48] As a result, wartime marriages often followed on soon after initial meetings in the dance hall. For example, one Glasgow woman remembers her own experience at the Barrowland ballroom: 'I met a sailor, out in Glasgow for a day out. He took me home. The following week, he took me to his home town, Burnley. He asked me to marry him in front of his mother, over the breakfast table . . . We were married within three weeks. It lasted 53 years.'[49] This was not uncommon. One woman who danced at the Covent Garden dance hall recalls a similar experience: 'I met my future husband on a blind date, he asked me to marry

[42] Ibid., 24.
[43] *Top Spin: a periodical devoted to the interests of north London dancers*, 1 June 1940, 2.
[44] PWA, Irene Fairall, Article A2729540, 10 June 2004.
[45] PWA, Betty Sutton, Article A3895860, 14 April 2005.
[46] PWA, Christopher Andrews, Article A4374713, 6 July 2005.
[47] PWA, Dorothy Cartwright, Article A4869840, 8 August 2005.
[48] PWA, Neville Harcourt Paddy, Article A4090024, 19 May 2005.
[49] PWA, Betty Clegg, Article A5320450, 25 August 2005.

him that night—I refused. Three weeks later, he asked me again—I said "yes."' They married three months later.[50]

However, despite the increasing role of the dance hall in helping wartime dancers to find 'life partners', there is some evidence that it served another function as a place to meet more 'casual dates' and satisfy a desire for companionship of a semi-romantic nature. Some took a more casual approach to dating during the war, though not necessarily one that meant more sexual activity, nor one that challenged the sanctity of marriage. The dance hall served a vital role in bringing the lonely together. During the war, as the conflict separated lovers, dating became flexible, and many people made new acquaintances at dance halls whilst still in relationships with someone else. For example, one woman from South London recalls how she went on a blind date with her friend to the Locarno, Streatham, whilst she was seeing another man, who was frequently absent working late nights on war work. Her blind date was also already dating, but his partner too was absent, evacuated to Bath. As she explained, he was 'lonely and willing to make the date just for a bit of fun and company'.[51] They ended up marrying, but many more used dance halls as a way of finding company 'for the duration'. Women going out whilst they were in relationships was something relatively new, and fairly common. The relative anonymity of the wartime dance hall made it possible. Women did not necessarily see their dancing dates as serious dates, just someone to have company with whilst their serious boyfriends were away fighting. For example, a Liverpudlian woman recalls how she carried on dancing whilst engaged:

> I was engaged and always wore my engagement ring, but several of them told me it was too small to be an engagement ring . . . And they wouldn't have it, oh no. In fact, one fella, I broke his heart because he really thought I was wearing it to keep people away . . . But it was good for me, insofar as I knew how much I loved my boyfriend and it was all fun.[52]

Some married women did this too. For example, a solider working for Army Welfare in Monmouthshire who organized dances to raise funds for servicemen remembers: 'At these events I met a girl or two, but most of them turned out to be somebody's wife waiting for him to come home from overseas.'[53] As one woman from London recalls, the motives of most of these liasons at the dance hall were innocuous and largely innocent. Even Americans who had a reputation for womanizing were '[f]or the most part lonely and eager for the brief solace of warm human contact, they would hold a girl close, dancing cheek to cheek, smelling excitingly of expensive aftershave and French cigarettes, murmuring sweet inanities. "You have the cutest little ears honey, like pink seashells."'[54]

For both the casual dater and the more serious, as before the war, the final dance of the evening still took on a particular significance in the evening's proceedings. In

[50] PWA, Terri Sanders, Article A2661590, 24 May 2004.
[51] PWA, Sheila Granger, Article A2298459, 16 February 2004.
[52] LDHI, Jane Campbell, b. 1922, 23 June 2009.
[53] PWA, Leonard McKay, Article A3326618, 25 November 2004.
[54] PWA, Margaret Tapster, Article A5827665, 20 September 2005.

virtually all dance halls, this dance, ceremoniously announced, was a waltz, played to lowered lights. The desire to have somebody to dance with for the last dance was great. One Glasgow dancer recalls: 'That was when a lot of the guys asked the girls if they could walk them home, that's why they met up with people. If you didn't get asked to be walked home you went on the bus with your pals.'[55] Wartime circumstances often intruded on the choice of partner, however. In Liverpool during the war, for example, with limited transport facilities and frequent disruptions, it became increasingly common for men to ask where their prospective 'last dance' partner lived, before asking for a dance. If it was too far from his own area, the man would move to another girl.[56] Sometimes women used this as a way of putting off men they did not like. Bert Smith (b. 1926) from Liverpool points out: 'The girls always had a back up with the boys . . . one fella said to the girl "And who's taking you home?" She said: "You can if you want." So he said "OK" and he got outside and he said: "Where do you live?" and she said "Prestwich". That's about fifteen miles away! He said: "Goodnight!"'[57]

During the period from 1945 to 1960, the linking of dance halls with romance was even more deeply entrenched. Many dancers certainly considered the atmosphere in dance halls to be conducive to love. As Jack Hogan (b. 1936) comments, there was a special tone, especially in the larger dance halls: 'It was much more atmospheric, from a romantic point of view. It was a nice ambiance . . . the band stand was lovely . . . the ambiance was lovely, they would have the mirror balls when the slower dances were on . . . '[58] We should remember, however, that some dance halls were better than others for potential romance. Agnes McHugh (b. 1934) remarked: 'I think you had to go somewhere like the Plaza where the lighting was muted, couples went there and regarded it more as a romantic place, rather than the hustle and bustle of the Glasgow dance halls I went to.'[59] Most dance halls, however, deliberately sought to emphasize the romantic aspect of their appeal. For example, Andy Lothian, longstanding bandleader at the Dundee Palais from the 1930s to 1960s, would sometimes announce that someone had got engaged and that they had met in the dance hall. Lothian would also allow time for requests of 'special tunes' connected to particular courting couples, and announce them as such.[60] In Liverpool in 1959, one hall introduced a 'couples only' policy for dances on Saturday nights. Only married or engaged couples were allowed. In order to be romantic, violinists wandered among the tables and mingled with the dancers. There was a 'Cupid's Corner' with soft lights and cocktail bar decorated with a giant wedding cake (see Figs. 7.1 and 7.2) There was also dancing in the dark and a special 'dream time' session when couples requested their favourite memory jerking tunes.[61]

55 GDHI, Jean Meehan, b. 1921, 14 June 2011.
56 LDHI, Vera Jeffers, b. 1925, 22 July 2009.
57 LDHI, Bert Smith, b. 1926, 23 June 2009.
58 DDHI, Jack Hogan, b. 1936, 11 March 2011.
59 GDHI, Agnes McHugh, b. 1934, 1 June 2011.
60 DDHI, Sandy Melville, b. 1934, 11 March 2011.
61 *DM*, 3 November 1959, 15.

Fig. 7.1. Romance and the dance hall: Cupid's Corner, 1954
Source: Scotsman Publications Ltd.

Fig. 7.2. Romance, youth and the dance hall: Teddy Boy and girl, Mecca dance hall, Tottenham, *Picture Post*, 29 May 1954
Source: Getty Images.

Particular dances lent themselves to more romantic encounters too. Slow dances such as the waltz were particularly popular amongst those who wanted to get closer and be more romantic. Even as changing musical trends brought more energetic dances such as Jive, the Twist and so on, the slower dances retained their appeal. As Margaret Taylor (b. 1938) recalls, 'when there was a slow dance . . . the lights were dimmed and the big beautiful ball in the ceiling came on. Then you would dance cheek to cheek. I remember doing that with my husband to be when he learnt to dance.'[62] Kath Hogan (b. 1936) also held a special affection for the waltz. She remembers: 'It was always romantic doing the waltz and being held close . . . You held a partner close and the music itself lent to romance in the slow dances.'[63]

As in previous generations, the last dance remained perhaps the most significant dance of the evening, as far as romance was concerned. Dancers attached great importance to it. Jack Hogan (b. 1936) recalls: 'That was important, very important. That was when you sussed out over the night who you would want to take home. Then you would make a bee line for who you fancied to take home.'[64] The same was true in Liverpool, as Marie Kernan (b. 1942) remembers: 'when they played the last song, the band, it was always a slowy, and they used to say: "Right, whose getting a tail home?" The person in the band would say. A tail home was someone who liked you, a fella who liked you all night, and he'd say to you: "Can I walk you home?" And that was a tail home. And then he'd take you home. And he'd take you right to the door. And then he'd just kiss you and say: "I'll see you next week." Then he'd have to walk all the way back.'[65]

Yet, securing the last dance was not always a guarantee that a date had been found. Again, distance and consideration of the area which the dancers came from could often kill off a blossoming romance: 'If you met someone who lived at the other side of town and you thought it was too far sometimes you would say "I'll see you outside" and then you would be off, because it was too far . . . '[66] Local opinion could often be turned against those who did this too often, however. Peer pressure often worked to make last waltz couples keep their promise of walking the woman home. In Dundee, for example, if a date made at the dance did not turn up outside at the allotted meeting place after the dance, this was referred to as 'duffing'. Girls made sure that such men would be ostracized, using gossip networks: 'if you got duffed, you immediately told all your pals, and in Dundee parlance as far as I was concerned: "That wiz his erse oot the windie." He just got ignored from then on in.'[67]

These conventions remained remarkably unchanged throughout the period from the end of the First World War until the mid-1950s. However, in the later part of the 1950s, the revolution in dancing styles represented by such dances as the Twist started to dramatically transform the way in which people danced. These dances

[62] GDHI, Margaret Taylor, b. 1938, 31 May 2011.
[63] DDHI, Kath Hogan, b. 1936, 11 March 2011.
[64] DDHI, Jack Hogan, b. 1936, 11 March 2011.
[65] LDHI, Marie Kernan, b. 1942, 21 July 2009.
[66] DDHI, Jack Hogan, b. 1936, 11 March 2011.
[67] M. Stewart, *'O' is Fir Ingin* (Edinburgh: Black & White Publishing, 2010), 142.

ushered in a new era of solo dancing. Without the requirement of partner dancing, the conventions of the previous thirty years or so were overturned. It was no longer necessary to secure a partner to dance, and thus the major advantage of dancing in introducing strangers to each other—the prescribed conventions for couple formation—disappeared. Now it became more difficult to meet members of the opposite sex, and dancers had to pursue different strategies for meeting. Whilst it is true that social conventions had also changed by this time, so that people were more at ease with approaching strangers, this only partially compensated for the disappearance of a whole code of behaviour designed to put men and women together. The move to solo dancing also meant, inevitably, that any dancing 'coupling' could be extremely transitory—you were not 'tied' to the same person even for the duration of a single dance any more. This of course led to an even greater casualization of the dating game. Not everyone liked the changes. Ivor Laycock (b. 1939), a dance band musician, complained: 'I always thought the idea of dancing was to grab a bird and away you go! This separate dancing, the guy would dance with a girl but if you turned around they were dancing with someone else!'[68] Moreover, the new solo dancing meant that couples did not hold each other whilst dancing—physical distance was maintained between dancers. Some disliked the Jive for the same reason: 'I always thought, you didn't hold the girl, just her hand. I liked the more conventional dancing.'[69] Of course, as time progressed, solo dances became increasingly sexualized, and this compensated for the lack of physical closeness. This also had the effect of making dancing more about sexuality, rather than romance.

THE DANCE HALL AND INTIMACY

Links between dancing and sex were long established, and as we shall see later, this caused considerable moral alarm throughout the period.[70] However, in order to assess the extent to which such reactions were unfounded or otherwise, we need to explore the various ways in which dancing and dance halls permitted intimacy between those involved.

Even though they went out of their way to find evidence of it, most Mass Observation reports from the 1930s pointed to a lack of overtly sexual behaviour in dance halls.[71] A 1939 report from the Streatham Locarno, for example, remarked: 'There doesn't seem to be much sex about—dancing the thing—not sex dancing specially.'[72] Similarly in a Rye Lane night club called 'Stones', a place with a bad reputation, there was a similar lack of action: 'No evidence of sex here. Dancing definitely not sexy. Lights extinguished for waltz... Even then obs. saw no sex.

68 GDHI, Ivor Laycock, b. 1939, 26 May 2011.

69 DDHI, Dolores Brown, b. 1939, 22 April 2011.

70 See Chapter 8.

71 Mass Observation's use of the term 'sex' was fairly loose; it referred to various stages of intimacy ranging from kissing to actual sexual intercourse.

72 M-O A: MJD: 38/1/A, 'Big Apple Ball, I2', 17 November 1939, 9.

Danced and looked in all dark corners whilst dancing but couldn't see anything of sex nature—no petting, or even chaps with arms round girls . . . There was no evidence that sex was the reason for the people visiting the hall. Most came there to dance as far as one could judge from appearance.'[73]

With the attendance of supervisors in the larger dance halls and attendants in cloakrooms and toilets, regulation of dancers' behaviour was often tight. In the Tower Ballroom, Blackpool, for example, in 1937 it was noted that '[f]ive uniformed attendants stand round the edge of the ballroom floor, one at each side of the stage, one beside a pillar half way down the floor, and one at each end of the corridor opposite the stage'.[74] Such attendants paid particular attention to the way dancers held one another, and sanctioned dancers who danced too closely. As one Bolton dance hall manager commented: 'There isn't any room for the funny business in the Modern Dance Hall, the people watch too keenly for that.'[75]

Yet despite this, the dance hall did permit notable levels of 'sexual' intimacy between its patrons. Dancing itself allowed a level of intimacy between men and women that was rare in other public situations. Indeed, part of the huge appeal of the new dances that emerged just before the First World War was that they were partner dances often requiring quite considerable degrees of intimacy. Unlike sequence dancing, the foxtrot, the waltz, the quickstep, and so on required men and women to hold each other for the duration of the dance. These dances also required men and women to position their bodies close to each other, and to move around the dance floor with legs, hips, and arms touching or passing close to one another. Countless critics saw such dancing as overly sexualized.[76] Tom Harrisson, for example, thought that dancing was a substitute for sex: 'The old element of sexual approach still exists in the dance, but the new form gives dance a new meaning. Either fulfilment, in the primitive dance found in copulation, is found now in the dance itself, or its very nature makes fulfilment impossible. In either case it is a partial substitute for more intimate sex relations.'[77]

Although the development of the English style sought to eliminate any overt intimacy, individual dancers danced the standard dances in a variety of ways, and with varying levels of intimacy. In 1939, for example, Mass Observation noted nine different ways in which men held their female partners for the same dance, some holding their partner's waist, and some placing their hands on their partner's bottom.[78] Clearly, MCs could not eliminate all opportunities for those who wanted a little more intimacy whilst dancing. Some dancers did hold their partners a little closer, move their hands to 'non-approved' places, and conduct their dancing with a greater emphasis on 'getting close'. Moreover, such intimacy was often taking place between people who were strangers—mere acquaintances put together for the duration of a dance, something which one Mass Observer experienced at the

[73] M-O A: MJD: 38/1/I, 'Stones, Rye Lane IX2', 6 March 1939, 8–9.
[74] M-O A: Worktown: 60/D, 'Dancing', 1938, 11.
[75] M-O A: MJD: 5/F, 'Alfred Clarke, Empress Hall, Bolton', 1938, 8.
[76] See Chapter 8. [77] M-O A: Worktown: 60/D, 'Dancing', 1938, 8.
[78] M-O A: MJD: 38/1/B, 'AH Paramount II6', 31 March 1939, 1b.

Streatham Locarno in 1939: 'Ob was allowed to enter the preliminary stages of petting, arm round shoulders, hand held, though he had only known her for about half hour . . .'[79] Clearly, one effect of the dance hall could be to speed up the stages in the dating process.

More important than this, however, dance halls permitted dancers to gain experience with a large number of people quickly, and led to a notable 'casualization' of the process of heterosexual coupling. This fostered a tendency to think of members of the opposite sex in more obvious sexual terms. The dance halls' programme of ever changing dances throughout the evening allowed people to move from dancer to dancer easily. The number of individual dances in an evening could be high, up to forty or forty-five. Each dance offered a fresh opportunity to find a dancing partner. Tom Harrisson observed this, noting the 'breaking [of] the music at frequent intervals, each time introducing a new mood and tempo, and with that the habit of changing one's partner'.[80] The dance hall made it much easier to acquire experience with lots of different women, or men. For example, in May 1939 Mass Observation followed three male and three female dancers at the Locarno Streatham.[81] In the course of an evening's dancing, these six dancers danced with a total of 58 different partners, all members of the opposite sex. 'Girl A' danced for 30 out of 41 dances, with 11 different partners. 'Girl B' danced most, for 33 out of the 41 dances and she also had the most partners, 20. 'Girl C' danced least, dancing for 26 of the 41 dances, and had fewest partners, dancing with only 8. The men danced much less than the women and had fewer partners. 'Man A' danced most, 24 out of 43 dances. He had only 4 partners. 'Man B' danced only 10 dances out of 28 (he left early) and also had 4 partners. 'Man C' danced for 15 out of 37 dances, with 9 different partners. Women even more than men then were gaining experience of physical closeness and interaction with the opposite sex.

For many, this process was just about finding someone to dance with, and it had little impact on the way that they viewed members of the opposite sex. For some in the dance hall, however, the high turnover of dance partners was making them 'more choosy' and was accompanied by a greater emphasis on physical attributes. This often led to the grading and rating of their potential partners. This made the dance less about long-lasting romance, shifting the emphasis from partnership to sex. The following is an account of a Manchester dancer in Blackpool in 1937/8—it illustrates the very unromantic nature of many dance hall pairings:

> Immediately enter, girl sitting on first settee looks me in the eyes and a tiny flicker one corner mouth looks away. I pass before time to stop, slow up, turn round, go back, and with a hot feeling on back on neck 'Can I have this please?' in mutter. Gets up immediately, tall, fawn coat, and swings away through crowd . . . I follow and she waits on floor arms ready. She does not look at me . . . we dance off and fall into normal dance hall long short short short. She is rather short on long beat. Sign of poor dancer . . . notice as she speaks has much rouged lips, good complexion, but peculiar

[79] M-O A: MJD: 38/1/A, 'SS Locarno I12', 18 April 1939, 1.

[80] M-O A: Worktown: 60/D, 'Dancing', 1938, 8.

[81] M-O A: MJD: 38/1/A, 'Locarno Dance Follows I34', 9 May 1939.

rat trap formation of mouth, almost as though no teeth . . . Lips come over teeth most of time even when speaking . . . I think: she's no such good dancer and no so good lookin. Must get rid of her at end of dance . . . By now I am fed up with woman. Band stops again. Walk off. As we get to edge of floor, she stops looks at me. I feel uncomfortable, but instead of stopping say 'see you again' and dart off . . . as I walk round see good looking brunette leaning against pillar. Think 'I'll dance with that next' and stand within striking distance . . . Band strikes up. Nip cig. Push through and touch girl in purple dress on arm. She looks at me and then walks on floor . . . She has full evening dress, I notice. Sign of good dancer as a rule. She is not quite so hot close to but passable. Very dark eyebrows and hair. Full lips but too large a conk. She dances close but not so well as her dress suggests. Enjoy first part of dance. We do not speak. Dance recommences, it is a foxtrot. Discover she cannot do one or two steps . . . She begins to pall, too, my left arm aches and her dancing gets worse. Dance in silence. I look at women dancing round. Look a tough crew. Notice one whippet with plastered hair, earrings, a low evening dress, looks about 40 . . . I make detour round other side to face them, and pick least ugly of them.[82]

Many dancers were well aware of the function of dance halls as a place to pick up. Talking of Blackpool's holiday makers in 1937 Mass Observation stated: 'the boys and girls who have failed to "get off" in the course of the day make another attempt in the Tower and other ballrooms at night.'[83] In addition, despite the disppointment of some Mass Observers at not finding more evidence of 'sex', it is clear that the dance hall was not completely devoid of opportunities for intimacy. The following are reports from the Streatham Locarno in 1939:

The girl is perspiring freely . . . The man takes the opportunity to place his hand on her back. Man 'So long as it don't run . . . ' He continues to place his hand on different parts of the girl's body, under the cloak of solicitation for her.[84]

Chap has his arm round her shoulder. He kisses her neck. She squirms about erotically. He moves his hand down her upper arm and under her arm pit. Squeezes it through and on to her breast. She lets him keep it there for a few seconds, staring ahead. Then forces his hand away. He brings it back on to her shoulder. She forces it off again. They sit apart on the settee for 2 minutes. He starts kissing her neck again. She squirms once more. He repeats his movement, putting his hand on her shoulder working it down her arm and under her armpit and on to her breast. She moves his hand off and holds it. He keeps his fingers free and tickles her breast.[85]

Most sexual activity occurred outside of the dance hall, however, on the way home. Most would probably engage in petting and kissing but sexual intercourse before marriage was still taboo, although it was common. It is likely, however, that many people acquired initial sexual experience with those they met at the dance halls. As Mass Observation noted in Blackpool in 1937:

The evening's dancing is over and the crowd leaves the electric light and warmth of the ballroom for the darkness and cold freshness of the promenade. But an observer finds

82 M-O A: Worktown: 60/D, 'Blackpool', 1937/8, 23–4.
83 M-O A: Worktown: 60/D, 'Dancing', 1938, 9.
84 M-O A: MJD: 38/1/A, 'JA Locarno I46', 1 July 1939, 1.
85 M-O A: MJD: 38/1/A, 'AH Locarno I47', 1 July 1939, 1.

> proof that the new relations made during the evening do not end here, necking goes on and lead in some cases to what? 'Outside one young girl being dragged along between two lads having passed out with too much drink.' 59 necking couples on way home from tower. (Note: About 1.5 miles of promenade). One comment 'You want a tight fuckin' tonight'. (Observer Report CM 4/9/37)[86]

Certainly, there was plenty of rumour at the halls about how far dancers were willing to go. A male dancing professional working in the Streatham Locarno suggested that the number of people who were looking for sex was large:

> AH mentioned a girl he had seen trying to get off with two of the professionals. Cyril replied: 'Oh yes, one of the fast kind—that pokes with all and everyone. About 5% of the women in Locarno don't poke, and about 2% are virgin—if that' . . . some of the women are so easy, you only have to say: 'Would you like to come and have a coffee?' . . . Some of them even ask us . . . They say 'When are you coming to sleep with me.' They do, really.[87]

In Blackpool the situation was similar; perhaps behaviour here was even more uninhibited due to the holiday spirit:

> . . . two chaps were dancing and then came up and said, 'There's plenty of tash here' (tash—meaning girls who fuck). They also told me that if you get a 'set-home' it's alright here.[88]

Sex was certainly on the mind of some of the dancers, as a Mass Observer noted in the Peckham Pavilion in 1939. Overheard at the café during the dance interval: '"she wants a Swiss roll and the other says you know what she wants," pause, "Jessie says you know what she wants," the other chap said "Yes, I know what she wants but it is not the time and the place."'[89] Some in the Church also considered that dance halls were places where the young gained sexual experiences, and that this was undermining their commitment to marriage. Reverend George Potter, vicar of St Chrystostom's Peckham, told Mass Observation in 1938:

> The young people don't marry the first one they kiss, of course there's a lot of hugging goes on after they have had drink at the dances in the halls . . . I think the youngsters don't think so much of marriage now, that's when they go about hugging and kissing as they do, some people won't face these things . . . Practically every boy in here has had connections with girls, they tell me so.[90]

The dance hall, therefore, provided an arena for varying degrees of sexual activity. Some attended the halls in order to find sexual partners and were prepared to go at least some way to satisfy these demands. On the whole, however, sexual activity and behaviour within the dance hall was restrained and respectable and often awkward. Any subsequent action was usually pretty innocent too, restrained by social

[86] M-O A: Worktown: 60/D, 'Dancing', 1938, 29.
[87] M-O A: MJD: 3/G, 'Interview: Cyril Amersham', 25 June 1939, 2.
[88] M-O A: Worktown: 48/C, 'An evening with a friend drinking and dancing', 2 April 1938, 6.
[89] M-O A: MJD: 38/1/E, 'Peckham Pavilion: V17 S. S. 15/14/39', 15 April 1939, 2.
[90] M-O A: TC: MJD: 38/1/I, 'Interview with Parson re dancing and sex', 26 October 1939, 3.

pressures as well as familial practicalities. Marjorie Hooley (b. 1917) dancing in Liverpool in the 1930s recalls:

> Oh, you'd only do a bit of kerfuffling in the parlour, hoping my father wouldn't come out, you know... But not going to bed with them or anything like that. Oh good grief no. There was nothing like that. And if a fella got funny with you, you know, it'd go round all the girls. You know, you'd say 'be careful of that fella.'[91]

During the war, the challenges to conventional sexuality were potentially great. Social life was re-organized, gender boundaries were challenged, and the ever-present threat of death, together with the arrival of thousands of foreign servicemen, threatened to undermine traditional restrictions on sex before marriage. It was believed by some that wartime moral standards had fallen.[92] Some feared that there was more sex going on than ever before. Mass Observation, for example, noted widespread perceptions that promiscuity was 'rife'.[93] William Temple, Archbishop of Canterbury, writing in 1943, believed that there had been 'a really alarming collapse in... sex morality'.[94] Statistics seemed to verify that there were changes to conventional morality too. Cases of VD and syphilis had risen, for example, with their occurrence estimated to be 50 per cent higher in 1941 than in 1939.[95] Divorce figures also grew, from 6,092 in 1938 to 15,221 in 1945.[96] Illegitimacy also grew, to 255,460 in 1940–5, 102,000 more than in the period 1934–9.[97]

If there was some liberalization in attitudes towards sex, was this reflected in the palais? The evidence from the dance hall is that the war did not bring about a revolution in sexual activity, but there were some alterations in the atmosphere. Certainly some wartime changes made the dance hall and dancing more 'sexualized', i.e. focused on sex and sexuality. For example, during the war, many dance halls became the venue for 'beauty contests', which not only increasingly objectified women, but also accentuated glamour and 'sex appeal', rather than romance and life partnerships. Mecca's role in the creation of the Miss World competition in the post-war world is well known.[98] Eric Morley created the competition initially as an attraction of the 1951 Festival of Britain before launching the global competition that was to achieve worldwide success. However, what is less appreciated is that Mecca was building on experience organizing such competitions first gained during the war. Beauty contests were a regular feature of Mecca's wartime programme of dance hall entertainments, designed to attract media attention and bring in new

[91] LDHI, Marjorie Hooley, b. 1917, 23 June 2009. [92] See Chapter 8.

[93] M-O A, FR2205, 'Sex, Morality and the Birth Rate' (January 1945) cited in G. Field, 'Perspectives on the Working Class Family in Wartime Britain, 1939–1945,' *International Labor and Working Class History* (Chicago, IL) vol. 38, Fall 1990, 16.

[94] *Quarterly Leaflet of the Church of England Moral Welfare Council* (August 1943), 4 cited in Field, 'Perspectives', 16.

[95] S. M. Laird, *Venereal Disease in Britain* (1943), 34 cited in Field, 'Perspectives', 17.

[96] O. R. McGregor, *Divorce in England: A Centenary Study* (1957) cited in Field, 'Perspectives', 18.

[97] *National Council for the Unmarried Mother and her Child: Annual Reports* (1938–46) cited in Field, 'Perspectives', 19.

[98] See J. Nott, 'Heimann, Carl Louis Bertram Reinhold (1896–1968)', *Oxford Dictionary of National Biography* (Oxford: Oxford University Press, 2004).

customers. For example, in 1941 Mecca held a competition to search for 'London's most beautiful girl' at its Royal Opera House dance hall in London and by April 1942, encouraged by its success, beauty contests were being held in its dance halls throughout the country. Competitions were held regularly for the rest of the war. Other dance halls followed suit too, copying Mecca's idea, and the practice gained particular popularity in Scotland. Sometimes, finalists from such competitions were put to the popular vote following the publication of their photographs in the local press, and such women acquired short-lived local celebrity. The impact of such competitions is hard to judge. What is clear is that the language used in press reports of these beauty contests illustrates an unprecedented degree of objectification of women. This no doubt linked the dance halls with 'sex' in the minds of some. A report from a beauty contest held in the Streatham Locarno in 1942 illustrates this point. It salivates:

> First a blonde, then a brunette takes your eye—then how about this demure one with dimples—at last you make up your mind that they're all equal as they stroll by with infectious smiles, just oozing 'IT'... The girls line up for their second test. This personality 'business' over the 'mike' is intended to sort out any dumb Dora's, and you must have pep to catch public fancy... Here come the 'glamourettes' one by one, reading their party piece, some serious, some winsome, some perky.[99]

During the war dancing accentuated the trend towards the 'casualization' of heterosexual coupling, as the practice of gathering 'hostesses' for troops became increasingly common. This also led to a focus on superficial and transitory relationships between the sexes, and could have encouraged a more 'casual' approach to dating. In April 1940 in Sheffield, for example, a dance club opened for soldiers in the city, and the *Daily Mirror* remarked that 'large stores and business houses are being invited to turn to select squads of nice girls—mannequins, typists and assistants —who can dance well and entertain the soldier boys'.[100] Similarly, in December 1942 in Manchester, adverts were placed in the local press asking for women to volunteer as hostesses at a dance for American troops. About one hundred were found.[101] Girls were used to make other foreigners feel at home too. South Africa House in London had a Girls Escort Service, with twenty women, nicknamed 'Femescorts' by the *Daily Express*, whose job it was to accompany troops from South Africa to entertainments in the capital, including dancing. They were given funds of £1 per boy.[102] This had the effect of 'commodifying' women to an extent that would have not been permissible before the war.

As well as the clearer focus on 'sex' outlined earlier, the wartime dance hall saw other changes that made greater sexual activity more likely. The more 'mixed' nature of wartime dance hall crowds meant that some felt less inhibited in sexual matters than before. In peacetime, familiarity with other dancers, together with local and family connections, acted as an informal censor on behaviour amongst

[99] *DN*, 28 March 1942, 1. [100] *DM*, 12 April 1940, 5.
[101] *DT*, December 1942, 147. [102] *Daily Express*, 9 February 1940, 3.

dance hall patrons. The greater transience of large sections of those present at dances meant that some felt less social pressures to behave appropriately. At the same time, the pressures of war speeded up the rules of the dating game. It is likely that some people were bolder and more assertive as a result. This trend was exacerbated by practical dance hall management problems. As we have seen, staffing was a constant problem in wartime dance halls due to the effects of conscription and mobilization. Although most dance halls would try to maintain order through the employment of an MC, this role could sometimes be neglected when staff shortages were particularly acute.

There is little evidence to suggest, however, that the dance hall became a venue for increased public sexual behaviour. Despite the loosening of social pressures already outlined, there remained sufficient peer pressure to limit public exhibitionism. More sexual behaviour might be taking place, but as before the war, it was taking place outside the dance hall, not in it. In the dance hall itself, activities remained limited. As one dance hall cloakroom attendant from Dovercourt, Essex, remarked: 'At the end of the evening, the local girls would often pop up to the balcony for a quick cuddle with their lad before he went and rejoined his ship.'[103] In some halls, even that was forbidden, a female dancer from Glasgow observing that in the Albert dance hall during the war '[t]here was no kissing, nothing like that'.[104] Also, not all wartime dance halls were without prying eyes to keep control of behaviour. For example, at the Casino dance hall in Birmingham, situated almost opposite the city's magistrates courts, one dancer recalls 'members of the Birmingham "city fathers" used to watch from a balcony above the dance hall to make sure nothing untoward happened—even a man putting his arm around a girl counted as untoward'.[105] As British and American servicemen used to frequent this dance hall, there were two American, two Canadian, and two British military policemen on hand at all times too. Usually, people went outside venues to places nearby in order to engage in anything more serious. In Belfast for example, one man recalls the 'abuse' of air raid shelters:

> There was a dance hall at the top of our street, Richview dance hall. It was frequented by the Americans. Usually the Americans took the Girls for a kerfuffle into the air raid shelters. I don't know how the devil we would have got into them![106]

Similarly in Bristol during the war Americans and local girls who had met in city centre dance halls would usually retire to Church Lane (near to the official dropping off and picking up point for the GIs) to have sex.[107] As before the war, the dance hall's chief role was as a place of introduction, not for actual sexual activity. For the majority of its patrons, the dance hall remained a primarily

[103] PWA, Jim Howard, Article A2836163, 14 July 2004.
[104] GDHI, Rae Birch, b. 1922, 8 August 2011.
[105] PWA, Sylvia Merriman, Article A2064700, 20 November 2003.
[106] PWA, Robin Collins, Article A6014350, 4 October 2005.
[107] PWA, Delphine Rowden, Article A4073889, 16 May 2005.

romantic venue, and even the walk home would be innocent. As one female Liverpudlian dancer noted:

> We very often walked home with young men that we'd only met at the dance... they'd have their arm round your waist... but they would never attempt to go further than that... and they'd take you home to your door, and they'd give you a kiss and a cuddle, and ask if it was possible to see them again. Sometimes it was, sometimes it wasn't. And they'd say goodnight and they'd go.[108]

Was such relative innocence retained in post-war dance hall relationships? The 'sexual revolution' did not really come to fruition in the period under investigation here, with big changes in traditional attitudes towards sex not taking place in Britain until the later 1960s and more fully in the 1970s and 1980s. However, traditional notions of marriage, pre-marital sex, and attitudes towards sexuality in general were being challenged long before this. By the 1960s these challenges were starting to bring legislative changes, if not widespread attitudinal changes. In 1960, the government famously lost its obscenity trial to try and ban Penguin's publication of *Lady Chatterley's Lover*. The contraceptive pill was made available on the NHS in 1961, and in 1967 laws prohibiting abortion and homosexual sex were repealed. There is some indication that attitudes amongst the young were changing and that the dance hall was, by the early 1960s, a key venue for finding sexual partners. As early as 1953, R. F. Logan and E. M. Goldberg's study of young men, *Rising Eighteen*, identified new attitudes towards sex. Now the notion of 'mutual sharing' between men and women was popular, 'be it at the level of petting, pre-marital or marital intercourse. The majority did not acknowledge the older sanctions of formal engagement and marriage, which may have previously restricted sexual expression. In fact almost all the youths said they approved of pre-marital intercourse with a "steady" girl friend, though not with a casual acquaintance, provided "both partners felt the same".'[109]

Schofield's later study of sexual attitudes amongst the young showed that intercourse was occurring at an earlier age. Of the sample, very few (0.9 per cent of boys, 0.1 per cent of girls) had had sex before the age of 14, only 6 per cent of boys and 2 per cent of girls at 15. Amongst boys who had had sexual intercourse, 36 per cent had been 17/18 when they first had it, 32 per cent 16, 20 per cent 15 and 12 per cent 14 and under. Amongst girls, 55 per cent had first had sex ages 17/18, 26 per cent aged 16, and 19 per cent under 15.[110] The majority of girls (82 per cent) said they had been 'going steady' with the partner when they had their first sex, 16 per cent said it was with an acquaintance, and 3 per cent said the boy was a 'pick up'. Amongst boys, 45 per cent said they were going steady, 34 per cent that it was an acquaintance, and 16 per cent with a 'pick up'.[111] Schofield's survey also

[108] LDHI, Vera Jeffers, b. 1925, 22 July 2009.

[109] R. F. Logan and E. M. Goldberg, 'Rising Eighteen in a London Suburb: A Study of Some Aspects of the Life and Health of Young Men' (1953) 4(4) (December) *The British Journal of Sociology* 332–3.

[110] M. Schofield, *The Sexual Behaviour of Young People* (London: Longmans, 1965), 59–60.

[111] Schofield, *Sexual*, 61.

confirmed that dances were popular places to meet sexual partners. When asked where they had met their first sexual partner, the replies showed that of boys, 18 per cent met the girl outdoors, 11 per cent at a dance, 10 per cent at a party, 8 per cent at school, 8 per cent at a club, 7 per cent at a cinema, and 9 per cent said they had grown up together (29 per cent couldn't remember). Of the girls, 14 per cent said they met the boy outdoors, 14 per cent at a dance, 11 per cent at a party, 6 per cent at a club, 5 per cent at a cinema, and 7 per cent they had grown up together (43 per cent mentioned miscellaneous places/couldn't remember).[112] Most had intercourse in the home of one of the partners.

Changing boundaries regarding sexual behaviour might reasonably be expected to have been reflected in behaviour in the dance hall. Yet, for most of the period from 1945 to 1960, there were very few changes to the level of intimacy shown in dance halls. As one dancer recalls: 'you didn't show open affection at the dance hall. If you liked someone you held hands, but that was all.'[113] In the majority of dance halls, intimacy remained both discreet and largely innocent in nature. The experiences of dancing teenagers from Richmond, Surrey, interviewed by the *Daily Mirror* in 1959, support this. Fourteen-year-old Robert, for example, proclaimed: 'I only talk to girls, I never smooch. Time enough for that when I am married.' Alan James, a 17-year-old apprentice also stated: 'I never hurry to get to know a girl. I dance with her several times. If we finish up having an interesting conversation I invite her to the pictures or else we go for a walk. I always see my dates home afterwards.'[114]

Why wasn't there more intimacy in the post-war dance hall? First, social conventions were strong and acted as subconscious censors on the behaviour of most dancers. People were deeply concerned about their personal reputations. Most of Britain's towns and cities at this time still contained strongly bonded communities, closely knit networks of people brought together by common work, leisure, and housing conditions and experiences. Most dance halls were patronized by a regular clientele, and a keen sense of community grew up amongst these regulars too. Inevitably, with most working-class groups living in such close quarters, gossip was a common feature of local life and culture. Who danced with whom that week at the palais, and who was dating whom were topics discussed and debated in the workplace, in the family home, with the neighbours, and in the palais itself. Under such circumstances women in particular were keen to protect their reputations. Thus, to engage in overtly intimate activities whilst in the dance hall was frowned upon by most. As Pat Spencer (b. 1933) from Liverpool commented: 'You didn't want to be kissing on the floor, because that would look, they would think you would look easy. If you didn't know the fella.'[115]

The other key reason for a lack of more passionate intimacy was the continued control of dancer's behaviour by stewards and MCs. If anything, given the panic over youth culture during the 1950s, dance hall managements became even stricter.[116]

112 Schofield, *Sexual*, 61–2.
113 DDHI, Alistair Brown, b. 1930, 22 April 2011.
114 *DM*, 29 March 1959, 2.
115 LDHI, Pat Spencer, b. 1933, 31 July 2009.
116 See Chapter 10.

Certainly in Dundee in the 1950s, for example, it appears that there had been little relaxation in the strict moral codes employed by dance hall managements. Overt intimacy was checked for and stopped. Sandy Melville (b. 1934) recalls: 'In the JM if you got too close the stewards would come along and part you, saying "that's enough." You didn't get a kiss in the dance hall. If you were getting a wee bit too close they would stop you.'[117] In Liverpool too, dancers were watched closely. For example, Eunice Spencer was employed by a Liverpool dance hall to act as a 'kiss killer'. She explained in 1953: 'If I see anyone kissing or dancing too close I tap them on the shoulder and say "Please, do you mind? We don't allow that."'[118]

For the most part, such measures seemed to have been effective; however, this did not stop men trying to go further in the halls. As one female dancer remembers: 'I shouldn't say this, but they all tried. Which is normal really. And things like that. But with one thing you could say no and they would respect that.'[119] As before the war, dancing did provide some opportunities for intimacy, however. Slow dances were often the best, as a Mass Observation from 1947 noted: 'In the slow waltz now in progress the lights have been dimmed, and partners seen to be clasping each other as tight and as close as possible.'[120] Jack Hogan (b. 1936) concurs: 'You could have a bit of a smooch whilst you were dancing, because you were dancing close together.'[121] As before the war, dancers found areas in the dance hall where they could kiss. As Agnes McHugh (b. 1934) recalls of Glasgow's dance halls: 'There were some dark areas where you could have a cuddle, other places were better lit and you couldn't do that . . . You could get away with [kissing] because of the dark areas. I don't think if you were caught necking anyone would have come up and stopped you. You may have been sanctioned by the other dancers looking at you.'[122] However, the dance also could lead to intimacy at an earlier stage of acquaintance than was normal outside. Often the spirit of the moment could take over a dancer. For example, Pat Spencer, an 18-year-old from Liverpool in 1950, remembers meeting her future husband: 'I was, anyway, a bit too confident at that time, because when I came off the dance floor, they were seated. I didn't know who these chaps were, cos it had only been my second visit there. And he was sitting there, Jack, with his brother, I didn't know it was his brother then, and somebody else, and he just said to me "sit on my knee" and you know what? You did do! Sat on his knee.'[123]

There was also some evidence that necking and other forms of petting were now more acceptable in the dance hall. As Patrick Doncaster and Tony Miles wrote in the *Daily Mirror* in 1956, 'serious petting' started at age 14, and in Manchester six out of ten boys expected a little petting on a first date. More significantly, it went on: 'They have brought necking into the open . . . in the cinema . . . in the park . . . on the dance floor.' One youth from Bolton claimed that there was no more necking than in the past, but that now it was more open: 'It's just that we

[117] DDHI, Sandy Melville, b. 1934, 11 March 2011.
[118] *DM*, 4 December 1953, 5.
[119] LDHI, Pat Spencer, b. 1933, 31 July 2009.
[120] M-O A, FR2473, *Report on Juvenile Delinquency* (1947), 48.
[121] DDHI, Jack Hogan, b. 1936, 11 March 2011.
[122] GDHI, Agnes McHugh, b. 1934, 1 June 2011.
[123] LDHI, Pat Spencer, b. 1933, 31 July 2009.

don't hide it so much. If we want to cuddle we do it openly in a dance hall or cinema.'[124]

Particular dances also offered the opportunity for more sexualized dancing. In 1953 a new dance, The Creep, became briefly popular. Its moves were not particularly intimate, but the points of contact between the dancers became controversial. In the dance the partners stood about a foot apart, the boy's left hand held the girl's right arm straight out and low down, so that their hands were level with the middle of their thighs. The man then put his right wrist on the woman's hip and let his hand hang loosely. The two bent their knees slightly and then crept off around the room. Although this seemed innocent enough, the *Dance News* attacked The Creep for its 'sexual overtones': '[I]t is something that needs to be watched as there is just that little bit too much sex about it which is not quite nice.'[125]

As in previous periods, most 'action' came after the dance, as one female Liverpool dancer remembers: 'After, yes. I always shoved them against the wall so I could get an easy get away.'[126] As Professor Meyer Fortes, Professor of Social Anthropology at Cambridge, participating in a 1951 *Picture Post* discussion about 'Sex and the Citizen' stated: 'I think the facts are that a good deal of physical sexual experience does go on amongst the very best type of young peoples . . . I think we have got to face that fact.'[127]

CONCLUSION

The dance hall's most significant social function was as a venue where working- and lower-middle-class men and women could meet. Rapidly assuming a role as Britain's most important 'marriage bureau', the dance hall remained central to courtship throughout the early twentieth century. Whilst there were varying degrees of intimacy available to dancers within the dance hall, most encounters of this nature did not take place within the venue itself. Instead, the dance hall reinforced the centrality of heterosexual coupling, and marriage, in British society. In this respect, despite its detractors—to whom we turn next—it was wholly supportive of conventional morality, whilst allowing that morality to change with the times.

[124] *DM*, 8 February 1956, 9. [125] *DM*, 15 October 1953, 7.
[126] LDHI, Pat Spencer, b. 1933, 31 July 2009. [127] *PP*, 20 October 1951, 43.

PART III

CONFLICTS AND CONTROL: MORAL PANIC AND THE DANCE HALL, 1918–60

Chapter 8

Morality, Gender, and the Dance Hall, 1918–60

INTRODUCTION

Soon after they began to emerge in unprecedented numbers in towns and cities throughout Britain following the First World War, public dance halls and dancing more generally rapidly acquired a reputation for being 'immoral'. These twentieth-century fears were the continuation of a long-standing link made between dancing and sin. In the Renaissance, as Liz Oliver points out, dancing was frequently used as a metaphor for copulation. In the sixteenth century, moralist John Northbrooke had warned: 'Through dancing many maidens have been unmaidened . . . (dancing) is the nursery of bastardy.'[1] The waltz and the tango had created an outrage in nineteenth-century Britain for similar reasons. Criticized on moral grounds by those opposed to the waltz's close hold and rapid turning movements, religious leaders almost unanimously regarded it as vulgar and sinful. Even George Bernard Shaw is reputed to have called dancing 'a perpendicular expression of a horizontal desire'.[2]

Similarly, in the twentieth century concerns about dancing tended to be focused on the notion that dancers were exposing themselves to accusations of sexual impropriety, either through the 'eroticism' of the new dance forms or the widespread mixing of men and women in the dance halls. As A. H. Franks remarked: 'Most social dance has its firm foundation in the sexual impulse.'[3] Additionally, there was a wider attack on the new dances and dance halls that reflected concern with changing gender boundaries. Dancing became critical to images of 'new women' who were seen to emerge after the First World War. The 'Flapper', the 'Good Time Girl', the 'Palais Pearl', and the 'Snooty Cutie' were all popular archetypes of women who enjoyed dancing and whose behaviour in the dance hall created considerable concern amongst critics. Men's changing image and relationship with women were also reflected and shaped by dance hall experiences. Concerns grew that dancing was 'feminizing' men and eroding older standards of masculinity. All will be discussed here.

[1] Quoted in L. Oliver, 'From the Ballroom to Hell: a Social History of Public Dancing in Bolton from *c.*1840–1911' in (1995) 2(2) *Women's History Notebooks* 15.

[2] G. Melly, *Revolt into Style: The Pop Arts in Britain* (Harmondsworth: Pengion, 1972), 63.

[3] *Daily Mail*, 9 May 1963, 12.

THE 'IMMORALITY' OF DANCE HALLS

The opinions of a panel survey of Mass Observation contributors taken at the end of the 1930s illustrate some of the reasons for negative views of dance halls. First, some general comments from those surveyed illustrate the range of complaints. 'They are poorly lit, stuffy and overcrowded'; 'rough and rowdy'; 'all low-down dives'; 'they assist in overemphasising sex in modern life'.[4] The majority of those with adverse opinions of dance halls considered them 'disreputable and immoral'. 'They would appear to be hot beds of vice'; 'They are places where the worst side of human nature is shown, among young people especially. They are to me places where sex is enjoyed like a pleasure . . . '[5] The open and free mixing of the sexes at dance halls was considered particularly objectionable. A 21-year-old female clerk from Bromley remarked:

> Whereas dance halls in poorer districts take young people off the streets, are they doing a very great service by putting those young people in closer and more intimate touch with the opposite sex? I do so hate to see girls, so obviously dressed 'to kill', bunched together like cattle around the door of a public dance hall: just waiting, and ogling, for the men . . . [6]

Class distinctions were a significant factor in forming opinions about dance halls. Of those holding negative opinions of public dance halls in the Wandsworth Jazz Survey, a larger proportion was middle-class (26 per cent as opposed to 12 per cent among working-class interviewees). Many middle-class people considered that public dance halls were unsafe, certainly not the place for 'decent' people:

> I think of them as the haunts of the less desirable sections of the lower 'classes' . . . The resort of the rowdier sections of the lowest middle and upper working classes . . . People go on there from pubs and there are 'free fights'.[7]

However, we must remember that such negative opinions were only ever held by a minority of people. In the Mass Observation survey just mentioned, for example, even though middle-class observers were twice as likely to regard dance halls negatively as working-class observers, three quarters of those middle classes asked did not hold negative views at all. Most people were able to draw distinctions between good and bad halls. One Yorkshire dancer in 1939 explained:

> In Bradford there are 3 kinds of dance halls. First, those run by professional dancing teachers. These are respectable well conducted affairs in the main intended to teach people to dance. The second kind consists of those halls run for profit, in a fairly large way. They are not quite as well conducted as the first kind but are not wild. The third kind is those halls which are run in the suburbs by various young men who have formed a band and wish to make a bit of money. Several of the halls are converted

[4] M-O A: DR: 'Jazz 2, July 1939', various. [5] Ibid.
[6] M-O A: DR: 'Jazz 2, July 1939', 'M. Harris'.
[7] M-O A: DR: 'Jazz 2, July 1939', 'F. Meaden'.

'Army' huts. These halls attract a lower class than others and are inclined to be rather wild.[8]

In spite of this, dancing generally got a bad press. It was from a minority of clergy, politicians, and writers that negative views were publicized by a press keen to cash in on the sensational appeal that dancing had, particularly during the 'dance craze' of the 1920s. Talk of dance halls as 'dens of vice' sold newspapers. Editors deliberately highlighted polemical views about dancing in order to provoke reactions from their readers. Despite coming from a minority these views were sufficiently widespread in public debate to make those in the dance industry nervous and defensive, as we shall see shortly. They even elicited intervention from the government on a number of occasions. Furthermore, the poor reputation that dance halls gained during the 1920s and 1930s was to shape negative views of them for a generation to come, despite a considerable effort on the part of the dance industry to 'clean up' its act.

A key reason for the link between dancing and immorality made so strongly in the 1920s was the tainted association of the new dance culture with the marginal culture of nightclubs and 'jazz' (by which was meant all modern dance music and its associated dances). Although the new music and dances which arrived in Britain after the First World War were to spread most widely via dance halls and the new media of records and radio, they initially took root most strongly amongst the nightclub culture of central London. The numerous fashionable clubs and restaurants which opened in the West End and elsewhere following the First World War were perhaps the most visible symbol of an altered moral climate. With the lifting of wartime Defence of the Realm Act regulations in 1920, there was a great expansion in their numbers. 'Nightclubs' worked under the pretence of being private members' clubs but in practice they were open to anyone who could afford them, and it was easy to join at the door. True to their name, nightclubs opened late, and stayed open until three or four o'clock in the morning, serving food in order to get around the licensing laws, and providing late night music, cabaret, and dancing. They caused considerable concern. William Joynson Hicks, Home Secretary between 1924 and 1929, described nightclubs as the 'Plague spots of London'.[9] The Bishop of London denounced them as the 'haunts and hunting grounds of sharks and loose women', whose aim was to exploit 'the follies and weaknesses of those who are induced to visit them'.[10] Certainly, there were close connections with the underworld. Kate Meyrick, one of the most famous London nightclub hostesses, owner of the '43' and other clubs, noted actors, sportsmen, aristocrats, and members of fading European monarchies amongst her clientele. She also highlighted how, in the same clubs, they rubbed shoulders with gangsters and members of the IRA.[11]

[8] M-O A: DR: 'Jazz 2, July 1939', 'A. Hewes'.
[9] *The Times*, 18 November 1925, 11.
[10] *The Times*, 31 January 1925, 13.
[11] K. Meyrick, *Secrets of the 43: Reminiscences with Mrs Meyrick* (London: John Long, 1933), 52–62.

Although the *raison d'être* of the nightclubs was to offer drinking, music, and dancing, there were clearly other motives for attendance. The journalist Sydney Moseley, writing in 1920, certainly considered the main impetus for male attendance at nightclubs as sexual. He wrote that '[n]ine men out of ten who frequent night haunts do so to indulge a physical craving. The question of sexual passion is crucial.'[12] Even though it seems likely that Moseley was exaggerating, male and female prostitutes were to be found in many nightclubs, giving rise to rumours of sordid behaviour. In the first of a series of prosecutions against nightclubs by the London County Council in 1922, the prosecuting solicitor gave a lively description of the clientele of the Blue Hall Dancing Club, Archer Street, W1. It was frequented by:

> . . . women of a questionable character . . . there are practically nightly scenes of drunkenness and disorder inside and outside the premises, and . . . indecency of a most objectionable character takes place within the premises.[13]

Similarly, at Bow Street Police Court in February 1924, police described the atmosphere of the Moulin Rouge Dance Club, off Leicester Square, seeing dancing as integral to its seediness:

> There were 15 women and 20 men dancing to the music of a 'Jazz' band. Two of the men were drunk, and nearly all of the women were well known to the police. The witness had several dances with women; the general conversation in the room was of a gross character. Women were soliciting men in the hall.[14]

Key to the poor reputation of nightclubs, but also dance halls, was the issue of 'dance hostesses'. Many of the larger dance clubs and nightclubs in central London employed attractive female hostesses. Officially they were there to act as waitresses, to dance with patrons, to talk to and entertain those who entered alone. Yet dance hostesses were much more than just that. They were chosen deliberately as bait to draw in male patrons. Hostessing could be a lucrative business, some women earning up to £80 a week—a fortune when a kitchen maid could earn as little as £2 a month. Furthermore, it is clear that many such hostesses *did* also provide sexual services and it was this activity that was perhaps key to the poor reputation many nightclubs had. The National Vigilance Association was particularly interested in this issue and they monitored nightclubs and dance halls for potential irregularities, believing that thousands of women a year were being lost to the so-called 'White Slave Trade'.[15]

Yet dance hostesses could also be found in public dance halls where the use of professional dance partners also served to give dancing a poor reputation. By 1939 it was estimated that there were around 600 dance partners in Britain's dance halls.[16] Like hostesses, dance partners were employed by the halls to partner those

[12] S. Moseley, *Night Haunts of London* (London: Stanley Paul & Co., 1920), 116.
[13] *The Times*, 27 April 1923, 11. [14] *The Times*, 1 February 1924, 7.
[15] WL, London: 4NVA/3/1, F. Sempkins, 'Traffic in Women and Children', nd.
[16] *PP*, 23 September 1939, 35.

who came alone and needed someone to dance with. They could be hired out per dance or per hour for a small charge, sometimes booked in advance, at other times hired on the spot. Both male and female dancing partners were available and they were usually 'penned off' in a corner of the ballroom, coming out only when they had been hired. Most were skilled dancers, indeed Victor Silvester had started off as such a dance partner. Some were merely there to offer dance instruction or partnership, but others offered more than dancing. Certainly the public opinion of dance partners was poor. The men were commonly believed to be 'gigolos' and the women 'prostitutes'. Several high profile scandals concerning these dance partners served to reinforce negative images of dance halls during the interwar period. One of the most important was a scandal which took place at the Kosmo Club in Edinburgh in 1933. The Kosmo Club was the oldest dancing club in Edinburgh. Opened in 1923, it had a large dance hall plus another smaller darkened hall with two exits, one to an adjoining garage. Dance partners were in regular use. In 1933 police raided the club and brought a case against the owners who were accused of living off the prostitution of their employees. The club had arranged a system whereby men could select and hire out one of the dance partners for 30 shillings, then leave the club to go to pre-arranged places (houses or boarding rooms) for 'immoral purposes'. The profits were then split two to one between the club and the dance partners. Fourteen dance hostesses were listed as being involved in the affair between 1 December 1932 and October 1933. They were charged under the Immoral Traffic Act of 1902.[17] The case caused scandalous headlines throughout Britain, with the press following the case and the trial closely, eager to reveal 'shocking' details. The *Daily Herald*, for example, reported how one of the girls had been hired out by an Egyptian who 'thrashed her because she would not submit to him'.[18] The *Daily Express* shrieked 'Dance Club Girls Tell of Night Bathing Parties: Visits to Portobello at 2am'.[19] Mr Adair, summing up, said that this was a 'case of white slavers taking women into their employment without consideration of their moral upbringing. A case of placing them in temptation in the hope that they will succumb.'[20] The owners were found guilty and the club closed down. In the wake of the scandal, rules were tightened up on the hiring of partners, and many halls decided to get rid of them altogether. During the war necessity meant they all but disappeared. Hireable dance partners did remain in business despite this though and re-emerged in some nightclubs. Even as late as 1959 a report on nightclubs by *The Economist* could suggest: 'The question of hostesses is one of the most hotly debated in the night club business... it is a management's policy towards hostesses that determines the standing of a night club.'[21]

Dancing and dance halls were further discredited by the link with drugs that was made at the nightclubs and in the wider dance music scene. Between 1920 and 1923, drugs gained a high profile in Britain and one inextricably linked with

[17] NAS, HH 16/1 Kosmo Club, 'Indictment Against Arthur Bernard, Edwin Jones and James Black', November 1933, 1–3.

[18] *Daily Herald*, 28 November 1933, 12.

[19] *Daily Express*, 29 November 1933, 7.

[20] *Daily Express*, 7 December 1933, 5.

[21] *The Economist*, 11 April 1959, 105.

nightclubs and dancing. The Dangerous Drugs Act had been introduced in 1920 and from 1921–23 there were an average of sixty-five cocaine prosecutions a year.[22] A Parliamentary Report into nightclubs undertaken in January 1921 found evidence that drug use was taking place in some nightclubs in London.[23] In April 1922 *The Times*, under the headline 'Drugs at Dancing Resorts', pointed to the continuing problem, stating that drugs could be purchased by those who frequented nightclubs and fearing an epidemic of addicts.[24] Indeed, 1922 witnessed a series of drug panics as stories of 'Cocaine Girls' filled the newspapers. In March, for example, Freda Kempton, a twenty-three-year-old nightclub hostess and cocaine addict, committed suicide by drinking cocaine. Her case caused an outcry, not least because she had been from a respectable middle-class family before she became addicted. Kempton's position as a dance hostess was seen as central to her downfall. Her tragic story prompted the *Daily Mail* to launch a campaign against drugs in order to save Britain's youth, and women in particular, from a similar fate. Of particular note, Kempton had been supplied by 'Brilliant Chang'—a Chinese gangster who styled himself London's 'Dope King'. Chang supplied most of London's underworld with drugs, operating via various nightclubs and safe houses. Following a long game of cat and mouse, Chang was finally sent to prison in 1924. The previous year had also seen the high profile arrest made against another of London's leading drug barons, Jamaican Edgar Manning, who was said to play in the jazz band at Ciro's, one of London's top nightclubs. For the press this was the stuff of dreams—exotic foreigners, violence, sex, and vice, and all against the backdrop of jazz dancing and nightclubs.

This association between drugs and dancing continued to be made, though on a much smaller scale, during the 1950s. In April 1950 new drugs scandals developed in the press concerning the use of drugs in London's jazz clubs and dance halls. Noel Whitcomb, for example, writing in the *Daily Mirror*, condemned what he described as a growing trend amongst teenagers who 'hang around dance halls' to smoke marijuana. He warned: '"reefers" are being sold in terrifyingly large numbers to kids of fifteen or sixteen by foreign racketeers who hang about outside and inside some of the popular dance halls.' He drew parallels with the 1920s and 30s: 'It is the old West End club game of dope peddlers reaping fortunes by making addicts—only on a rottener, lower down scale.'[25] As with that moral panic, there was a race element involved. The new complaints about dance halls and drugs centred around black men getting white women hooked on marijuana.[26] The President of National Federation of Jazz Organisations, the Marquis of Donegal, issued a strong rebuttal of the claims in the *Daily Mirror*, arguing that '[t]o hold a group of jazz clubs responsible for the pernicious vice of a few individuals is to cast an entirely unmerited slur on promoters, musicians and members of scores of clubs throughout the country'.[27]

[22] M. Kohn, *Dope Girls: The Birth of the British Drug Underground* (London: Lawrence & Wishart, 1992), 168.
[23] *The Times*, 29 April 1922, 12. [24] *The Times*, 26 April 1922, 14.
[25] *DM*, 15 April 1950, 6. [26] See Chapter 9.
[27] *DM*, 19 April 1950, 8.

As we shall see in Chapters 9 and 10, dance halls also came to be seen as immoral due to an association with violence and their importance as a place of racial mixing, also seen negatively by critics. These negative images of dance halls proved hard to shift. As one Dundee dancer of the 1950s remarked: 'Years previously, I think dance halls had had a reputation as being brothels. I don't think that was ever the case in Dundee, but it permeated and lasted a while.'[28] A middle-class woman who brought a case against Sherry's dance hall in Brighton in 1950 for running dancing on Sundays, depicted the hall in terms reminiscent of the moral panic of the 1920s: 'The band was playing, the lights were dim and the atmosphere was somewhat exotic', she told the horrifed judge, who responded, disapprovingly, that they sounded 'very oriental'.[29] Other judges also continued to condemn dancing and even dances in village halls did not escape suspicion. In 1950 one judge described them as 'orgies of immorality . . . It is perfectly obvious that the behaviour going on at these dances is simply unbelievable. It is this kind of behaviour you would see at a monkey house.'[30]

PREVENTING IMMORALITY IN THE DANCE HALL

Driven by the notion of widespread immorality in dance halls, moves were taken to try and clean them up. Action came from various groups, chief amongst them local licensing authorities, the police and an active 'morality' lobby. Dance hall managements also began to actively prevent 'immorality'.

The renewal of licences for music and dancing was a key tool via which local magistrates and police could try to control dancing and dance halls. Regulation and control of dance halls was made in England and Wales by the licensing committees of magistrates in any given district. They had been empowered by the Local Government Act of 1888 to provide licences for places of public entertainment. Dance halls required music and dancing licences, sometimes provided as music, singing, and dancing licences, which were issued and renewed annually, subject to the approval of Licensing Justices of the Peace. Magistrates could attach their own conditions to the licences. In Scotland the situation was similar, with powers granted by the Local Government Act (Scotland) 1889 establishing licensing committees controlled by local magistrates. In addition to these main tools of regulation, there were additional pieces of legislation that could be used to control the dance hall. An attempt was made in 1922 to insert a clause into the Criminal Justice Bill which would make explicit a provision of the Disorderly Houses Act 1751, whereby unlicensed public dances could be penalized in the High Court or the common law misdemeanour of 'keeping a disorderly house' applied to close them down.[31] Though it was removed, some authorities, notably Middlesex

[28] DDHI, Sandy Melville, b. 1934, 11 March 2011. [29] *DM*, 21 February 1950, 7.

[30] *The Essex Newsman Herald* (Chelmsford), 21 November 1950, 4.

[31] NA HO45/11088/437236, 'Music and Dancing Licenses', December 1922.

County Council and London County Council, through acts of Parliament, assumed responsibility for enforcing these laws.

There was a clear moral conceptualization of the law in relation to dance. Many of the restrictions imposed by magistrates were driven by 'morality'—they were making moral judgements based on their own, often class-based, prejudices. Key to their moral conceptualization of the law, local authorities frequently prescribed rules and regulations concerning the conduct of individuals once at dance halls. Some examples from several major British cities illustrate how prescriptive these regulations were, all relying on middle-class perceptions of the subjective notion of 'decency'. In Birmingham, in 1932, rules for licence holders stipulated that 'good order and conduct' had to be kept. The licence terms stated:

> The licensee shall maintain and keep good order and decent behaviour in the premises during the hours of public performance. Nothing shall be done, acted, recited, sung or exhibited which is licentious, indecent, profane or improper, or likely to produce riot, tumult, or breach of the peace.[32]

Just exactly what 'decent behaviour' was, was left to be interpreted by the middle- and upper-class licensing magistrates in the committee. There were also rules meant to prevent 'unsavoury' characters from entering dance halls and other places of public entertainment: 'No common prostitute, reputed thief, or other notoriously disorderly person shall knowingly be admitted into or permitted to remain in the property.'[33] In Glasgow too there were similar rules about behaviour and conduct, focused on the subjective notion of 'decency'. A 1932 licence stated: 'nothing shall be allowed . . . which is licentious or indecent' and that 'the Licensee shall not knowingly suffer any . . . improper conduct in the places licensed, and shall maintain therein good order and decency'.[34] As part of this attempt to prevent indecency, Glasgow dance licences, infamously, stipulated that women could not enter a dance hall unless accompanied by a man. The extremely paternalistic nature of those who regulated dance halls is nowhere better illustrated than in the moves of other Scottish regulators in the 1920s. Such paternalism was underpinned by a clear class prejudice whereby the lower-class frequenters of dance halls were treated with both suspicion and condescension. In 1927 the Scottish Justices and Magistrates Association issued a statement on its policy ideas entitled 'Dancing: Dangers of Unrestricted Liberty':

> Corporations have often to follow in the wake of their citizens' pursuits like careful modern parents, preventing liberty from becoming licence; as it were protecting the family in its playroom from unhealthy atmosphere, unguarded fires, and obstacles they may trip over. Like modern parents. Also, they must stear clear of mollycoddling, of too many verbotens and irksome restraints. When a recreation becomes a passion,

[32] CBA PS/B 4/1/1/4, *Regulations for the Management of Institutes, Church Rooms, and Places Licensed for Music, Singing and Dancing, and with or without Licences for Stage Plays and Cinematograph Exhibitions, Licences D and E,* 25 October 1932, 1.

[33] Ibid.

[34] NAS, DD5/984: 'Dance Hall Licence by the Magistrates' Committee of the Corporation of the City of Glasgow', 125.

> and men and women, boys and girls, wish to indulge in it to the limits of fatigued excitements, our Magistrates have no easy task to set the tactful guardians of our welfare.[35]

Such was the level of moralizing, that some sections of the dance hall industry were unhappy with the growing level of police interference in their businesses. In October 1925 the Liverpool Association of Dance Hall Proprietors and Licensees sent a deputation to the Theatre and Public Entertainments Committee to ask that uniformed and plain-clothed police officers stop entering private dance functions.[36] Their strongest complaint was against police interference in the conduct of dancers. The deputations suggested:

> that at public dances the Police should not act as censors; or express their opinion as to how ladies should be dressed; or act as judges as to the immorality of modern dancing.[37]

As a whole, however, the dance hall industry adopted a different strategy for dealing with this interference and regulation. Rather than opposing and criticizing, most dance halls adopted a long-term strategy of trying to make their industry 'respectable'. In doing so, they were also driven by a middle-class notion of morality. They tried to work with local licensing authorities and police, and even took pre-emptive action, taking on the role of censor and regulator in order to prevent local authorities feeling the need to do so. The advent of commercially run, standardized palais de danse with self-imposed codes of behaviour served to regulate and control the atmosphere in which most people were dancing and hearing live dance music. Businesses were keen to prohibit any kind of bad behaviour in their dance halls and so they employed stewards and Masters of Ceremonies to regulate the behaviour of patrons. Throughout the period, they worked hard to show themselves as respectable, also courting local 'establishment' opinion by hosting many charity fundraising events in dance halls.

THE 'IMMORALITY' OF DANCE

A further key reason why dance halls and dance clubs had a reputation for immorality was the link between the dances performed there and sex. We can see a remarkable continuity in the charges levelled against particular dances throughout the period 1918–60. Consistently, dancing was caricatured as something wild and sensual and requiring provocatively close physical contact between men and women. Dances were seen as 'sinful'.

Certainly the proximity that dances created between men and women was part of their appeal. As we have seen, the new social dances of the early twentieth century

[35] *Glasgow Herald*, 25 October 1927, 3.

[36] LRO, 347 MAG 1/1/15, Theatre and Public Entertainments Licensing Committee, 'Proceedings 1923–28', Minutes 26 October 1925, 65.

[37] Ibid.

were made for couples and this increased the room for physical contact between the sexes. As dance teacher Jack Crossley recalled in 1947, comparing the old dances with the new:

> the dancers did not stand close to each other . . . in fact most of the dances then were danced with both the lady and the gentleman facing the same direction, the only contact being with the man's right hand and the lady's left hand, whereas today it is essential that the man should convey his partner, by the very movements of his hands and body, the steps he has in mind.[38]

The new social dances required close bodily contact between men and women and thus increased the opportunities for sexual contact between the two. For example, early social dances the 'Bunny Hug' and the 'Grizzly Bear' required dancers to embrace and hug each other. More significantly the foxtrot, introduced to Britain in 1914, required that dance partners held each other, close and tight. Victor Silvester, a leading figure in ballroom dancing, recalls the variety of ways in which it was danced:

> . . . there were men who held a girl by her finger-tips with the other hand very low on her waist line. There were others who placed one hand between the girl's shoulder blades and stretched her arm to its full length. Some men would embrace a girl in a bear-like hug so that she could barely breathe, much less dance.[39]

Similarly, the modern waltz and quickstep involved close contact and gyrating movements. Santos Casani in his *Self Tutor* of 1927 gave the following advice for how to hold and guide when dancing. Guiding came not from the arms, but from the body:

> The direction you choose must be indicated to your partner by a movement of the body from the hip upwards. That is, if you wish to steer the body to the right your body should turn right, your left shoulder swinging clockwise. The lady accepts the indication from the hip upwards and follows it with a movement from the hip downwards. That is, while she is placid in your arms, her feet must follow the new line of dance set by your turn.[40]

Even this 'correct' way of dancing required the woman to take her lead from the man's hips, thus expecting a considerable degree of physical intimacy, especially 'shocking' as the etiquette of the dance hall allowed for the free mixing of strangers in such a way. Contact between dancers was central to the new dances. Victor Silvester describing the correct way to dance a slow foxtrot noted:

> The couple dance opposite and level with each other. The man should lean very slightly forward from the ankles—not the waist, and the girl leans very slightly back

[38] J. Crossley, *Pictorial Dance Tutor: A beginner's guide to ballroom dancing* (London: Sir Isaac Pitman & Sons, 1947), 2.

[39] V. Silvester, *Dancing is My Life* (London: Heinemann, 1958), 85, quoted in T. Cresswell, '"You cannot shake that shimmie here": producing mobility on the dance floor' (2006) 13 *Cultural Geographies* 66.

[40] S. Casani, *Casani's Self-Tutor of Ballroom Dancing* (London: Cassell & Co., 1927), 8–9.

from the hips—not the waist; both should keep their hips well forward, and no space should be discernible between them from hips to chest.

He went on:

The man's R. arm is round the girl, and his R. hand just under her shoulder blades... The man's L. hand holds the girl's R. hand in a natural manner with the back of his hand backward, and the wrist must not bend. The girl rests her L. arm and hand along the man's R. and with her L. elbow just below his.[41]

For the tango, holds were even closer:

The man holds the girl with his R. arm further round her than in other dances, and with his L. hand lower... The girl is held on the man's R. hip which is kept forward... When starting a promenade the girl's R. side and man's L. side are slightly away from each other... and the man's R. hip and the girl's L. hip are kept close to each other.[42]

For some observers, this was too much. Writing in *The Times* in September 1922, for example, J. D. McAughton, a member of the Scottish District of the British Association of Teachers of Dancing, argued that the way in which such dances were executed in dance halls was not dancing but simply 'hugging to music'. He concluded that dance halls were degrading, indecent, immoral, and deliberately sensual.[43] Robert Douglas, writing in the *Liverpool Echo* in 1926, concurred, arguing that they were no place for shy men: 'The young man may very well find himself dancing with and embracing a female whose bareness is at once the subject of common gossip amongst other people in the room... A dance can be a very embarrassing affair indeed for the shy man.'[44]

The Churches were also particularly concerned. Frederic Spurr, writing of *The Christian Use of Leisure* in 1928, stated that the question of whether to dance or not was one that divided the Christian community. He argued:

What is capable of being a boon may become an evil when it is made the ally of our baser passions. There are in the modern world descendants of Salome, who practise a great art in a vile way, for the purpose of awakening the devil in man and of gaining from him favours which in sane moments he would never dream of granting. And there are men also who... act in a similar manner. They frequent ballrooms and make dancing the occasion for stimulating the passion of young girls and playing upon the sexual excitement that is thus aroused. Any minister or doctor of experience can bear witness to the fact that many social tragedies had their birth in the ballroom. In the public dancing places, where miscellaneous crowds gather and mingle, the greatest danger lies.[45]

This was part of a wider attack by some in the Churches on modern dancing. A member of the clergy, presiding over a meeting of the Maidenhead 'Preventive and Rescue Assocation' in March 1919, for example, strongly condemned the new dance craze as 'one of the most degrading symptoms of the present day', a sign of a

41 V. Silvester, *Modern Ballroom Dancing* (London: Herbert Jenkins, 1927), 100–1.

42 Silvester, *Modern*, 127.

43 *The Times*, 21 September 1922, 8.

44 *Liverpool Echo*, 13 February 1926, 4.

45 F. Spurr, *The Christian Use of Leisure* (London: Kingsgate Press, 1928), 55–6.

'very grave disease which was infecting the country'.[46] Similarly, Bishop Weldon declared in 1920 that the use of dances as a means of raising money for war memorials was 'little less than a national humiliation'. Thus, the popularity of dancing was seen by many leading Christian figures as symptomatic of a general collapse in moral standards. In 1919, Sir Dyce Duckworth of the Church Army, which aimed to raise the standard of Christianity and religious observances in Britain, was convinced that 'wild dances', and music 'only fit for West Indian Savages' were 'palpable indications that the morals of old England had become degraded'.[47]

This transformation in the rules and aesthetics of social dancing was reflective of, and helped shape, a significant shift in gender relations and discourses of sexuality. The new partner dances for men and women, with their close bodily contact, sexualized dancing to a level that would have been unacceptable in the Victorian era. Whilst it is not accurate to describe the 1920s as a period of sexual revolution, it did witness the emergence of a more enlightened attitude towards public expressions of sexuality. The courting couple could now more acceptably express their love for each other in public, unlike the public restraint expected in Victorian society.

The issue of 'proximity' stubbornly clung on amongst critics, despite the subsequent relaxation in societal attitudes. Still, in 1950, Douglas Kennedy of the English Folk Dance and Song Society was advising readers of the *Daily Mirror* on the 'art of holding a girl without making her breathless'. He suggested that dancers could avoid 'the devil's interests' in such matters and actually using the correct form of dancing was a way of encouraging 'civilized' behaviour. He went on:

> It can rescue good manners and project a sense of chivalry. A man can learn how much art there is in the simple business of holding a girl so that she is supported and still able to breathe and harmonise her actions with his.[48]

Using dances for 'smooching' and 'petting' became a common source of complaint in the 1950s. In November 1951 23-year-old Margaret Thelwall, President of the Young Catholic Workers Association in Preston, made allegations that 'dancing in the dark' sessions gave rise to 'all kinds of unhealthy opportunities', including 'forty minutes kisses'. She threatened to lead a protest to the local Watch Committee. By now, however, dance hall managements were well prepared to rebut such claims, mostly unfounded. V. Mellin, manager of the dance hall in question, retorted 'it is ridiculous to say anything "unhealthy" happens. There is far more cuddling in a cinema.'[49] Similarly, in 1955, Detective Chief Inspector David Bradley of Huddersfield told the local licensing committee that he had been shocked by what he had seen at a dance in the town hall: 'It was disgusting and demoralising. No decent parent would like his child to go. Several young people were behaving in a matter that any respectable parent would deprecate. They were spooning in public obviously because of drink.'[50] Such objections were based on subjective moral judgements that took no account of behavioural differences dependent on

46 *The Times*, 15 March 1919, 7.
47 *The Times*, 18 March 1919, 7.
48 *DM*, 3 January 1950, 3.
49 *DM*, 6 November 1951, 3.
50 *DM*, 3 September 1955, 3.

both class and age. As we have already established, the dance hall was a largely innocent and well-conducted environment, especially by the 1950s. However, there *were* clearly some who saw the dance hall as a place to engage in displays of intimacy.[51] As the *Daily Mirror* complained in 1953: 'The dance hall is not a petting parlour. It isn't a pub. It isn't a gymnasium. And it is no place for show offs. People who go to the palais to do their courting, prop up the bar all night or act the fool, can ruin the evening for everybody else.'[52]

As well as placing men and women in close proximity to one another, one other persistent complaint against the new social dances of the twentieth century was that their movements were 'erotic' and 'unrestrained'. Certainly by utilizing a completely new set of body movements, the new dances were far freer than the dances of the nineteenth century and undermined older notions of 'respectability' by appearing 'uncontrolled'. For example, notable aspects of the African tradition in dancing on which many of the new dances were based, such as exaggerated hip and pelvis movements, can clearly be seen in early social dances like the 'Turkey Trot', which involved the man 'trotting' towards his partner, flapping his arms in the manner of an aroused fowl, while his partner did the same in retreat. The vitality and free expression of new dances, such as the Charleston, was also a cause of concern. Such dances were equated with dangerously uncontrolled sexuality and eroticism by critics. Patrick Chalmers, describing the new dance in March 1926, wrote: 'In its extreme form it is a wild and frenzied affair, done at terrific speed, with shoulder "shimmies," head shakes, arms waving, legs and feet flying in all directions.'[53] Similarly, a *Daily Mail* correspondent condemned the dance, emphasizing the lack of self-control it induced: 'Here were some thirty couples lurching, wriggling, and kicking their legs wildly from side to side, the perspiration streaming down their face . . . '[54] Such displays of wildness in public places offended the sensibilities of some. Major Cecil Taylor, president of the Imperial Society of Dance Teachers, complained that the Charleston was making the ballroom 'vulgar'.[55] Lady Walpole supported his comments: 'The dance is vulgar and absolutely absurd and should be banned in London ballrooms . . . Women should not stoop to that kind of thing and make themselves ridiculous. When doing the Charleston, women get into crooked postures which make their figures very graceless.'[56] Similar complaints came from a Mrs Wilfred Ashley who argued: 'Dancing must comprise grace, rhythm, and deportment—the couples wriggling and writhing in their Charleston agony achieve none of these attributes of dancing.'[57]

Similarly, during the war, the Jitterbug was condemned because it seemed to indicate a lack of self-control that was regarded as morally dubious. There were direct parallels drawn with the Charleston, one reporter even calling the Jitterbug a '1943 hotted up version of the Charleston'.[58] At a Jitterbug contest in Glasgow in 1941 a newspaper reporter exclaimed: 'Dancers' feet were going like lightning.

[51] See Chapter 7. [52] *DM*, 9 October 1953, 10. [53] *Daily Mail*, 12 March 1926, 8.
[54] *Daily Mail*, 13 November 1926, 8. [55] *Daily Mail*, 21 July 1925, 7.
[56] *Daily Mail*, 27 April 1926, 7. [57] *Daily Mail*, 28 April 1926, 7.
[58] *Daily Mail*, 5 October 1943, 3.

One youth whirled his girl on the floor and stepped over her. Another threw his in the air, her feet missing the face of another girl by inches. Couples danced back to back, then boy seized girl and almost threw her in amongst band. All this to a chorus of screams and shouts from onlookers.'[59] Collie Knox condemned such contests as 'the acme of madness . . . another name for hysteria'.[60] East End magistrate Basil Henriques labelled the Jitterbug as 'wild and raucous' and a 'sex exciter for negroes'.[61] When banned in some Dundee dance halls in 1944 one dance promoter argued that it was being outlawed because it caused 'riotous repercussions on those who practise it'.[62] Similarly, in Derby the local Dance Halls Association banned it because it 'lowered standards' of behaviour and dancing.[63] A Derby dancer labelled those who danced it as 'witch doctors cum fire-dancers', a reference to the racist complaints made against the dance and dealt with fully in the next chapter.[64]

In the post-war era, Jiving was similarly condemned. In language reminiscent of twenty years earlier, in 1946 the Rev. H. Hardman of Fleetwood condemned Jive as 'the work of the devil'. He went on: 'This so called dance is a debased form of art which stimulates the lowest passions.'[65] Likewise, Father Joseph Sunn of New Southgate made comparable remarks that year about swing dancing, claiming that 'old time dances are cleaner and healthier than jazz, swing and Jitterbug'.[66] The abandon and the physicality of the Jive were singled out for particular condemnation. In 1947 dance teacher Norton Colville explained that the 'throw away' move was what caused most trouble. He wrote: 'We see a couple, dangerously hurtling about, the man using much strength throwing the girl away rather more than arm's length away so at the end of every other bar or so it seems that they are playing "tug-o'-war" with each other. Hence, these very crude and ugly positions.'[67]

Interestingly, even the move towards solo dancing, where men and women actually moved further apart and did not hold each other, was condemned. As in previous decades, authority figures made value judgements about cultural forms, associating certain dances with lower moral standards. This was due to the accusation that solo dancers were dancing with even greater abandon than ever before. The Twist was one of the first solo dances to be condemned. In the dance the hips, torso, and legs were swung together forward and back, with the arms in a fairly static position. The feet could also twist back and forth, and one leg could be periodically lifted off the floor. Speed and vertical height were also adjustable. It was the repeated gyrating of the hips and torso, usually whilst facing your partner, that made the dance so 'scandalous' in critics' eyes, however. In 1963, for example, a High Court Judge told a court that 'nice girls' did not do the Twist, they did the

59 *The Sunday Post* (Glasgow), 2 March 1941, 5.
60 *Daily Mail*, 4 June 1940, 7.
61 *Daily Mail*, 27 April 1944, 2.
62 *Dundee Courier and Advertiser* (Dundee), 7 February 1944, 3.
63 *Derby Evening Telegraph* (Derby), 22 October 1943, 4.
64 *Derby Evening Telegraph* (Derby), 10 February 1945, 3.
65 *LDN*, 27 April 1946, 1.
66 *LDN*, 15 June 1946, 2.
67 *Ballroom Dancing Annual 1947* (1948), 11.

waltz and slow foxtrot instead.[68] Like the Charleston and Jitterbug before it, vicars and bishops lined up to condemn it and ban it. In August 1962 for example, the Rev Robert Keal, Vicar of Sutton-on-Trent, Nottinghamshire, said he would ban the Twist in the church hall where he organized dances.[69]

MAKING DANCES 'RESPECTABLE'

In addition to trying to regulate dance venues and behaviour within them, throughout the period, deliberate attempts were made to alter the dances performed in Britain's dance halls. Professional dance teachers made concerted attempts to reformulate and control dance steps in order to make them more 'acceptable' to their critics and in order to regain the 'respectability' of their profession. Their most notable work came in developing a standardized 'English style' during the 1920s, but they also attempted to 'tame' other dances in subsequent decades.

Of greatest significance for the reputation and form of dancing in twentieth-century Britain was the development of a standardized set of dance steps and formalization of dancing standards first developed in the 1920s, known as the 'English style.' It was a development led by professional dance teachers and their reasons for creating it are important. Via a series of informal conferences in the 1920s, these groups demanded action to improve the reputation of dancing due to the image of 'immorality' with which it had become associated. The first 'Informal Conference' of the Teachers of Ballroom Dancing, held in May 1920, expressed outrage at the 'artistic bolshevism' displayed by the new dances flooding in from the United States. The 200 dance teachers from around Britain who had met at the invitation of Philip Richardson, editor of *The Dancing Times*, were determined, as Richardson put it, 'that something should be done to call a halt to freakish dancing before it became something worse'.[70] Two important resolutions were passed that were to alter popular dancing in Britain forever. The first resolution was a clear statement of intent: 'That the teachers present agree to do their very best to stamp out freak steps.'[71] The second resolution set out the means by which the dancing profession intended to transform the reputation of dancing:

> That this meeting of teachers do select a committee whose duty it shall be to consider which shall be the recognized steps of each dance and report their decision to another general meeting to be convened after the summer holidays.[72]

The conference received widespread press coverage and this, together with three further informal conferences that year and in 1921, led to a national campaign from dance teachers against 'objectionable dancing'. A total of six Informal Conferences

[68] *Daily Mail*, 15 January 1963, 7. [69] *Daily Mail*, 13 August 1962, 3.

[70] P. Richardson, *A History of English Ballroom Dancing (1910–45): The story of the development of the modern English style* (London: Herbert Jenkins, 1947), 41.

[71] Richardson, *A History*, 44. [72] Ibid.

were held between 1922 and 1928, together with numerous other conferences arranged between those years. The establishment of an 'Official Board' made up of leading members of the various dance teaching groups and associations was also agreed upon. This signified a desire on the part of the dancing professionals to change the image of dancing in the public's mind, by shaping key dances into less controversial forms. As James Donald of Aberdeen argued at a conference in 1923: 'Let us preserve the dance by maintaining strict supervision of it.'[73]

Of most significance, the committee of experts established by the Informal Conferences resolved to standardize the most popular dance steps and to eliminate 'undignified moves'. It was decided that the basic steps of the foxtrot, tango, and waltz (and later the quickstep) should be standardized. The freedom of expression so closely associated with the new dances was to be eliminated. Victor Silvester, then a leading dance teacher, worked tirelessly at this standardizing process. He wrote:

> We spent hours discussing basic principles—the correct hold and such finer points as body sway, contrary body movement and footwork—all of which we put down on paper. We decided the most suitable figures for the different rhythms, and we laid down what was good and bad form. Then, to ensure that our code of ballroom procedure and behaviour became widely known, we incorporated it in a syllabus for a teacher's examination which prospective members of the branch had to pass before they could be admitted.[74]

Once agreed upon, the new steps were popularized using a variety of methods. The ISTD issued wall charts and booklets with illustrations of the correct sequence of dance steps, correct positioning of the body, and the correct hold for partners. The media were also utilized. *Dancing Times* printed articles and photographs of the standardized forms, and by the end of the 1920s most popular national newspapers contained a regular column on dancing, which illustrated how the 'professionals dance'. Regional newspapers also supported the efforts of the dance teachers, with regular columns often written by local members of the dance teachers' associations. As we have seen, a myriad of different guides and handbooks to dancing were also produced. Finally, dance competitions sponsored by official dance teacher associations also aided the regulating process, with official rules for their conduct laid down by the Official Board in 1924.

The aim of this standardization and codification process was to minimize the room available to dancers for individual expression and to eliminate 'freakishness'. It was a response to the critics who claimed that popular dancing was uncontrolled, wild, undignified, and needlessly sensual. The dancing profession wanted to prove itself as responsible, professional, and serious. It wanted to make dances ordered, dignified, and respectable. The English style dancing was primarily concerned with the perfect execution of steps, rather than the expression of the dancers' mood or

[73] *Sunday Sun*, 24 June 1923, 3.

[74] V. Silvester, *Dancing*, 86, quoted in T. Cresswell, '"You cannot shake that shimmie here": producing mobility on the dance floor' (2006) 13 *Cultural Geographies* 66.

emotions. Lack of spontaneity and a controlled, less emotional dancing experience were central and seen as representative of the national character. They also show a concerted focus on the notion of 'respectability' as a motivation for shaping Britain's dance culture.

The precedent set by the dancing profession in the 1920s, together with the formation of various official and semi-official committees of 'experts', laid the foundations for continued attempts to regulate dance forms by teachers. Thus, whenever a new dance emerged which threatened the order and discipline established by the English style, attempts were made to either ban it or control it. We can see similar patterns of condemnation then regulation with other big dance developments. The Charleston and Jitterbug were perhaps the most important. Maxwell Stewart described this process in 1927: 'Steps we may borrow from all over the world . . . But we make them our own . . . The fact is that we are not good at finding dances of our own, but we are excellent at taming those of other people.'[75]

Even at the earliest stage of its introduction into Britain, dance teachers were trying to 'tame' the Charleston. When Annette Mills and Robert Sielle, sponsored by the *Dancing Times*, introduced the dance to the public in 1925, they showed it first in its original stage solo form, then the wild ballroom form popular in New York dance halls, and finally as the more sedate version danced by dance teachers in America.[76] They recommended the latter version to the press and to dancers. By October 1926 the *Dancing Times* was publishing illustrations showing two versions, the wilder original and the new 'flat version'. The illustration shows clearly the difference between the dances, with the original far more vivacious and taking up far more room. Unfortunately, as far as dance teachers were concerned, the Charleston as initially adopted by dancers in Britain's ballrooms was rowdy, taking its example from the wild solo examples of the dance shown in cabaret and on stage. By the end of 1926 there was an organized effort to push a standardized version of the dance. The resulting standardized Flat Charleston was largely the brainchild of Josephine Bradley and Victor Silvester. With its more controlled and subdued movements—the feet never left the floor, hence it was 'flat'—the press commented on the Charleston being 'made respectable'. The *Derby Daily Telegraph* for example remarked: 'With the modification of the steps principal objections to the Charleston have been eradicated, and the dance has been made "respectable" without any writhing or kicking movements.'[77] To demonstrate just how balanced the tamed version was, and to illustrate that it did not require much room in the dance hall, Santos Casani famously danced the Flat Charleston on the top of a London taxi whilst travelling through the West End, a moment captured by British Pathé Newsreels.[78]

We can see a similar process in response to the Jitterbug during the war. In Blackpool B. S. Hayward noted that the threat of an 'epidemic of Jitterbug' had

[75] *Nottingham Evening Post*, 9 April 1927, 7.
[76] *DT*, September 1950, 753.
[77] *Derby Daily Telegraph*, 18 September 1926, 3.
[78] 'The Flat Charleston Made Easy', *British Pathé*, 15 March 1927, Media URN 36710.

receded due to 'an immediate and very firm suppression' by local teachers.[79] In March 1940 Alex Moore noted the emergence of a 'quiet form' of the dance emerging in British ballrooms and welcomed its exuberance as a non-threatening addition to the ballroom programme which had 'not the slightest possibility' of ousting the English style from Britain's dance halls.[80] This mild form of Jitterbug was also noted in Nottingham's dance halls where Frank Hanford argued that it was 'a good way for dancers to express something a bit off the beaten track'.[81] By April 1940, Mecca's Adele England, originator of the Lambeth Walk, was demonstrating her 'Ballroom version' of the Jitterbug, and other leading dance teachers also took to the dance and adapted it.[82] Most famously, it was later even taken up by Victor Silvester in 1944, who, encouraged by Edgar Jackson the pro-Swing editor of *Melody Maker*, welcomed the dance as something new and interesting, before introducing his own ballroom version.[83] By 1944, then, the Jitterbug was much altered and in fact on the decline as a separate dance, having been around, on and off, for about six years. It was via this process that the Jitterbug evolved into the Jive, which was to the Jitterbug what the Flat Charleston had been to the Charleston.

DANCING AND CHANGING GENDER BOUNDARIES

Dancing was also condemned because it was indicative of and helped shape changing gender boundaries. In particular, the revolution in dancing styles that had occurred after the First World War was a sign of new attitudes towards women and symptomatic of changes in women's identities and experiences. How women dressed, how women moved, where they went and who with, were all issues that were central in responses to the emergence of dancing as a popular pastime. In particular, dancing became integral to the image and experience of 'new types' of women that emerged after the First World War. We will examine the anxiety created by these developments, by focusing on three of them. In the period after 1918 the 'new woman' or 'Flapper' emerged as a stereotypical image of the new woman. During the war the 'Good Time Girl' became identified as problematic. Following the war, concerns were focused on the new, increasingly independent woman, caricatured as the 'Palais Pearl' and then the 'Snooty Cutie'. A passion for dancing was central to all three images of 'problematic' women.

We start with the interwar period. The 1920s was a decade in which women entered the public sphere to an unprecedented extent. There was a renegotiation of the division between public and private spheres and contemporary debate about the 'new woman' was widespread. Not surprisingly, both changes were resisted by some. As we have seen, dancing was one of the key areas whereby women could enter the public sphere in a space that was female dominated. This and other

[79] *DT*, March 1940, 357–61. [80] *DT*, March 1940, 357. [81] *DT*, March 1940, 360.
[82] *DT*, May 1940, 488. [83] *MDD*, March 1944, 23.

transgressions into the formerly 'male sphere' were condemned by some critics. Tom Burke, for example, complained:

> The young London girl now goes everywhere and goes alone if she wishes. No public amusement is barred to her. You see her at the racecourse, the greyhound course, the dirt-track, the boxing match, the wrestling match, the football match, the night club . . . the palais de danse, the smoking rooms of tea shops, the brasserie, and even in your own club. You can't keep her out of anything.[84]

This new 'leisured woman' was the subject of a debate between G. K. Chesterton and Lady Rhondda introduced by George Bernard Shaw at the Kingsway Hall, London, in January 1927. Chesterton condemned the modern woman for neglecting her role in the home as a mother. He observed disapprovingly: 'A woman can spend her time drinking cocktails, going to the night club, dancing the Charleston, and doing all the things that many women seem to imagine will fill their lives gloriously.'[85] These 'modern girls' were condemned by other young women for wasting their lives and opportunities on dancing: 'The modern society girls . . . are the most terrible type of all, for they are born with magnificent opportunities for making the world a better place—and throw them away on the Charleston or a hair wave, and are bored at twenty.'[86] Involvement of women in 'jazz dances' was of particular concern and dancing was thus central to images of the 'new woman' and criticism of her (see Fig. 8.1). For example, writing for the *Sunday Chronicle* in 1924 in a piece called 'Violet Quirk goes to a dance and brings back disturbing impressions', Miss Quirk made the following observations concerning women:

> These women cannot know how revolting they appear, as they shuffle around the room with striding legs too far apart, rigid bodies and fixed staring eyes. They are so closely clasped by the men that free movement is impossible. Yet only a few years ago girls, among themselves, unanimously condemned the partners who didn't keep their proper distance. They drew a sharp line between dancing and embracing. They didn't give to the casual stranger that which they reserved for a chosen man.[87]

She concluded with the following advice: 'Before mothers give permission to their girls to go alone to jazz dances, let them know first where they are going, or else go with them.'

Women's evident enjoyment of both dancing and the dance halls themselves were a sign of a new self-confidence. This caused concern for many who feared for the survival of the family and the institution of marriage. Dancing, as with the cinema, was attacked because it took young women out of the home and gave them 'false values'—glamour, escape, romance, etc. Doctors and health experts were concerned that dance halls were ruining the health of young women and endangering their fertility. These new dancing girls were also criticized because they

[84] T. Burke, *London in My Time* (London; Rich and Cowan, 1934), 176.

[85] *Daily Mail*, 28 January 1927, 12. [86] *Daily Mail*, 10 May 1926, 10.

[87] *Sunday Chronicle*, 24 June 1924, quoted in J. Godbolt, *A History of Jazz* (London: Paladin, 1984), 32–3.

Fig. 8.1. Gender and Dance: 'Do Young Girls Care about Politics?', W. K. Haselden, *Daily Mirror*, 13 December 1920
Source: © Mirrorpix.

appeared to be self-confident. The hard-nosed, confident dancing girl became the focus of complaints from many young men. In Dundee, for example, one man wrote in 1920:

> If a gentleman is a novice at dancing and visits one of the local dance halls he is in for a sorry time. Ridicule greets him in every corner, along with turned up noses and snappy remarks, such as—'We have our own set and partners.' These are common expressions used by Dundee girls. There is too much of the 'stand aff my fut' attitude about the local ballroom girl.[88]

During the war, societal anxieties about changing gender roles were played out in the dance hall as several features of wartime dancing culture were seen as ominous signs of wider changes. The supposed 'masculinization' of women during the war

[88] *DET*, 23 February 1920, 9.

was one such anxiety. For example, even though women dancing with women had been a common and acceptable feature of interwar dance halls, during the war, same sex dancing was seen as an example of changing gender roles, and considered worrying. So frequently were 'girls dancing as man' that in March 1941, dance teacher Phyliss Haylor wrote an article in the *Dancing Times* giving guidance for women on 'how to take man', indicating the best steps to learn and how to lead them.[89] Journalists satirized the new dancing roles of women, seeing them as part of a wider masculinization of women.

The way women looked in the dance hall was also an important feature of these anxieties. Mobilization of women into heavy industrial work, labouring on farms, and service in the armed forces all had the potential to challenge gender boundaries and identities. In particular, the wearing of uniforms and overalls, and more utilitarian hairstyles designed not to interfere with machinery, led to the 'masculinization' of women's appearance in daily life. As Pat Kirkham has shown, this caused concern at an official level, and attempts were made to re-assert feminine identity through a 'Beauty and Duty' campaign, whereby valuable shipping space was set aside for the importation of cosmetics, corsets, and so on.[90] In the dance hall, there was an expectation for women to remain looking feminine, and when this was not possible such transgressions were often resented by both men and the women involved. One group of women whose appearance was criticized quite regularly were the Land Girls, who were seen as 'tough girls'. It is clear that some women resented their new-found 'masculine' appearance as they were often shunned if they took their new outfits into dance halls. In November 1941 for example, one Land Girl from Maidstone, Kent, wrote of her visit to a London dance hall:

> I had no other clothes to wear except my land outfit, and knowing that most people are wearing uniform these days, thought I should be in order too. From the comments of some of the dancers there, I felt pretty awful about my rig-out. Perhaps it is time some of the public realised that we girls in the Land Army are doing our bit just as much as Civil Defence Workers.[91]

Such criticism of 'masculine' clothing was common. For example JT of Clapham wrote to *Dance News* in September 1941: 'These are free-and-easy days, I know, when more and more women are wearing slacks for work and recreation. But please, must we have them at dances. To my mind they are entirely out of place here and should be banned.'[92]

In addition, the perception that women were becoming more assertive continued to cause consternation in wartime. The desire of a few women to turn traditional dance hall etiquette on its head and to ask men to dance, rather than wait to be asked, was thus seen as problematic. As we have seen, the 'Equal Rights' campaign in the dance hall largely grew out of the practicalities of a shortage of men dancing.

[89] *DT*, March 1941, 340.

[90] See P. Kirkham, 'Beauty and Duty: Keeping up the (Home) Front' in P. Kirkham and D. Thoms, *War Culture: Social change and changing experience in World War Two Britain* (London: Lawrence & Wishart, 1995).

[91] *DN*, 8 November 1941, 2.

[92] *DN*, 30 September 1941, 2.

Although it failed to catch on, its introduction did create debate. Elsewhere the shortage of men could lead to an increasing competitiveness amongst women, and a new assertiveness. For example, competition between civilian girls and WAAFs for men in dance halls could be intense.[93] In Chester, a 'table system' for getting men was introduced, which also shows more assertiveness amongst some women. A soldier who was a 'victim' of it recalls:

> You walked in the Dance Hall and they could tell a dancer so you got grabbed and seated at a table with a group of ATS, WAF or Land Girls . . . They bought your beer all night but you belonged to them and danced with all of them in turn. The fisticuffs at the end of the night as to who took you back to barracks had to be seen to be believed . . . You could try and stay independent but try fighting off a dozen women who were determined to own you for the night.[94]

To many critics this new assertiveness was considered at best as distasteful, and at worst a sign of a new 'immorality'. Sonya O'Rose has shown how there was a particular focus on the behaviour of women, and an attempt to stigmatize dancing as a key feature of the 'new immorality', most closely associated with so-called 'good time girls'.[95] Women's sexuality was regarded as dangerous, disruptive, and a danger to the nation. The Good Time Girl thus became the wartime equivalent of the Flapper. Like the Flapper she was largely a construct. However, 'going out' and having a 'good time' became particularly sensitive issues for all women during the war. Was it patriotic to have fun whilst so many people were suffering? Was not dancing bad for the war effort? Worse, were such women not being unfaithful whilst their sweethearts were risking their lives for the country? As the name suggests, however, the Good Time Girl seemed particularly hedonistic, often focused on flaunting herself in order to enjoy herself. As Mass Observation noted in its 1943 survey of pubs in central London: 'These girls are out chiefly for an exciting evening, with someone to pay for their entertainment. All the indications point to their being well aware of what they are doing.'[96] It continued: '[T]hey are only looking for men who will buy them presents. That's why they go for Colonial soldiers or the Americans, because they've got the money.'[97]

As dancing was one of the most popular activities for young women, it inevitably became a focus of criticism and an attribute of the 'Good Time Girl'. For critics, her dancing was seen as a sign of the Good Time Girls' increased financial and social independence; her selfish attitude of enjoying herself whilst others suffered; and her sexual immorality. Good Time Girls used dancing as a way of expressing their indecency and as a way of 'snaring' men, either for sexual or material reasons. Mass Observation noted how WAAFs used dances as a key venue to pick up the men they were interested in. The report provided details of how WAAFs manoeuvred

[93] M-O A, FR757, 'WAAF Life', June 1941, 6.

[94] PWA, Frank Mee, Article A2553761, 23 April 2004.

[95] S. O. Rose, *Which People's War? Citizenship and National Identity in Britain 1939–1945* (Oxford: Oxford University Press, 2003).

[96] M-O A, FR1835, 'Behaviour of Women in Pubs', June 1943, ii–iii.

[97] M-O A, FR1835, 'Behaviour of Women in Pubs', June 1943, 4.

themselves at dances in order to pick up the man they had identified as most prized. Working in pairs they would position themselves close by, engage in deliberately loud conversation about topics they believed their chosen man would be interested in, making sure to refuse offers from others nearby until asked.[98]

Inevitably, having a good time and dancing became the subject of some criticism. For example, in 1941 Sir William Jenkins, Labour MP for Neath attacked organizers of late dances in Britain's industrial areas. He argued that late dances in South Wales were leading to absenteeism there. He could not understand how girl workers could be expected to get up at five or six in the morning when they were encouraged to spend their evenings dancing until after midnight. That women were becoming more assertive is indicated by their response to Jenkins' criticisms. *Dance News* sought the opinions of female war workers in Edinburgh, from the Fountainbridge area, who attended evening and afternoon dance sessions. One of them said: 'Sir William should come along and see us enjoying ourselves some evening. He would get a surprise! Dancing, far from making us tired, has the opposite effect and takes us out of our wartime routine. We are actually far fresher for work in the morning after a good night's dance relaxation.'[99]

A sign of official concern at the 'problematic' dancing woman, in Glasgow in 1943, the police reintroduced an old Victorian bylaw whereby dancing licences were granted on the condition that no woman could enter a dance hall unless accompanied by a man. The *Dancing Times* commented that 'by insisting on the full enforcement of this old Act, the authorities were only encouraging an undesirable type of woman to loiter around the outside of these halls and importune men in order to gain admission'.[100] The Scottish Ballroom Association sent a deputation to the city council, who rescinded the clause, arguing that it unfairly affected women in the Services and war work.

Dancing thus acquired the reputation as a dubious feature marking out 'modern women' who were discontented with traditional roles. For example, in March 1945 Councillor Mrs Helen B. Shaw of the Lanarkshire Education Committee remarked that '"Miss 1945" in Scotland preferred to be an exponent of the Waltz, Tango and the Foxtrot rather than to be able to cook a good dinner or earn honours in housewifery'. She added: 'I want young people to have as much relaxation as possible, but—as educationalists—we should see to it that girls are capable of running homes of the future.' She was commenting on the fact that out of over 5,000 girls attending classes in the county youth service scheme, only 90 were studying first aid and nursing, and 147 cookery, while 940 girls were taking dancing classes.[101]

Whilst single women were singled out for particular criticism, married women were also attacked for dancing. Women with husbands in the armed forces were often censured for attending dance halls whilst their husband was away on active

[98] M-O A, FR1029, Tom Harrisson, 'Article for Modern Reading: WAAF Observer', January 1941, 4.

[99] *DN*, 9 December 1941, 3.

[100] *DT*, February 1943, 249.

[101] *Danceland*, April 1945, 8.

service. Issues of fidelity combined with the perception of women's increasing independence, to create hostility, not always just from men, but also from other women. For example one 'soldier's wife' from the Midlands who was on munitions wrote in 1941 to *Dance News*: 'I am fond of dancing and occasionally go with friends to a local hall. On these visits I meet many people and it is surprising how many seem to think that with my husband's allowances and my own wage I am rolling in wealth. Some people in fact have made pointed references to it and spoiled my enjoyment.'[102] A *Danceland* editorial from March 1942 illustrates how the issue of married women dancing in wartime was a contentious one. Whilst recognizing that dancing helped such women to overcome feelings of loneliness and isolation it encouraged its readers to make sure that women whose husbands and boyfriends were away went dancing as part of a larger group. Being part of a dance party was acceptable. Implicit was the idea that married women who went dancing alone or only with a single friend were making themselves susceptible to allegations of infidelity. Of married women, it stated:

> We see many in our dancehalls with parties of friends and it is right that they should seek entertainment and congenial company. It is in such surroundings and with good friends that war wives and sweethearts can find a relief from the loneliness that can do so much harm if not alleviated. It is up to the other members of the party to see that they are given a good time and not left without opportunities to dance.[103]

If the issue of dancing wives was contentious then the issue of mothers dancing was doubly so. Yet in wartime some dance halls made facilities available to enable parents to dance. In a tour of English and Scottish dance halls made in 1944 it was noted that some provided a 'children's corner' where parents could leave their children with a nurse whilst they danced.[104] Inevitably the idea of 'dancing mothers' who neglected their children whilst living it up in dance halls caused consternation amongst some. Collie Knox of the *Daily Mirror* condemned dancing mothers as immoral for neglecting their children, arguing that they were bad for the war effort as it was de-moralizing for troops to read about women who behaved in this way. Mecca, consistent in its policy of standing up for women, defended married women who danced, claiming that their numbers had been exaggerated:

> These so called Dancing Mothers are . . . but a fractional part of this country's womanhood . . . . Wives, young and middle aged, have only one thought: somehow, in the midst of all their duties and manifold and nerve-racking difficulties, to keep intact and sacrosanct a Home to which their men can return . . . Having toiled all day long for many long days, why on earth should not a wife go dancing? It is monstrous to make time-off synonymous with child neglect.[105]

Such concerns about women dancing continued after the war. In the post-war period concerns about changing gender boundaries rested, in the dance hall, on two stereotypes of women associated with dancing. The first, found in the earlier part of

102 *DN*, 2 December 1941, 1.
103 *DN*, 21 March 1942, 2.
104 *Danceland*, May 1944, 2.
105 *Danceland*, July 1944, 2.

the period—from the end of the war up until the mid-1950s—was the 'Palais Pearl'—the woman who spent most of her free time dancing, was obsessed with getting men, and 'freeloaded' on them at considerable expense. The second type of women criticized in this period emerged with the growing affluence of the later 1950s and early 1960s. The 'Snooty Cutie' was a symbol of a new independence, both economic and social, amongst young women. Not surprisingly, she was condemned, as had been the 'Flapper' before her.

The early post-war dancing woman was repeatedly condemned for being insincere and mercenary. In March 1949, for example Jean Christie, writing in the *Daily Mirror*, criticized those women who complained about the men who took them out dancing, and despite having considerable amounts spent on them, resented men for wanting to 'own' them. She also attacked the fashion amongst some women to affect an air of bored disinterest, believing that enthusiasm made them appear 'unsophisticated'. She wrote:

> How disloyal they were to the boys who were paying for the night out... Disloyalties like Pat's and Joan's have become smart currency today. Why do girls like to pretend to be ever-so-bored when they're really having a good time?... Men prefer natural women. And it's far, far smarter to be sincere.[106]

The demanding nature of female dancers was also criticized by a judge who claimed that they were making dancing too costly for men. Discussing the issue of excessive drinking, Judge Scobell Armstrong, speaking to the Cornwall and Isles of Scilly Combined Police Authority in June 1951 warned that many young men were fighting shy of going out dancing because they found it so expensive to keep their female partners in spirits all evening. He estimated that young women wanted at least five gins an evening, and that the cost of a night's dancing for men was around 30 shillings.[107] Robert Muller, writing in the *Picture Post* in 1954 linked this to the 'commercialization' of courting: 'Courting has become organised, industrialised, almost civilised out of existence. Whole industries make their profits out of other people's courting.'[108] Perhaps motivated by concern at the increasing presence of women drinking and enjoying themselves in public, some men were critical of the newly confident women of the post-war period.

Such fears became focused on what Marshall Pugh of the *Daily Mirror* labelled, in 1950, the 'Palais Pearls' of the dance hall. Such women were condemned for their hardened, predatory attitude and behaviour. Palais Pearl used her looks to snare men. She was dressed to kill, as Pugh put it: 'she bought nothing in the clothes line which wasn't tight and bright.' Her hairstyle 'became more uproarious week by week'. Such women became well rehearsed in chatting up men. Pugh went on: '[O]ther ham actresses at her local palais soon taught her a slick line in small talk... until *all* her conversation was slick and fast, and her ideas as phoney as the

[106] *DM*, 25 March 1949, 8. [107] *DM*, 26 June 1951, 3.
[108] *PP*, 11 December 1954, 28.

break in a crooner's voice.' Whilst good to dance with, Pugh warned men of the dangers of such women, who, he believed, would not make good wives:

> Do you think she would prefer a tea cloth to a Tango? Or care to swap the palais crooner for an ironing board? For five years home has been the place between her office and the dance floor; the place where she put on her war paint and refused to help with the dishes. Is that likely to change? She'd never care for a quiet night in by the fire, or a walk on the heath. To her, the countryside is merely the space between dance halls.[109]

Pugh was not alone in his criticism. A male dancer, Jerry from Newcastle-upon-Tyne, wrote to the *Daily Mirror* in 1956 to complain about the Palais Pearls:

> The girls at my local dance hall on Saturday nights are dressed to kill. They've obviously spent all day doing their hair and making up—but the girls who think they're film stars won't even look at an ordinary chap like me on Saturday nights. They want a 'catch' who is rich and handsome.

He was joined by 'Prospective Suitor' from Manchester who complained: 'Where do all the nice girls get to these days? . . . Only the gold diggers hang around the towns at night. It is getting awfully difficult for a man to find a future wife.'[110] The fears that such women were undermining marriage were echoed by some 'experts' too. Kenneth Walker, a surgeon and philosopher, saw a link between rising divorce rates and the appearance of women who were aping men in their behaviour and attitudes. He concluded: 'It is possible that the present rise in the divorce rate is partly accounted for by an increase in the incidence of the masculine type of woman.'[111] The legacy of the Good Time Girl was alive and well. Here women were being condemned because they seemed to be enjoying themselves to the full at the dance hall. Dancing was singled out, yet again, as a symbol of moral and social decline. In particular, such women were seen to transgress their traditional roles as wives and mothers, preferring the 'bright lights' of the dance hall to the comforts of home and family. This was an old accusation, but one that seemed to assume new currency in the climate of perceived social dislocation caused by the war. The austerity of the period also added to the venom with which women were attacked, as material possessions were hard to come by and much coveted.

Women were in a no-win situation, however, for as greater economic independence for single women began to emerge in the later part of the 1950s, this did not eliminate criticisms. Once they had discovered new affluence, women were condemned for this too. Their behaviour in the dance hall was one of the most visible signs of their changing gender roles.

In February 1960 the *Daily Mirror* highlighted a new trend whereby women were paying for their boyfriends on nights out. Labelling them 'Boom Girls' it told readers that they were ordinary factory girls. 'The teenage girl in a model frock brought her £1000 red sports car to a stop outside the dance hall. She handed her escort £5. With her money he paid for their tickets, cigarettes, rounds of drinks and

[109] *DM*, 30 November 1950, 4.
[110] *DM*, 7 December 1956, 2.
[111] *PP*, 30 April 1955, 39.

a snack at the buffet. It happened in Leicester. The girl wasn't a rich industrialist's daughter—just a factory girl having her weekly night out at the Palais.' Its investigation in Leicester pointed to a boom in business for the 18,000 girls who worked in the city's hosiery business. For these mostly 15 to 22-year-olds, a 45-hour week on piece work could see them taking home 'bulging pay packets' containing up to £20, and making them more affluent than their boyfriends. As Roy Winfield, manager of the Palais confirmed: 'These girls are earning fabulous wages—and most of them believe in spending well. In a week we get about 5000 here.'[112]

Increasing economic independence was also accompanied by growing social confidence amongst women. In particular, women started to become more critical of men and their methods of approach and behaviour when dancing. Turning down men for dances became more common than in the past. As a male dancer complained in 1956: 'Before the war ballroom dancing was a pleasure, but now girls constantly refuse requests to dance. I was rejected seven times in a few minutes at one dance. Why doesn't the MC turn out these rude females?'[113] Labelled 'Snooty Cuties', in 1960 some of these women explained why they refused men. Shirley Yates, 18, from Manchester stated: 'I often refuse dances. A lot of it has to do with a lad's attitude. I like to be asked properly. I don't like this "come-on-kid" attitude. And I'm sometimes put off by the ridiculous things they wear.' Doris Marchbanks, 18, from Liverpool complained: 'They hug you and maul you. They think they own you when you get up to dance. That last partner used my ear as a microphone for fifteen minutes.'[114] A girl from Anfield, Liverpool: 'Dance halls are like slave markets—men just eye us poor females up and down and pass on as if we were up for auction.'[115]

Such changing attitudes were greeted in a variety of ways from the boys involved. John Jarvis, 17, from Manchester who had been turned down five times in an hour remarked: 'I don't mind them saying NO so much. It's when they just look you up and down and shake their heads disdainfully. It just makes you feel stupid.'[116] A male dancer from Ilford retorted: 'How stupid can these girls get? They should feel honoured that a boy should ask them for a dance. It shows them they have something that the boys admire.' [117] The right of women to refuse a dance was still considered a controversial issue during the 1950s. A *Daily Mail* column contemplated the rights of women in this respect in 1957, observing of a woman who turned down a man only to dance with another one immediately: 'She has a right to refuse, but no "right" at all to refuse discourteously and gauchely. She has yet to learn the social graces.'[118]

So far we have talked exclusively about changing notions of femininity. However, dance halls also helped in the emergence of redefined notions of masculinity and allowed important changes in the relationships between men and women throughout the twentieth century. As we have already noted, boys became

[112] *DM*, 10 February 1960, 21.
[113] *PP*, 11 August 1956, 38.
[114] *DM*, 11 March 1960, 13.
[115] *DM*, 18 March 1960, 13.
[116] *DM*, 11 March 1960, 13.
[117] *DM*, 18 March 1960, 13.
[118] *Daily Mail*, 8 January 1957, 6.

interested in dancing at a young age, and although taking to it later than girls, dancing and dance halls allowed them to interact with females in a positive way. With its mostly orderly environment, the focus on 'wooing girls', and its glamorous surroundings, the dance hall was leading to the emergence of large numbers of smartly dressed, well-behaved, sometimes chivalrous men. Predictably however, these positive developments were regarded with suspicion by some. The relative dominance of women in the dance hall, the 'feminine' environment, and the association of dancing with 'female' values such as grace and beauty meant that many saw dancing as a sign of the feminization of Britain's men.

Such concerns were first voiced at the height of the 1920s dance craze. The context of interwar Britain is important for explaining the sometimes obsessive focus on masculinity. There were fears and complaints that Britain had become 'soft' and that the country was being 'feminized'. The aftermath of the First World War certainly caused challenges to traditional notions of masculinity. The slaughter of thousands of young men had led to a widespread revulsion to the 'masculine' concepts of conflict and war. Throughout the period then, anti-war feelings ran high. Moreover, thousands of returned soldiers injured both physically and mentally created new images of men. Disabled veterans were a common sight in communities up and down the country and they were living symbols of a challenged masculinity. A new focus on 'domesticity' so prevalent in interwar Britain was also regarded as a sign of Britain's feminization. The shifting of the economy away from the traditionally 'masculine' heavy industries towards the new light industries and the growth of the service sector not only opened up more job opportunities for women, but was part of the redefinition of 'men's work'. Together with the growth of suburbia, new home appliances, and the new leisure industry, some intellectuals berated the feminization of the country.[119] Wyndham Lewis, for example, warned men to remain vigilant to threats against their masculinity in his 1926 *The Art of Being Ruled*: 'Men were only made into "men" with great difficulty even in primitive society: the male is not naturally "a man" any more than the woman. He has to be propped up into that position with some ingenuity, and is always likely to collapse.'[120]

Within this wider context then, the growth of dancing amongst Britain's men, particularly the young, was seen as evidence of this 'feminization' (see Fig. 8.2). There were several elements of men's association with dancing that were regarded as problematic. First, particular dances or dance forms were regarded with suspicion as they involved public displays of 'feminized' movements. The carriage of men when dancing could be taken as a challenge to traditional notions of masculine behaviour. Predictably, men who engaged in these new modes of behaviour were labelled as homosexual. In 1928, for example, Victor Silvester highlighted how men could expose themselves to accusations of effeminacy if they got their steps wrong. Talking about the execution of the dance move called the 'contrary movement',

[119] C. Ferrall, *Modernist Writing and Reactionary Politics* (Cambridge: Cambridge University Press, 2001).

[120] P. W. Lewis, *The Art of Being Ruled* (London: Chatto and Windus, 1926), 279–80.

Fig. 8.2. Gender and Dance: 'Dancing Men of Yesterday and Today', W. K. Haselden, *Daily Mirror*, 13 December 1920

Source: © Mirrorpix.

he warned men not to introduce it in the wrong place. He wrote: 'I know a man . . . who, when doing an ordinary walk forward in the Slow Foxtrot, introduces it on every step. It gives the appearance of the worst effeminacy . . . we do not want "fairies" in the ballroom.'[121] Party dances seemed to attract particular ire from critics. With their playful approach to dancing and often 'juvenile' movements, it was considered unseemly for grown men to do them in public. A Mass Observer thus described the demonstration of the Big Apple by 'two foolish looking young gents in tails' in terms which drew attention to the challenge to traditional masculinity: 'A rather pansy affair, not very interesting and without spontaneity. However, people laughed at a peculiar gesture, often repeated, on the part of the dancers. They lifted up the leg of their trousers, sometimes one leg, sometimes both

[121] *DT*, February 1928, 684.

together, and disclosed little white socks and some pinky flesh.'[122] If men dancing with women created concerns that masculinity was being undermined, then even more alarm was caused when men danced with each other in the dance hall. Though not common, this did occur. Mass Observation, for instance, found several instances where men danced with each other during its surveys of dance halls in London. At the Rye Lane dance club in Peckham, for example, young men danced with each other when learning to dance. Some men even danced with each other after they could dance properly, especially in the new swing dances of the later 1930s. It was noted: 'Only one pair of chaps danced together regularly. Once a chap got up with the negro lad and they danced hot for about a minute, kicking their feet out all over the place. Both roared with laughter.' Whilst the observer did not believe that this was a sign of effeminacy he noted that 'they allowed that here but not at the bigger public places', implying that men dancing with each other was regarded with hostility.[123] Yet even in one of the 'bigger places', the Paramount Tottenham Court Road, some men danced with each other, again usually during swing dance programmes.[124] This was not just a London phenomenon either. It was claimed that in Wales men quite commonly danced with each other in the dance hall. Their reasons for doing so and the challenge to their masculinity are illuminating. The following report is of a conversation with a Welshman dancing in London:

> G talks with Obs . . . about dances back home.
>
> 'There it was common for chaps to dance with each other. I used to dance with one chap—did so for about 3 months. He took the lady's part and when he asked a woman for a dance he used to start backwards—he got so used to the lady's part.'
>
> 'Did the fellows dance with each other because there was a shortage of women?'
>
> 'No. It is very common in South Wales for the chaps to dance together, that's all.'[125]

Whilst for the men concerned such couplings were predominantly the result of homo-social interactions and the desire to practice, or in the case of swing dances to let themselves go, for outsiders such incidents were usually treated as a sign of latent homosexuality. Such evidence highlights, however, that even in heavy industrial areas such as South Wales, traditional notions of working-class masculinity were perhaps more fluid than outside middle-class observers realized.

Another area of concern for critics was the changing relationships between men and women that were occurring in the dance hall, and in wider society. As early as 1919 Richard Ward writing in the *Daily Mirror* expressed concern that women were leaving men behind and that old gender certainties were in flux. He exclaimed: 'While women have been marching forward men have been standing still! . . . Will the sexes turn round? Is woman on the way to shouldering all the responsibility? Will evolution make her the "stronger sex" . . . ?'[126] As we have seen,

122 M-O A, MJD: 38/1/A, 'Streatham Locarno I1', 17 November 1938, 5.
123 M-O A, MJD: 38/1/I, 'Stones, Rye Lane', 6 March 1939, 8, 4.
124 M-O A, MJD: 38/1/B, 'Paramount', 24 April 1939, 1.
125 M-O A, MJD: 38/1/E, 'Peckham Pavilion V9', 28 February 1939, 6.
126 *DM*, 26 February 1919, 5.

the dance hall allowed women to renegotiate their public interactions with men in a way that gave them greater freedom and power. Unsurprisingly, some regarded these developments negatively. In particular, the shyness of many men in asking for a dance was taken as evidence of their lack of courage and the emergence of a generation of 'emasculated' men. We have already noted how men could be extremely reticent to ask women to dance in the dance hall. Male dancers in Liverpool explained some of their reasons for avoiding dancing in 1928. Fear of being snubbed was the major reason. One dancer wrote that many men were 'a little diffident about asking a girl for a dance lest they be turned down', another concurring by stating: 'Men hate a refusal, and if they get one it is often sufficient to give them cold feet for the rest of the evening.'[127] Whilst such explanations seem reasonable, to those looking for evidence of the decline of manliness, they were signs of ominous developments. Men who were too shy to ask for a dance or who couldn't get a female dancing partner were treated with condescension, often by women. Dorothy Dix writing in 1927, for example, stated: 'Anything half way good in trousers goes, so any youth who finds himself dateless may well hold a heart to heart session with himself and find wherein lies his offence.'[128]

Furthermore, men's interest in dancing was also condemned because it was seen as a sign of the rejection of more acceptably 'masculine' pastimes and attitudes. Renee Radford noted the emergence of a new breed of men, fashion conscious and interested in dancing, as early as 1927.

> The cloth-capped and mufflered works' boy of the older generations has passed. The winged collar and butterfly tie and dancing pumps are now more familiar, just as the modern works' youngster in this district, whether he be a collier or steel worker or tinplate worker or what not, knows that Italian-run cafe better than the public-house—much better, too.[129]

Rather than welcoming such 'modern youngsters' many were alarmed at the erosion of older notions of masculinity that they seemed to represent. In his 1931 study of juvenile delinquency, for example, S. F. Hatton berated the influence of dance halls in creating 'soft' young men: 'I deplore all attempts to effeminize young manhood, and am a little ashamed of some of the youths of today who are more given to the softer delights of the cinema and the dance hall, than the more vigorous and manly sporting instincts of boxing, football, and such-like pastimes.' He blamed women for shaping men and creating the 'soft-faced, mealy-mouthed, dolled-up pomaded puppet as a dancing partner'.[130] Others condemned the 'dancing dude' as a pitiful role model for young men. During debates over the Cinematograph Bill of 1927 that was to introduce a quota for British films, Colonel Josiah Wedgewood told the standing Committee of the House of Commons that

127 *Liverpool Echo*, 12 January 1928, 12. 128 *Sunday Sun*, 22 May 1927, 7.
129 *DT*, April 1927, 83–4.
130 S. F. Hatton, *London's Bad Boys* (London: Chapman & Hall, 1931), 23.

American films could be beneficial to British men, because of the masculine role models they contained. He argued:

> The he-man is the essence of the American film. He is the self-made man who struggles to the top. He is a type that we want more of and a wholly good example to set before our young people. Let us have that sort of hero rather than the dude who never works but spends his time horse-racing, hunting and dallying in dance halls.[131]

Such concerns were played out throughout the subsequent decades too. Whilst the war might have been expected to reinforce traditional 'masculine' values, in fact, as we have seen in our discussion of women, it created new challenges. The necessity of having women working in heavy industry, their increasing economic and social independence, or at least the perception of it, forced many to think that women had been 'masculinized'. At the same time, those men who did not go off to fight, or those too young to join up, were also regarded with some suspicion, especially if they danced.

Whether or not to allow men in the services to dance was an issue that caused debate within the hierarchy of the armed forces. Was it good for the image of the armed forces for servicemen to be seen dancing in uniform? Was this activity 'masculine' enough for those who were about to go into armed combat? The military authorities made some concessions to 'modernity' when they allowed men to dance. In 1940, W. Heath of the London Welfare Branch of the War Office was making the case for dancing for servicemen:

> One of the finest exercises for the troops is to dance. They are brought into association under good conditions. They have the opportunity of listening to bright, breezy music. In good class dance halls they have cheery illuminations with picturesque decorations and everything combined to give an atmosphere of happiness and jollity . . . the whole thing is a system of physical training taken under pleasant conditions.[132]

That winter, Anthony Eden argued that dancing was one of the entertainments that should be available to soldiers.[133] By 1941 the War Office was encouraging dancing as a way of overcoming boredom. 'If possible,' it stated, '"sleeping out" passes should be given to the married men whose wives go along to a dance with them.'[134] Serving soldiers in Scotland were offered regular dancing practice when an East Lothian club was started at the suggestion of Lieut-General Thorns, GOCinC Scottish Command. Such was its success that by 1942 it was noted that it had 'received many letters of appreciation from the Services'.[135] Despite the official support, some men joining considered their interest in dancing problematic. *Modern Dance and Dancer*, for instance, remarking on an RAF man who felt embarrassed to tell his officers that his chief recreation was dancing, defended dancing as 'masculine' by comparing it with other more traditionally male pastimes: 'Physically there is no

131 *Manchester Guardian*, 13 April 1927, 9.
132 *MDD*, September 1940, 9.
133 *MDD*, December 1940, 3.
134 *DN*, 2 August 1941, 4.
135 *DN*, 21 February 1942, 1.

difference between football and dancing. Both require nimble feet, individualistic thought, careful planning, and above all good teamship.'[136]

As we have seen, too much dancing was seen as unmanly too, because it implied shirking the responsibilities of war. Hence 'lounge lizards' were attacked for being unpatriotic, too intent on enjoying themselves rather than assuming their traditional role as defenders of the nation and women and children.

Masculinity after the war was similarly under attack. Richard Hoggart's 1957 *Uses of Literacy* famously berated the new 'Juke Box Boys' of the period as passive, feminized, and impotent ciphers of a new Americanized mass culture. These 'new men' were attacked from all sides. As we shall see in Chapter 10, they were attacked for being too masculine and violent, yet at the same time criticized because of their coquettishness and vanity, seen as symbols of their feminization. Many of these concerns were played out in the dance hall, a major public arena for the creation and display of new youth phenomena and the changing relationships between men and women.

As before the war, shyness was taken as a sign of a less masculine breed of young men. In 1948, Rosemary Young of Windsor complained: 'Where are all the tall, charming and interesting cavaliers of the dance floor? At dances now you see male wallflowers who are scared to "have a go."'[137] Similarly, in 1950, for example, female dancers in Southport complained to local dance hall managers, asking them to introduce more 'ladies' invitation' dances in order to overcome the problem. As the *Daily Mirror* reported: 'The girls . . . complain that boys eye them wistfully but cannot pluck up enough courage to say "Will you have this dance with me?" . . . most of them huddle in a corner and just stare all evening.'[138] Brian Spinley's 1953 investigation of adolescent behaviour in one of London's slums also showed how girls had to chase boys, though not necessarily because of shyness. The notion of the boy as an objectified 'prize' that girls had to have was prevalent in such communities. As Spinley noted:

> The adolescent boys make few advances to girls, the latter have to take the initiative and make strong efforts to attach to themselves masculine admirers. All the effort of courtship seems to be made by the girls. In this social group there is no conventional idea that a girl grants favours, instead it is the boy who bestows the favour of his company.[139]

There was a reversal here too of the older notion of girls freeloading on boys. Now, as Spinley observed, girls bought gifts for boys: 'Boys spend little money on girls . . . Girls give the boys many presents, ranging from cigarettes to more elaborate gifts at Christmas. The boys . . . take these presents as their due . . . '[140] By the later 1950s men's increasing interest in fashion, especially when dancing, was held up as a sign of their increasing feminization and as evidence of a change in gender

[136] *MDD*, June 1942, 12.

[137] *PP*, 11 December 1958, 5.

[138] *DM*, 21 September 1950, 7.

[139] B. M. Spinley, *The Deprived and the Privileged: Personality Development in English Society* (London: Routledge, 1953/1998), 74.

[140] Spinley, *The Deprived*, 73–4.

boundaries. The presence of increasing numbers of 'glamour boys' was highlighted as a growing trend in Britain's dance halls. Marjorie Proops, for example, claimed in 1957:

> For years, we women have been in the limelight and our menfolk, in their sober, dark clothes, have been a neat, quiet backdrop to our glamour. But the signs all point to a masculine revolution on the fashion front . . . You've only got to go to any dance hall to see the fellows in their nearly-knee-length jackets and pretty hair-styles to realise that it is not just the odd one or two extrovert blokes trying to show off.

Proops, however, did not see this as a sign of feminization: 'don't get the idea that these lads are a lot of cissies. They do tough jobs all right.'[141] If not a sign of 'cissiness' then the new fashion conscious boy was perhaps indicative of a new attitude of 'display' from men. Spinley's 1953 study of boys from the slums also pointed to a new vanity. He remarked: 'This vanity does not become marked until puberty . . . The greatest pride is taken in the hair; it is worn long and cut in various fashions, each of which has a name and can be recognized by the boys . . . The styles in clothing are wide shoulders, full trousers, long drape jackets, gaudy ties worn with large loose knots and the top button of the shirt undone . . . Much money is spent on clothing, and in saving up for a new suit many other pleasures will be gone without or obtained through the generosity of a friend.'[142]

One reason for this newfound interest in fashion amongst young men was probably to attract girls. As one young male dancer from Harlesdon, London, observed in 1959, the most fashionable were more likely to get the girls: 'I wear a suit, collar and tie. But at a dance the lads in jeans, loud shirts and creepers invariably get a yes from the girls whereas I get a NO. Other lads say its pays to look like a Brando or James Dean.'[143] This was certainly backed up by sociologist Dr Josephine Macalister Brew who argued that there were 'too many boys craving the attention of too few girls' and that this had led to 'personal adornment' amongst boys. The *Picture Post* remarked, in 1955: 'Girls love it. A shop girl in Lambeth assured me that none of her girl friends "would dream of looking at a boy who wasn't wearing drainpipes."'[144] So, the more competitive need to attract women was perhaps one important factor in the rise of the new glamour boys. In another article on 'Boy Gangsters' the magazine called such men vain, labelling them 'dandies'—'They are vain, very vain, and the boy who is handsome in the conventional or flashy way is much admired.' It went on: 'They believe that girls will admire their daring and their gaudy clothes.'[145] We should also bear in mind that clothes rationing had recently ended (in March 1949) and that pent-up demand for clothing was thus released. This combined with a new sense of prosperity. As young people were amongst the most affluent, and because they were amongst the most concerned with their appearance, it was not surprising that there was a sudden and very visible rise in the wearing of 'sharp' clothes.

141 *DM*, 29 May 1957, 11.
142 Spinley, *The Deprived*, 73.
143 *DM*, 28 February 1959, 2.
144 *PP*, 24 September 1955, 47.
145 *PP*, 10 October 1953, 17.

CONCLUSION

Some of the most vociferous attacks on dance revolved around its association with immorality, either through the proximity of those dancing, or the eroticized movements of the new social dances. There was a clear class dimension to such attacks. Most critics were middle class and most had very little experience of the dance culture that they condemned so heartily. Those who did encounter Britain's dance halls did so through the prejudiced and clouded lens of middle-class propriety. What they saw shocked them, but only because they were brought up in a totally different moral order. For those who went looking for it, changing gender identity was also visible in the dance hall. The emergence of 'new' women and men in the twentieth century was greeted with inevitable alarm from some conservative quarters, and perhaps because they were most visible in the palais, the dance culture that also emerged alongside them was similarly condemned.

Chapter 9
Race and the Dance Hall

INTRODUCTION

Dancing and race were inextricably linked for a number of reasons. Most obviously, dancing in Britain was influenced by exposure to foreign dance forms, many of which came from black American culture. Whilst for most people these developments were not regarded as problematic, for a few they caused considerable concern. Dancing and dances became a convenient way to express wider ideas about race and racial theory circulating in British society at the time. Particular dance steps and rhythms, for example, were seen to typify racial characteristics and their popularity with white British dancers generated some concerns about racial purity. More significantly, the racial debate concerning dance forms helped to perpetuate, extend, and reinforce racial images. Dance music and dances were key to shaping British stereotypes about black people in the early twentieth century. Secondly, the dance hall was one of the first popular public venues where the increasingly racially diverse nature of British society in the twentieth century became obvious. It was in the dance hall that many whites and non-whites in Britain first came into close contact with one another and the tensions created by a new sense of racial diversity could be expressed. Importantly, racial mixing and tension in British dance halls pre-date the arrival of black American GIs during the Second World War, and post-war immigration, although those episodes remain significant landmarks in British race relations.

DANCE AND CULTURAL RACISM, 1918–60

The early twentieth century represented a major turning point in the history of British popular culture. As we have seen, between 1910 and 1920, dancing and dance music in Britain had been transformed by the widespread popularity of revolutionary new styles of music and dance which had arrived from the United States, as first 'ragtime' then 'jazz', and the numerous new social dances that developed alongside them, took hold of and captured the public imagination.[1] This was followed in the 1920s by a new invasion as the Charleston, Black Bottom,

[1] As has been well documented, ragtime, jazz, and the associated dances evolved from America's South and Midwest, part of the legacy of slavery. Forced into 'juke joints' and 'honky tonks', black Americans evolved unique musical and dancing styles incorporating African and white European

and other dance crazes flooded in from America, followed by swing, Truckin', and Jitterbugging in the late 1930s. Jive and then Rock 'n' Roll followed in the 1940s and 1950s. Whilst British popular culture had been exposed to outside influences before this period, the scale and extent of foreign influence in the first decades of the twentieth century was unprecedented. As Ross McKibbin points out, this was one of the key moments 'when American influence was so strong as to change the way the English thought of music and dance'.[2] The same applied to those in the rest of Britain. Unlike the previous era where popular culture had contributed to a strengthening of national identity, now it threatened to undermine it. There were inevitable concerns about the new influences on British culture, and much debate about British national identity, more often than not linked to concerns about Britain's political and economic position. As the twentieth century progressed, this process continued and expanded.

Dancing and dance music were two of the most obvious symbols of the increasingly transatlantic nature of British culture following the First World War. For the majority of the British population the most obvious and meaningful encounters with the increased global power of the United States were via popular culture—the cinema, popular music, and the new social dances. These influences threatened to 'Americanize' British culture. Throughout the interwar period then there was a sustained anti-American line taken by certain critics and it was mixed with a race element. It must be noted when considering these negative reactions to jazz and dance that they were only ever the views of a small minority. Most people who danced or listened to these new cultural forms had little interest in such debates. Furthermore, it is not certain that the complainants were representative of the groups from which they came—the majority of clergy, cultural critics, politicians, and intellectuals did not actively enter into a public discourse about these forms. However, contemporary journalists certainly did see the attraction of spreading the more colourful views of those who did take issue with popular dances, as they realized the huge interest in them that the general public at large had. Moreover, as we shall see, however unrepresentative complaints about them might have been, those professionals who had an interest in the dancing industry were certainly deeply concerned about them.

Although there were numerous foreign influences shaping the new post-war dances in Britain from the end of the First World War onwards (Latin American, Spanish, even Eastern European), the association between the new dances and black culture was the most dominant one. This centred around the dances' early links with 'jazz', the *leit motif* of the immediate post-war years. 'Jazz' was seen as black music, 'jazz dances' were seen as the dances of black people. Indeed, as early as 1919, the *Observer* had defined jazz as 'a number of niggers surrounded by noise',

traditions. See for example, K. J. Ogren, *The Jazz Revolution: Twenties America and the Meaning of Jazz* (New York: Oxford University Press, 1989).

[2] R. McKibbin, *Classes and Cultures: England 1918–1951* (Oxford: Oxford University Press, 1998), 390.

Fig. 9.1. Race and dance: 'Present Day Dancing and Its Origins', W. K. Haselden, *Daily Mirror*, 13 January 1927

Source: © Mirrorpix.

criticizing it for being 'crude and vulgar'.[3] Similarly, in 1920 Cecil Sharp, director of the English Folk Dance Society, described the new dances that accompanied jazz as 'the expression of the nigger' and also condemned them, contrasting them with the English folk dance tradition, arguing that '[w]e are a higher race, and our expression ought to be different'.[4]

The arrival of new dances in Britain around the time of the First World War was accompanied almost immediately by a fascination with the national and racial origins of these phenomena. Newspapers and dancing manuals went to great lengths to explain to their readers where dances came from, often using highly questionable information (see Fig. 9.1). For example, the origins of the Black Bottom were described thus in the *Daily Mail* in 1926: 'The silted mud on the tidal

[3] *The Observer*, 16 March 1919, 14.

[4] *Manchester Guardian*, 5 January 1920, 10.

bed of the Mississippi Rover is as black as Thames mud, but firmer. It is firm enough near the banks for a Negro to dance upon. And Negroes have been dancing on it. Hence a new dance—Black Bottom.'[5] For the Charleston the same reporter claimed: 'Its rhythm is one of the primitive things—as simple as a laugh. Negro slaves were doing it before the American Civil War. Years ago darkie piccaninnies pranced it outside the subways of Harlem, New York's coloured quarter.'[6] Even particular steps or dance moves were put down to 'Negro characteristics', usually reinforcing particular images of black people. Of the Charleston it was reported: 'The Charleston's peculiar foot twist originated in the foot twist the Negro slaves gave when they came out of the cotton fields and cleaned their feet of mud.'[7] However, in an article on the 'Negro Steps of the Charleston' a correspondent for the *Aberdeen Press and Journal* claimed that the foot twist was called the 'grape vine twist', taking its name from the wild grape vines that it claimed grew in the 'cotton districts' below the Mississippi delta, and used by black children to make swings.[8] Other 'negro steps' in the Charleston were the little back kick called 'dogging', a side step called the 'Buzzard lope', and a 'little sort of scratchy step' called 'Chicken in a Bread Tray', being 'several quick, short steps, followed by a longer back movement of the foot'.[9] Such discussions reinforced images of the new dances as products of a primitive black culture, an issue to which we will return shortly. This obsession with portraying dance trends as part of a continual process of black cultural 'invasion' did not end with the end of the arrival of new social dances in Britain in the 1920s either. Even as late as 1955 the same language that had been used to describe jazz dances was in mainstream use. In August 1955, for example, the *Daily Mail* described a performance of a West End show, 'Braziliana' at the Piccadilly Theatre, in the following way:

> Scarcely has 'The Jazz Train' steamed out of this station than another coloured express pants in—lighter-skinned, but just as extrovert and noisy. These are South American Negroes instead of North, but their music stems from the same source, namely Darkest Africa. There are savage tribal dances, mild sophistication represented by sambas, and fuller sophistication. Determined, even deafening, and full of colour, but rather an unsatisfactory show.[10]

The idea that the new dances essentially 'came from the jungle' was established early on in Britain and endured in the popular imagination for some time. R. W. S. Mendl, in the first British book on the subject, *All About Jazz* (1927), argued that 'the savage dance to the accompaniment of singing and clapping of hands' was the early counterpart 'of the galaxy of modern youth and beauty dancing to the Savoy Orpheans'.[11] Similarly, in 1935, the *Dancing Times* ran a series of articles on 'The History of Jazz Dances' by Ivan T. Sanderson, 'a young Cambridge zoologist who, as leader of the Percy Sladen Expedition, recently penetrated several

[5] *Daily Mail*, 13 November 1926, 8. [6] *Daily Mail*, 20 September 1926, 8.
[7] *Daily Mail*, 13 November 1926, 8.
[8] *Aberdeen Press and Journal*, 27 December 1926, 3. [9] Ibid.
[10] *Daily Mail*, 10 August 1955, 3.
[11] R. W. S. Mendl, *The Appeal of Jazz* (London: P. Allen & Co., 1927), 63.

hundreds of miles of unexplored jungle among the Cameroon Mountains of West Africa where he made contact with the original home of Jazz'.[12] Sanderson traced the evolution of modern dancing in purely racial terms, from its origins in the 'jungles of Africa', via Spanish, French, and Portuguese influences in the slave trade to Anglo-Saxon 'refinement' in America.

Such discussions of dancing served to reinforce racist images of black people and black culture in Britain. Several themes emerged in this process of stereotyping. Speaking on '[t]he development of negro art and artists in the United States' in Bristol in 1927, visiting American writer Walter White identified three common stereotypes of black people—the 'happy care-free buffoon', the 'vicious primitive brute', and the 'humble servant type'.[13] To these we can add the widely held view that black people had an innate sense of rhythm and were somehow more naturally suited to dancing. All of these images proved remarkably resilient throughout the whole of the period under investigation.

The orthodox view of musicologists, dancing masters, and pseudo-racial theorists was that black people possessed an innate sense of rhythm, and that this rhythmic element had led to the development of the syncopated jazz music and dances that were sweeping the world. For example, in 1927 Victor Sylvester, answering the question 'Why do we always get our dances from the niggers?' explained that it was because 'niggers commence to dance as soon as they have learnt how to walk. They have music and rhythm instilled in their bodies when they leave the cradle.'[14] F. A. Hadland, writing in the *Dancing Times* in the same year on the 'Negro Influence in Dancing', also suggested that dancing was an innate feature of African life and culture. 'It dominates everything and takes the place which prayer occupies in European religions,' he wrote, 'It is almost the only way of representing their affections and sensibilities.'[15] The arrival of the Lindy Hop also allowed further discussion of black American influence in dancing and for the re-appearance of some worn racial stereotypes. In a 1943 article on the dance, *Picture Post* argued that only black people could really do this kind of dancing:

> Dancing is to the coloured people what sport is to the British, or warfare to the Germans—their truest form of self-expression. It is a racial heritage, tracing back to the dark ritual of the tom-tom. For all its apparent spontaneity, it is both a traditional and progressive art—a folk art that is inspired by emotion rather than reason. Above all, it is a careless rapture. Like the negro music of the jam session, its heights are reached by an intensity of feeling rather than by technical virtuosity, and this is where white dancers, however good, fall short if they encroach on so racial an idiom as swing. They are too self conscious . . . They never really 'go to town'—they are never quite 'in the groove.' The rapture is not quite careless enough. There is something in them which holds back: a sort of cerebral discipline which reflects in a rigidity, apparent behind their most exuberant antics . . . while the white man deliberately sets out to dance, the coloured man passes into a state of dancing and is of it, rather than with it.[16]

12 *DT*, January 1935, February 1935.
13 *Western Daily Press*, 4 November 1927, 4.
14 *DT*, September 1927, 643.
15 *DT*, April 1927, 73.
16 *PP*, 18 December 1943, 20–1.

On the accompanying photos of expert black dancers, it commented: 'These really do capture something of the supercharged raptures, at once childish, exotic, eccentric, witty and passionate which go to make up the muscular rhapsody we see every time a negro dances.'[17] The notion that black people were 'natural' dancers, with a natural sense of rhythm and passionate enjoyment of dancing remained strong in post-war Britain too. In 1947 a Mass Observation report of a London dance hall noted: 'there seems to be great competition to dance with the Blacks, the reason being, I should imagine, their superb sense of rhythm and their natural ease of keeping in time with the music.' It continued: 'These Blacks are certainly dancers in the truest sense of the word. The look on their faces as they "Jive" is a revelation. They are the picture of blissful joy and utter contentment. Smiling most generally all the while and occasionally letting out a whoop or a yell.'[18]

Black culture was also seen as 'childlike' and playful, and by implication, simple and unsophisticated. In describing the origins of the 'new negro dance' the Black Bottom, in November 1926, Patrick Chalmers of the *Daily Mail* wrote: 'The Negroes, childlike, easily moved to joy or sorrow, finding both emotions in simpler things than the more sophisticated and more civilised peoples, fall much more easily than the white peoples into a joy dance.'[19] One letter writer, defending the dance, used similar stereotypes: 'I fail to see what is wrong in copying a dance of the Negroes of America . . . Negroes, I believe, are usually healthy, carefree, happy beings. So perhaps, after all, they can teach us something about dancing.'[20] Following the Second World War popular stereotypes of West Indian culture seen in the new immigrants conformed to these earlier images of black people as childlike and playful. The music and dancing associated with Calypso were particularly important in creating such images. In 1947, the *Daily Mail* reported on the 'Calypso Crazy' carnivals in the Port of Spain, Trinidad, where '[f]or 48 hours only the aged and weak will go to bed, the rest will sing, dance, and drink rum'. It went on to describe the revels and preparations of 'these likeable, loyal Trinidadians' who had 'rumba rhythm in their souls and snappy lyrics in their heads'.[21] The following year 'Caribbean Rhapsody', a musical dance show at the Prince of Wales Theatre, allowed for the trotting out of further racial images of West Indians as playful and uninhibited. Katherine Dunham the 'coffee-coloured calypso dancer' was described 'leading, directing, dancing—with her hips, her stomach, her naked toes. The story she tells is a fundamental one—daring and uninhibited' and came from 'the hot, throbbing swamps of the West Indies'.[22] By the 1950s Calypso singers were often employed in cabaret at the top restaurants of London's West End and there was a Calypso Club operating in the West End too by 1952.[23]

17 *PP*, 18 December 1943, 22.
18 M-O A, FR2473, *Report on Juvenile Delinquency* (1947), 49.
19 *Daily Mail*, 13 November 1926, 8. 20 *Daily Mail*, 10 January 1927, 8.
21 *Daily Mail*, 3 February 1947, 2. 22 *Daily Mail*, 5 June 1948, 3.
23 *Daily Mail*, 8 April 1950, 3 and 7 May 1952, 1.

The issue of 'primitivism', which we have already hinted at, was also raised by critics. Popular stereotypes portrayed black people as sexually wanton, unable to control their sexual urges, predatory, and unnatural. Fears of myscegny were widespread in twentieth-century Britain. The new social dances amplified these concerns and their critics exploited these popular stereotypes. Sensuality and primitive sexuality remained central to images of the new dances. A general lack of self-control, seen as central to black culture, was thus an important characteristic in condemnations of dance. The energy and vitality of the Charleston, for example, were widely feared. One description from 1926 remarked: 'In its extreme form it is a wild and frenzied affair, done at terrific speed, with shoulder "shimmies," head shakes, arms waving, legs and feet flying in all directions.'[24] A correspondent for the *Daily Mail* shreiked in April 1926 that the Charleston was '[a] series of contortions without a vestige of charm of grace, reminiscent only of the Negro orgies from which it derives its creation'.[25] He went on: 'Here were some thirty couples lurching, wriggling, and kicking their legs wildly from side to side, the perspiration streaming down their face . . . '[26] A flurry of letters reached the *Daily Mail* protesting against the dance. One writer proclaimed: 'With the addition of war-paint and feathers the Charleston would rival the antics of a tribe of savages. Let us have dances to conform with our standard of civilisation.'[27]

Similarly, during the war, Norah Alexander of the *Daily Mail* described jitterbugs as 'the dancing dervishes of our day'.[28] The link between black culture, dance, and sex, so prevalent in pre-war deliberations on jazz dancing, resurfaced.

Furthermore, the emergence of new dances based on black cultural traditions was seen, by a few, as a threat to white culture. The Rev. E. A. Guest, a missionary from West Central Africa visiting London in 1928, condemned the Charleston and Black Bottom for undermining the reputation of the white races in the eyes of colonial subjects. He argued:

> when boys from West Africa come to this country to be educated and see British people dancing immoral dances they return home with bad ideas of us . . . It is not a good thing for Britain to copy immoral dances from a country which we try to educate and build up.[29]

It was claimed that 'good people' did not do the new dances. In 1920, for example, one local dance correspondent in Aberdeen claimed that married men and their wives did not like the 'new fangled negro dances of a questionable character'.[30] In 1919 it was claimed that '[e]ven if it be granted that well-bred people can "Jazz" in an unobjectionable manner, the example they set as leaders in social circles should prompt them to renounce the evil thing'.[31] This 'invasion' of black dances was also seen as a threat to British cultural traditions. Cecil Sharp, Director of the English Folk Dance Society, argued in 1923 that 'negro dancing had to a large extent

24 *Daily Mail*, 12 March 1926, 8. 25 *Daily Mail*, 13 April 1926, 7.
26 *Daily Mail*, 13 November 1926, 8. 27 *Daily Mail*, 1 May 1926, 8.
28 *Daily Mail*, 13 October 1945, 2. 29 *Liverpool Echo*, 4 February 1928, 7.
30 *Aberdeen Daily Journal*, 20 August 1920, 4. 31 *Derby Daily Telegraph*, 5 March 1919, 3.

ousted English folk dances'.[32] Maxwell Stewart, world champion ballroom dancer in 1926, also complained that 'more civilised' dances were being driven out. He complained that the 'craze for negro rhythms' was 'elbowing out' other 'and in many cases better' rhythms and dances.[33] Similarly, when swing music and dances began to arrive in Britain in 1937, Harry Kahn, writing in the *Modern Dance and Dancer*, warned that it threatened the standards of dancing in Britain and the newly evolved English style. It was fine for 'negroes' he complained, but not for whites:

> Of negroid origin, 'swing' is naturally most suitable when performed by negroes. To them it is a natural form of expression. But despite the fact that the negro has contributed largely towards world art, this latest creation can never evolve progressively, for it is essentially retrograde in character and in the interests of true dancing should be retained only as a novelty.[34]

DANCE AND ANTI-AMERICANISM IN BRITAIN, 1918–60

As well as racist prejudice serving to label them as dangerous, the fact that the new social dances were from America was another reason for the resistance that they received from some quarters in Britain. Exacerbated by the new confidence of the United States after the First World War, fears were widespread of an American invasion of culture. These fears were maintained and grew during the Second World War and after it. Consequently, an insistent nationalistic note of anti-Americanism ran through much of the period's harshest objections to dancing, as in so much else. Let's start by examining the extent to which British dance culture became Americanized in the period 1918–60 and place that development within the context of British anti-Americanism.

Certainly, the growing Americanization of dancing in Britain at the start of the twentieth century is undeniable. The new popular dances (and the dance music that went with them) were largely American in origin. A correspondent writing in the *Manchester Guardian* in 1923 lamented:

> We are Americanised in our dancing. It is America which invents the fashions and sets the grade. New steps and modifications devised in the States and tried out in ballrooms there, consistently appear here a month or two later. All the new dance music developments... have had their birth in America; whilst the American bands and dance music composers decide the tunes we shall hear and the manner of their execution. Dancing... is, indeed, a very considerable American industry now.[35]

Fred Astaire also noted the Americanization of dancing in Britain in 1928: 'America, it is usually admitted, leads the fashions in dancing... News travels fast

32 *Western Morning News and Mercury*, 24 January 1923, 5.
33 *Nottingham Evening Post*, 12 March 1927, 7.
34 *MDD*, February 1938, 12.
35 *Manchester Guardian*, 15 July 1923, 9.

these days. I can see no fundamental difference between the style of dancing in the London West End clubs and in New York. Dancing is becoming an international art.'[36] In the 1930s, evidence of an apparent 'American invasion' came from other popular dances such as the Big Apple, The Susie Q, Truckin', and later swing dancing. Whilst we must remember the significant emergence of dance trends that allowed a British dance culture to fight back, notably the development of the English style and the Lambeth Walk, it is clear that for many in interwar Britain, objections to dancing were based on their dislike of its perceived Americanization. This transformation of British dance culture helped shape, and was reflective of, a wider antagonism towards the United States at this time. Whilst racist concerns may well have been confined to a small group, anti-Americanism was much more widespread in political and cultural circles in the 1920s. Politically, anti-Americanism was running high in the aftermath of the 1923 changes to War Reparations that treated Britain more harshly than any other combatant of the First World War. The resurgent economic power of the United States during the 1920s also added to British anxieties, as markets lost during the First World War were never recovered. With Britain's Empire facing new challenges due to the rise of independence movements, it appeared that the geo-political certainties of the previous century or so were being dramatically altered. Culturally, America threatened Britain too. The spread of cinema in particular had generated some loudly heard complaints about the threat to Britain's cultural survival. The 1927 'Quota Act' for the cinema, which aimed to curb the dominance of Hollywood, was one response.

If anything, the war increased fears of Americanization, and with good reason. Whilst British dance culture had been exposed to, and transformed by, American and black American influences between the two wars, it had been exposure 'at a distance', largely via the new mass media of film, radio, and recordings. However, the arrival of large numbers of white and black American troops during the Second World War had the potential to transform dancing in Britain again, this time via 'intimate' and personal encounters (see Fig. 9.2). British dance halls were full of Americans and they demanded the dance music that they were used to back home, dancing in their own inimitable styles. Now dancers could be influenced directly—they could dance with and be taught by Americans in person. Predictably, this led to a revival of the by now well-rehearsed racial and nationalistic debates concerning popular culture seen before the war. Dance teachers were concerned that the English style that had become predominant in British dance halls by 1939 was going to be overtaken by a new American invasion. Some in the dancing world believed that they were in danger of losing control of British ballrooms to American servicemen. S. Ramsden complaining about American influence in Derby's dance halls wrote: 'We do not wish to deprive the Americans of their pleasure in dancing, but they ought to conform to our rulings and get into our way of ballroom dancing.'[37]

[36] *Daily Mail*, 17 October 1928, 6.

[37] *Derby Evening Telegraph*, 1 March 1945, 4.

Fig. 9.2. Race and dance: American and British at a service dance, 1943
Source: Imperial War Museum.

The impact on British dancing was, as we have seen, not that great, but the degree of interaction with American culture was considerable and highly visible. Moreover, a noteworthy minority rushed to adopt American styles. In Liverpool the arrival of large numbers of American troops altered the dancing habits of some fairly rapidly. Even before their arrival interest in American styles grew. In October 1942, for example, the *Dancing Times* noted a growing demand for lessons in swing dancing by girls 'who doubtless want to be in a position to keep pace with any American partners who may come along'.[38] The Grafton Rooms ran an 'American Dancing' night that month, with demonstrations of American styles, and a swing dance competition was also held. One of the biggest Liverpool stores also gave an exhibition of American dancing by Corporal J. Nairn, formerly from a noted New York dance team. By March 1943 the number of Americans asking for Jitterbug dancing to be held led Malcolm Munro of the Grafton Rooms to introduce a 'Jitterbug Night'.[39] Similarly, the number of Americans at the Paramount Tottenham Court Road, London, had led to a revival of interest in the dance that same year.[40] Covent Garden Opera House and the Hammersmith Palais were also

[38] *DT*, October 1942, 41. [39] *DT*, March 1943, 293. [40] *DT*, August 1943, 520.

centres for Jitterbug dancing, with American soldiers using the halls every afternoon and evening to practice Jitterbugging with English girls, despite periodic bans from the management.[41] In addition to the influence of Americans in British dance halls, American dancing styles could be picked up at the various American Red Cross clubs that sprung up throughout Britain, described by Alex Moore as 'Little Americas'.[42] Other recreational facilities provided for the Americans also helped the spread of the dance, and American culture more generally. Anglo-American friendship clubs sprang up in towns and cities across Britain. For example, in 1944 a British 'Welcome Club' was opened in Shenstone, Staffordshire, for American serviceman, and the opening night dance included a Jitterbug contest.[43] In Walsall an American nightclub, said to be an exact replica of a nightclub on Broadway, New York, was opened by the Americans, with American food, drinks, and cabaret.[44] In Cheltenham 'Anglo-American Entertainments' were put on at the Holy Apostle's Hall Charlton Kings with music supplied by the American Red Cross Dance Orchestra and the 'Swing Wings', and a Jitterbug competition and Jitterbug demonstrations given by Corporal Frank Wroblewski.[45]

Yet this process of Americanization did not end with the war. As we have already noted, the post-war period saw the continued presence of Jive in British dance halls and this was joined by other American dance styles, notably square dancing, which became popular up until the mid-1950s. Following the war, this Americanization of British dance culture took place against the backdrop of an anti-Americanism influenced by the huge growth of American geo-political power. In the space of just over two decades, Britain had gone from apparent pre-eminence in global affairs, to a poor third behind the new superpowers of the Soviet Union and the United States of America. A letter in the *Picture Post* of 1952 showed that some in Britain reacted to loss of power by adopting condescending views towards the USA. American popular culture (including dance culture) was seen as central to this cultural inferiority:

> It has been said by the Americans that we cast with a superiority to them and treat them like kids. In my opinion, we are superior to them. The vast majority of people in these islands do not wish to live the American way of life, which includes jiving, jitterbugging, be-bop, the wearing of silly looking clothes and weird haircuts.[46]

Yet, as before the war, the extent of Americanization had been exaggerated. In 1958 Drew Middleton of the *New York Times* in an article about the Americanization of Western Europe concluded that in Britain this had been a largely superficial process. Despite the fact that 'the young men and women trooping into a local dance hall may be dressed very much like those heading for the high-school gymnasium at home', he noted a resistance to more meaningful cultural exchange. He concluded that only the 'worst' aspects of American culture had reached Britain

[41] *Daily Mail*, 5 October 1943, 3. [42] *DT*, January 1944, 171.
[43] *Lichfield Mercury*, 2 June 1944, 4. [44] *Lichfield Mercury*, 17 August 1945, 4.
[45] *Cheltenham Chronicle and Gloucestershire Graphic*, 2 January 1943, 4.
[46] *PP*, 26 July 1952, 8–9.

and that this was responsible for a deeply held anti-Americanism in some quarters. Dance and youth culture were seen as particularly emotive in this respect. 'The inclinations of young people,' he noted, 'to stay up late, dance to loud music, drink too much and experiment sexually are attributed to "the American influence."'[47]

As with the racist images outlined earlier, condemnation of dance was also linked to stereotypes about American culture and society prevalent in Britain at the time. Dance was taken to be indicative of different national temperaments, with American dancing and national character seen as largely inferior to those of the British.

Throughout the whole of the period under investigation it was argued that American dancing was less refined and less stylish than British dancing. Critics of 'American dances' drew attention to their lack of sophistication. As early as 1919 a correspondent writing in Newcastle newspaper the *Sunday Sun* attacked the new dances:

> all of which are ridiculous and nonsensical concoctions devoid of any beauty and genuine feeling . . . They are mostly of American origin, and the eccentric temperament of that country has adopted them from the illiterate uncivilised negroes . . .[48]

American dancers were labelled as lazy, lacking in style, and 'chaotic' in their approach to dancing. Alex Mackenzie, a Scottish ballroom dance teacher, proclaimed in 1928, following his observations of New York dancers, his 'astonishment at the complete disregard of style and bewilderment at the haphazard method of progression'.[49] Margaret Winter concurred: 'The ballroom dancing as a whole seems so different here; it strikes one as more vivacious if less scientific than in England.'[50] Similarly, during the war when many more British dancers gained first-hand experience of the dancing skills of Americans, critics argued that, though skilful, they were not as stylish as the British. Dance teacher Eve Tynegate-Smith contended: 'The better American dancers are very clever at all kinds of rhythms and swing and jitterbug figures, but among these experts I have not seen any that can compete with our trained dancers. They cannot compare with them for footwork, movement, body line, grace or style.'[51]

More menacingly, it was believed that American dances were wild and chaotic and thus disruptive. We have already seen how racism created the impression that the Charleston and other dances were primitive. In addition to condemnation of dances on the grounds that they were black, there were complaints because they were American. The President of the British Association of Teachers of Dancing complained about America's influence in 1926: 'The dancing of America is largely to blame for the antics of many . . . today. In America, if you say it loud enough, it is so, and when the word goes forth that dancing is to be "peppy," because some great dance musician says so, bands accept it, and dancers quicken up.'[52] Remarkable similarities can be observed in reactions to the Jitterbug. Even before the arrival of American servicemen in Britain during the war, the Jitterbug was being singled out

[47] *New York Times*, 6 April 1958, 17. [48] *Sunday Sun*, 24 October 1926, 7.
[49] *DT*, October 1928, 53. [50] *DT*, September 1927, 643.
[51] *DT*, December 1942, 129. [52] *Daily Mail*, 5 July 1926, 8.

for its 'primitiveness'. The *Dancing Times*' columnist 'Sitter Out', writing in December 1939, called it 'the frenzied exaggeration of the worst form of rhythm dancing' and compared it directly to the 'great wave of freak dancing' which had become popular at the end of the First World War, putting its appearance down to the peculiar psychological conditions prevalent in wartime. He observed:

> It has been said that all dance is originally the motor reflex of intense excitement and that in the case of many of the most primitive peoples the dancers depended upon the exhilarative power of rhythmic movement. It is therefore not at all surprising that the present time of great mental stress should witness a mild invasion of our ballrooms of 'jitterbug' dancing.[53]

Others in the dance world were less easy going. Dance teacher Alex Moore also drew comparisons with the 'jazz dancing' of the immediate post-First World War period, and condemned the physicality of the dance. Commenting on an All England Jitterbug Competition held in London in March 1940 he complained:

> It was about the most disgusting and degrading sight I have ever seen in a ballroom. Leapfrog, double somersaults, 'kicking the ceiling,' and 'peckin' were but a few of the 'steps' used by the competitors in their efforts to gain applause.[54]

As with the Charleston before it, crudeness and primitiveness were seen as major features of the new dances. Describing swing, Truckin', Jitterbugging, and Jive in 1944, R. C. Brenan explained that they were 'the untutored muscular response of the slum child to the barrel organ, the interpretation of rhythm in movement at its crudest, ugliest and most primitive form, dancing—if we may so debase the term—without art, grace, beauty, pattern, technique or terminology'.[55] Links between dancing and 'addiction', and loss of control, made during the 1920s, were also made with the Jitterbug. For example, in a *Picture Post* article, 'What it Means to Be a Jitterbug', reporting on American dancers in August 1943, it was claimed that dancers were 'flinging themselves into paroxysmal exercises . . . it is as if every one is plunged simultaneously into an opium dream, out of which strange mutterings are heard, such as . . . "You're Killing Me."'[56] As with jazz and swing, the American Rock and Roll was also described in terms that emphasized a 'primitive', 'instinctive' appeal. In 1956 *Picture Post*, in an article entitled 'Presley Fever', described the new music above a photograph of youths Jiving in the streets outside Manchester's Gaiety Cinema after a performance of the film Rock Around The Clock: 'Whatever "Rock'n'Roll" may be, it does emphasise an overriding, persistent, throbbing beat—a beat that will start anybody's feet tapping. When teen-agers hear it they go off in an uncontrolled rampage of destruction.'[57]

In addition to being unstylish, wild, and primitive, American dances were seen to be unsuited to the British and indicative of important differences in national temperament. Differences in the way the same dances were danced here and in

[53] *DT*, December 1939, 141.
[54] *DT*, March 1940, 357.
[55] *MDD*, February 1944, 17.
[56] *PP*, 7 August 1943, 16.
[57] *PP*, 22 September 1956, 43.

America were highlighted by dance experts. In 1926, for example, one British dance teacher remarked: 'The Charleston as it is danced in the States, is hardly to be classed with its British counterpart. It is only necessary to visit any of the "down town" dancing saloons of Chicago and New York . . . In these establishments the dancers work themselves up into a perfect frenzy. Strange contortions, steps, and "shimmies," which would not be permitted for one minute in a British ballroom, are the rule, not the exception.'[58] Similarly, Margaret Winter writing in 1927 considered the Black Bottom unsuited to the 'frigid' English temperament: 'Black Bottoms renderings in England often remind one of invalids whose perfect health necessitates their native air, because it *is* a negro dance and the English environment is a bit frigid for its best development.'[59] Later too, in the 1930s, Victor Silvester doubted that the Big Apple would appeal to English dancers because it required them to dance alone 'and English dancers are as a rule shy of performing solo'. Pointing out the temperamental differences between the two nations Silvester remarked: 'The Englishman likes evolving his own combinations and variations, but he does not like turning them into an exhibition . . . the Americans can still teach us a lot about rhythm, though we beat them every time as regards style.'[60] Similarly, Maxwell Stewart claimed in 1927: 'It is the fundamental shyness of the English which brings them to the front as shining examples of good dancing. They do not lose sight of themselves. Their self-consciousness . . . is always there. They have at the back of the minds, even when they are thoroughly enjoying themselves, the ideals of reserve and polish.'[61]

It was for these nationalist and racist reasons that the process of standardization in dancing style and the evolution of the English style was begun. It was self-consciously labelled in such terms too. Dancing teachers deliberately tried to distance dancing from its 'suspicious' foreign cultural associations. The standardizing process already outlined was thus presented as a 'civilizing' process. In an article on the 'Negro Influence in Dancing' in the *Dancing Times* in 1927, for example, F. A. Hadland explained that any new dance 'had to be refined and adapted to civilised life before it could be countenanced in European ballrooms. The rowing movements of the arms, shaking shoulders, and close embraces, the incessant tom-tom beating and clatter had to be modified.'[62] The codification of dancing that took place was deliberately presented as a British response to the foreign invasion of national dance culture. Speaking in 1921, Major Cecil Taylor, President of the ISDT, argued:

> England has long been the dumping ground for Continental and American concoctions, and the time has come for this to cease. British teachers have the faculty of invention, and London should henceforth become the cultured dancing centre of the world.[63]

58 *Sunday Post*, 25 April 1926, 3. 59 *DT*, August 1927, 507.
60 *Nottingham Evening Post*, 17 December 1937, 6.
61 *Nottingham Evening Post*, 9 April 1927, 7. 62 *DT*, April 1927, 73.
63 *The Times*, 26 July 1921, 12.

Expressing the national spirit in dance was something that leading dance teachers believed they had achieved. Thus, the dance profession argued that the process of codification had created a distinctive national style of popular dancing.

RACIAL CONFLICT IN THE DANCE HALL, 1918–39

In addition to these debates concerning cultural forms, the dance hall itself became a focus for concerns about racial mixing. Throughout the period 1918 to 1960 the dance hall was the site of some of Britain's earliest sustained episodes of racial mixing (see Fig. 9.3). However, as a venue for close interaction between men and women, intimately associated in the public mind with sex, when a racial dimension was introduced, many of these encounters proved highly problematic.

In port cities and towns during the 1920s and 1930s, dance halls were some of the few venues where different nationalities and races might potentially mix in a period before widespread immigration into Britain. It has been estimated that the black British community probably numbered no more than eight thousand in 1939, mostly concentrated in the ports of Liverpool, Cardiff, Newcastle, and

Fig. 9.3. Race and Dance: Paramount Dance Hall, Tottenham Court Road, London, 1949
Source: Getty Images.

London.[64] These communities originated largely as result of immigration during the First World War, when many black men were employed as sailors, soldiers, and factory workers, although some black communities had been in Britain for considerably longer than this. There were also other ethnic minority populations in Britain at this time, chiefly Chinese, Indians, and, notably in the north-east of England, Arabs. In addition, temporary visiting foreign nationals, often non-white, could be found when naval and mercantile vessels docked in British ports.

Visiting seamen and other naval personnel were usually frequenters of local dance halls, adding a cosmopolitan dimension to British dancing experiences outside London's West End, allowing interaction between locals (chiefly women), and often causing conflict with local men. Some examples from the period help illustrate the tense nature of race relations in Britain during this time. In June 1924 the *Manchester Guardian* reported that 'racial jealousy' had led to a knife fight among American sailors anchored in Torbay who were dancing in a Torquay dance hall.[65] A large number of Filipino sailors had gone to the dance hall and paired off with white girls. Later several white American sailors arrived and objected to the Filipinos dancing with the local women. A fight with a stabbing ensued. American shore pickets were sent in to control the situation, with the result that the Filipinos were ejected from the dance hall and the white Americans were allowed to continue to dance. Two years later a similar episode led to a white American sailor from the US destroyer Lardener shooting dead a Filipino outside a Gravesend dance hall.[66] Sometimes, ignorance of British dance culture, together with jealousy from local men, also caused conflicts with visiting sailors. In June 1926 twenty-five Argentinian sailors were charged with rioting and disorderly conduct by the Liverpool Police Court following a fracas at a dance hall in Great George Street.[67] The sailors were from the warships Pampa and President Sarmiento, docked in Liverpool and Birkenhead at the time, and had started regularly attending the same dance hall whilst they were docked, with the result that some hostility developed between sailors and local men. The sailors armed themselves with a number of weapons and attacked a British man, following a misunderstanding of the etiquette for the 'Excuse Me' dance, where men could take a woman partner off another man by tapping her on the shoulder. The result was a serious fight. The *Manchester Guardian* reported: 'this is not the first time Argentine sailors have been involved in lively scenes at this dance hall, and the girl dancers declare that a good deal of jealousy has developed between the Argentines and young Englishmen who go there to dance.' Yet whilst local men might have resented the presence of these foreigners, it would appear that some local women were keen to build relationships, as the newspaper report concluded: 'A number of smartly dressed English girls waited outside to greet the smiling Argentinians when they left the court.'[68]

[64] D. Reynolds, *Rich Relations: The American Occupation of Britain 1942–1945* (London: HarperCollins, 1995), 216.

[65] *Manchester Guardian*, 25 June 1924, 10.

[66] *Manchester Guardian*, 3 September 1926, 4.

[67] *Manchester Guardian*, 14 June 1926, 11.

[68] *Manchester Guardian*, 22 June 1926, 12.

The fact that some English women in port city dance halls did find foreigners and men from ethnic minorities attractive was the cause of considerable concern. In Middlesbrough, for example, there was a small but highly visible Japanese (and to a lesser extent Chinese) presence in the town during the 1920s, as boats regularly pulled into this iron producing town from Japan and the east. Up to 400 East Asians could be present at any one time and some had settled permanently, in the Marton Road area. In 1927 the *Sunday Sun* explained their attraction to local women and emphasized that it was the dance halls that 'bring the white girls and the foreigners into close association'. It blamed 'dance mad' local girls for taking the initiative, not the visiting sailors:

> Middlesbrough has its share of foolish girls. Charleston mad girls. Mad on dance halls. Mad on their tawdry dress. Mad to flirt with little yellow men from the East . . . Far too many girls . . . go out of their way to dally with the slant eyed yellow men . . . The truth appears to be the lure of fine clothes and a good time is sufficient to lead many Middlesbrough girls astray.[69]

Indeed, those white women who danced with men of other races were considered to be of particularly low morality, and their attraction to foreigners seen as a kind of 'addiction'. For example, F. A. Richardson's 1935 investigation into the social conditions in British docks concluded: 'These types probably attract women of low type . . . Once a girl has been in company with a coloured man she seems to prefer them to other types of seamen.'[70] Some dubious racial stereotypes were also behind much of the moral fear created by black men and white women dancing together. It was commonly believed that black men had insatiable sexual appetites, were unable to control their sexual urges, and that they preyed on white women, turning them to prostitution for their own ends.[71] Thus, there was widespread opposition to any form of interracial sexual contact. As J. W. Gregory noted in 1925, there was: 'an instinctive aversion to the mating of white women with coloured men, and especially with Negroes . . . ' amongst the British population.[72] Many were convinced of the need for action to prevent these liaisons and there were calls by some in authority for the government to take action. From 1936, Chief Constables at major seaports were required to monitor their non-white populations and file reports on their behaviour.[73]

These sexual fears were exacerbated by economic tensions, especially in the seaports. The fear of cheap non-white labour undercutting wages in the merchant

[69] *Sunday Sun*, 17 April 1927, 5.

[70] F. A. Richardson, *Social Conditions in Ports and Dockland Areas. A Survey for the Joint Council of the British Social Hygiene Council and the British Council for the Welfare of the Mercantile Marine* (1935) cited in M. Banton, *The Coloured Quarter: Negro Immigrants in an English City* (London: J. Cape, 1955), 37.

[71] Clive Harris, 'Images of Blacks in Britain, 1930–60' in S. Allen and M. Macey, *Race and Social Policy* (London: ESRC, 1988).

[72] J. W. Gregory, *The Menace of Colour: A study of the difficulties due to the association of white and coloured races, with an account of measures proposed for their solution, and special reference to white colonization in the tropics* (London: Seeley, Service & Co., 1925), 228.

[73] Harris, 'Images', 31.

fleet had been one of the major causes of violence which spread throughout Britain in 1919 when 'Race Riots' broke out in Glasgow, South Shields, Salford, Cardiff, Barry, Newport, Liverpool, and in Limehouse, Poplar, and Canning in London. Such fears were probably behind the high level of racial prejudice prevalent in interwar Britain. In 1928 R. T. Lapiere, an American social scientist, conducted a survey of racial attitudes in Britain, focusing on people in London, Birmingham, Liverpool, and North Wales. Out of 315 interviewed, only fourteen (4.44 per cent) were 'without prejudice', forty-seven (14.9 per cent) were 'doubtful', while the vast majority (over 80 per cent) were 'with prejudice' towards black people.[74]

As a result of the stereotypes, fears, and prejudices described earlier, some dance hall owners introduced 'colour bars' to prevent the races mixing and to reduce racial tensions. In 1927, Edinburgh was the scene of one such controversy. Following the lead of one or two prominent halls, by May 1927 most dance halls in Edinburgh were refusing admission to Asiatic and African residents, mostly students studying at Edinburgh University, not because of any complaints against their conduct, but on account of their racial origin. In one case it was stipulated that 'coloured people' would be allowed entrance at the afternoon sessions only if accompanied by a white resident. One dance hall manager justified his policy thus:

> If a coloured person comes to your premises wanting admission you may know for a fact that he is respectable and would be quite a suitable patron. It is not easy to refuse him admission; but, on the other hand, if he was allowed in the chances are that some white patrons would object. The result is that we have decided to favour the majority of our patrons, and put on a colour ban.[75]

This line of argument was often used to justify racist prejudice among dance hall owners. A colour bar in Glasgow in 1929 was similarly defended:

> I have been in the dance hall business for a great number of years, and from the very start I have never allowed coloured students to enter my premises. I have my own patrons to consider. They, like myself, do not wish to dance in a hall where coloured men are admitted . . . I would not allow any of my girls to dance with them, so I do not see why I should give my regular patrons an opportunity of accepting coloured men as partners.[76]

Such lines of argument suggest that many resented the presence of non-whites in dance halls. In the Edinburgh case, however, the colour bar caused a considerable controversy. The Secretary of the Edinburgh Indian Association, Dr Rahman, sent a telegram to the King's Private Secretary to highlight the issue, and in May 1927 the General Assembly of the United Free Church attacked the colour bar, and the issue was also debated by the General Assembly of the Church of Scotland. The issue was taken up by Britain's third parliamentarian of Indian birth, the Communist MP for Battersea North, Shapurji Saklatvala, who warned about the

[74] R. T. Lapiere, 'Race Prejudice: France and England' (1928) 7(1) (September) *Social Forces* 106–7.

[75] *Manchester Guardian*, 21 May 1927, 16.

[76] *Manchester Guardian*, 20 December 1929, 5.

damage to Britain's position in its colonies that such a policy would create. The result, in June, was that Edinburgh Town Council unanimously passed a motion expressing their very strong disapproval of the ban, and the Lord Provost was asked to consult with local dance hall managers, together with representatives of Indian students, in order to resolve the situation. As a result a compromise was reached whereby 'coloured men' were to be allowed to attend dance halls 'under certain conditions'.[77] Elsewhere, dance hall managers proved less willing to yield to outside pressure. For example, despite the issue being taken up in Parliament by Labour MP for St Pancras North, James Marley, the local dance hall manager operating a colour bar remained defiant:

> I have lived abroad, and I know that a Zulu chief would resent a white man intruding in his kraal. For the same reason I resent the intrusion of a coloured man into my dance hall. Our hall is for white people only, and we stand absolutely by our decision not to admit coloured people, no matter how eminent or distinguished they may be.[78]

Marley's position was protected by law too, as a similar episode at the Locarno, Streatham was to prove in 1930. On being refused entry to the dance hall on grounds of his race, Dr A. M. Shah, an Indian, wrote to the India Office to complain. The Home Office and the Prime Minister became involved in the case which ultimately got nowhere, the Home Office telling Dr Shah that any place of public entertainment had the right to grant or refuse admission 'at its own option', with no terms being attached to licences to prevent them from doing so.[79]

In addition to colour being an issue in dance halls, anti-semitism was also a feature of racial tension, albeit on a small scale. Jews were the second largest minority in Britain (after the Irish) in the interwar period, and there were around 370,000 settled in Britain by 1939, largely in working-class areas of London, Leeds, and Manchester, but moving into the suburbs in these decades.[80] One Jewish dancer from Manchester recalls that there were numerous fights in Dyson's dance hall throughout the 1930s, usually concerning girls. He noted that mixing between Jews and non-Jews was not always welcomed: 'if a Jew would go up to a Christian lass for a dance and she said she didn't want to and somebody come up and she give him the dance, it would cause a bit of friction and vice versa.'[81] In the summer months particularly, racial tensions could erupt in Britain's cities and the dance hall was often a key issue in 'territorial' disputes. For example, rising tension in the Cheetham Hill district of Manchester between gangs of Jewish and Christian youths who had been frequenting various dance halls boiled over in July 1927. The feud had developed between Jewish and non-Jewish dancers both resentful of

[77] *Manchester Guardian*, 1 July 1927, 7.

[78] *Manchester Guardian*, 28 October 1929, 13.

[79] NA, HO45/24748, 'Locarno (Ltd.) Dance Hall—Ban on Coloured Visitor', 20 June 1930, 2.

[80] Panikos Panayi, 'Immigrants, Refugees, the British State and Public Opinion During World War Two' in P. Kirkham and D. Thoms (eds), *War Culture: Social change and changing experience in World War Two Britain* (Lawrence & Wishart, 1995), 201–2.

[81] NWSA: Interview with Lou Black, Manchester Jewish Museum (MJM):J40, nd.

each other's presence in what they considered to be 'their' dance halls. Over a series of evenings one week in early July, tensions mounted so much that police had to be called to several stand-offs between rival gangs, where two arrests were made after anti-semitic threats were made by two Christian youths, possessing garden tools as weapons.[82]

In a period before widespread immigration then, the dance hall nevertheless occupied an important role as one of the most public places for interaction between people of different races in Britain. Although this was largely confined to ports and larger university cities where small ethnic minorities had settled, such experiences were important. They reveal a widespread suspicion of foreigners amongst certain sections of British society, and racial prejudice amongst many dance hall owners and dancers. On the other hand, many dancers, particularly younger women, welcomed the opportunities of dancing with people from different cultures.

RACIAL CONFLICT IN THE DANCE HALL DURING WORLD WAR II

The dance hall's role as a potential site of racial mixing, and also racial tension, became greatly increased during the Second World War. During the war, the issue of race and dance became a 'reality' in Britain to an extent that was not possible before. It was most visibly manifested when three million US troops, amongst them around 130,000 black Americans, arrived in Britain from 1942 onwards. Like the rest of the population, dancing was one of the favourite leisure time activities of both black and white American troops and their presence in British dance halls caused headaches for the British and American authorities. A policy of segregation brought about a level of racial tension hitherto unheard of in Britain's dance halls. In addition to Americans, the British government recruited non-white labour from the Dominions to help plug manpower shortages on both the Home Front and in the Forces. This increased the presence of black and Indian people in many British towns. They were not the only foreigners in Britain however. There were large numbers of Canadian, Polish, French, Czech, and other troops which added to the cosmopolitan air of wartime Britain. The presence of so many outsiders at a time of intense risk led to inevitable conflicts. Hostility to foreigners ran high in Britain throughout the war. However, not all of these encounters were negative—some Britons embraced the newly racially diverse population, seeing it as a welcome injection of 'variety', albeit one they expected would only be temporary, and welcomed those who came to help Britain in its hour of need.

Both the American and British governments anticipated that the arrival of black troops in Britain during the war would create a potentially problematic situation. The British government tried to persuade the Americans not to bring over large

[82] *Manchester Guardian*, 9 July 1927, 15.

numbers of black troops and they were supported by the US Army authorities in Britain. However, the US War Department overruled both, and from May 1942 black American troops began to arrive in Britain. Concerns about racial mixing came from two fronts. The most obviously racially motivated policy was adopted by the American government and US Army, under the control of General Eisenhower. The American Army which arrived in Britain in 1942 was a segregated one, and whilst recognizing that an official 'colour bar' did not exist in Britain, the US Army brought into effect a policy of segregation in British towns and cities that was to have an impact on dance halls. Several methods were used to keep black and white American troops apart when off duty. A system of 'rotating passes' was introduced, with black troops allowed to go into local towns on different nights than whites. In Tewkesbury, for example, in 1942 white troops were given passes into the town every Tuesday, Thursday, and Saturday, and black troops every Monday, Wednesday, and Friday. Sundays were rotated black and white.[83] In situations where this was not possible, a town's leisure facilities were to be allocated along the lines of race—so certain pubs and dance halls were meant for whites only, and others for blacks only. Another method was to allocate certain facilities on a rotating basis, so that in local town halls, for example, there were 'black' dances one week and 'white' dances the next.[84] Such rules were not couched in purely racial terms; instead dances were arranged on different nights for a certain company or unit (which were all single race). As General J. C. H. Lee, in charge of the Services of Supply unit, who commanded most black troops in Britain noted: 'While colour lines are not to be announced or even mentioned, entertainments such as dances should be "by organisation."'[85] The US military authorities could also effectively create a colour bar on dance halls by banning coloured troops from visiting particular halls. One example of this came in Glasgow in 1944 when a complaint was made at the Glasgow Trades Council that several dance halls in the city were giving preference to white over black soldiers. The dance hall management revealed that this situation was forced on them when it had had to call in the American military authorities after a fight between white and black soldiers. The authorities then responded by putting the hall out of bounds for black soldiers, thus applying the colour bar themselves.[86]

The British government also had considerable concerns about the potential mixing of races that the presence of large number of black American troops provided. Officially, the British government opposed the segregationist policy of the US Army in Britain and in September 1942 the Home Office contacted all Chief Constables to remind them that discrimination against black troops was not government policy, and that police should not ask those in charge of places of entertainment to refuse entry on the basis of race. Moreover, it asked that police officers 'should not make themselves responsible in any way for the enforcement of

[83] Reynolds, *Rich Relations*, 223.
[84] J. Gardiner, *Over Here: The GIs in Wartime Britain* (London: Collins & Brown, 1992), 149.
[85] Reynolds, *Rich Relations*, 222.
[86] *Danceland*, August 1944, 3.

such orders'.[87] Yet whilst the official policy was to distance itself from US Army segregation, the British government also sought to limit the contact between black US troops and the British population. Women and dance halls were particular concerns. Thus in 1942 the War Office advocated a propaganda campaign to inform British troops of the reasons behind US Army racial policy and to advise women in particular to avoid contact with black GIs. In Southern Command, for example, a senior officer advised that soldiers 'should not make intimate friends with them, taking them to cinemas and bars' and that women should not 'associate with coloured men . . . they should not walk out, dance or drink with them'.[88] Moreover, it advocated the use of 'whispering campaigns' using the Women's Voluntary Service, Housewives Committees, etc. to scare women away from associations with black servicemen on the grounds of sexual dangers and the dangers of venereal disease.[89]

On the ground, Britain's record of racial interaction during the war was a mixed one. Certainly, many people in Britain disliked the American policy of racial segregation. They could not see what was wrong with drinking and dancing with black Americans. As Eisenhower himself later commented:

> The British population, except in large cities and among wealthy classes, lacks the racial consciousness which is so strong in the United States. The small-town British girl would go to a movie or a dance with a Negro quite as readily as she would with anyone else, a practice that our white soldiers could not understand. Brawls often resulted and our white soldiers were further bewildered when they found that the British press took a firm stand on the side of the Negro.[90]

White Americans gained a reputation amongst sections of British society for harsh treatment of blacks. In Manchester, for example, it was rumoured that black soldiers had been stabbed or even castrated for dancing with white women.[91] As a result of growing tension, in 1943 the US Army pressed the British government to 'educate' the British people about blacks because they were so concerned about the growing number of racial incidents in which British civilians were taking the side of the black GIs. The British government, who had refused a previous request the year before, agreed, in order to reduce miscegenation.[92] Serious efforts were made to manage the behaviour of British women in particular, both in and out of the armed forces. For those in the services, military discipline was used. Local police forces kept reports on women soldiers discovered in the company of black GIs, with dance halls frequently inspected for evidence. By January 1944 an ATS order was produced 'forbidding its members to speak with coloured American soldiers except in the presence of a white'.[93] The law was also used against civilian women to discourage mixing. Wartime Defence Regulations were used, with prosecutions for

[87] NA HO45/25604, 'US forces personnel stationed in the UK: possibility of friction between white and coloured troops', 1942–44.
[88] Ibid. [89] Ibid. [90] Gardiner, *Over Here*, 155. [91] Ibid.
[92] Reynolds, *Rich Relations*, 228. [93] Ibid., 229.

trespass if women were discovered with black GIs on US military bases being the most commonly used device.[94]

The arrival of the Americans in Britain also affected dance hall relations with the colonial immigrants who had been brought to Britain to help with the war effort. Ten thousand West Indians, for example, joined the British war efforts as soldiers, sailors, and airmen. There was a large West Indian contingent in the RAF and West Indian women also served in the ATS. There was also considerable need for skilled and semi-skilled workers in the factories and elsewhere. Nearly 1,000 technicians from the Caribbean and nearly 1,000 timber workers from British Honduras were brought over.[95] The experience of West Indian civilians in the north-west of England illustrates the fluctuating state of race relations in the dance hall during the war. Some 345 West Indians came to Liverpool from 1941–3 under a scheme organized jointly by the Ministry of Labour and the Colonial Office to increase production. Later smaller numbers went to Manchester, Bolton, and surrounding areas.[96] Initially, there was tension as the new black population, with few ties and far from home, wanted to make full use of the local dancing facilities to relax and meet their fellow workers and local girls. However, a colour bar existed in the most popular dance hall in Liverpool and this caused a great deal of resentment. Despite initial problems, however, there followed a period of about a year during the major part of 1942 where there appears to have been some diminution in the expression of prejudice and discrimination against the West Indians. As A. H. Richmond noted: 'They were free to use the majority of dance halls and public houses in the city, and, in fact, became regular and well-liked patrons of a number of them. Similar good conditions appear to have operated in Manchester, Warrington, and Bolton, where the other West Indians were living.'[97] However, the arrival in the north of England during 1943 of large numbers of American troops led to a serious deterioration in the state of race relations. For one thing, the arrangements for segregation at dance halls introduced by the US Army did not prevent white American troops from coming into contact with black British and colonial troops or civilians. The black colonial workers were much less likely to accept white American prejudice. As Richmond concluded:

> [I]t seems that the American Negro was much more prepared to avoid conflict with the American white by leaving a dance hall or restaurant when white Americans arrived; but such acceptance and submission to whites was not part of the culture pattern of the West Indian Negro, who was much more likely to stand up to the contemptuous attitude expressed by some of the American white troops by equally contemptuous retorts; this often led to an exchange of physical blows.[98]

[94] Ibid.

[95] I. Spencer, 'World War Two and the making of multiracial Britain' in P. Kirkham and D. Thoms (eds), *War Culture: Social Change and Changing Experience in World War Two Britain* (London: Lawrence & Wishart, 1995), 209, 212.

[96] A. H. Richmond, *Colour Prejudice in Britain: A Study of West Indian Workers in Liverpool, 1941–51* (London: Routledge & Kegan Paul, 1953), 23.

[97] Richmond, *Colour*, 86. [98] Richmond, *Colour*, 87.

These tensions had a knock-on effect, poisoning relations between local white populations and blacks of all nationalities, civilian and military too. One West Indian writing to the welfare officer of a factory in Liverpool in 1942 complained:

> . . . now it is worse. The Americans have got some power over things that I can't understand. There used to be a few dance halls that we could go to after a week's work, or whenever one felt like dancing. In these dances one could have fun with other people and meet the boys that are living far away. Now when we enter these halls all one can hear is 'No Negroes'. When we ask why, this is always the answer, 'Well, you see, the Americans don't like the Negroes in the same place where they have fun.'[99]

In late 1943 a series of similar episodes in Warrington and Liverpool caused so much resentment amongst colonial workers that politicians and the Colonial Office became involved. A series of clashes between West Indians and American white troops at the Grafton Rooms, Liverpool had led to a colour bar. One of the West Indians involved, George Roberts, protested and tried to gain admittance again with his Home Guard uniform. He was refused. In protest he said he would no longer do Home Guard duties if he was not 'good enough' to gain entry to the dance hall of his choice. Roberts was prosecuted for the offence of refusing to do Home Guard duties and a fine of £5 imposed. A similar incident occurred in Warrington the following month. A party of American soldiers demanded the ejection of one of the Jamaican technicians who was dancing with a white girl. He was well behaved and quiet. The manager of the dance hall refused the request of the American soldiers. Soon after the incident the manager received a letter from the local commanding officer of the US Army: 'It is not our intention to dictate the policies of privately owned establishments, but in the interest of eliminating trouble in which our troops may be involved we would appreciate your co-operation in prohibiting Negroes from attending the dances.'[100] The dance hall manager, who believed in tolerance, instead banned all troops American, British, and Dominion but later had to go back on this policy as he nearly went out of business.

The treatment of the other large group of black civilians brought to Britain to help during the war effort was also similarly checkered. The 1,000 British Honduran forestry workers who were located in Scotland were both welcomed by some and resented by others. Although situated far from large urban centres, the workers had access to dances and created their own dance culture. The Colonial Office noted that the jazz band from the Duns camp, for example, played at local dances and that the workers also held their own dances to which locals were invited.[101] Mrs James of Bielgrange recalled: 'Those who remember the Hondurans at local dances say that they were well behaved' but went on to note that '[i]nvolvement of local girls with Hondurans was generally frowned upon.'[102] Despite these objections, local women and the black workers inevitably formed

[99] Richmond, *Colour*, 88. [100] Richmond, *Colour*, 89.

[101] Marika Sherwood, *Many Struggles: West Indian workers and service personnel in Britain (1939–45)* (London: Karia, 1985), 117, 122.

[102] Sherwood, *Many*, 116.

partnerships, sexual or otherwise, with some even marrying. Such 'fraternization' alarmed those in authority. The welfare team of the Colonial Office reported, in October 1941, that a deputation of local ministers of the Kirk suggested that East Linton and Duns camps be made 'out of bounds' due to 'unpleasantness . . . sexual and alcoholic' but the commanding officer argued that this was not necessary. The Duke of Buccleuch, however, complained to Harold Macmillan, Under-Secretary of State for the Colonies, about the Hondurans on his estates in August 1942. He too was particularly concerned about their mixing with white women, complaining: 'I think it can be admitted that loose relations between black men of totally different standards, both moral and material, and our simple country girls has unpleasant features and that improper intercourse with decent young women should be strongly discouraged.' Sir Harold Carrington, Deputy Director of the Home Grown Timber Department in Scotland, also went around notifying parents and ministers of the 'undesirability of such marriages'. In November 1942 some of the camps were raided and some local women evicted. Many of the timber workers were sent back home.[103]

Within the wider community, dance hall race relations were often strained too. Often Britons 'hid' behind the US policy of segregation in order to justify applying colour bars in their dance halls. For example, on 7 September 1942 the *Daily Herald* reported a ban on black GIs attending dances in the town of Eye in Suffolk. Although locals blamed the US Army for this colour bar, it had actually been an illegal decision made by the local council.[104] Such instances were not rare. The League of Coloured Peoples' *Newsletter* reported in March 1944 that an unofficial colour bar was operating at public dances held at Watford Town Hall. It noted: 'Incidents have occurred in which Army officers have walked out when coloured men, many of them serving soldiers, came in. Girls have refused to dance with them. Alderman E. C. Last, chairman of the Town Hall Management Committee, complained: "If I hear of definite cases where dance promoters are operating a colour bar, I shall ask my committee to refuse further permission to hire the hall."'[105]

Individual dancers rather than dance hall management could also object to the presence of black people in dance halls. One particular hot spot for trouble in London began to develop in Mecca's dance hall the Paramount Tottenham Court Road. The Paramount began to attract increasing numbers of black dancers, who made the place their own, dancing with white women on a regular basis. Tensions grew with local white men, who resented this encroachment on 'their territory'. Mecca thus introduced a policy whereby black men had to bring a partner before they could be admitted.[106] This partial colour bar came to the attention of the Colonial Office, who contacted Heimann to tell him of their criticism of his policy, and requesting that he reverse it. He did. As large numbers of American troops began to arrive after mid-1942 the dance hall became the site of increasing numbers

103 Sherwood, *Many*, 113. 104 Reynolds, *Rich Relations*, 225.
105 *Newsletter*, No. 54 (March 1944), 96.
106 R. Fairley, *Come Dancing Miss World* (London: Neamme, 1966), 71.

of fights from various sections of the clientele: between black and white locals; between black and white US soldiers; and between locals and American blacks. By 1943 things reached a crisis point, with constant feuds and on one particularly bad weekend a stabbing and a shooting outside the Parmount and a pitched battle in Leicester Square. Fearing for their lives, Paramount manager Harry Chaperlin and Carl Heimann decided to impose a 48-hour ban on all black people, 'in their own interests' and to dissipate the tensions. Again, the Colonial Office intervened, arguing that Mecca was introducing a colour bar. Mecca's response was that they 'only barred people, whatever colour they were, who created disturbances on our premises—and, of course, we banned many white people who did not conform'.[107] The temporary colour bar remained, and was followed by another attempt to impose a 'must bring a partner' admissions policy for coloured people ('this was always the sparking-off point—when the [white] girls were asked to dance'). Again, the Colonial Office objected and this time Heimann and Chaperlin were invited to meet with representatives from the League of Coloured Peoples. After a tense meeting the black group accepted Heimann's policy and his statement that he had no prejudice, and that he wanted to protect the interests of all concerned.

Wartime racial tensions in the dance hall also involved mistrust of white foreigners. As we have seen, the white GI was often less preferred than his black counterpart amongst some Britons. The 'flashiness' of the foreign solider was often a source of irritation to the hard-pressed, ration-restricted British men. In the dance hall differences in pay, rations, and clothing became obvious. Andy Lothian, popular danceband leader in Dundee, remarked: 'In 1940, Polish submarines docked in Dundee and the influx of Polish and American sailors and soldiers caused a lot of resentment amongst the local lads. These visitors wore flashy uniforms and often as not had a packet of nylon stockings in their pockets or a packet of cigarettes, which impressed the girls used to British wartime rationing.'[108] As venues for exhibition and display, dance halls brought cultural differences to the fore. With a reputation as expert dancers, feigning knowledge of the latest steps from New York, American soldiers were particularly resented by British men. Competition for women was fierce.

One of the earliest incidents caused by the arrival of American troops occurred in August 1942 in Antrim, Northern Ireland. Private Owen McLoughlin, a 24-year-old in the Pioneer Corps, was stabbed to death in a fight between British and American soldiers after a dance. Rivalry in the dance hall had built up all evening. The coroner was anxious that the incident would not damage relations between the two Allies, stating: 'I trust that the unfortunate incident will not mar good relations between the British and American forces, and that every officer and NCO will see that such events as this do not recur.'[109] His wishes were not to come true. In

[107] Ibid.

[108] E. Casciani, *Oh, How we Danced! The History of Ballroom Dancing in Scotland* (Edinburgh: Mercat Press, 1994), 98.

[109] *Manchester Guardian*, 5 August 1942, 8.

October 1943 a 'dance hall battle' occurred in Liverpool, when bottles, glasses, chairs, and knuckle dusters were uses as weapons following arguments between Americans and locals. This resulted in the arrest of thirteen American sailors.[110]

RACIAL CONFLICT IN THE DANCE HALL DURING A PERIOD OF MASS IMMIGRATION, 1945–60

In the period after 1945, Britain experienced its first wave of mass non-white immigration, as large numbers of blacks from Africa and the West Indies arrived, together with substantial numbers of Indians and Pakistanis. Unlike their wartime predecessors, these immigrants were not temporary. Their arrival marked a significant change in the racial make-up of British society and was to have a substantial impact on race relations within dance halls, as with many other aspects of daily life in Britain. Encouraged by the labour shortage in post-war Britain, together with the 1948 British Nationality Act and official sponsorship from British firms, immigrants began to arrive in large numbers from the later 1940s onwards. In 1949 the 'coloured' population of Britain was estimated, by both the Colonial Office and the League of Coloured People, to be about 25,000, including students. Although distributed throughout the UK, two significant early concentrations were to be found in communities in the 'Tiger Bay' area of Cardiff (*c.*7,000) and the South End of Liverpool (8,000). Smaller non-white communities were also found in all the main ports, including London.[111] By 1951, however, the census showed some 138,072 people in Britain who had been born in the Caribbean and the Indian subcontinent—16,188 from the Caribbean, 110,767 from India, and 11,117 from Pakistan.[112] Between 1951 and 1957 an estimated 87,500 West Indians arrived in Britain and by 1966 there were approximately 450,000.[113] As greater numbers arrived, the pattern of settlement also changed, with immigrants settling beyond the traditional port areas and university towns. More and more of Britain became acquainted with the growing racial diversity of its society. Sizeable concentrations were to be found in the West Midlands, particularly Birmingham and its environs; the east Midlands, in Nottingham, Derby, and Leicester; and in the north, Bradford and other parts of Yorkshire, and Manchester, Liverpool, and the mill towns of Lancashire.

Dancing and dance halls played a vital role in the history of post-war British race relations. Many clashes and some of the most notorious race riots began following dancing disagreements. As Sydney Collins's 1957 survey of ethnic minorities in the north-east of England argued: 'In the recreational sphere, only in dance halls has

[110] *Manchester Guardian*, 28 October 1943, 3. [111] *PP*, 2 July 1949, 23.

[112] C. Holmes, *John Bull's Island: Immigration and British Society, 1871–1971* (Basingstoke: Macmillan, 1988), 226.

[113] N. Deakin, *Colour, Citizenship and British Society* (1970), 31 cited in P. Addison, *No Turning Back: The peacetime revolutions of post-war Britain* (Oxford: Oxford University Press, 2010), 120.

overt prejudice been experienced by coloured persons on Tyneside.'[114] Sheila Patterson also noted in London that:

> [c]asual contacts in such places of recreation as bars, cafes, and dance halls do of course provide the main opportunities for friction and open clashes between migrants and local people, just as they do between local people. Such places tend to attract a fair proportion of the young, the lonely, and the maladjusted of both sexes, and it is inevitable that from time to time incidents should occur, particularly if competition for a desirable commodity such as a dancing partner flares into overt conflict.[115]

As the majority of the early West Indian immigrants were single males, most of the conflicts were the result of rivalry for female dancing partners. Commenting on the introduction of a colour bar at the Streatham Locarno in August 1958, one social investigator remarked: 'The measure was said to have been introduced because of rivalry between coloured and white dancers over girls, which resulted in fist and knife fights at some halls. Street brawls of this kind had occurred in July 1958 and on earlier occasions outside the Locarno.'[116] She went on to conclude that black people 'are still not so sure of a welcome in dance halls where the sexual motivation is more directly involved'.[117]

Sexual competition was a major element in racial prejudice and conflict. As one commentator put it: 'coloured immigrants and white men in Britain regard each other as sexual competitors.'[118] As the number of immigrants increased, then, the sense of competition also rose. Moreover, this tapped into the most enduring stereotypes of and prejudices against black immigrants—those concerning sexuality. In particular it was believed that black men had larger sexual organs and could give greater sexual satisfaction to women. Banton, for example, remarked: 'In Manchester . . . white women who associate with coloured men are firmly convinced of the potency of coloured men's organs of procreation and the extraordinary satisfaction they can provide.'[119] It was also asserted that black men were sexually aggressive. A social worker in Brixton, 1959, commented: 'Local people don't like the coloured men's attitude to women. You can't go along certain streets, even in broad daylight, without every second one making remarks and suggestions, whether you look the type or not. And local people say they're getting more noisy and aggressive as the numbers go up.'[120]

This led to fear and admiration amongst many white women, and jealousy among white men. The dance hall played a dual role in both re-affirming and breaking down these sexual stereotypes. For example, it is clear that some white women were greatly attracted by the idea of black men as 'wild' and sexually

[114] S. Collins, *Coloured Minorities in Britain: Studies in British Race Relations based on African, West Indian and Asiastic Immigrants* (London: Lutterworth Press, 1957), 110.

[115] S. Patterson, *Dark Strangers: A Sociological Study of the Absorption of a Recent West Indian Migrant Group in Brixton, South London* (Harmondsworth: Penguin Books, 1963), 248.

[116] Patterson, *Dark*, 245. [117] Ibid.

[118] M. Banton, *White and Coloured: The behaviour of British people towards coloured immigrants* (London: J. Cape, 1959), 131.

[119] Banton, *White*, 132. [120] Patterson, *Dark*, 237.

exciting and would thus agree to dance with them in public. As Banton remarked: 'Whites who wish to cast off their inhibitions will often seek out coloured people for company . . . ' The way in which black men danced was vital to this attraction. Banton continued: 'In London, well-to-do women have been known to support coloured men living in dockland, to visit occasionally a notorious Negro dance-hall, and to invite ill-lettered but powerfully built Negroes from Stepney to Mayfair parties. The more primitive they make themselves out the more are they welcome.'[121]

Apparently, many white girls danced with black men for 'novelty' and excitement too. Michael Banton concluded:

> The cases . . . exemplify the image of the coloured man as the exciting stranger. The girls in the dance-hall were perhaps attracted to the novelty of dancing with a Negro in the style of which they are masters. To dance with someone trying to be English—and never quite succeeding—had much less appeal.[122]

Indeed, there is some evidence that white women were more favourably disposed towards black men than white men were. In Banton's 1959 survey, 23 per cent of females (19 per cent of males) had 'very friendly' attitudes towards immigrants, and more than twice as many men (8 per cent) as women (3 per cent) were considered unfriendly.[123]

Yet despite this, there was considerable social pressure acting on white women that made them think twice before dancing with black men in post-war Britain. To mix socially with black men was potentially 'declassing', and it was widely believed that only 'bad' or socially outcast women did so. A number of surveys of race relations in the Britain of the 1950s commented on such prejudices and pressures. For example, A. H. Richmond's study of West Indian workers in Liverpool between 1941 and 1951 found that whilst some women were friendly with black men in the workplace, they were fearful outside, many of them cutting them dead: 'a girl would often seriously hesitate about accepting an invitation to a cinema or a dance because of the attitude their friends or their family would adopt if they found out that she had been out with a coloured man.'[124] Such hesitancy was also found in a later study of West Indian immigrants in Brixton, South London in the period 1955–8: 'some coloured men complain that white girls frequently refuse to dance with them, only to accept offers from white men immediately afterwards. Such statements are difficult to verify. In some cases they may be accurate, in view of the widespread local disapproval of association between white men and coloured men.'[125] In Cardiff too, it was found: 'Here, as elsewhere in Great Britain, the main reason for avoiding personal contact with or physical approximation to a coloured man or woman is probably fear of losing social status.'[126]

[121] Banton, *White*, 129. [122] Banton, *White*, 130. [123] Banton, *White*, 209.

[124] A. H. Richmond, *Colour Prejudice in Britain: A Study of West Indian Workers in Liverpool, 1941–51* (London: Routledge & Kegan Paul, 1953), 78.

[125] Patterson, *Dark*, 245.

[126] Kenneth L. Little, *Negroes in Britain: A Study of Race Relations in English Society* (London: Kegan Paul, Trench, Trubner & Co, 1947), 105.

As a result of these prejudices and social conventions, it could be difficult for black men to find female dance partners in dance halls. Yet, an overview of the racial conflicts originating in dance halls in post-war Britain reveals that a majority of cases were caused by the fact that black and white *were* dancing together. As Hill suggests, this tended to motivate interventions from white men:

> When any occasion arises presenting a possibility of an association between a dark-skinned man and a white girl this situation immediately arouses the white man's protective instinct. He looks upon himself as being divinely appointed to protect the purity and innocence of girls of his own race from being ravaged by the savage lusts of the black man.[127]

As before and during the war, dance hall managements thus regularly imposed colour bars in response to fears about racial mixing from dancers and as a result of their desire to prevent trouble in their halls. The dance hall in the 1950s became a microcosm for the wider societal debate concerning race relations, now extended and involving more of the population, with the majority in society resisting the emergence of racial diversity within their community, and a liberal minority fighting for greater tolerance. The debate created by colour bars in dance halls was an important part of the eventual introduction of anti-discrimination laws in Britain, but also no doubt played a part in the decision to introduce restrictions on immigration in 1962.

The Scala Ballroom in Worcester Street, Wolverhampton, was the scene of one particularly controversial colour bar, sparking debate both in Britain and abroad. Questions were asked in the Parliament of India and complaints were made also in the West Indies, whilst at home it prompted moves by Labour MPs to enact new legislation. In 1958 the Scala had refused to admit Udit Kumar Das Gupta, a local Indian engineering draughtsman, to a dance. As a result Das Gupta wrote to the Mayor of Wolverhampton who told the local licensing magistrates that they would have to decide whether or not the licence of the dance hall would be renewed. The issue divided opinion. The Wolverhampton Labour Party opposed the renewal of the licence on the ground of 'racial discrimination and prejudice' and the local Labour MP John Baird also took up the matter, drafting a Private Member's Bill in the House of Commons to make colour bars in dance halls and other public places illegal.[128] There was also opposition from a member of the Wolverhampton Town Council, the Secretary of the Wolverhampton Branch of the International Friendship League, and the Secretary of the Wolverhampton Free Church Council. Despite these protests, however, the local licensing committee renewed the Scala's licence for music and dancing, thus implicitly supporting the colour bar imposed there. The defiant dance hall manager explained:

> Before anyone condemns us they should ask themselves whether they are genuinely sincere. They could ask themselves what they would do if on calling at the Scala to

[127] C. S. Hill, *How Colour Prejudiced is Britain?* (London: Panther Books, 1965), 231.

[128] R. Glass, *Newcomers: The West Indians in London* (London: Centre for Urban Studies, Allen & Unwin, 1960), 81.

collect a teenage daughter she could be seen dancing with a coloured man employed as a labourer. We must acknowledge that there is prejudice and when it is overcome coloured people will be admitted.[129]

A Gallup Poll on the introduction of this colour bar was taken in June 1958—it shows that the manager was out of step with public opinion: 22 per cent approved of the colour bar, 62 per cent disapproved, and 16 per cent did not know what they thought.[130] However, the dance hall manager claimed that in a straw poll of dancers taken in the dance hall itself, one hundred were in favour of the bar and only five against it.[131] This was not the end the matter, either. In protest, the Musicians' Union told its members not to play there, but the local branch decided to allow local members to carry on working. As a result, the leaders of the three bands playing at the Scala were expelled from the Union. The local branch re-admitted them; the Union then expelled them again.[132] The following year a change of ownership and an end to the colour bar were announced, largely as a result of public pressure.

The Scala incident highlighted the ineffectiveness of the law and led to increased demands for new legislation. Colour bars were not illegal in Britain. Whilst there was no law that allowed discrimination, there were also no laws which defined it and explicitly prohibited it. Thus, it was perfectly legal to deny jobs to non-whites, to refuse accommodation to non-whites, or even to make abusive statements about them. The issue of colour bars in dance halls, public houses, etc. was left to local decision makers and central government repeatedly avoided responsibility for the issue. Instead, licensing judges could take complaints about discrimination into account when they considered the renewal of a licence. There were, however, no specific rules of conduct for the managers of licensed premises, nor guidance on the issue of discrimination from any official body.[133] This meant that there was considerable variation in official local attitudes towards colour bars.

As the largest dance hall business in Britain, the Mecca chain also became intimately involved in the management of disputes concerning race in the post-war period, and it found itself at the centre of considerable controversy. In some of its dance halls it was able to foster good relations with influential individuals in the black community that allowed it to manage race relations without resorting to restrictions. For example, in the historically troublesome Paramount Tottenham Court Road, London, one ringleader of trouble who had been barred asked for re-admittance on the promise of good behaviour, becoming an 'unofficial lieutenant' calming down disputes when black people were involved. He would calm the situation by appealing to black dancers, saying 'this is a place where coloured people are allowed to come and we are treated with respect—and you can dance with a

129 *Manchester Guardian*, 15 June 1958, 13. 130 Patterson, *Dark*, 245.
131 *DM*, 18 June 1958, 19. 132 Glass, *Newcomers*, 81.
133 See for instance PRO HO45/24748, 'Coloured Servicemen refused admission to public entertainments', June 1946, which explicitly states that there is no legal position on 'colour bars' following a case in Cardiff in 1946, and that the Home Office would like to keep it that way.

coloured girl or a white girl and nobody questions it'.[134] Yet elsewhere, growing feuds between black and white resulted in Mecca introducing restrictions on entrance to its dance halls. In 1958, amidst the rise of race tensions and the race riots, Mecca introduced a 'partner' policy in its dance halls in Sheffield, Nottingham, Birmingham, and Streatham, which was based on its wartime experiences of dealing with racial tension. All non-white men had to enter the dance hall with their own partner, white or non-white, and were not allowed to change that partner once they were in the dance hall. The policy was obviously designed to stop black men approaching white women they did not know, on the grounds that this would cause trouble, either by 'offending' the white women who were asked to dance, or by 'offending' white men who disliked white women being asked by black men to dance. Eric Morley justified the policy as 'a precaution against violence' but it caused considerable controversy.[135]

In Sheffield, the Trades and Labour Council, which represented 100,000 workers, asked Sheffield City Council to withdraw the licence of Mecca's Locarno dance hall there, and also asked the Musicians Union to 'blacklist' it on account of alleged racial discrimination. Whilst the Musicians' Union leaders did not ask its members to refuse to play at Mecca's halls (a lucrative source of income), Mr Francis, assistant secretary, did express the union's criticism of the policy in the *Daily Worker*:

> The union does not agree with restrictions imposed by Mecca. If a situation arises where it is necessary to impose certain restrictions, then we think they should apply to everyone, regardless of colour . . . In this case, a temporary regulation might have laid down that everyone must bring a partner, and this would apply to both white and coloured dancers. In that way, discrimination might have been avoided.[136]

The mainstream press also latched onto the story. The *Times* was critical. 'If not exactly a "bar", all that sounded remarkably like a least a "colour restriction" did it not?' it asked Mecca. 'Mr Heimann thought it would be true to say that, but he posed the problems which could arise otherwise in a hall with 600 white boys and 100 coloured boys without partners. He insisted that he had no objection to coloured people as such. He would take the same step, if need be, with Irish, Scots, or Jews. It was really a question of mixing with strangers. "Man, from the beginning of time, has always been suspicious of strangers."'[137]

The same policy was introduced to Mecca's new Locarno Ballroom in Bradford in 1961 and was condemned by the Methodist Superintendent of the Bradford Mission, Dr Maurice Barnett, as a sign of 'apartheid and racial discrimination'.[138]

In the absence of a stronger lead from government, it is clear that dance hall managers were at the sharp end of often tense race relations at the beginning of the first post-war wave of mass immigration. The experience of prejudice and colour bars in dance halls, however, was leading to increased demands for new legislation

[134] Fairley, *Come Dancing*, 74. [135] *Daily Mail*, 1 July 1958, 3.
[136] Fairley, *Come Dancing*, 76–7. [137] Fairley, *Come Dancing*, 76.
[138] *Daily Mail*, 28 September 1961, 9.

to tackle the problem of discrimination. Following the race riots of 1958 the groundswell of opinion from the immigrant population for new anti-discrimination laws was joined by the Labour Party, who, in September 1958 called for legislation 'making illegal the public practice of discrimination'. Although the Conservative government refused, the tide of public opinion was turning against them. In April 1958 a group of twelve Labour MPs led by Mr Fenner Brockway, proposed a Private Member's Bill to prevent discrimination in public places, which it defined and which included dance halls. The suggested penalties were rather slight—and the Bill aimed to educate rather than punish; however, it did not get a second reading.[139] It wasn't until 1965 that Harold Wilson's Labour government passed the Race Relations Act outlawing racial discrimination in dance halls and other public places. In the meantime, however, the Conservatives, with Labour support, had introduced restrictions on the number of immigrants allowed into the country, with the Commonwealth Immigrants Act of 1962 putting an end to unrestricted entry.

CONCLUSION

Dancing and dance halls are essential to the consideration of race, racism, and racial interaction in twentieth-century Britain. As a cipher of wider debates about racial theory and as a vehicle for the spreading of racial stereotypes, dance performed a significant role in the creation of a language, and attitudes, of racism. Moreover, the dance hall was perhaps the most significant public space for the playing out of this racism, and racial interaction, as Britain became increasingly multi-racial and multi-cultural.

[139] Glass, *Newcomers*, 161.

Chapter 10

The 'Youth Problem' and the Dance Hall, 1918–60

INTRODUCTION

> We are living in an age of excitement and craving for pleasure, when amusements and the gaiety of the evening hours of our big cities and towns wield a powerful influence over boys and girls in their early teens. Some of our so-called amusements—particularly the cheap dancing halls—are not the most desirable centres for them to idle away the nights.[1]

So complained the *Hull Daily Mail* in April 1920 in an early comment that was to be repeated in various forms many times in the following decades. Indeed, dancing and dance halls were instrumental to the perception of a 'youth problem' in Britain throughout the period 1920 to 1960. 'Dance' became convenient shorthand by which to vilify youth and was seen as symptomatic of a lowering of moral and cultural standards amongst young people. This chapter will explore the reaction against dance halls based on an assumed link with gangs, hooliganism, and juvenile delinquency more generally. The widespread involvement of large sections of the young, working-class population in dancing and attendance at dance halls was also seen as problematic because it reflected the emergence of a newly confident and relatively affluent group intent on expressing itself. Thus, dance culture was linked to the emergence of what critics regarded as a selfish, over-indulgent generation 'addicted' to the 'wrong sort' of leisure. As we shall see, however, the impact of 'dance' and the 'problem' of youth were both grossly exaggerated by critics and the media.

DANCING, 'ADDICTION', AND SELF-INDULGENCE

It was in the inter-war period that the concept of a 'dance mad' youth first came to prominence, fuelled by the growth of public dance halls. There can be no doubt that the most ardent fans of dancing were the young of both sexes, and that for the keenest dancers, only the limitations of time and money curtailed their demand for dancing. Rather than seeing such changes in leisure habits as positive, however, the

[1] *Hull Daily Mail*, 6 April 1920, 4.

idea that dancing was a harmful 'addiction', indicative of a lack of self-control, was one that had widespread currency amongst critics. Lady Aimee Scott, for example, writing in the *Sunday Sun* in 1929, claimed that 'dance mad young people' did not know why they danced so much, and that they were being swept along by a consuming force over which they had no control. She claimed:

> thousands of young men and women, working all day and dancing all night . . . had drifted along, not because it was 'life' . . . but because . . . [they] had been led into such a current as long as [they] could remember, and amusement of an excitable kind had lured [them] in a way that [they] had been unable to resist, and which in turn, had reacted upon [their] nervous conditions.[2]

Youth's association with modernity and 'excessive' leisure consumption were part of a growing awareness that they constituted a separate group from the rest of society. In the interwar period, observers from George Orwell to J. B. Priestley and the social surveyors noted the emergence of a new youth, less defined by their class than before, and more willing to spend their money on distinctive leisure pursuits, of which the dance hall was one of the most important. Moreover, this new youth was at the forefront of a supposedly more Americanized, lawless, and promiscuous society. The authorities increasingly went out of their way to find evidence of juvenile delinquency, and they found it. Statistics showed a seemingly alarming increase in youth crime. In Manchester in just four years (1933–6) there was a rise of 162 per cent, from 338 to 885, in the number of crimes involving juveniles. In Liverpool, there was a similar rise, of 103 per cent, from 1,013 to 2,055 juvenile crimes.[3] Such rises prompted woeful predictions about the future prospects for crime, with a more lawless society envisaged as a result of the younger age of criminals. The popular press picked up on the statistics and spread sensational headlines concerning the new lack of respect for the law and authority.

Moreover, as Smithies has noted, the growing materialism and affluence of society, and particularly the young, was seen as part of the cause of this increase in juvenile crime and bad behaviour. Consumerism and commercialized leisure were seen as bad. Thus, repeatedly throughout the 1920s and 1930s, local magistrates declared that there was 'too much dancing' and that it was detrimental for young people, threatening to undermine their work ethic. As a result, many magistrates sought to limit the number of dancing venues in their areas of jurisdiction by refusing to grant licences for new halls. In October 1925, for example, the chairman of the West Hartlepool bench of magistrates argued that dancing was becoming 'too popular', stating that 'there was a strong feeling that this kind of thing was moving too rapidly and that they were becoming surrounded by dancing saloons'.[4] Justices of the Peace were often under pressure from vocal local residents to restrict the provision of dancing facilities in a district and petitions were usually mounted by an energetic, complainant middle class. Often 'public opinion'

2 *Sunday Sun*, 2 June 1929, 3.
3 E. Smithies, *Crime in Wartime* (London: Allen & Unwin, 1982), 171.
4 *Manchester Guardian*, 1 October 1925, 17.

was used to justify the prejudices of those on such licensing committees, who were, however, driven by a moralizing agenda. In 1926, for example, permission for a dance hall in the Sparkbrook area of Birmingham was turned down. The chairman of the Public Entertainments Committee, Samuel E. Short, who was clearly opposed to the extension of commercial pleasure seeking in the city, adjourned an initial discussion of the issue, where there was very little opposition, to allow time for local residents to voice their opposition. Predictably, a vocal middle-class lobby group subsequently opposed the plans and the dance hall was rejected.[5] Magistrates also had the power to determine how long people could dance by setting limits to normal dance hours in any locality and by controlling extensions for late night dancing. Some local magistrates were particularly draconian, and their restrictions often provoked anger in local communities. In Liverpool, at a quarterly meeting of the justices in October 1928, Dr T. Clarke condemned the large number of applications for extensions of hours. The applications, he argued, 'appeared to indicate that the opportunities for recreation were excessive and detrimental to the welfare, not only of those who took the enjoyment, but the general community'. In common with other justices, he was particularly concerned about the impact of late night dancing on the work ethic. He could not see:

> how young people could remain up dancing until one or two a.m. and get home . . . so as to get to bed about three a.m., and then be fit to do their work, mental or physical, on the following day with efficiency. Many of these habitués of dancing halls did not turn up at work the next day; they spent it in bed.[6]

In addition to being seen as a harmful addiction, then, young people's hunger for dancing was condemned because it was the 'wrong sort of leisure'. The idea of leisure as an opportunity to mould 'model' citizens—the concept of rational recreation examined by historians such as Peter Bailey—had first emerged in the nineteenth century with industrialization and urbanization.[7] The rising amounts of leisure time and the commercialization of pleasures seen in the twentieth century threatened to shift the focus of free time away from 'educative' leisure forms towards the mere escapist and trivial. Thus much criticism of dancing was directed at its supposedly puerile nature. In March 1920, for example, the City of Edinburgh Council of Social Service held a public meeting on the matter of recreation, highlighting how the problem of 'unwholesome amusements'—including dance halls—was potentially corrupting young people who sought distraction from their poverty and poor living conditions.[8] Dancing was considered neither beneficial to building good character nor improving health. In 1937, T. F. Coade, headmaster of Bryanston School, at a conference on new ideas in education at Somerville College, Oxford, attacked what he saw as 'neurotic ravings for mere sensation', arguing that there was now 'a generation of escapists—people who seek in football crowds,

[5] *Birmingham Gazette*, 18 January 1927, 7. [6] *Liverpool Echo*, 15 October 1928, 7.
[7] P. Bailey, *Leisure and Class in Victorian England: Rational recreation and the contest for control, 1830–1885* (London: Routledge and Kegan Paul, 1978).
[8] *DET*, 3 March 1920, 9.

cinemas, dance halls, cocktails bars . . . to slake a thirst that cannot be satisfied in that way'.[9]

The idea that dancing was the 'wrong sort of leisure' was also current amongst those who provided clubs and institutions for the young and who were alarmed at a falling off in numbers due to the attraction of dancing. The question of how to respond to this growing 'problem' of youth leisure elicited numerous ideas. Many social welfare groups argued that the 'dance hall menace' had to be met by providing attractive alternatives, emphasizing the need for properly run clubs for young people. The need to compete with dance halls for the attention of youth was widely recognized. In June 1927 the Conference of the National Association of Boys' Clubs, held in Buxton, debated the problem of attracting youths when faced with the competition of new amusements. The conference recognized the powerful appeal of commercialized leisure forms and especially that of dancing. B. Henriques of the St George's Jewish Settlement noted that 'the difficulty was to compete with the noise, excitement and thrill of the dance halls'.[10] Churches and religious figures were also alarmed by the huge popularity of dancing among young people, and the impact it had on church attendance. The Free Church of Scotland warned that the new leisure freedom meant that adolescence 'was never . . . fraught with more danger than at present' but advised against trying to compete with dance halls. Church representatives declared, at a meeting in Edinburgh in 1937, that 'the attempts of some of the denominations to hold their young people by competing with the cinema and dance hall by providing amusement in their own halls for their own youth are not likely to be successful. The sacred and the secular do not harmonise readily, and the Church better adhere to her own function and retain her old and tried methods of administering to the rising generation.'[11] It is clear, then, that commercialized leisure activities, of which the dance hall was one of the most potent symbols, were an important element in the vilification of youth in the interwar period.

During the war, too, similar arguments were made concerning the dance hall's role in the emergence of selfish, over-indulgent young people, addicted to pleasure seeking. Moreover, the dire straits in which the nation found itself added an extra dimension to this criticism of pleasure seeking, which was seen by some as unpatriotic and detrimental to the war effort, as we have seen already in relation to women. Youth was attacked too. As one critic, a female war worker from Huddersfield, put it:

> I have long felt that it is a disgrace to what we call our 'War Effort' that people should fritter their time away dancing night after night . . . Young men and women herded together in a stuffy atmosphere in close proximity to one another, is hardly conducive to the moral well being of the race . . . The spare time of all of us . . . soldiers, sailors, airmen, men and women workers is better spent in healthful sleep or exercise than in flaunting around in these haunts.[12]

[9] *Manchester Guardian*, 4 April 1937, 30.
[10] *Manchester Guardian*, 20 June 1927, 12.
[11] *Manchester Guardian*, 31 March 1937, 10.
[12] *DM*, 20 March 1941, 4.

Such 'decadence' was now regarded as a sign of a dangerous new affluence amongst the young. Now high wages, not unemployment, were seen to be behind delinquency. The Home Office and the Board of Education both regarded high wages for youths as problematic. Other experts did too.[13] 'Raising the wages of adolescents . . . from £3 to £6 a week gave boys far too much money to spend and drunkenness was increasing . . . The wages of these young workers must come down' argued a Southwark Juvenile Court probation officer.[14] Others complained of over-indulgence. Dr H. F. Brisby, the medical officer at Leeds Prison, talking about the link between high wages and juvenile delinquency argued that 'too much money without responsibility or the necessity of learning its value leads in some cases, where self-control is wanting, to a lack of appreciation of property rights and values with regard first to one's own property and then to that of others'.[15]

During the war, the debate about youth leisure became dominated by two other concerns. First, the number of 'positive' leisure and recreation opportunities was reduced as many youth organizations and groups were closed due to the requisitioning of buildings, a lack of supervisory staff, and the dislocation caused by evacuation, bombing, and shortages. This meant that the danger of young people falling into the wrong sorts of leisure was felt to be particularly acute. Second, during the war concern about youth leisure increasingly became focused on the issue of absent parents and its impact. In Liverpool in January 1944 a quarterly meeting of JPs requested that the Ministry of Labour exempt mothers with children under 16 from any compulsory work during times they would be at home 'in the view of the large number of young adolescents suffering from lack of parental guidance'.[16] This parental problem was seen to be behind the perception that the age at which young people went to public dances was getting younger. In Weymouth, for example, in 1943, the attendance of girls under 14 at dances held in the local town hall was condemned as a problem in itself, but also related to the wider issue of 'absent parents' due to war work. Mrs R. L. Sharpe, leader of the local YWCA, told the local press that 'the main problem was that of mothers who were out at work at night and relied on dances and the cinema to keep their children occupied in the evening'.[17]

The combination of fewer alternatives and the absence of strong family networks led to the emergence of two problematic youth types during the war, both associated strongly with dancing. These were so-called 'shelter girls' and 'lounge lizards'. In October 1940, for example, young girls from Liverpool were the focus of media concern. It was claimed that gangs of girls were spending their nights with undesirable men in public air raid shelters, causing a new problem for local authorities and social workers where they spent nights 'dancing, singing and keeping awake those who have come to sleep'.[18] Similar complaints were made

13 Smithies, *Crime*, 177.
14 *Police Chronicle and Constabulary World*, 4 April 1941 cited in Smithies, *Crime*, 177.
15 *The Police Review*, 30 April 1943 cited in Smithies, *Crime*, 177–8.
16 LRO, 347 MAG 1/1/18, 'Minutes 1940–64', Quarterly Meeting, 28 January 1944.
17 *Western Gazette*, 2 April 1943, 5.
18 *DM*, 28 October 1940, 3.

about dancing youths living it up in Birmingham's public air raid shelters. In 1943, alarm about delinquent girls spread to Bath too. The city had become a popular recreation haunt for the many American troops stationed in the area and the inevitable excesses of some Americans, and some locals, caused concern. Local 'morality' pressure groups lobbied the City Council for action. The local press followed up these stories too, blaming too much money: 'wartime conditions... were having [an] appalling effect... on some girls in all parts of the country... children of school age were becoming utterly spoilt... Too much money and many soldiers with money to fling about were... factors leading to their downfall.' 'Some were undoubtedly suffering from sexual mania... The trouble was they could get any job they wanted at more money than the job was worth.'[19]

'Lounge lizards' were another focus of media attention. These were young people so called because of the time they spent lounging around in bars, dance halls, and other places of entertainment. For example, teenage boys and girls were banned from dancing at the Willsden Co-operative Youth Club in 1945, the club leader calling their behaviour whilst dancing an 'unwholesome influence over the younger members'. He went on: 'These young lounge lizards, around 17 and 18 years, have not had good home supervision, owing to the war. Boys are the worst offenders. They are usually the ones at a loose end—but they don't come to learn dancing.'[20] Others saw dancing itself as the reason for moral concern, again making a connection with sex. When the Methodist Church Conference voted to allow young people to dance on church premises in Birmingham in 1943, there were some who complained. Lord Rochester claimed that 'dancing has been known to lead to impurity of thought, desire and practice' and that he wished to fight against such impurities. He went on: 'There are few forms of pleasure in modern society which make that battle more difficult than dancing. This is not a time to lower our standard when there is such a collapse of the sex standards of our country.'[21]

The return to peacetime conditions did not end criticism of young people dancing either. After the Second World War, long established prejudices against the impact of dancing on young people were thus given new currency as Britain entered an era of unprecedented prosperity. In this period, the concept of an over-indulgent, selfish young population became even more widespread than before. Indeed, concerns about the 'age of affluence' became increasingly concentrated on the behaviour of young people, and dancing was central to images of decadence. In the popular imagination, spurred on by the press, a newly affluent generation of young people was represented as 'living it up' to an extent that was 'unhealthy'.

One of the first post-war debates about juvenile delinquency came in the House of Commons in November 1945, just months after the end of the war. It picked up on all of the major concerns about youth culture prevalent at the time. During the debate, dance halls were listed amongst the many causes of juvenile delinquency. Labour MP for Stretford Herschel Lewis Austin blamed poverty and lack of parental control. Yet he also saw relative affluence amongst youth as a factor,

[19] *Bath Weekly Chronicle and Herald*, 27 March 1943 cited in Smithies, *Crime*, 183.
[20] *DM*, 15 December 1945, 3. [21] *DM*, 13 November 1943, 4.

blaming 'abnormally high wages, which gave young people an overrated opinion of themselves'. Commercialized, Americanized culture, and readily available entertainments such as the cinema and dance halls, were, according to Austin, creating a generation whose moral outlook was warped:

> We have seen the development of a cheap, shallow, superficial outlook in our young people. What I see today is the Piccadilly Circus spirit, allied with the honky-tonk of the saloons of America. Almost every parent to whom I have spoken has expressed concern about the decadence of our young people.[22]

He therefore proposed a minimum age of eighteen for attendance at public dances, in line with policy regarding entrance to public houses, claiming that 'public dance halls, particularly during war-time, had a bad effect on young people'. Similarly, in 1951 a report commissioned by the British Medical Association and the Magistrates' Association into the problem of the 'adolescent delinquent boy' saw dancing as a 'malinfluence' on teenagers. Pointing to a multitude of causes, notably bad parenting and broken homes, the report also laid blame on 'a craving for light and colour and amusement and a desire to be "one of the boys" that leads to the dance hall, the slot machine alley or the cinema'.[23]

They were not alone; other contemporary commentators in all fields remarked on what was thought to be the materialization of a new consumer culture, largely targeted towards the affluent teenage market during the 1950s. Famously, the connection between post-war youth and affluence was made in Mark Abrams' 1959 *The Teenage Consumer* which examined youth spending patterns during the late 1950s, calculating a 50 per cent rise in overall earnings. He discovered male teenagers made an average of £8 a week, females made an average of £6, while their collective yearly spending was around £830 million, establishing the notion of unprecedentedly affluent teenagers.[24] Despite its limitations (it did not take into account regional differences or compare such figures with pre-war ones), Abrams' study cemented the notion of a newly rich young generation confirmed by official figures which showed that the average real wage earning of teenagers rose at twice the adult rate between 1945 and 1950. The difference between the new generation and the older one, brought up in the hardships of the depression and war, was striking. Bryan Reed, in his advice book for teenagers, *For Teenagers Only* (1958) criticized the waste and selfishness of the new young generation: 'young people never had more money or leisure than they have today, and . . . on the whole they don't know what to do with it . . . there are far too many young people today whose lives are pretty empty and dull and purposeless . . . They don't know how to use their leisure time.'[25]

In addition to the newly heightened concern that dancing was indicative of over-indulgence, the long established claim that it was the 'wrong sort' of leisure

[22] *Manchester Guardian*, 3 November 1945, 3. [23] *Daily Mail*, 1 June 1951, 2.

[24] Cited in B. Osgerby, 'From the Roaring Twenties to the Swinging Sixties: Continuity and change in youth culture, 1929–59', in B. Brivati and H. Jones (eds), *What Difference Did the War Make?* (Leicester: Leicester University Press, 1993), 82–3.

[25] B. H. Reed, *For Teenagers Only* (London: Epworth Press, 1958), 15.

persisted. Thus, in 1946 a local government report condemned the effect of dancing on teenagers, seeing it as harmful. 'Some dances, and dancers, seem to overemphasise the sexual aspects of dancing,' it argued. 'On the physical side there is the question of vitiated atmosphere, late hours and undue excitement. On the moral side there is the question of boys and girls, and particularly girls, making chance acquaintances who may be of doubtful character.'[26] Fearful of its negative influence, attempts were made to stop the very young from dancing by concerned groups. In Nottingham in January 1957, for example, local education authorities, councillors, magistrates, and police had to take action to stop about 400 children aged 9 to 16 from local school who were absconding during their lunch hour to take rock 'n' roll classes at the palais de danse. The headmaster of the Becket Roman Catholic School complained that the dancing sessions were not compatible with the 'atmosphere of culture we set before our boys'.[27]

As before the war, dancing was also condemned because it was taking young people away from youth clubs and organized leisure. In July 1949 the King George's Jubilee Trust commissioned universities to investigate why youth club membership was so dramatically low in a survey that covered the whole of Britain. It declared that '[t]he scream of the "hot" trumpeter in the dance hall, and the super-charged "love interest" in American films is proving a big counter-attraction to the clubs'.[28]

DANCE, YOUTH VIOLENCE, AND HOOLIGANISM

Of more concern to most than youth's selfishness was an apparent predilection for violence and hooliganism. Dancing and dance halls were central to the discussion of such misbehaviour. Indeed, dancing soon became a symbol of a young generation 'gone astray'. Thus, during the 1920s, dancing and the dance hall became convenient scapegoats amongst police, magistrates, and others. A young criminal's predilection for dancing was frequently highlighted as one of the reasons for a descent into criminality and as an indication of poor character. For example, when talking of the 'evils of dancing' in 1928, Herbert Smith, President of the Miners' Federation, and president of the bench of magistrates in Barnsley told a 'gang' of young colliery workers accused of theft that '[a]s one who has felt the necessity for education I advise you to forsake your dancing classes for evening schools'. The mother of one of the accused also blamed dance halls for their going astray. 'What goes on at these halls,' she argued, 'is disgraceful.'[29] As we have already seen in relation to women, young offenders were often barred from dance halls as part of their sentencing. In May 1927, for example, Sheffield probation officers banned young probationers from visiting cinemas and dance halls, seeing them as central to the cause of delinquency.[30]

[26] *DM*, 15 October 1946, 2. [27] *Daily Mail*, 24 January 1957, 5.
[28] *DM*, 30 July 1949, 9. [29] *Manchester Guardian*, 6 April 1928, 11.
[30] *Manchester Guardian*, 2 May 1927, 6.

How true were these accusations? Certainly dance halls were the venue for the gathering of youth 'gangs', and often led to territorial disputes of a violent nature. A city with a particularly bad reputation for violent gang culture in the early part of the twentieth century was Glasgow.[31] As early as 1916, the *Manchester Guardian* reported concerns about 'numerous wild gangs', containing both young men and young women, who had become 'the night terror of Glasgow'. Dance halls were often central to the reporting of this 'social problem' as they were one of the main public gathering points for such gangs. For example, following an argument in a 'low dance hall' in Glasgow in October that year, a young woman known as 'the Queen of the Redskins' stabbed another female gang member fourteen times, and the police were 'severely handled' before being able to make an arrest.[32] Razor gangs were a problem that beset Glasgow throughout the 1920s and 1930s and violent attacks in dance halls involving razors were a fairly frequent occurrence. In November 1921, for example, there was a disturbance at a dance hall in the north of Glasgow, where razors were produced. One man was cut about the head and face, the other in the neck.[33] In August 1923, a dance hall commissionaire was slashed under the armpit with a razor by two youths who had been refused entry by him the previous night.[34] Gang violence in dance halls was not confined to Glasgow, however. In Hamilton, four men, members of a young 'hooligan gang' in Blantyre known as the 'Glad Eyes' were sentenced in 1926 after a fight broke out a dance in the Co-op Hall there. One of the gang attacked the crowd of dancers with a bottle, injuring three dancers.[35] Outside Scotland, there is plenty of evidence of violent gang behaviour in dance halls too. In April 1922, for example, a man was stabbed by two members of a gang in one of London's West End dance halls.[36] That some dance halls attracted 'toughs' is therefore without doubt.

Another contemporary concern that linked dance halls with 'problematic' youthful behaviour was the less violent but similarly serious problem of 'rowdiness' and 'hooliganism'. Dance halls were seen as a particularly troublesome part of this problem due to their late closing hours. For example, in 1925 in Cumberland, the Chief Constable, Eric Spence, and the Carlisle Diocesan Conference both discussed the question of dancing and its relation to the moral life of young people. The Chief Constable publically protested against the disorder associated with dancing. He pointed out that when dances finished, sometimes at 2 and 3 am, the young dancers often assembled outside and continued their merriment, with 'crowds of girls and boys trooping through the streets in a noisy fashion' causing annoyance as 'hard working citizens are deprived of their sleep'. The Chief Constable threatened that unless this type of disorder ceased, licences for extended dancing hours would be opposed by the police in an attempt to 'end the hooliganism that has become so rampant'.[37] Similar situations were repeated throughout Britain. In Warrington in

[31] A. Davies, *City of Gangs: Glasgow and the Rise of the British Gangster* (London: Hodder & Stoughton, 2013).

[32] *Manchester Guardian*, 28 October 1916, 8.

[33] *Glasgow Herald*, 17 December 1921, 12.

[34] *Sunday Sun*, 19 August 1923, 3.

[35] *Glasgow Evening Times*, 11 January 1926, 1.

[36] *Manchester Guardian*, 18 April 1922, 10.

[37] *Sunday Sun*, 1 November 1925, 3.

1926, there were complaints from residents about 'unruly conduct in the early hours of young people when they are leaving Warrington's dance halls'.[38] The same year Bootle's deputy town clerk told police that more than 3,000 lamps, 2,000 mantles, and 250 glass globes had been damaged that year 'due mainly to the actions of young madcaps returning from Dances'.[39] It was not only in urban areas that such things occurred either. In 1931, dances in the Cumberland village of Borrowdale were condemned because of the rowdiness they caused, with young farm labourers frequently brought before courts in Keswick for disorderliness. The chairman of the bench Anthony Spedding complained: 'It was a great disgrace to the village and to those who ran the dances.'[40]

What happened to youth violence in dance halls during the war? In many ways it is hard to tell with accuracy as the press often avoided printing details of incidents for fear of upsetting the war effort. Certainly, the perception of a wartime rise in crime was widespread. Even before war broke out it was anticipated that its disruption would see juvenile delinquency rates rocketing, and in the early years of the conflict this happened. The numbers of juveniles found guilty in magistrates' courts in England and Wales rose between 1939 and 1941, amongst under-17s rising from 52,814 in 1939 to 72,105, an increase of 36.5 per cent. For those aged 17 to 21 there was a rise from 58,902 to 69,096, an increase of 17.3 per cent.[41]

Just why this rise occurred was a central concern, and dance halls were often cited as part of the problem. As we have seen, during the war, the association between dance halls and violence was exacerbated by racial tensions and there were a large number of violent incidents, even deaths, involving black and white, British and foreign servicemen and civilians. There were also other violent incidents involving only young native Britons too. In Hull in 1942 for example, a 19-year-old 'gang member' was fined £1 for assaulting the owner of the Danse de-Luxe dance hall in the city and a further £2 for assaulting a special police sergeant during the same incident. The youth had been ejected from the dance hall on several occasions for disorderly conduct and took his revenge by bringing a gang of youths to force entrance to the hall. He succeeded in entering, then assaulted the dance hall owner with a chair. Later the youth, together with ten other youths and four girls, assaulted the police sergeant, dragging him to his knees then punching him several times.[42] Similarly, in Mansfield police complained that they were having 'continual trouble' with people leaving a dance hall at Underwood, and that an officer had to be sent there on Saturday nights to keep order. In May 1940 three youths were fined for causing an obstruction and being drunk and disorderly outside the dance hall.[43] It is surprising that there were not more gangs, as on the outbreak of the war, the government had decided to release all borstal boys who had served not less than six months of their sentence. In all, 2,817 boys were freed. Many were reconvicted in a short space of time. By September 1946, 50 per cent of those discharged in

[38] *Liverpool Echo*, 5 February 1926, 4. [39] *Liverpool Echo*, 16 February 1926, 5.

[40] *Manchester Guardian*, 22 August 1931, 16.

[41] NA, HO 45/20250 cited in Smithies, *Crime*, 176.

[42] *Hull Daily Mail*, 23 January 1942, 1. [43] *Nottingham Evening Post*, 16 May 1940, 1.

1939 had been reconvicted, while 56 per cent of girls were back inside by December 1943.[44]

After 1945 dancing and dance halls became even more closely associated with the 'problem of youth' as concern about juvenile delinquency reached new heights. Fears were widespread of a youth crime epidemic, caused in part by the disruption to normal family life brought about by the war. Crime statistics seemed to support and promote people's fears; in 1955 the number of offences involving young people under the age of 21 was 24,000; however, by 1959 this had risen to 45,000.[45] Leslie Wilkin's findings for the Home Office were published in 1960's *Delinquent Generations*, in which he asserted that children born between 1935 and 1942 were more susceptible to crime, and like Hoggart, he implicated youth attire as contributing to the supposed crime surge.[46] T. R. Fyvel's 1963 *The Insecure Offenders* also declared that the apparent post-war 'crime wave' was a delayed manifestation of wartime trauma, indicating that absent or dead fathers or working mothers all contributed to the collapse of the socialization process.[47] In November 1945 the Church of England Commission on Youth also highlighted what it considered to be a new 'youth problem'. One of Britain's worst problems, it argued, was the 'race of young hooligans which has arisen during the war—street corner toughs, more animal than human, haunting the little streets of our cities and towns'. It argued that these youths were mostly from unhappy homes, and that they drifted from job to job, working spasmodically, and treating employers and foremen with rudeness and contempt.[48]

Most discussions of juvenile delinquency and youth culture in the post-war period start with the Teddy Boys and the so-called 'Rock 'n' Roll' riots of 1956. Dance was central to both of these youth problems. Let's start with the 'violent' reaction to the screening of the American film 'Rock around the Clock' in 1956. Here both the film and the violence associated with its screening were driven by dancing. The film itself was concerned with dance music and dance styles, its central narrative being that dance music had become old fashioned and 'sluggish'. The film then charted the arrival of a new, exciting music—'rock 'n' roll'—and its spread from a wayside local dance hall across the whole of America. It particularly pitted the young against the older generation and revelled in the new cultural phenomenon. Its focus on dance was picked up by contemporary reviewers. *The Times* review of the film, for example, drew attention to the 'freakishness' of its dancing: 'with odd contortions and odder noises the film extols the virtues of "rock 'n' roll" and mirrors American youth finding fulfilment in what seems to be a mingling of primitive dance and ritual.'[49] More central to reinforcing the link between dancing and violence, the reaction to the film, dubbed as a series of riots, created national headlines and national debate. Using well-rehearsed arguments, links were made between youth, dance, and uncontrolled behaviour. In 1956, the *Daily Mail* reporting on 'riots' that had broken out in London and Manchester

[44] H. D. Wilcock, *Report on Juvenile Delinquency* (1949), 129 cited in Smithies, *Crime*, 179.
[45] P. Lewis, *The Fifties* (London: Heinemann, 1978), 118. [46] Osgerby, 'From', 81.
[47] Ibid. [48] *Daily Mail*, 10 November 1945, 3. [49] *The Times*, 15 September 1956, 4.

following screenings of 'Rock around the Clock' claimed that 'the rhythm drunk teenagers jammed the roads by throwing fireworks and jiving in the city centre's main streets'.[50] *The Times* also drew links between dancing and uncontrolled behaviour, reporting on how gangs of about 1,000 youngsters had 'Jived' through the streets of Manchester and Bootle, halting traffic, after seeing the film.[51] Similar scenes were reported in Birmingham, Belfast, Bristol, Liverpool, Carlisle, Bradford, Blackburn, Preston, Blackpool, Bootle, Brighton, Gateshead, and South Shields.[52]

These 1956 riots brought an even closer focus on the Teddy Boy, the quintessential symbol of post-war youth culture. The Teddy Boy emerged as a folk devil during the 1950s, and was closely associated with dancing and dance halls. That some Teddy Boys were violent is without doubt, and much of this violence originated or took place in dance halls. In 1954, for example, a series of incidents in dance halls in south-east London led to Teddy Boys being banned from entering dance places. One dance hall had been invaded by more than thirty youths, six of whom attacked one of the dancers, knocking him unconscious and hurting several others.[53] The following year rival gangs of Teddy Boys fought in the Streatham Locarno, with the police being called and several youths and the box officer manager badly injured.[54] In Bath, magistrates put a 9 pm curfew on three Teddy Boys responsible for a disturbance at the Pavilion dance hall, as well as jailing another for assault and a further ten were fined.[55] Numerous examples can be found of 'Teddy Boy violence' in dance halls throughout the rest of the decade. Yet, the Teddy Boys were not the only link that dance halls had with youth culture and violence in post-war Britain. In 1956 under the headline 'Dance Hall Thugs' the *Daily Mirror* asked whether public dances had become 'impossible' because of the presence of youth 'bottle and razor gangs' causing trouble there. It pointed out that most dance halls had to employ 'strong arm staff' to quell 'hooliganism'. Claiming that 'rowdysim to music' was 'rampant' it gave evidence of youth disorder in dance halls throughout the country. At Camden Town, a 17-year-old boy was beaten up after his girlfriend refused to dance with a gang of louts. In Halifax a policeman received a broken nose when quelling a dance floor brawl. In Streatham, police were called to a dance hall four times in one evening to deal with youth fights. At Bradford three teenage girls were knifed in a battle outside one of the town's ballrooms. Band leader Teddy Foster, thirty years in the business, claimed that the problem was reaching new heights: 'this hooliganism is at its worst ever. Once, at Liverpool, I counted eighteen fights in ten minutes. It was like a battlefield. These toughs swagger into the dance halls like cowboys entering a Wild West saloon.' Another bandleader, Ralph Davies, refused to play at public dances because of the violence: 'I refuse to provide music for ballroom brawls', he explained.[56]

Afraid of the impact of this violence on their business, dance halls adopted new strategies to try to stamp it out. At Mecca, for example, during the 1950s Heimann and Fairley introduced a number of house rules designed to eliminate troublemakers.

[50] *Daily Mail*, 10 September 1956, 5. [51] *The Times*, 11 September 1956, 8. [52] Ibid.
[53] *Daily Mail*, 27 April 1954, 5. [54] *Daily Mail*, 4 February 1955, 5.
[55] *Daily Mail*, 31 May 1951, 3. [56] *DM*, 27 January 1956, 9.

Mecca policy was to bar all of those involved in disputes, regardless of who was responsible for causing the problem. In London's Lyceum on the Strand, for example, rival gangs from nearby Elephant and Castle would cause considerable disorder. Mecca put a blanket ban on any of them entering the hall. The partners also took time out to talk individually to persistent troublemakers, if asked to by their managers. This tactic often worked, with tough gang members respecting such straight talking and mutual respect developing between both parties. Mecca also found that women were often better at diffusing tensions than men. Rather than sending in the 'heavies' Mecca adopted a policy of using usherettes to talk with troublemakers and 'hostesses' to keep order. These new hostesses were not the dancing partners of old, but older, married women employed as MCs—dressed in beautiful evening gowns they patrolled the dance halls on the look out for trouble yet appearing non-threatening.[57]

As we have seen, before the war most dance hall owners had privately resented the restrictions imposed on their business by magistrates, police, and courts, yet in the post-war period they turned to those groups in an attempt to control the problem. Now, they argued, not enough was being done by legal authorities to solve the problem, and they pressed for a higher level of intervention. Some examples from Scotland highlight this. In 1954 the North British Ballrooms Association (NBBA), the trade organization of commercial ballrooms in the north, south, and east of Scotland, headed by Mecca's Alan Fairley, had worked with Edinburgh magistrates in order to try to overcome disorder in the halls. There was some disagreement on how to solve the issue. Edinburgh magistrates thought that overcrowding was a major cause of trouble and considered the imposition of a limit to the numbers who could be admitted to dance halls. In addition they wanted to make it a condition of licence holders that there was no admittance after 10 pm on Saturday nights. The NBBA were consulted by the Edinburgh magistrates and it in turn consulted with proprietors in the city to ask for their opinion. Whilst agreeing to a limit on the numbers who could enter halls they strongly opposed the suggestion of a 10 pm Saturday night entrance bar. Instead they suggested that police be given the powers to enter dance halls at any time they wanted, and to deal with troublemakers in the same way as in pubs. The magistrates rejected these suggestions. In December 1959 the North British Ballrooms Association decided again to appeal for greater intervention, this time from a higher authority, the Secretary of State for Scotland. In particular they drew attention to the nuisance caused by gangs of Teddy Boys and the impact that it was having on their business. The NBBA criticized the inadequacy of sentences imposed on offenders by the magistrates. Sentences were often very lenient. In Aberdeenshire, in October 1958, for example, three youths on being refused admission to a dance hall in Strichen assaulted the girl in the pay box; two of them were fined £2 each and the third, who had a previous conviction, £3. Similarly, a man who had hit an

[57] R. Fairley, *Come Dancing Miss World* (London: Neamme, 1966), 88.

attendant with a chair, causing the loss of an eye, was sentenced to only twenty-eight days. Norman Duncan, Secretary of the NBBA protested:

> We feel that as responsible business people with well organised businesses providing a service which is enjoyed by many people, both young and old we are entitled to the necessary protection from the authorities . . . The attitude of the magistrates . . . is discouraging not only to the ballroom proprietors . . . but also to the constable on whose assistance he has to depend.[58]

Duncan demanded that the 'minimum sentence' for a disturbance should be considerably increased and that there be a shift in responsibility for prosecuting offenders, moving from the burgh courts to the sheriff's courts. Whilst the Secretary of State was sympathetic to the dance hall owners, he turned down their requests, believing that the courts were the best judges of what penalties should be set. More trouble occurred the following year in Scotland when an Edinburgh baillie found two Aberdeen youths not guilty of breach of the peace in the Palais de Danse, Fountainbridge, after they assaulted an attendant, blaming instead the bouncers. 'It is my impression,' he argued, 'that dance hall bouncers tend to precipitate trouble and create provocation. I would like to see them conduct themselves with more restraint.'[59] This elicited another appeal from the NBBA to Niall Macpherson, Parliamentary Under Secretary to the Secretary of State for Scotland, who argued that this action gave the impression to troublemakers that they could do as they wished. The protest also argued that managements were now no longer able to retain experienced members of their staff who have left 'because they fear they cannot expect the judicial support necessary if their efforts to maintain good order in dance halls are to be of any avail'.[60] Their requests for harsher punishments were turned down, however.

DEFENDING YOUTH DANCING

Yet, not everyone was convinced that dancing was bad for young people. Ranged against the numerous groups who saw a link between juvenile delinquency and dancing were others who considered it to have positive effects amongst the young. Some saw links between the decline in drinking and new leisure habits. In 1928, for example, arrests for drunkenness in Manchester and Salford had dropped substantially and were at their lowest level since 1919. The *Manchester Guardian* attributed this to the rise of the dance hall and other leisure activities involving a mixing of the sexes:

> The days when the swing doors of the public house were the easiest exit from a pent and arduous life in an industrial city are passing. The crystal set, the dance hall, the

[58] NAS: DD5/984, letter, N. Duncan to N. Macpherson, MP, Parliamentary Under Secretary of State for Scotland, December 1959, 3.
[59] *Edinburgh Dispatch*, 5 August 1960.
[60] NAS: DD5/984, letter NBBA to N. Macpherson, 12 August 1960.

movies, and the motor coach provide more attractive variants on the humdrum life than ever did the public house. Moreover, the growing partnership of women in all popular activities plays its part. A generation that dances the year in nimbly has little patience with the fuddled footsteps that welcomed in the past. We grow more sober though not less gay.[61]

Also, not everyone was convinced that the young people of the day were 'wicked' or self-indulgent. In 1921, writing in Newcastle's scandal rag, the *Sunday Sun*, J. H. Varwell attacked the critics of modern youth as Victorian 'fuddy duddies' who were following in a long line of people who had claimed that Britain was 'going to the dogs'. He wrote:

> The fact is that there is nothing in all this incessant talk about the decadence of the younger generations. That has been the favourite maxim of all the sour old fogeys since the Flood . . . The veterans censure in the youngsters those qualities they no longer possess themselves . . . Some folks are so constituted that all change is abhorrent to them.[62]

There was even official support for dancing amongst young people, with several studies concluding that it was good for health, physical and mental. In 1933, for example, in his annual report on the Schools Medical Service, Sir George Newman, Chief Medical Officer of the Board of Education, advocated that dancing be encouraged in schools, seeing it as a vital form of physical education. Moreover, he considered that well conducted dancing was a model form of recreation that had considerable benefits. He argued: 'With the introduction of the shorter working hours, there will be a big compulsory increase in leisure. Dancing will do much to teach the present younger generation how to utilise this leisure to the best advantage.'[63] Generational conflict was not the only outcome of young people dancing, either. In fact, some young people were actively encouraged by their parents to dance. For example, a Glasgow teenage girl dancing in the 1930s recalls that her mother encouraged her to go dancing: 'I had freedom to go where I wanted and I had lots of friends to visit . . . I was keen on dancing or at least my mother was. I don't know why she encouraged me to go . . . My mother was very keen on dancing.'[64]

If dancing was seen by some as positive for youth, we should also remember that the extent to which there was a rise in juvenile delinquency might have been exaggerated. In the interwar period, the rise in juvenile crime statistics was in part due to the impact of changes in the law brought about by the Children and Young Person Act of 1933, which raised the minimum age of criminal responsibility from seven to eight years, and extended the jurisdiction of the juvenile court to young persons up to the age of seventeen.[65] As a result, delinquents who might in the past have been dealt with in a more informal manner by the police were now being brought before the court. As an Assistant Secretary at the Home Office

61 *Manchester Guardian*, 2 January 1929, 8. 62 *Sunday Sun*, 26 June 1921, 4.
63 *DM*, 3 December 1934, 5. 64 GDHI, Rae Birch b. 1922, 8 August 2011.
65 Smithies, *Crime*, 171.

remarked: 'Experience shows . . . that each time a new statute relating to the young has been put into effect, the immediate result is an apparent rise in the number of offences. This "rise" is not due to any "wave" of crime among juveniles, but to a desire on the part of those concerned with putting the law into motion.' He summed up that there was 'no justification for jeremiads about a decay in the moral fibre of the young'.[66]

The importance of dancing to young people, and its positive potential, were also recognized by some during the war. Increasingly during the war, dancing, 'properly organized', came to be seen by some as a solution to youth problems, not a cause of them. In May 1941, for example, the *Daily Mirror* reported on an experiment in a Surrey country village to 'civilize' youths from London's docklands by the use of dancing. Two hundred and fifty youths from East Ham had been evacuated to a Surrey school camp, where the headmaster, William Skipsey, taught them ballroom dancing. 'It is teaching the boys not to be rough with the girls and rationalised the children's attitudes towards sex,' he argued. 'Ballroom dancing has solved many problems. The children are not longer shy, and it has taught the boys to be gallant.'[67] In the spirit of the post-war reconstruction debate so prevalent during the war, questions were asked about what provision should be made for Britain's youth, and again, dancing was recognized to be of vital importance to their well-being. In 1944, for example, following up on its earlier blueprints for a welfare state in Britain, beneath a half page photograph of youths dancing in a Rotherhithe Youth Club, *Picture Post* asked: 'Are We Planning a New Deal For Youth?' It advocated the creation of state-sponsored youth centres where the young could spend their leisure hours, meet friends, and get rest and recreation. Such ideas were already coming to fruition during the war itself. Dancing was seen as central to the attraction of youth clubs. Building on experiments begun in 1942, there had been a rise of interest in youth clubs and by 1944 over 50 per cent of those aged 14 to 18 belonged to some youth or educational organization.[68] Thus, in some quarters complaints about the influence of dancing on the young were more nuanced, with commercial dance halls, and not dancing per se, seen as potentially dangerous.

Moreover, there is convincing evidence that the idea of a wartime 'youth problem' had been exaggerated. Most of the wartime juvenile crime was actually very trivial in nature. The Chief Constable of Plymouth, for example, stressed that much of it arose from 'a propensity for mischief and adventure' rather than anything more serious.[69] The Commissioner of the Metropolitan Police also insisted that 'adventure hunting' and 'mischief' rather than 'crime in the ordinary sense' lay behind most juvenile offences.[70] During later stages of the war, general levels of crime soared. However, juvenile crime actually fell at this point, thus undermining the more gloomy predictions about a new generation of criminals made earlier on. In England and Wales the number of persons found guilty fell by

66 *The Police Review*, 2 April 1937 cited in Smithies, *Crime*, 172.
67 *DM*, 3 May 1941, 3.
68 *PP*, 2 January 1944, 15.
69 *Police Chronicle and Constabulary World*, 4 April 1937 cited in Smithies, *Crime*, 178.
70 *Reports of the Commission of the Police of the Metropolis*, 1936, 23–4 cited in Smithies, *Crime*, 178.

32.3 per cent for those aged 17–21 between 1941 and 1944, and by 6.2 per cent for those under 17.[71] The reduction in the number of offenders between the ages of 17 and 21 was no doubt related to war service. But the decline of those under the age of 17 is noteworthy. In part this can be put down to the change in approach of the police after 1941. Such was the pressure on resources both of police time and the time of the courts that a fresh policy was essential. Increasingly, police forces began to issue cautions wherever possible, in order to keep children out of the courts.[72]

Following the war, ideas concerning the positive impact of dancing on young people gained even more currency, as the new Britain of the welfare state, dedicated to eradicating problems such as juvenile delinquency, put some of the more progressive wartime attitudes into practice. Dancing was part of the curriculum for boys at a Home Office approved school at Hayton, Cumberland, for example. Here dance classes were given and the six best dancers were allowed to go to dances in the village hall once a week. Dancing was used to re-socialize the boys, allow them to interact with girls, and to enforce discipline.[73] By 1955 the King's Jubilee Trust was siding with dance halls too. In its 'Citizens of Tomorrow' it investigated the influences on youths aged 15 to 18, between school and National Service. It saw such years as 'lost years', encouraging boys to look for a 'good time' and disruptive to their progress. However, the report stated: 'The well conducted dance hall or soft drink bar is a far better place for young people to spend their time in than the streets.'[74]

Dancing, when properly conducted and organized, was thus encouraged as part of the growing provision of youth clubs and other facilities for young people. In the new town of Crawley, for example, considerable effort was spent developing facilities for the young of the town. A series of ex-Army Nissen huts were turned over to the young of the town, and they used them for a variety of sports and recreational facilities, including dancing. The Old Tyme Dance Club made use of large, well-heated hut with a stage and dressing rooms, holding dances on a regular basis and organizing social dances for other youth groups in Crawley and the surrounding area. Such facilities were seen to have transformed the town's young people.[75] By the later part of the period, 'official' dance provision for youth could be very elaborate indeed. In 1963, for example, Bristol city authorities built youth centres with dancing facilities and coffee bars and the Ministry of Education used the city's example as a model for other local authorities to follow.[76] The following year Stevenage invested £137,000 in its youth centre, the largest in Britain, simultaneously offering dancing, roller skating, boxing, and a theatre.[77]

It is also clear that not everyone saw youth's predilection for dancing as negative. For example, defending dancing against criticisms, the *Daily Mirror* in 1946 highlighted that 'advocates of dancing . . . say that swing music and dancing are

[71] PRO, HO 45/20250 cited in Smithies, *Crime*, 180. [72] Smithies, *Crime*, 180–3.
[73] *DM*, 7 September 1946, 4. [74] *DM*, 21 October 1955, 9.
[75] *The Times*, 18 February 1961, 9. [76] *The Times*, 22 August 1963, 10.
[77] *The Times*, 7 February 1964, 9.

driving immorality, rowdysim and juvenile crime from the streets. Tee-totallers point out that most of the halls are unlicensed, and that dancing keep young people away from public-houses. Perhaps the best argument of all comes from some of the young jitterbugs themselves. "Dancing," they say, "gives us a healthy escape from the slummy districts and drab houses where we are forced to live." '[78] As part of its editorial policy to side with youth, the *Daily Mirror* in an editorial of 1954 'Lay off the Youngsters!' argued: 'Maybe the dodderers can't be expected to turn to jive for inspiration or enjoyment. They would not know how to handle a "coolcat" if they met one. But better a coolcat than a sourpuss any day . . . Shivering shimmies, let the kids have a go! They are better off jiving in a dance hall than rotting in the streets.'[79]

A more balanced view of Teddy Boys was also taken by many. Hilde Marchant was particulalry positive about Teddy Boys and dance halls: 'it seemed to me, after several visits to this dance hall, and watching these young men at their daily work, there was little to criticise—a touch of vanity, perhaps, a gesture of exhibitionism, a release from the methodical, rather dull routine of earning a living. But harm and violence did not seem to be among them.'[80] Likewise, the mere existence of 'gangs' did not necessarily mean trouble; as one expert, psychiatrist Dr Peter Scott, explained in 1956, not all young people in gangs were delinquents. Dr Scott, who was addressing school medical officers at a meeting arranged by the Society of Medical Officers of Health, argued that it would be a great mistake to assume that all gangs were bad. His study of juvenile gangs in London, he said, had shown had they ranged and varied between the anti-social and the completely innocent. Most Teddy Boys, he argued, were simply seeking security, whilst trying to gain independence from parental control. Only a small percentage of those he had questioned were anti-social.[81] Similarly, Logan and Goldberg in their 1953 'Rising Eighteen' study of the life and health of young men identified 'the adolescent gang stage' when 'all their activities were restricted to certain small groups of youths whether in the Club, at the milk bar, watching in the dance hall, hanging around the street, or on cycling jaunts to the country' as normal and largely harmless.[82] Teddy Boys were also defended by the *Daily Mirror* along class lines. Their hard work and affluence were things to celebrate, the newspaper argued. Talking of Teds in a London dance hall Peggy Briggs wrote: 'These lads are labourers, factory workers, lorry drivers and mechanics. They all do an honest day's work. If, in their leisure hours, they try to capture just a spark of past splendour do you blame them for it?' She went on 'Besides, if a working lad has provided himself with an expensive velvet trimmed suit, a brocade waistcoat, a narrow tie, fob chain and hairstyle in keeping with his clothes, he will live up to them.'[83]

[78] *DM*, 15 October 1946, 2. [79] *DM*, 26 March 1954, 2. [80] *PP*, 29 May 1954, 25.

[81] *Manchester Guardian*, 21 April 1956, 4.

[82] R. F. Logan and E. M. Goldberg, 'Rising Eighteen in a London Suburb: A Study of Some Aspects of the Life and Health of Young Men' (1953) 4(2) (December) *The British Journal of Sociology* 323–45.

[83] *DM*, 17 April 1954, 7.

We should also consider the extent to which the scale of the problem was exaggerated too. We can get a better idea of the scale of the problem of youth violence and disorder in dance halls from a police survey of the number of dance hall offences in Scotland undertaken in 1959.[84] That it was undertaken at all was a reflection of the perception of problem amongst the police. Its results suggest that in Scotland at least, dance hall disorder was not a big problem. In Fife seventeen cases of disturbances in dance halls had come to the notice of the police that year, including seven in Kirkcaldy, with sentences ranging from thirty days in prison for an assault and fines from £2 10s to £5 elsewhere. Three dance hall offences were recorded in St Andrews, none with serious injury, though one man was imprisoned for fourteen days. In Edinburgh in 1959 fourteen persons were charged with offences in dance halls. Thirteen were prosecuted in the burgh court and fined sums ranging from £3 to £13, one was prosecuted in the sheriff court and sentenced to three months' imprisonment. In Midlothian seventy-five persons were prosecuted. Forty were prosecuted in the burgh courts. Two were imprisoned for twenty days and the remainder fined between 10s and £10. Prosecutions in the sheriff court totalled thirty-five. Three were sentenced to imprisonment, one for thirty days, one for forty days, and one for three months. The remainder were fined between £2 and £20. In Dundee 'there were very few cases'. In Aberdeen, the Procurator Fiscal was 'not aware that disturbances in dance halls have created any great difficulties'. Similarly police authorities in Stirling stated that 'disturbances in dance halls are not a major problem' reporting on eight cases for the whole year.

Elsewhere there was evidence that the scale of the Teddy Boy problem had been exaggerated too. At their peak there were only 30,000 Teds in the Greater London area, a proportion that was typical for the rest of the country.[85] Moreover, the increasing crime statistics cited by the government and newspapers can be shown to be artificially high as a result of the reclassification of crimes and new punishments being implemented. Stanley Cohen believes that in effect the juvenile crime wave became a self-fulfilling prophecy, as the public interest in teenage crime led to greater recording of juvenile convictions and over-reaction to it caused greater problems. The creation of Teds as folk devils triggered an escalating spiral of delinquency as their anti-social behaviour became what society expected of them.

CONCLUSION

Youth's predilection for dancing throughout the twentieth century was greeted with consistent apprehension from some quarters. Linked to a more general charge that young people were increasingly self-indulgent and hell bent on pleasure, dancing become synonymous with a perceived youth problem in Britain. Moreover, dancing and dance halls were seen as important to a rise in juvenile

[84] NAS, DD5/984, 'Summary of Procurator Fiscals' reports on dance hall offences', 47.

[85] T. Fyvel, *The Insecure Offenders: Rebellious youth in the welfare state* (London: Chatto & Windus, 1961), 69.

delinquency. Whilst there is no doubt that some errant youths did cause trouble in dance halls, they were in no way representative of the younger generation as a whole. This vilification of dancing and the scapegoating of young people was a subconscious reflex response by society to the anxieties caused by war, economic dislocation, and, subsequently, rising prosperity.

Conclusion

At the outset I established four central objectives at the heart of this study. The first was to examine the expansion of the dance hall industry and the development of a mass audience. The second, perhaps most important, was to investigate the impact of dancing and dance halls on individuals and communities. The third and fourth were to assess the cultural impact, and reactions to, the huge explosion of interest in dancing.

Taking the development of a mass audience first, it is clear that during the period 1920 to 1960 there was an unprecedented audience for dancing. At no point before had so many people, from so many different sections of society, danced as much as they did in these decades of British history. Dancing moved from a craze to a habit, cementing itself as part of the fabric of daily life in Britain. Why was this so, and what does it tell us about British society at this time? Fundamental to explanations of the growing audience for dancing is economic change. Rising prosperity was behind much of the growth in dancing's popularity, as an increasingly affluent working and lower-middle class chose to spend their money on a wide range of leisure activities, of which dancing was second only to the cinema, and was eventually to eclipse even that institution in popularity. However, this was a very British type of economic development and affluence. Just enough to keep people out of poverty and give them more in their pockets, but unlike the growth of consumerism in the United States, for example, at least until after the Second World War, not sufficient to allow them to satisfy any acquisitive instincts they might have had.

Paradoxically then, the British love of dancing was both a reflection of a working class with more money and time, but also one with a craving for pleasure driven by economic insecurity. Dancing fitted the bill for such a situation because it was affordable, because it offered very good value for money, and because it was extremely pleasurable. Once the British working class became properly affluent, or at least more economically secure, which only happened after the Second World War and the creation of the welfare state, their love affair with the dance hall fell away. With its popularity 'artificially' prolonged by the years of austerity up until the 1950s, the dance hall was ultimately a victim of rising prosperity. No longer 'living for the moment' and with the security of full employment, the working class turned away from such communal pleasures and towards home buying, homemaking, family-life, and 'individualism'. Though such things had been developing embryonically since the 1920s, it was only during the 1960s that they began to assume an importance sufficient to shift previous patterns of behaviour. In discussing the development of this mass audience for dancing, however, we must not neglect to afford importance to the role of commercialism and the far-sightedness of certain businessmen. The dance hall industry that evolved to cater for this increasingly affluent nation of dancers is worthy of considerable praise. Inevitably there were those who were out to exploit and make as much money as they could, but the biggest names in the industry, particularly Mecca, were first-class businesses—in every respect. The men behind Britain's palais de danse were responsible for holding on to and extending a mass market at times of considerable economic and physical disruption. Businessmen such as Heimann and Fairley adopted the most up-to-date business methods from the United States, relying heavily on advertising and publicity, and constantly updating the appeal of what they offered following research into audience tastes. Moreover, whilst trying to maximize their profits, they were clearly offering an extremely good 'product' at a very affordable price. Mecca and others really cared about the dancing experience they were providing and devoted considerable effort to ensuring that it was as good as it could be. Carl Heimann's philosophy of giving 'Savoy Hotel standards to the masses' was one that he believed in wholeheartedly. In this, the dance hall industry was reflective of an increasing democratization of British life.

Turning next to the impact of dancing on individuals and communities, we have seen that the most prolific dancers were working or lower-middle class, young, and female. Cultural change was clearly helping to redefine class, gender, and, as we shall see, national identity. Examining first the importance of dancing to women, this was perhaps one of the most significant legacies of the dance hall. For women, dancing was a wholly liberating experience and played a significant role in their struggle for emancipation. Dancing allowed women to enter the public sphere in unprecedented numbers and in a venue that allowed them to renegotiate their relationships with men. If debates and discussions about dress codes and standards of propriety whilst dancing were designed to restrict this renegotiation of gender relations, they were more than overcome by the empowerment dancing gave to women. Women dominated the dance hall in more ways than one. It was a female leisure activity par excellence, offering a form of physical activity that was both physically and mentally the equivalent of sport for men. Through their attainment of dancing skills women's self-worth was vastly improved. Through their adoption of particular dancing styles and dance hall appearances, women's identities were playfully explored and experimented with. Through their interactions with men, on equal if not 'superior' terms, women in the dance hall were redefining how the two sexes saw each other. Moreover, dancing allowed women to explore their sexualities in ways that were wholly liberating for them, whatever the voices of critics were to say. It is for all of these reasons that whole generations of British women look back at their dance hall experiences with real fondness, sometimes tinged with regret that they had to give it up when they got married or had children.

If the dance hall was helping to make 'new women', however, it was equally important in the emergence of 'new men' throughout the twentieth century. Although it alarmed some die-hards, the smartly turned out, well-behaved (largely), polite generation of young men who had been schooled in the dance hall were another wholly positive product of the popularity of dancing in Britain. The violence so closely associated with dance halls in the press was by no means representative of the behaviour of the vast majority of men who went dancing. Although the process was slow, the familiarization of young men with women at an early age via dance schools and dance academies brought about a new mutual respect between the two. Moreover, in terms of men's identities, dance halls with their highly prescribed conventions and 'respectability' allowed the working-class male an alternative model of behaviour than that found in traditional leisure outlets and modes of life. This is not to say that men were being 'feminized'—such a conclusion would be a misinterpretation of the processes at work. Masculinity was being renegotiated, as it always is. Thus, throughout the twentieth century in the dance hall, we can see the gradual emergence of a masculinity based on dignified conduct, civility, polite and respectful interaction with women, and a concern with appearance and fashionability. That fights and squabbles still broke out in dance halls throughout all of the period examined, illustrates how these 'new' modes of behaviour ran alongside a more 'traditional' masculinity born out of brutal living conditions, harsh working environments, and the exploitation of working-class men in general. In the dance hall though, working-class men were exposed to an equally liberating force as women were. These palaces of dance, together with the accompanying erosion of brutality represented by the ending of pre-welfare state social conditions in Britain, were an important factor behind the emergence of new male identities.

The other major group for whom dancing had a significant impact was youth. Here again it is hard to overestimate the importance of dancing, both socially and culturally. In social terms, dancing was vital to the socialization of young people from the 1920s onwards, offering them early forms of independence. Dancing was vital in the transition from childhood to adulthood, and many youths of both sexes spent large amounts of their formative years in the dance hall. Peer and individual identities were shaped by dancing experiences and the palais allowed instruction in the adult pleasures of dating and, unofficially, drinking and smoking. In addition, dancing was at the centre of the emergence of a distinctive youth culture in Britain, a process that started as early as the 1920s. Young people made the dance hall their own. The dances they adopted, the way they danced them—and where—together with the way they looked—and spoke—were central to all of the key youth cultures of early twentieth-century Britain. Their craze for the Charleston, the Jitterbug, and the Jive marked young dancers apart from their older counterparts. Moreover, the critical responses that youth's dancing behaviour attracted merely served to reinforce their distinctiveness. Their determination to have as much fun as they could in the face of such criticism also belies a new-found confidence amongst working-class youths. As major beneficiaries of the economic and social changes behind the explosion of interest in dancing, young people were increasingly affluent and confident. The popularity of dancing amongst youth was both an important reflection of these changes, and also helped to drive them.

In addition to having these profound impacts on individuals and communities, the dance hall performed other key social functions, chief amongst which was its role as a place for members of the opposite sex to meet. Its prescribed conventions and central requirement of heterosexual coupling made the dance hall *the* place to meet. Despite the protestations of a largely middle-class morality lobby, there was nothing sordid about the dance hall. Middle-class fuddy-duddies in Cheltenham or Aberdeen might have seen in them the collapse of moral standards, but dance halls were mostly places of innocence, romance, and conventional morality. Moreover, the dance hall actually helped entrench marriage in twentieth-century British society. It probably extended its life too. Whole generations of Britons can point to the beginnings of life-long companionships in their local dance hall. Furthermore, with its atmospheric lighting, mood music, and partner dances, the dance hall encouraged a new focus on 'romance' in British society. This was a relatively new phenomenon, not particularly common prior to the twentieth century, at least not for the vast majority of men and women in Britain, whose motives for marriage were often much more practical than notions of 'love' and 'romance'. Being courted, dancing to romantic music, wearing glamorous clothes—the dance hall encouraged all of these new modes of behaviour in relationships and it was supported by whole industries that brought such experiences to everyone, not just the rich. This is not to say that the dance hall did not also allow for the freer expressions of sexuality however. Indeed, the very start of the explosion of interest in dancing at the beginning of the twentieth century was driven by new dances that were indicative of a new attitude towards public expressions of sexuality. Throughout the 1920s and into the 1960s, dance halls provided the opportunity to get close with strangers. They also increased the number of interactions between members of the opposite sex in ways that inevitably led to a casualization of the dating process and a focus on superficial qualities such as looks and style. Again, such developments were wholly positive. The more experience of dating men and women gained in dance halls, the better they were at discovering who they found suitable and who they did not. Such experiences were vital in the long run for the survival of marriage as an institution.

Inevitably, however, these transformations had their critics and as we have seen, dancing caused a 'moral panic' amongst a small number of anti-democratic critics.[1] Clear patterns emerge from these critical reactions, and the regularity with which they occurred and their seemingly unchanging nature, are instructive. The moral, social, and cultural responses to dancing in the period 1920–60 illustrate how popular culture has the capacity to shock, alarm, and agitate. Persistent attempts were made to regulate and control dancing forms, dancers' actions, and the spaces in which people danced. Attempts by dance professionals to reformulate dancing along lines they found more 'acceptable' also tell us important things about the new patterns of cultural production, and the emergence of a 'mass audience' for popular culture. Attempts to make popular dance in Britain more formalized, and to make performance reliant on greater levels of skill and learning, were an attempt to resist

[1] This includes critics of both the right and left (including Orwell, some in the Labour Party, and Hoggart) whose notion of 'democracy' was often patronizing, narrowly defined, and unsympathetic towards the working class and commericalized popular culture.

the primacy of commerce in the control of culture. There was an important class dimension to this. The concerted attempts to introduce 'better forms' of music and dance reflected middle-class sensibilities and notions of respectability. Moreover, this search for respectability had implications for changing social mores regarding gender and sexuality. Thus, particularly in the attempts to control dancing, we can see efforts to return to older standards of propriety, albeit with some acquiescence to the greater public visibility and freedom of women following the First World War. Similarly, the battle over the physical space of the dance hall conducted by magistrates and police illustrate the survival of a patronizing middle-class paternalism that refused to see the liberating influence of the palais on British society. In the long run, both of these impulses failed. They do, however, illustrate that the middle-class notion of 'rational recreation' was still very much alive in twentieth-century Britain. In addition, they underline that a central aspect of middle-class British identity was an overwhelming obsession with order, decorum, and the taking of pleasures seriously. In no other country in the world was an activity so potentially spontaneous and emotionally charged as dancing contained, controlled, and regimented as in Britain.

These reactions also tell us much more about how dancing and dance halls both reflected and helped to shape changing British national identity too. It is undeniable that the 1920s marked a major turning point in the history of British popular culture—political, technological, and economic changes had ushered in a new era of 'late modernity', bringing exposure to an increasingly cosmopolitan, Americanized, transatlantic culture. Dancing was perhaps the most tangible experience of this encounter with American culture that the majority of British people had. Together with the cinema, American culture was a persistent presence in British daily life from the 1920s onwards. However, this process of change and its impact on national identity was not straightforward, inevitable, or easy. In particular, this study allows us to make several important qualifications about the nature and extent of cultural change in Britain at this time. First, the history of dancing in Britain from the 1920s onwards suggests that the Americanization of British culture was contested, resisted and, moreover, that its penetration varied from group to group. As has been shown, clear attempts were made to produce distinctive 'national' dancing cultures in the face of an unprecedented wave of Americanization. Whilst American dances had undoubtedly transformed British culture, they were not adopted seamlessly into national life. British dance teachers worked hard to imbue these international mediums with specifically 'British' idioms, and they self-consciously labelled this process as such. This relates them to wider contemporary debates about Americanization in Britain during the period and the importance of resisting foreign control of new forms of communications and culture, which had led, for example, to the introduction of the Quota Act for films in 1927. Significantly, in contrast to Hollywood films, this study has also shown that, at one level, large sections of the British public seemed to prefer Anglicized versions of dances to their original American counterparts. However, this was not a simple rejection of American and preference for British culture. So, whilst the standard dance programme of the English style was the preferred programme of most British dancers, it was adopted by dancers on their own terms, and the values ascribed to it by dance teachers were not necessarily accepted by everyone who danced it. Furthermore, the majority of lower-middle- and working-class 'social dancers', and most especially the young, were much more welcoming of certain American dance crazes than professional dance teachers and 'keen dancers'. The Americanization of British dancing habits was therefore neither wholesale nor straightforward.

One further extremely important aspect of this redefinition of Britishness was the increasingly racially diverse nature of British society. Although the period of later mass immigration is not covered in this book, it is clear that the Britain of 1960 was far more racially diverse than that of 1920, at least in England. Dance and the dance hall had a key role to play in shaping the nature of this transformation. Dances were a convenient way to express ideas about racial theory. The widespread discussion of dancing in racial terms in local and national newspapers helped create, extend, and spread racist stereotypes about black people in Britain. Even before large numbers of black immigrants arrived, therefore, there were a series of pre-existing prejudices widespread amongst the British population which dance had helped define. Whilst the majority of the population were not wedded to the more extreme racist viewpoints of some intellectuals and politicians, they were probably subconsciously influenced by the popular images of black culture that dance created and reinforced. Moreover, dance was a particularly powerful vehicle through which such ideas spread, because it was less obviously theoretical and intellectual in nature than a treatise or lecture. Rather than abstract discussions on racial theory, dances could 'illustrate', through 'lived experience', the supposed 'primitiveness', 'joyfulness', or 'eroticism' of the black American culture from which they mostly originated. Whilst most British dancers probably did not see such things as particularly problematic, they nevertheless assumed a position of condescension towards black people via these stereotypes and images. All of this was to have a bearing on real-life relations between black and white people in Britain. Indeed, the dance hall played a further role in the development of race relations by acting as the key space where white Britain encountered black Britain in the twentieth century in any sustained and meaningful way. Outside the workplace, the dance hall was the most significant meeting point for immigrants and the local populations into which they moved. Significantly, this study has shown that conflict between black and white, as well as shared love of dancing, was not something that arrived in Britain with American GIs during the Second World War. In port towns and cities throughout Britain, inter-racial encounters in the dance hall were an established feature of daily life for decades before this.

Whilst there was much negative about these encounters, especially in the pre-war period, there is also a positive side to dancing's role in race relations in Britain. Though it has not been possible to examine it in any detail here, the dance hall helped the eventual smoothing of race relations in Britain in a number of ways. First, many official bodies used dances as a way of integrating newly arrived immigrants when they arrived in Britain. Although they had limited success, they were the first signs of the way in which dancing could help create points of contact between black and white peoples. Second, dancing was an important feature of the cultural identities of immigrant populations. Via the development of their own ways of dancing, and their own venues and dance clubs, immigrant populations not only reinforced their own identity in the midst of a new and strange environment, they also increasingly won the respect of local populations. Indeed, perhaps even more crucial to improved race relations, the dance hall and dancing provided a common point of interest between people of varied backgrounds. Love of dancing was a shared cultural instinct and one that helped overcome a myriad of differences. This may not have been an easy transition and was fraught with difficulties, but slowly the different peoples of Britain learnt, in the words of Roma Fairley, to 'shake down' together in the palais.[2] The fact that this happened spontaneously and in a space at the heart of British daily life made it more effective than any well-meaning officially sanctioned programme promoting better race relations.

Moreover, this reminds us that the idea of dancing contributing to a common culture in Britain from the 1920s onwards is also problematic. Undeniably, dancing had nationwide appeal and this, together with the influence of the new mass media, meant that people of all social groups and geographical backgrounds could potentially draw from the same common cultural stock. During the 1930s, for example, the Prince of Wales could dance a foxtrot in the Mayfair Hotel to the music of Ambrose and His Orchestra whilst to that very same music, broadcast into the homes of millions around the country via the BBC, crofters, railway workers, clerks, and teachers could potentially dance the same steps too, at exactly the same time. In an age where we are used to communicating with the other side of the world instantaneously we must not underestimate the novelty and power that these new forms of cultural exchange could have, and were perceived to have.

Yet we must be cautious. Rather than a single national dance culture emerging, there were a range and variety of dancing cultures that overlapped and complemented each other. Where one lived, how old one was, what class or gender one was—all were key determinants in the shaping of dance culture, together with the propensity of the individual to dance as they wished. As the period progressed, and certainly by the 1950s, this diversification in dance cultures became even more pronounced. Thus, whereas previously I have argued that the early twentieth century saw a common culture emerging in Britain that united diverse groups, I now consider the situation more complex. Certainly the example of dancing in Britain shows that the concept of 'cultures in common' is more appropriate than the idea of a 'common culture'.[3]

Nevertheless, even withstanding these caveats, it is clear that the degree of cultural uniformity in Britain brought about by the explosion of interest in dancing throughout the twentieth century was perhaps greater than it ever had been. Despite the distinctions outlined earlier, it is clear that from 1920 to 1960, teenagers in Dundee were as likely to be able to fit in at a dance in Bristol as

2 R. Fairley, *Come Dancing, Miss World* (London: Neamme, 1966), 78.

3 J. J. Nott, *Music for the People: Popular Music and Dance in Interwar Britain* (Oxford: Oxford University Press, 2002).

they were in Glasgow. Likewise, the palais found in Aberdeen were as similar to those in Liverpool as they were to those in Edinburgh. This was new. In this sense then, there was very clearly a 'national' British dance culture evident in the period 1920–60 and it was important in strengthening Britishness. Local cultural distinctiveness was being eroded and, in particular, England, Scotland, and Wales were being brought closer together through their engagement with this common cultural stock. In very important ways this culture was also increasingly democratic, reflecting the emergence of a Britain where social stratification was being weakened. The dance hall was democratic in a number of ways. Its price made it affordable to everyone and unlike the cinema, music hall, or theatre, there was one admission price and one entrance. Once inside there was one communal space open to all, with no exclusivity and no delineation of clientele along socio-economic lines. Clearly, however, some dance venues were more exclusive than others, and it is without doubt that class distinctions were an important factor in determining which dance location dancers would choose to frequent. Nevertheless, the twentieth-century explosion of interest in dance and the proliferation of dance halls throughout Britain opened up social dancing to working-class communities to an unprecedented extent. Working-class dancers were being given, and increasingly demanding, higher standards in their leisure activities and in their leisure venues. The expansion of entertainment and recreation improved the quality of life of those it touched, in ways comparable and complementary to the availability of cheap food and better housing, cheaper clothing and, later, social and economic security. The dance hall vastly increased the social and cultural possibilities of the working class in twentieth-century Britain. They represented, at a cultural level, an important shift in class relations too. As the period progressed, it was the working class who set the standards and trends in the dancing world, not the minority of 'Society' dancers who crammed the leading hotels and restaurants. The dance hall was a key vehicle in the coming to centre stage of popular culture in twentieth-century daily life in Britain. The influence of popular dance culture was striking. Its symbols were everywhere. News of dances, dance music, and dance halls filled the newspapers and gossip columns of magazines. Images of dancers and dancing filled the screen and the advertising hoardings up and down the country. Dancing infiltrated every aspect of daily life in Britain throughout the whole of the period 1920–60. In this respect, they are the most telling sign that several aspects of 'late modern' culture, its commercialism, populism, and 'democracy', had arrived, irreversibly, in Britain by the 1920s. The dance hall, then, both reflected and helped create the emergence of a Britain where the working class were at the centre of daily life, whether it be socially, culturally, or politically.

Bibliography

PRIMARY SOURCES

Archival Sources

Local Record Offices

City of Birmingham Archives, Birmingham
PS/B 4/1/1/4 Justices Meetings Minutes 1917–1932.
PS/B 4/1/1/5 Justices Meetings Minutes 1933–1952.

City of Glasgow Archives, Mitchell Library, Glasgow
E7/4/1, Register of Music Halls etc, 1934–52.
E7/4/2, Register of Music Halls etc, 1934–52.
Gf 381 GLA, Ritz Palais de Danse.
D-CA 8/988, F&F Palais de Danse.
D-CA 8/2636, Dennistoun Palais/Plaza.
D-CA 8/2753, Imperial Palais and Green's Playhouse.
D-CA 8/2930, Locarno Ballroom.

City of Manchester Archives, Manchester
M117/4/4/2, Register of Music, Dancing and Rooms 1902–37.
M117/4/4/2, Register of Music and Dancing Rooms, 1902–37.
M117/250, Manchester Licensing Committee Minutes 1920–32.
M117/252, Manchester Licensing Committee Minutes, 1952–66.
M117/216–218, Applications for Music Exemptions.

Liverpool Record Office, Liverpool
347/JUS/1/5, Register of Licenses for Music, Singing and Dancing 1919–26.
347/MAG/1/1/15, Theatre and Public Entertainments Licensing Committee, Proceedings 1923–28.
347/MAG/1/1/18, Theatre and Public Entertainments Licensing Committee, Minutes 1940–64.

Tyne and Wear Archives, Newcastle upon Tyne
MG.Nc.7/4, Licensing Minutes 1917–35.
MG.Nc.7/5, Licensing Minutes 1936–45.
MG.Nc.11, Register of Music, Singing and Dancing Licenses 1908–64.

Mass-Observation Archive, University of Sussex

Directive Replies
M-O A: Directive Reply: 'Jazz (Jan 1939)'.
M-O A: Directive Reply: 'Jazz 2 (July 1939)'.

File Reports
M-O A: FR11A, 'Jazz and Dancing', November 1939.

M-O A: FR20, 'Recording the War', January 1940.
M-O A: FR290, 'Women in Wartime', June 1940.
M-O A: FR295, 'On Jazz', 1940.
M-O A: FR301A, 'First Weekly Morale Report', 1940.
M-O A: FR449, 'Second Weekly Report For Home Intelligence', October 1940.
M-O A: FR533, 'Young People: A Social Survey in London', January 1941.
M-O A: FR538, 'Liverpool and Manchester', December 1940.
M-O A: FR559, 'Portsmouth and Plymouth', December 1940.
M-O A: FR633, 'Need for an Offensive Morale', April 1941.
M-O A: FR634, 'Broadcast for North American Service, 20.4.41'.
M-O A: FR722, 'Social Welfare in Blitz Towns', June 1941.
M-O A: FR733, 'The War in M.O. Diaries, Comparative Report', July 1941.
M-O A: FR757, 'WAAF Life', June 1941.
M-O A: FR877, 'Chatham', September 1941.
M-O A: FR884, 'Report on Ipswich Morale', September 1941.
M-O A: FR995, 'ATS', November 1941.
M-O A: FR1029, Tom Harrisson, 'Article for Modern Reading: WAAF Observer', January 1941.
M-O A: FR1031, 'The Great Man Chase', January 1942.
M-O A: FR1105, 'Morale in Donnington', February 1942.
M-O A: FR1496, 'Tube Investigation', November 1942.
M-O A: FR1632, 'Some Notes on the Uses of Leisure in Wartime', March 1943.
M-O A: FR1835, 'Behaviour of Women in Pubs', June 1943.
M-O A: FR2473, *Report on Juvenile Delinquency* (1947).
M-O A: FR3067, 'Work and Leisure', 1948.

Topic Collection: Music, Jazz and Dancing
M-O A: MJD: 1/A, 'Streatham Locarno: Big Apple Ball' 17 January 1939.
M-O A: MJD: 3/A, 'C L Heimann' (1938).
M-O A: MJD: 3/E, 'Facts about C L Heimann' (1938) and 'Byron Davies' (1939).
M-O A: MJD: 3/G, 'Interview: Cyril Amersham', 25 June 1939.
M-O A: MJD: 5/F, 'Manager Grafton Rooms Liverpool', 18 May 1939.
M-O A: MJD: 5/F, 'Manager Wimbledon Glider Rink', 13 February 1939.
M-O A: MJD: 8/B, 'Wandsworth Jazz Survey, July 1939'.
M-O A: MJD: 38/1/A, 'Big Apple Ball, I2', 17 November 1939.
M-O A: MJD: 38/1/A, 'Chaperlin', 17 November 1939.
M-O A: MJD: 38/1/A, 'Locarno AH 4.11.39'.
M-O A: MJD: 38/1/A, 'Locarno Dance Follows I34', 9 May 1939.
M-O A: MJD: 38/1/A, 'Locarno – Jitterbugs', 1 July 1939.
M-O A: MJD: 38/1/A, 'AH Locarno I47', 1 July 1939.
M-O A: MJD: 38/1/A, 'JA Locarno I46', 1 July 1939.
M-O A: MJD: 38/1/A, 'SS Locarno I12', 18 April 1939.
M-O A: MJD: 38/1/B, 'AH Paramount II6', 31 March 1939.
M-O A: MJD: 38/1/B, 'Paramount AH', 20 March 1939.
M-O A: MJD: 38/1/D, 'Clothing, Locarno I14 and I23', 19–21 April 1939.
M-O A: MJD: 38/1/D, 'Peckham Pavilion: Mollie Bourne', 19 August 1939.
M-O A: MJD: 38/1/E, 'Peckham Pavilion: V6', 7 February 1939.
M-O A: MJD: 38/1/G, 'Peckham Pavilion Questionnaire Survey Results', March/April 1939.

M-O A: MJD: 38/1/I, 'Interview with Parson re dancing and sex', 26 October 1939.
M-O A: MJD: 38/1/I, 'Stones, Rye Lane IX2', 6 March 1939.
M-O A: MJD: 38/1/I, 'Rye Lane IX6', March 1939.
M-O A: MJD: 38/2/C, 'Wapping', 13 August 1938.
M-O A: MJD: 38/4/H, 'Night in Soho', 14 April 1939.
M-O A: MJD: 38/5/D, 'Jazz since the war began', 13 November 1939.
M-O A: MJD: 38/5/F, 'Interview: Manager and Lessee of the "Empress Hall" XXXV', 15 July 1938.
M-O A: MJD: 38/5/H, 'Locarno School of Dancing Survey', 5 June 1939.
M-O A: MJD: 38/6/E, 'Jazz and Dancing – article draft'.
M-O A: MJD: 38/6/F, 'Jazz and Dancing, Draft'.
M-O A: MJD: 38/6/F, '*Danceland* Questionnaire Survey Results: 2', April 1939.

Topic Collection: Worktown
M-O A: Worktown: 48/C, 'An evening with a friend drinking and dancing', 2 April 1938.
M-O A: Worktown: 48/C, 'Co-op (Comrades Circle) Dance', 31 March 1937.
M-O A: Worktown: 48/C, 'Harlem Night at the Aspen Hall', 13 July 1938.
M-O A: Worktown: 48/C, 'Observations of Saturday Night', 3 April 1937.
M-O A: Worktown, 48/C, 'Shall We Dance?', *c* 1938.
M-O A: Worktown: 48/D, 'Manager. Aspin Hall. Bolton', 8 January 1940.
M-O A: Worktown: 57/D, 'Worktown Notes', 4 September 1937.
M-O A: Worktown: 60/D, 'Blackpool', 1937/8.

National Archives

National Archives, Kew, London
AIR 2/8865, 'RAF Dances For All-Ranks – Policy', 1944.
BT 31/24605/155007, 'Hammersmith Palais de Danse Ltd', (1919–32).
HO 45/11088/437236, 'Music and Dancing Licenses', December 1922.
HO 45/18141, 'Application of Public Entertainments (Restriction) Control in Rural Areas', 1939.
HO 45/24748, 'Coloured Servicemen Refused Admission to Public Entertainments', 1946.
HO 45/24748, 'Locarno (London) Ltd Dance Hall – Ban on Coloured Visitor', 1930.
HO 45/25604, 'US forces personnel stationed in the UK: possibility of friction between white and coloured troops', 1942–4.

National Archives of Scotland, Edinburgh
HH 16/1, Criminal case file: Asher Barnard, Edwin Jones, James Black (The Kosmo Club immorality case, Edinburgh), 1933–4.
DD5/984, Burgh Police (Scotland) Act, 1892. Dance Halls. Representations and Enquiries, 1953–60.

Oral History (Undertaken specially for this study)

Dundee Dance Hall Interviews, Dundee
Alistair Brown, b. 1930, 22 April 2011.
Dolores Brown, b. 1939, 22 April 2011.
Jack Hogan, b. 1936, 11 March 2011.

Kath Hogan, b. 1936, 11 March 2011.
Sandra Howarth, b. 1935, 29 April 2011.
Sandy Melville, b. 1934, 11 March 2011.

Glasgow Dance Hall Interviews, Glasgow
Rae Birch, b. 1922, 8 August 2011.
William Dewar, b. 1924, 27 June 2011.
John Lang, b. 1921, 3 August 2011.
Ivor Laycock, b. 1939, 26 May 2011.
Henry McGregor, b. 1922, 11 July 2011.
Agnes McHugh, b. 1934, 1 June 2011.
Jean Meehan, b. 1921, 14 June 2011.
Jean Murray, b. 1942, 19 July 2011.
Stewart Murray, b. 1940, 19 July 2011.
Mary O'Neill, b. 1920, 8 June 2011.
John Robb, b. 1927, 20 June 2011.
Margaret Taylor, b. 1938, 31 May 2011.
Irene Williams, b. 1929, 6 September 2011.

Liverpool Dance Hall Interviews, Liverpool Maritime Museum and Liverpool League of Well-Doers
Jane Campbell, b. 1922, 23 June 2009.
George Cauldwell, b. 1929, 23 June 2009.
Marjorie Hooley, b. 1917, 23 June 2009.
Vera Jeffers, b. 1926, 22 July 2009.
Marie Kernan, b. 1942, 21 July 2009.
Bettina Silverstone, b. 1929, 22 July 2009.
Bert Smith, b. 1926, 23 June 2009.
Pat Spencer, b. 1933, 21 July 2009.

Cheshire Dance Hall Interviews, Cheshire
Barbara Nott, b. 1943, 2014.
Terrence Nott, b. 1939, 2014.

Other Oral History Sources

Carlton Interviews, Rochdale
Carlton Interviews, Mrs Rose Blincoe, nd, Rochdale, Lancashire.

Manchester Jewish Museum, Manchester
Interview with Lou Black, Manchester Jewish Museum (MJM):J40, nd.

North West Sound Archive, Clitheroe
NWSA Oral History: 2001.0725, Neil Foster, b. 1940, 2001.
NWSA Oral History: 2006.0179, Maggie Hardy, b. 1931, 2006.
NWSA Oral History: 2001.0712, Lorna Macintosh, b. 1940, 2001.
NWSA Oral History: 2006.0145, Stella Morrison, b. 1933, 2006.
NWSA Oral History: 2001.0417, Millicent Thorp, b. 1937, 2001.

BBC WW2 People's War Archive, British Library
Christopher Andrews, Article A4374713, 6 July 2005.
Lily Bates b.1932, Article A3100140, 7 October 2004.
Dorothy Cartwright, Article A4869840, 8 August 2005.
Ken Clark, Article A2337167, 24 February 2004.
Betty Clegg, Article A5320450, 25 August 2005.
Robin Collins, Article A6014350, 4 October 2005.
Irene Fairall, Article A2729540, 10 June 2004.
Sheila Granger, Article A2298459, 16 February 2004.
Jim Howard, Article A2836163, 14 July 2004.
Audrey Lewis, Article A3346823, 30 November 2004.
Mary Matthews, Article A4055636, 12 May 2005.
Patricia McGowan, Article A2869770, 27 July 2004.
Leonard McKay, Article A3326618, 25 November 2004.
Frank Mee, Article A2553761, 23 April 2004.
Sylvia Merriman, Article A2064700, 20 November 2003.
Neville Harcourt Paddy, Article A4090024, 19 May 2005.
Delphine Rowden, Article A4073889, 16 May 2005.
Terri Sanders, Article A2661590, 24 May 2004.
Betty Sutton, Article A3895860, 14 April 2005.
Margaret Tapster, Article A5827665, 20 September 2005.

Women's Library, London

National Vigilance Association (NVA)
4NVA/1/1/07, NVA minutes.
4NVA/3/1, F. Sempkins, 'Traffic in Women and Children', nd.

PRINTED PRIMARY SOURCES

Newspapers, magazines and journals
The Aberdeen Daily Journal (Aberdeen)
Aberdeen Press and Journal
The Bath Weekly Chronicle and Herald (Bath)
Birmingham Dispatch
Birmingham Mail
Burnley Express and News (Burnley)
The Burnley News
Cheltenham Chronicle and Gloucestershire Graphic
The Cornishman and Cornish Evening Telegraph
The Courier and Advertiser (Dundee)
Daily Express
Daily Herald
Daily Mail
Daily Mirror
Danceland
Dancing Times
Derby Daily Telegraph
Derby Evening Telegraph

Dundee Courier and Advertiser
Dundee Evening Telegraph
The Economist
Edinburgh Evening News
The Essex Newsman Herald (Chelmsford)
Exeter and Plymouth Gazette
Glasgow Herald
Gloucester Journal (Gloucester)
Grantham Journal
Hull Daily Mail
Lancashire Dance News
League of Colonial Peoples Newsletter
Lichfield Mercury
Liverpool Echo
Manchester Guardian
Modern Dance and Dancer
New York Times
Northern Dance News Weekly
Nottingham Evening Post
The Observer
Picture Post
Sunday Sun
Sunday Post
The Times
Top Spin: a periodical devoted to the interests of north London dancers
Western Daily Press
Western Morning News and Mercury

Books, pamphlets, official papers

Anon., *Ballroom Dancing Annual 1947* (Dancing Times Ltd, 1948).
Anon., *Ballroom Dancing Annual 1948* (Dancing Times Ltd, 1949).
Anon., *Ballroom Dancing Annual 1951* (Dancing Times Ltd, 1952).
Anon., *Danceland 1941 Souvenir* (Danceland Publications, 1942).
Anon., *Kelly's Directory of Birmingham* (London: Kelly's Directories, 1920, 1925, 1935, 1939).
Anon., *Locarno School of Dancing Prospectus* (London: Mecca Publications, nd 1930s).
Anon., *Post Office Directory of Glasgow* (London: Kelly's Directories, 1920–35).
Anon., *Stepping Out* (London: Danceland Publications, 1940).
Atherton, J. and W., *Empress Ballroom and Palais de Danse, Wigan* (Liverpool: Private, 1926).
Banton, M., *The Coloured Quarter: Negro Immigrants in an English City* (London: J. Cape, 1955).
Banton, M., *White and Coloured: The behaviour of British people towards coloured immigrants* (London: J. Cape, 1959).
Barron Mays, J., *Growing up in the City: A Study of Juvenile Delinquency in an Urban Neighbourhood* (Liverpool: Liverpool University Press, 1954).
Bevington, S. M., *Leisure Pursuits outside the Family Circle* (London: National Institute of Industrial Psychology, 1939).
Brown, J., *Glasgow's Dancing Daft!* (Ochiltree, TX: Stenlake Publishing, 1994).
Burke, T., *London in My Time* (London: Rich and Cowan, 1934).

Cameron, C., A. J. Lush, and G. Meara (eds), *Disinherited Youth* (Edinburgh: Carnegie United Kingdom Trust, 1943).

Caradog Jones, D. (ed), *The Social Survey of Merseyside*, 3 (Liverpool: Liverpool University Press 1934).

Carey, A. T., *Colonial Students: A Study of the Social Adaptation of Colonial Students in London* (London: Secker & Warburg, 1956).

Casani, S., *Casani's Self-Tutor of Ballroom Dancing* (London: Cassell & Co., 1927).

Chaplin, P., *Darts in England 1900–39: A Social History* (Manchester: Manchester University Press, 2012).

Collins, S., *Coloured Minorities in Britain: Studies in British Race Relations based on African, West Indian and Asiastic Immigrants* (London: Lutterworth Press, 1957).

Crossley, J., *Pictorial Dance Tutor: A beginner's guide to ballroom dancing* (London: Sir Isaac Pitman & Sons, 1947).

The Crowther Report (1959) *A Report to the Central Advisory Council for Education (England)* (1959), HMSO, vol. II, Part 1.

Davidson, J. and M. Davidson, *Etiquette at a Dance* (London: W. Foulsham & Co., 1937).

Dennis, N., F. Henriques, C. Slaughter, *Coal is Our Life: An analysis of a Yorkshire mining community* (London: Eyre & Spottiswoode, 1956).

Fyvel, T., *The insecure offenders: rebellious youth in the welfare state* (London: Chatto & Windus, 1961).

Glass, R., *Newcomers: The West Indians in London* (London: Centre for Urban Studies, Allen & Unwin, 1960).

Gregory, J. W., *The Menace of Colour: A study of the difficulties due to the association of white and coloured races, with an account of measures proposed for their solution, and special reference to white colonization in the tropics* (London: Seeley, Service & Co., 1925).

Harrisson, T., 'Whistle While You Work' (1938) (Winter) *New Writing* 50.

Harrisson, T., 'Doing the Lambeth Walk', in C. Madge and T. Harrisson, *Britain by Mass-Observation* (Harmondsworth: Penguin, 1939).

Harrisson, T., 'Working Women in this War,' *Industrial and Personnel Management* (December 1939).

Harrisson, T. and C. Madge (eds), *War Begins at Home by Mass Observation* (London: Chatto & Windus, 1940).

Hatton, S. F., *London's Bad Boys* (London: Chapman & Hall, 1931).

Hill, C. S., *How Colour Prejudiced is Britain?* (London: Panther Books, 1965).

Jenkins, T., *'Let's Go Dancing': Dance band memories of 1930s Liverpool* (Liverpool: Liverpool Sound Series, 1994).

Jephcott, P., *Girls Growing Up* (London: Faber, 1942).

Kerr, M., *The People of Ship Street* (London: Routledge, 1958/1998).

Kuper, L. (ed), *Living in Towns. Selected Research Papers in Urban Sociology of the Faculty of Commerce and Social Science, University of Birmingham* (London: Cresset Press, 1953).

Langdon, C., *Earls Court* (London: St Paul, 1953).

Lapiere, R. T., 'Race Prejudice: France and England' (1928) 7(1) (September) *Social Forces* 102–11.

Lawson, A., *It Happened in Manchester: The True Story of Manchester's Music 1958–65* (Multimedia, 1998).

Little, K. L., *Negroes in Britain: A Study of Race Relations in English Society* (London: Kegan Paul, Trench, Trubner & Co., 1947).

Llewellyn Smith, H., and London School of Economics and Political Science, *New Survey of London Life and Labour*, ix (London: P. S. King and Son, Ltd, 1930–6), ix.

Logan, R. F. and E. M. Goldberg, 'Rising Eighteen in a London Suburb: A Study of Some Aspects of the Life and Health of Young Men' (1953) 4(4) (December) *The British Journal of Sociology* 323–45.
Marwick, A., *British Society Since 1945* (Harmondsworth: Penguin, 1990).
Mendl, R. W. S., *The Appeal of Jazz* (London: P. Allen & Co., 1927).
Meyrick, K., *Secrets of the 43: Reminiscences with Mrs Meyrick* (London: John Long, 1933).
Moseley, S., *Night Haunts of London* (London: Stanley Paul & Co., 1920).
Musicians' Union, *Music and the Borough Councillor* (London: Musicians' Union, 1947).
Patterson, S., *Dark Strangers: A Sociological Study of the Absorption of a Recent West Indian Migrant Group in Brixton, South London* (Harmondsworth: Penguin Books, 1963).
Reed, B. H., *Eighty Thousand Adolescents. A study of young people in the city of Birmingham, by the staff and students of Westhill Training College, for the Edward Cadbury Charitable Trust* (London: George Allen and Unwin Ltd, 1950).
Reed, B. H., *For Teenagers Only* (London: Epworth Press, 1958).
Richmond, A. H., *Colour Prejudice in Britain: A Study of West Indian Workers in Liverpool, 1941–51* (London: Routledge & Kegan Paul, 1953).
Schofield, M., *The Sexual Behaviour of Young People* (London: Longmans, 1965).
Seebohm Rowntree, B. and G. Lavers, *English Life and Leisure. A Social Study* (London: Longmans, Green & Co., 1951).
Silvester, V., *Modern Ballroom Dancing* (London: Herbert Jenkins, 1927).
Silvester, V., *Dancing is My Life. An Autobiography* (London: Heinemann, 1958).
Spinley, B. M., *The Deprived and the Privileged: Personality Development in English Society* (London: Routledge, 1953/1998).
Spring Rice, M., *Working-Class Wives* (Harmondsworth: Penguin Books, 1939).
Spurr, F., *The Christian Use of Leisure* (London: Kingsgate Press, 1928).
Stewart, M., *'O' is Fir Ingin* (Edinburgh: Black & White Publishing, 2010).
Taylor, C. F., *Round the Dundee Dance Halls from the 1920s* (Dundee: Private, 1987).
Zweig, F., *Labour, Life and Poverty* (London: Victor Gollancz, 1948).
Zweig, F., *The Worker in an Affluent Society* (London: Heinemann, 1961).

PRINTED SECONDARY WORKS

Addison, P., *No Turning Back: The peacetime revolutions of post-war Britain* (Oxford: Oxford University Press, 2010).
Aldgate, A., 'Ideological consensus in British Feature Films 1935–47', in K. R. M. Short (ed), *Feature Films as History* (London: Croom Helm, 1981), 94–112.
Bailey, P., *Leisure and Class in Victorian England. Rational recreation and the contest for control, 1830–85* (London: Routledge and Kegan Paul, 1978).
Bailey, P., *Music Hall: the business of pleasure* (Milton Keynes: Open University Press, 1986).
Baxendale, J., 'Popular Music and Late Modernity, 1910–30' (1995) 14 *Popular Music* 137–54.
Beddoe, D., *Back to Home and Duty: Women between the wars 1918–1939* (London: Pandora, 1989).
Bourke, J., *Working Class Cultures in Britain: Gender, class and ethnicity* (London: Routledge, 1994).
Bradley, J., *Dancing Through Life* (London: Hollis & Carter, 1947).
Briggs, A., *The History of Broadcasting in the United Kingdom*, rev edn (5 vols, Oxford: Oxford University Press, 1995).

Brocken, M., *Other Voices: hidden histories of Liverpool's popular music scenes, 1930s–1970s* (Farnham: Ashgate, 2010).
Buckland, T., *Society Dancing: Fashionable Bodies in England, 1870–1920* (Basingstoke: Palgrave Macmillan, 2011).
Buckman, P., *Let's Dance: Social, Ballroom and Folk Dancing* (London: Paddington Press, 1978).
Burke, T., *English Night-Life: From Norman curfew to present black-out* (London: B. T. Batsford, 1941).
Carey, J., *The Intellectuals and the Masses: Pride and Prejudice among the Literary Intelligentsia, 1880–1939* (London: Faber and Faber, 1992).
Casciani, E., *Oh, How we Danced! The History of Ballroom Dancing in Scotland* (Edinburgh: Mercat Press, 1994).
Cox, P., *Bad Girls in Britain: Gender, justice and welfare, 1900–1950* (Basingstoke: Palgrave Macmillan, 2003).
Cresswell, T., '"You cannot shake that shimmie here": producing mobility on the dance floor' (2006) 13(1) *Cultural Geographies* 55–77.
Cunningham, V., *British Writers of the 1930s* (Oxford: Oxford University Press, 1988).
Davies, A., *Leisure, Gender and Poverty: Working-Class Culture in Salford and Manchester, 1900–39* (Buckingham: Open University Press, 1992).
Davies, A., *City of Gangs: Glasgow and the Rise of the British Gangster* (London: Hodder & Stoughton, 2013).
Dawson, S., 'Islands of Leisure: British Holiday Camps in War and Peace', PhD, University of California Santa Barbara (2007).
Fairley, R., *Come Dancing Miss World* (London: Neamme, 1966).
Ferrall, C., *Modernist Writing and Reactionary Politics* (Cambridge: Cambridge University Press, 2001).
Field, G., 'Perspectives on the Working Class Family in Wartime Britain, 1939–1945', *International Labor and Working Class History* (Chicago, IL) vol. 38, Fall 1990, 16.
Fowler, D., *The First Teenagers: The lifestyle of young wage-earners in Interwar Britain* (London: Woburn Press, 1995).
Fowler, D., *Youth Culture in Modern Britain c.1920–c.1970: from ivory tower to global movement—a new history* (Basingstoke: Palgrave Macmillan, 2008).
Franks, A. H., *Social Dance: A Short History* (London: Routledge & Kegan Paul, 1963).
Frith, S., *The Sociology of Rock* (London: Constable, 1978).
Gardiner, J., *Over Here: The GIs in Wartime Britain* (London: Collins & Brown, 1992).
Glynn, S. and J. Oxborrow, *Interwar Britain: A Social and Economic History* (London: Allen and Unwin, 1976).
Godbolt, J., *A History of Jazz in Britain 1919–50* (London: Paladin, 1984).
Harris, C., 'Images of Blacks in Britain, 1930–60', in S. Allen and M. Macey (eds), *Race and Social Policy* (London: ESRC, 1988).
Hilton, M., *Smoking in British Popular Culture 1800–2000* (Manchester: A & C Black, 2000).
Holmes, C., *John Bull's Island: Immigration and British Society, 1871–1971* (Basingstoke: Macmillan, 1988).
Horn, A., *Juke Box Britain* (Manchester: Manchester University Press, 2010).
Horwood, C., *Keeping Up Appearances: Fashion and class between the wars* (Stroud: Sutton, 2005).
Humphries, S., *Hooligans or rebels? An oral history of working-class childhood and youth 1889–1939* (Oxford: Blackwell, 1981).

Jones, S. G., *Workers at Play: A Social and Economic History of Leisure 1918–1939* (London: Routledge & Kegan Paul, 1986).

Kingsley Kent, S., *Making Peace: The reconstruction of gender in interwar Britain* (Princeton: Princeton University Press, 1993).

Kirkham, P., 'Beauty and Duty: Keeping up the (Home) Front', in P. Kirkham and D. Thoms (eds), *War Culture: Social change and changing experience in World War Two Britain* (London: Lawrence & Wishart, 1995).

Kohn, M., *Dope Girls: The Birth of the British Drug Underground* (London: Lawrence & Wishart, 1992).

Langhamer, C., *Women's Leisure in England, 1920–60* (Manchester: Manchester University Press, 2000).

Lewis, P., *The Fifties* (London: Heinemann, 1978).

Lewis, P. W., *The Art of Being Ruled* (London: Chatto and Windus, 1926).

McCarthy, A., *The Dance Band Era* (Radnor, PA: Chilton Book Company, 1982).

McKibbin, R., *Classes and Cultures* (Oxford: Oxford University Press, 1998).

McMillan, J., *The Way it Was, 1914–34* (London: Kimber, 1979).

Martland, P., *Since Records Began: EMI the First 100 Years* (London: B. T. Batsford, 1997).

Marwick, A., *British Society Since 1945* (Harmondsworth: Penguin, 1990).

Melly, G., *Revolt into Style: The Pop Arts in Britain* (Harmondsworth: Penguin 1972).

Nott, J. J., *Music for the People: Popular Music and Dance in Interwar Britain* (Oxford: Oxford University Press, 2002).

Nott, J. J., '"The Plague Spots of London": William Joynson Hicks, the Conservative Party and the Campaign Against London's Nightclubs, 1924–29', in C. Griffiths, J. J. Nott, and W. Whyte (eds), *Classes, Cultures and Politics: Essays in Modern British History for Ross McKibbin* (Oxford: Oxford University Press, 2011).

Ogren, K. J., *The Jazz Revolution: Twenties America and the Meaning of Jazz* (New York: Oxford University Press, 1989).

Oliver, L., 'From the Ballroom to Hell: a Social History of Public Dancing in Bolton from *c.*1840–1911' (1995) 2(2) *Women's History Notebooks* 15–23.

Osgerby, B., 'From the Roaring Twenties to the Swinging Sixties: Continuity and change in youth culture, 1929–59', in B. Brivati and H. Jones (eds), *What Difference Did the War Make?* (Leicester: Leicester University Press, 1995).

Osgerby, B., *Youth in Britain Since 1945* (Oxford: Blackwell, 1997).

Panayi, P., 'Immigrants, Refugees, the British State and Public Opinion During World War Two', in P. Kirkham and D. Thoms (eds), *War Culture: social change and changing experience in World War Two Britain* (London: Lawrence & Wishart, 1995).

Pearson, G., *Hooligan: A history of respectable fears* (London: Macmillan, 1983).

Pennybacker, S., '"It was not what she said but the way in which she said it": The London County Councils and the Music Halls', in P. Bailey (ed), *Music Hall: The Business of Pleasure* (Milton Keynes: Open University Press, 1986).

Petrow, S., *Policing Morals: The Metropolitan Police and the Home Office, 1870–1914* (Oxford: Oxford University Press, 1994).

Priestley, J. B., *English Journey* (London: William Heinemann and Victor Gollancz, 1934).

Pronay, N. and D. W. Spring (eds), *Propaganda, Politics and Film 1918–1945* (London: Macmillan, 1982).

Redfern, P., *The New History of the C.W.S.* (London: J.M. Dent & Sons, 1938),

Reynolds, D., *Rich Relations: The American Occupation of Britain 1942–1945* (London: HarperCollins, 1995).

Richards, J., *The Age of the Dream Palace: Cinema and Society in 1930s Britain* (London: I. B. Tauris, 2009).
Richardson, P., *A History of English Ballroom Dancing (1910–45): The story of the development of the modern English style* (London: Herbert Jenkins, 1947).
Roberts, R., *The Classic Slum: Salford Life in the First Quarter of the Century* (Harmondsworth: Penguin, 1983).
Rock, P. and S. Cohen, 'The Teddy Boy', in V. Bognador and R. Skidelsky (eds), *The Age of Affluence 1951–1964* (London: Macmillan, 1970).
Rose, S. O., *Which People's War? National identity and citizenship in Britain 1939–1945* (Oxford: Oxford University Press, 2003).
St. John Rumsey, H., *Ball-Room Dancing* (London: Methuen, 1925).
Savage, J., *Teenage: The Creation of Youth Culture* (London: Chatto & Windus, 2007).
Scannell, P. and D. Cardiff, *A Social History of Broadcasting* (Oxford: Blackwell, 1991).
Sherwood, M., *Many Struggles: West Indian workers and service personnel in Britain (1939–45)* (London: Karia, 1985).
Smithies, E., *Crime in Wartime: A social history of crime in World War II* (London: Allen & Unwin, 1982).
Spencer, I., 'World War Two and the making of multiracial Britain', in P. Kirkham and D. Thoms (eds), *War Culture: Social Change and Changing Experience in World War Two Britain* (London: Lawrence & Wishart, 1995).
Springhall, J., *Coming of Age: Adolescence in Britain 1860–1960* (Dublin: Gill and Macmillan, 1985).
Stedman Jones, G., 'Working-class culture and working class politics in London, 1870–1900: Notes on the remaking of a working class' (1974) 7(4) *Journal of Social History* 460–508.
Stevenson, J., *British Society, 1914–45* (Harmondsworth: Penguin, 1984).
Stone, R. and D. A. Rowe, *The Measurement of Consumers' Expenditure and Behaviour in the United Kingdom, 1920–1938*, vol. ii (Cambridge: Cambridge University Press, 1966).
Strinati, D. and S. Wagg, *Come on Down? Popular media culture in post-war Britain* (London: Routledge, 1992).
Tinkler, P., 'Learning Through Leisure: Feminine Ideology in Girl's Magazines, 1920–1950', in F. Hunt (ed), *Lessons for Life: The schooling of girls and women, 1850–1950* (Oxford: Blackwell, 1987).
Tinkler, P., *Constructing Girlhood: Popular magazines for girls growing up in England, 1920–1950* (London: Taylor & Francis, 1995).
Walton, J., *The British Seaside: Holidays and Resorts in the Twentieth Century* (Manchester: Manchester University Press, 2000).
Ward, C. and D. Hardy, *Goodnight Campers: The history of the British holiday camp* (London: Mansel, 1986).
Waters, C., 'Manchester Morality and London Capital: The battle over the palace of Varieties', in P. Bailey (ed), *Music Hall: The Business of Pleasure* (Milton Keynes: Open University Press, 1986).
White, C., *Women's Magazines 1693–1968* (London: Joseph, 1970).
Wilson, J. F., *Building Co-operation: A business history of the Co-operative Group, 1863–2013* (Oxford: Oxford University Press, 2013).

Index